SUPERMAN

TALES FROM THE PHANTOM ZONE!

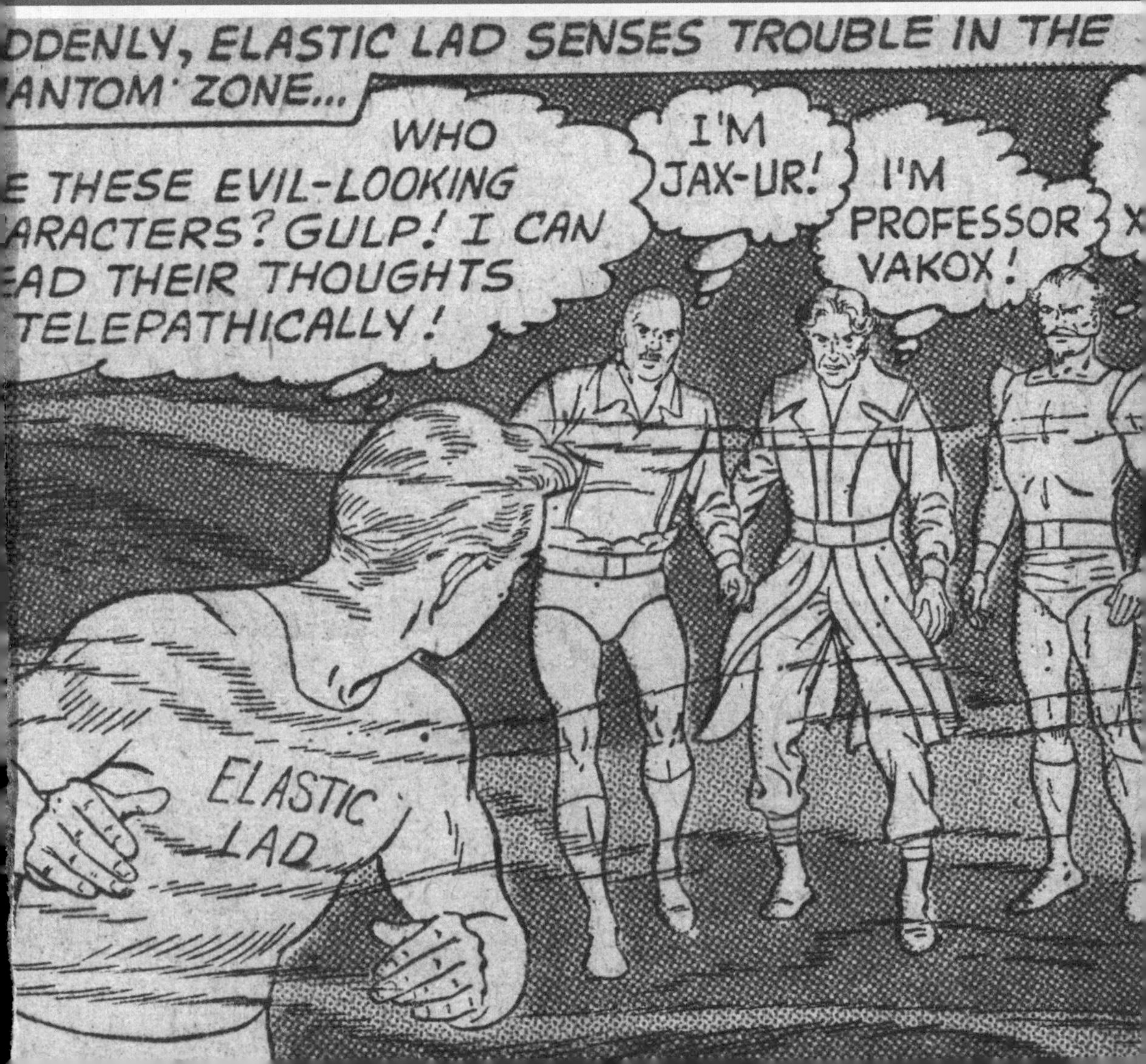
DDENLY, ELASTIC LAD SENSES TROUBLE IN THE
ANTOM ZONE...
WHO
E THESE EVIL-LOOKING
ARACTERS? GULP! I CAN
EAD THEIR THOUGHTS
TELEPATHICALLY!
I'M JAX-UR!
I'M PROFESSOR VAKOX!
ELASTIC LAD

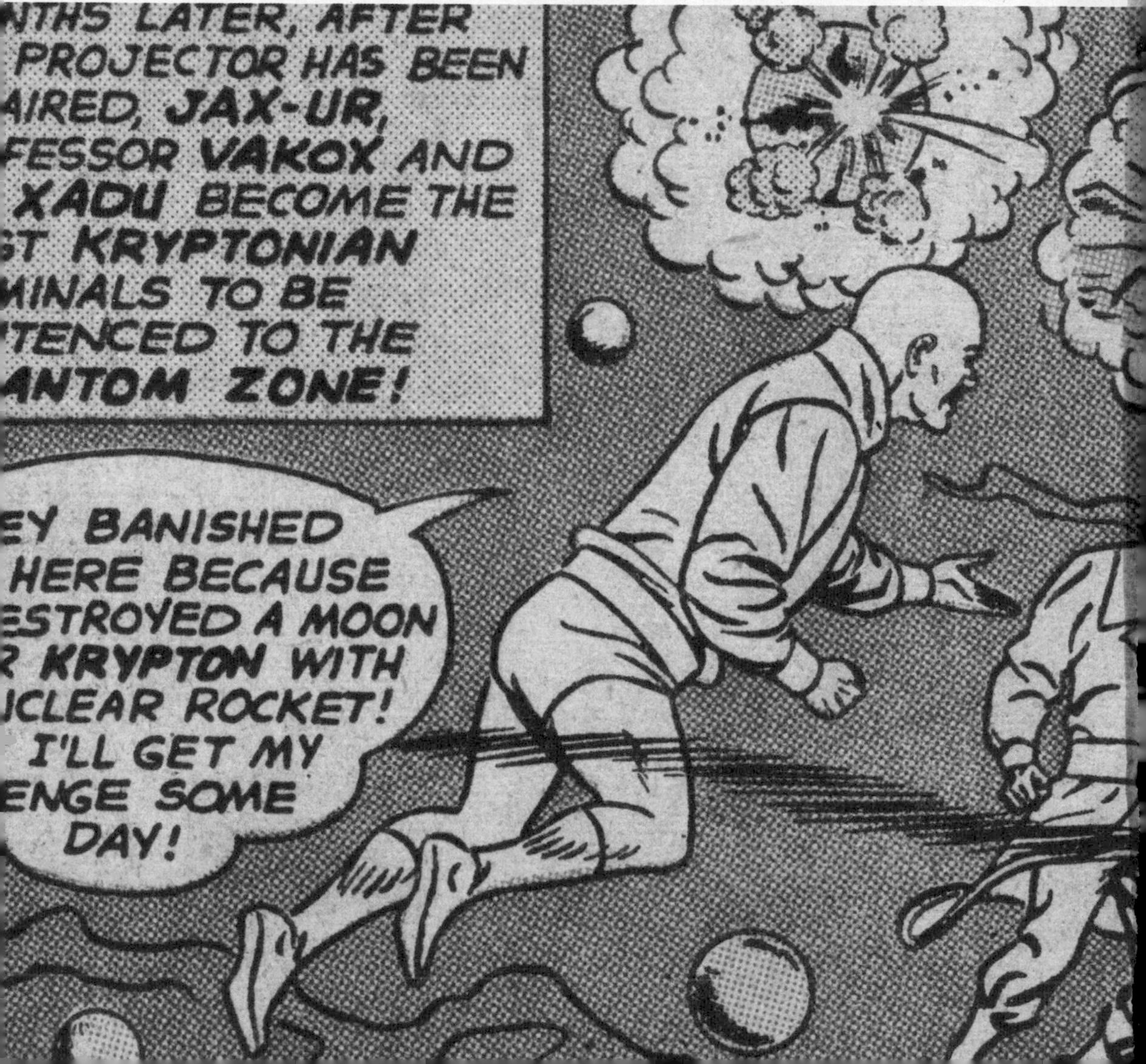

NTHS LATER, AFTER PROJECTOR HAS BEEN AIRED, JAX-UR, FESSOR VAKOX AND XADU BECOME THE ST KRYPTONIAN MINALS TO BE TENCED TO THE ANTOM ZONE!
EY BANISHED HERE BECAUSE ESTROYED A MOON R KRYPTON WITH UCLEAR ROCKET! I'LL GET MY ENGE SOME DAY!

SUPERMAN

TALES FROM THE PHANTOM ZONE!

SUPERMAN CREATED BY JERRY SIEGEL AND JOE SHUSTER

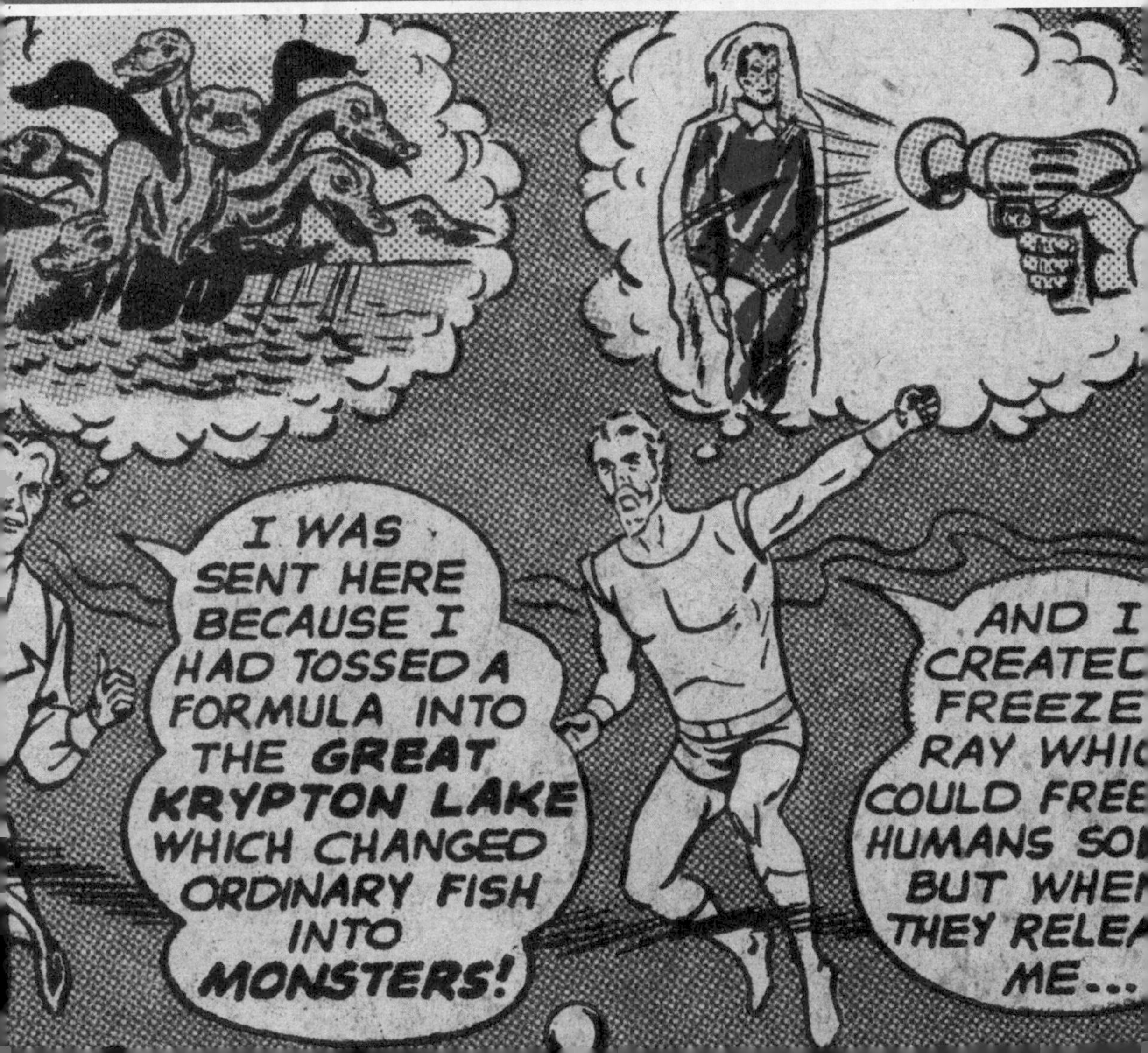
I WAS SENT HERE BECAUSE I HAD TOSSED A FORMULA INTO THE GREAT KRYPTON LAKE WHICH CHANGED ORDINARY FISH INTO MONSTERS!
AND I
FREEZE
RAY
COULD
HUMANS
BUT
THEY
ME...

Dan DiDio **Senior VP-Executive Editor**
Mort Weisinger Bob Greenberger **Editors-original series**
Bob Joy **Editor-collected edition**
Robbin Brosterman **Design Director-Books**
Paul Levitz **President & Publisher**
Georg Brewer **VP-Design & DC Direct Creative**
Richard Bruning **Senior VP-Creative Director**
Patrick Caldon **Executive VP-Finance & Operations**
Chris Caramalis **VP-Finance**
John Cunningham **VP-Marketing**
Terri Cunningham **VP-Managing Editor**
Amy Genkins **Senior VP-Business & Legal Affairs**
Alison Gill **VP-Manufacturing**
David Hyde **VP-Publicity**
Hank Kanalz **VP-General Manager, WildStorm**
Jim Lee **Editorial Director-WildStorm**
Gregory Noveck **Senior VP-Creative Affairs**
Sue Pohja **VP-Book Trade Sales**
Steve Rotterdam **Senior VP-Sales & Marketing**
Cheryl Rubin **Senior VP-Brand Management**
Alysse Soll **VP-Advertising & Custom Publishing**
Jeff Trojan **VP-Business Development, DC Direct**
Bob Wayne **VP-Sales**

Cover by Gary Frank

SUPERMAN: TALES FROM THE PHANTOM ZONE

DC Comics, 1700 Broadway, New York, NY 10019
A Warner Bros. Entertainment Company
Printed in Canada. First Printing.
ISBN: 978-1-4012-2258-1

SUSTAINABLE FORESTRY INITIATIVE Certified Fiber Sourcing
Fiber used in this product line meets the sourcing requirements of the SFI program. www.sfiprogram.org PWC-SFICOC-260

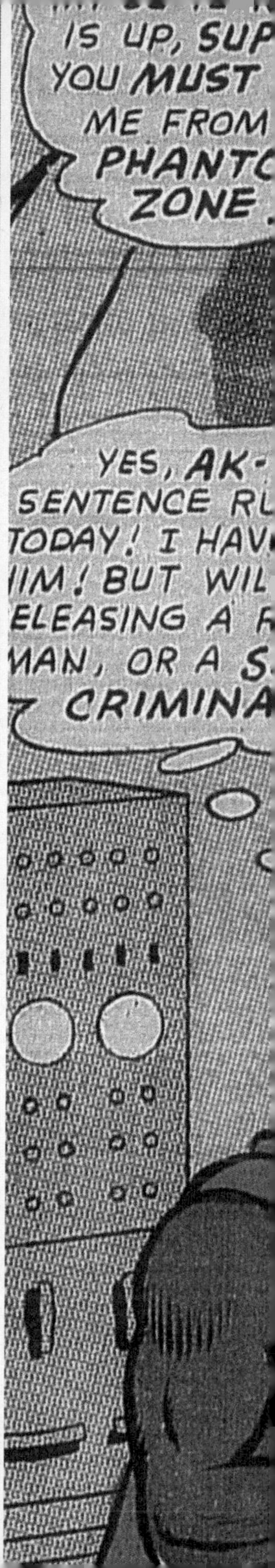
IS UP, SUP
YOU MUST
ME FROM
PHANT
ZONE
YES, AK-
SENTENCE R
TODAY! I HAV
IM! BUT WIL
ELEASING A
MAN, OR A S
CRIMINA

CONTENTS

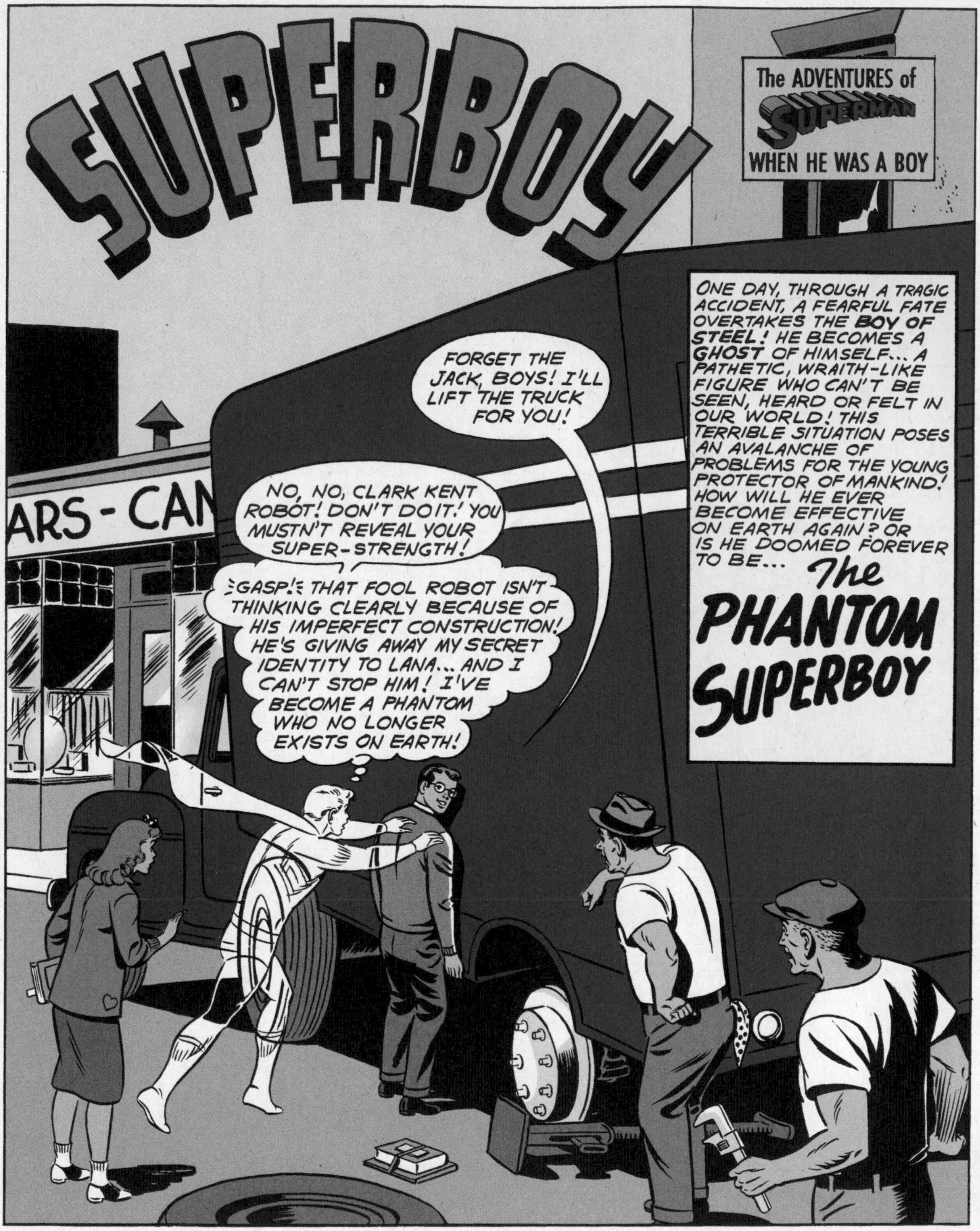
SUPERBOY
The ADVENTURES of SUPERMAN WHEN HE WAS A BOY
ONE DAY, THROUGH A TRAGIC ACCIDENT, A FEARFUL FATE OVERTAKES THE BOY OF STEEL! HE BECOMES A GHOST OF HIMSELF... A PATHETIC, WRAITH-LIKE FIGURE WHO CAN'T BE SEEN, HEARD OR FELT IN OUR WORLD! THIS TERRIBLE SITUATION POSES AN AVALANCHE OF PROBLEMS FOR THE YOUNG PROTECTOR OF MANKIND! HOW WILL HE EVER BECOME EFFECTIVE ON EARTH AGAIN? OR IS HE DOOMED FOREVER TO BE... The PHANTOM SUPERBOY
FORGET THE JACK, BOYS! I'LL LIFT THE TRUCK FOR YOU!
NO, NO, CLARK KENT ROBOT! DON'T DO IT! YOU MUSTN'T REVEAL YOUR SUPER-STRENGTH!
GASP! THAT FOOL ROBOT ISN'T THINKING CLEARLY BECAUSE OF HIS IMPERFECT CONSTRUCTION! HE'S GIVING AWAY MY SECRET IDENTITY TO LANA... AND I CAN'T STOP HIM! I'VE BECOME A PHANTOM WHO NO LONGER EXISTS ON EARTH!
ARS - CAN

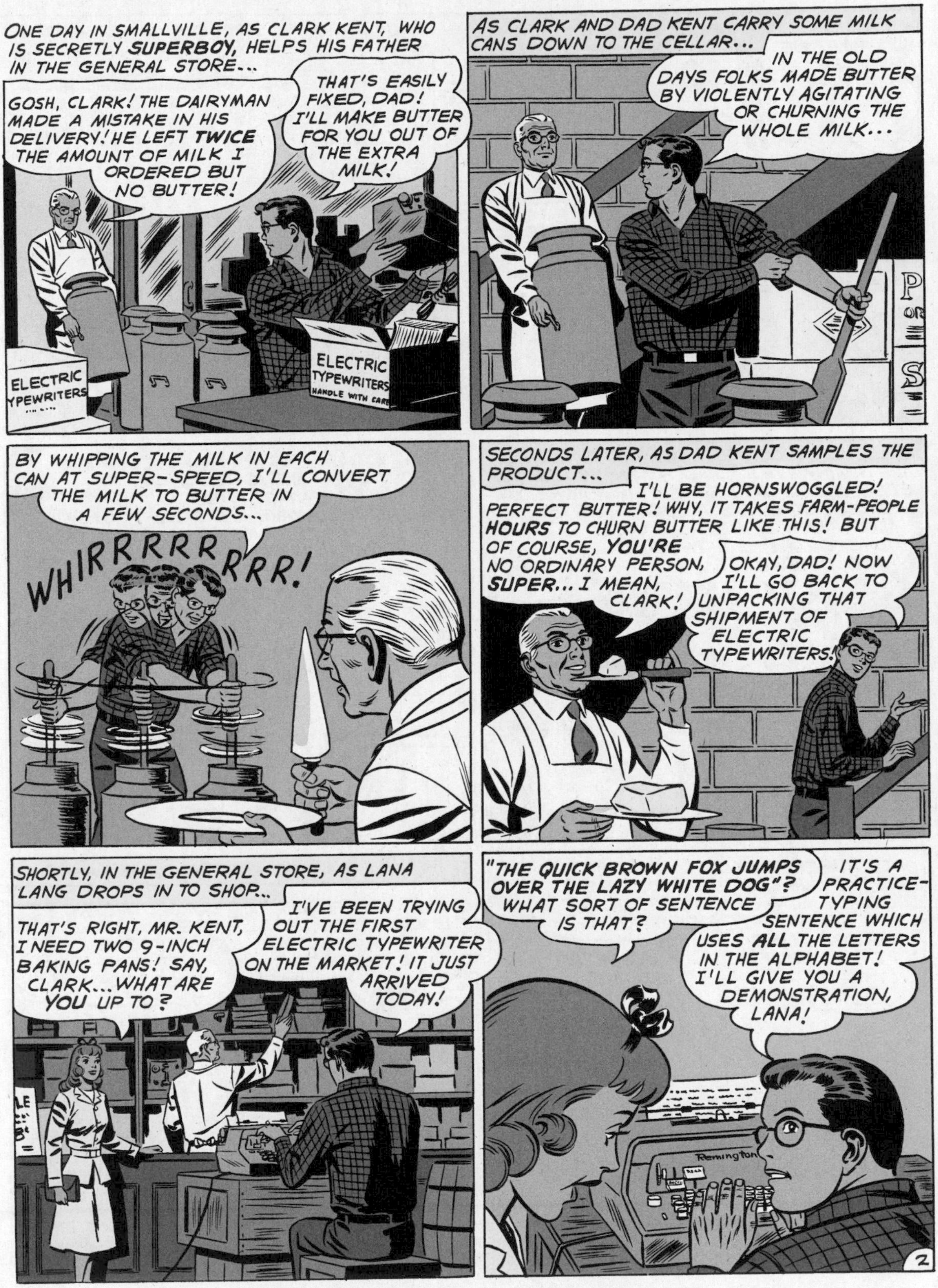
ONE DAY IN SMALLVILLE, AS CLARK KENT, WHO IS SECRETLY **SUPERBOY**, HELPS HIS FATHER IN THE GENERAL STORE...
GOSH, CLARK! THE DAIRYMAN MADE A MISTAKE IN HIS DELIVERY! HE LEFT **TWICE** THE AMOUNT OF MILK I ORDERED BUT NO BUTTER!
THAT'S EASILY FIXED, DAD! I'LL MAKE BUTTER FOR YOU OUT OF THE EXTRA MILK!
ELECTRIC TYPEWRITERS
ELECTRIC TYPEWRITERS HANDLE WITH CARE
AS CLARK AND DAD KENT CARRY SOME MILK CANS DOWN TO THE CELLAR...
IN THE OLD DAYS FOLKS MADE BUTTER BY VIOLENTLY AGITATING OR CHURNING THE WHOLE MILK...
BY WHIPPING THE MILK IN EACH CAN AT SUPER-SPEED, I'LL CONVERT THE MILK TO BUTTER IN A FEW SECONDS...
WHIRRRRRRRRR!
SECONDS LATER, AS DAD KENT SAMPLES THE PRODUCT...
I'LL BE HORNSWOGGLED! PERFECT BUTTER! WHY, IT TAKES FARM-PEOPLE **HOURS** TO CHURN BUTTER LIKE THIS! BUT OF COURSE, **YOU'RE** NO ORDINARY PERSON, **SUPER**... I MEAN, CLARK!
OKAY, DAD! NOW I'LL GO BACK TO UNPACKING THAT SHIPMENT OF ELECTRIC TYPEWRITERS!
SHORTLY, IN THE GENERAL STORE, AS LANA LANG DROPS IN TO SHOP...
THAT'S RIGHT, MR. KENT, I NEED TWO 9-INCH BAKING PANS! SAY, CLARK... WHAT ARE **YOU** UP TO?
I'VE BEEN TRYING OUT THE FIRST ELECTRIC TYPEWRITER ON THE MARKET! IT JUST ARRIVED TODAY!
"**THE QUICK BROWN FOX JUMPS OVER THE LAZY WHITE DOG**"? WHAT SORT OF SENTENCE IS THAT?
IT'S A PRACTICE-TYPING SENTENCE WHICH USES **ALL** THE LETTERS IN THE ALPHABET! I'LL GIVE YOU A DEMONSTRATION, LANA!
Remington
2

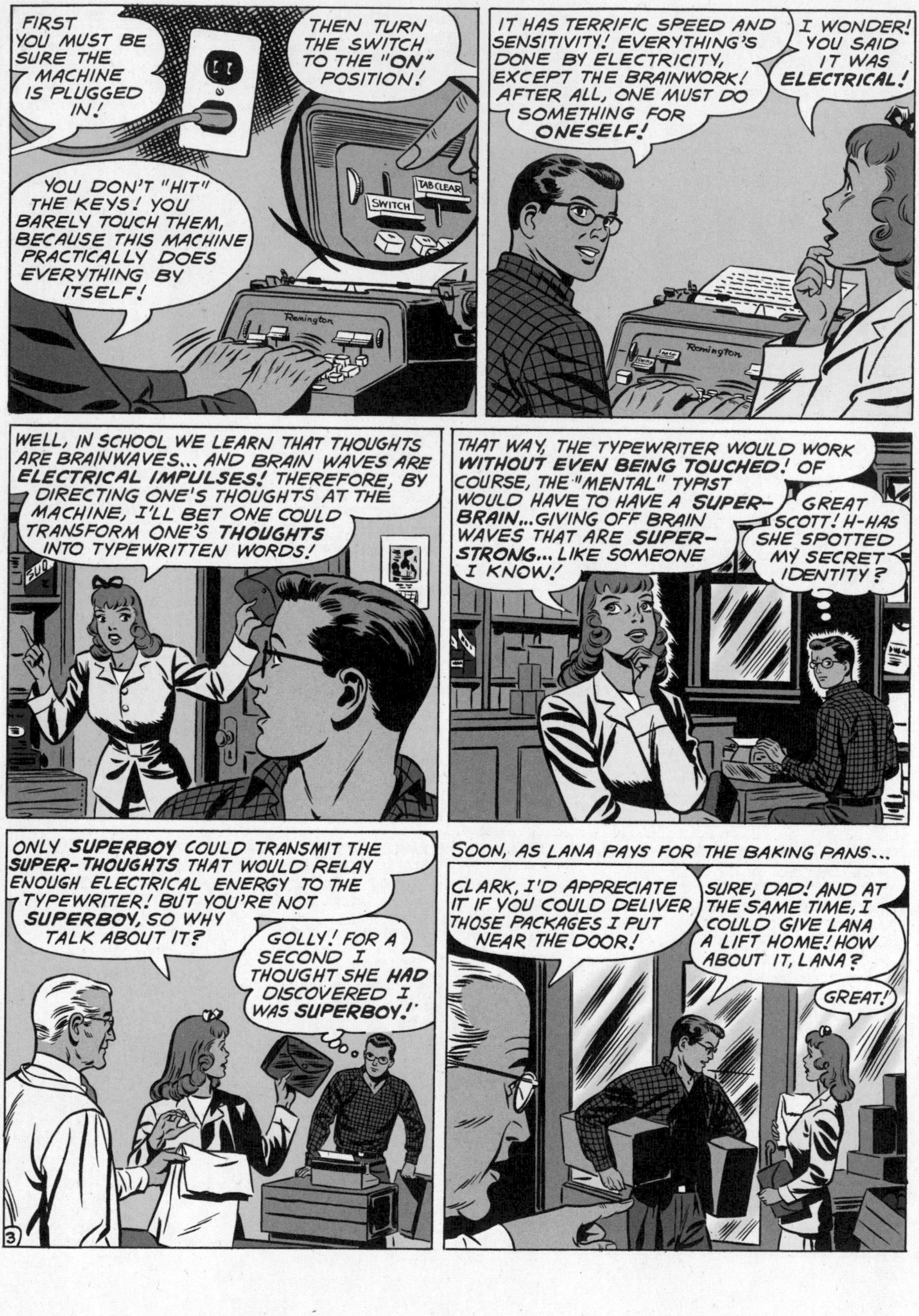
FIRST YOU MUST BE SURE THE MACHINE IS PLUGGED IN!
THEN TURN THE SWITCH TO THE "ON" POSITION!
TAB CLEAR
SWITCH
YOU DON'T "HIT" THE KEYS! YOU BARELY TOUCH THEM, BECAUSE THIS MACHINE PRACTICALLY DOES EVERYTHING BY ITSELF!
Remington
IT HAS TERRIFIC SPEED AND SENSITIVITY! EVERYTHING'S DONE BY ELECTRICITY, EXCEPT THE BRAINWORK! AFTER ALL, ONE MUST DO SOMETHING FOR ONESELF!
I WONDER! YOU SAID IT WAS ELECTRICAL!
Remington
WELL, IN SCHOOL WE LEARN THAT THOUGHTS ARE BRAINWAVES... AND BRAIN WAVES ARE ELECTRICAL IMPULSES! THEREFORE, BY DIRECTING ONE'S THOUGHTS AT THE MACHINE, I'LL BET ONE COULD TRANSFORM ONE'S THOUGHTS INTO TYPEWRITTEN WORDS!
THAT WAY, THE TYPEWRITER WOULD WORK WITHOUT EVEN BEING TOUCHED! OF COURSE, THE "MENTAL" TYPIST WOULD HAVE TO HAVE A SUPER-BRAIN...GIVING OFF BRAIN WAVES THAT ARE SUPER-STRONG... LIKE SOMEONE I KNOW!
GREAT SCOTT! H-HAS SHE SPOTTED MY SECRET IDENTITY?
ONLY SUPERBOY COULD TRANSMIT THE SUPER-THOUGHTS THAT WOULD RELAY ENOUGH ELECTRICAL ENERGY TO THE TYPEWRITER! BUT YOU'RE NOT SUPERBOY, SO WHY TALK ABOUT IT?
GOLLY! FOR A SECOND I THOUGHT SHE HAD DISCOVERED I WAS SUPERBOY!
3
SOON, AS LANA PAYS FOR THE BAKING PANS...
CLARK, I'D APPRECIATE IT IF YOU COULD DELIVER THOSE PACKAGES I PUT NEAR THE DOOR!
SURE, DAD! AND AT THE SAME TIME, I COULD GIVE LANA A LIFT HOME! HOW ABOUT IT, LANA?
GREAT!

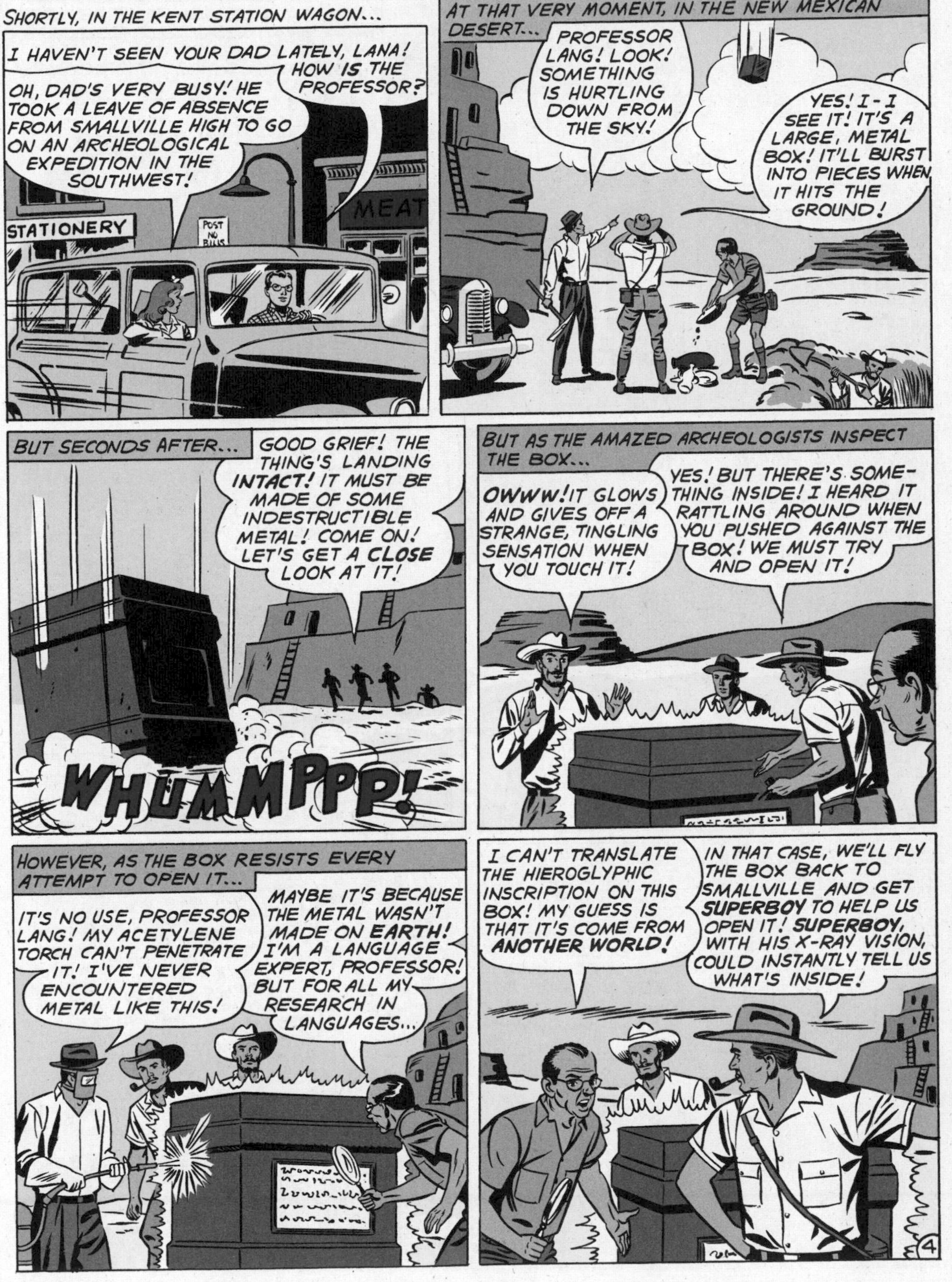
SHORTLY, IN THE KENT STATION WAGON...
I HAVEN'T SEEN YOUR DAD LATELY, LANA! HOW IS THE PROFESSOR?
OH, DAD'S VERY BUSY! HE TOOK A LEAVE OF ABSENCE FROM SMALLVILLE HIGH TO GO ON AN ARCHEOLOGICAL EXPEDITION IN THE SOUTHWEST!
STATIONERY
POST NO BILLS
MEAT
AT THAT VERY MOMENT, IN THE NEW MEXICAN DESERT...
PROFESSOR LANG! LOOK! SOMETHING IS HURTLING DOWN FROM THE SKY!
YES! I-I SEE IT! IT'S A LARGE, METAL BOX! IT'LL BURST INTO PIECES WHEN IT HITS THE GROUND!
BUT SECONDS AFTER...
GOOD GRIEF! THE THING'S LANDING INTACT! IT MUST BE MADE OF SOME INDESTRUCTIBLE METAL! COME ON! LET'S GET A CLOSE LOOK AT IT!
WHUMMPPP!
BUT AS THE AMAZED ARCHEOLOGISTS INSPECT THE BOX...
OWWW! IT GLOWS AND GIVES OFF A STRANGE, TINGLING SENSATION WHEN YOU TOUCH IT!
YES! BUT THERE'S SOMETHING INSIDE! I HEARD IT RATTLING AROUND WHEN YOU PUSHED AGAINST THE BOX! WE MUST TRY AND OPEN IT!
HOWEVER, AS THE BOX RESISTS EVERY ATTEMPT TO OPEN IT...
IT'S NO USE, PROFESSOR LANG! MY ACETYLENE TORCH CAN'T PENETRATE IT! I'VE NEVER ENCOUNTERED METAL LIKE THIS!
MAYBE IT'S BECAUSE THE METAL WASN'T MADE ON EARTH! I'M A LANGUAGE EXPERT, PROFESSOR! BUT FOR ALL MY RESEARCH IN LANGUAGES...
I CAN'T TRANSLATE THE HIEROGLYPHIC INSCRIPTION ON THIS BOX! MY GUESS IS THAT IT'S COME FROM ANOTHER WORLD!
IN THAT CASE, WE'LL FLY THE BOX BACK TO SMALLVILLE AND GET SUPERBOY TO HELP US OPEN IT! SUPERBOY, WITH HIS X-RAY VISION, COULD INSTANTLY TELL US WHAT'S INSIDE!
4

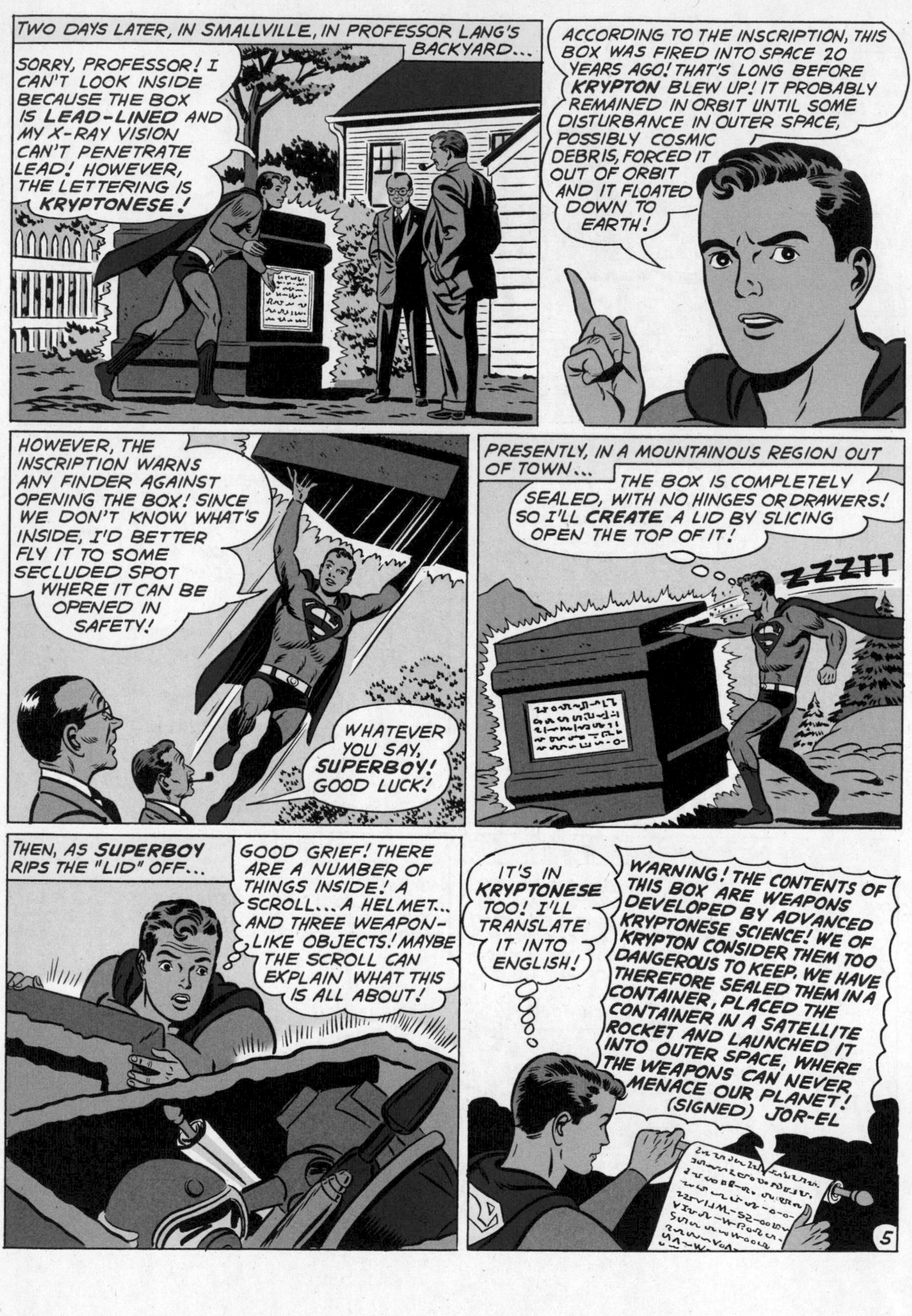
TWO DAYS LATER, IN SMALLVILLE, IN PROFESSOR LANG'S BACKYARD...
SORRY, PROFESSOR! I CAN'T LOOK INSIDE BECAUSE THE BOX IS LEAD-LINED AND MY X-RAY VISION CAN'T PENETRATE LEAD! HOWEVER, THE LETTERING IS KRYPTONESE!
ACCORDING TO THE INSCRIPTION, THIS BOX WAS FIRED INTO SPACE 20 YEARS AGO! THAT'S LONG BEFORE KRYPTON BLEW UP! IT PROBABLY REMAINED IN ORBIT UNTIL SOME DISTURBANCE IN OUTER SPACE, POSSIBLY COSMIC DEBRIS, FORCED IT OUT OF ORBIT AND IT FLOATED DOWN TO EARTH!
HOWEVER, THE INSCRIPTION WARNS ANY FINDER AGAINST OPENING THE BOX! SINCE WE DON'T KNOW WHAT'S INSIDE, I'D BETTER FLY IT TO SOME SECLUDED SPOT WHERE IT CAN BE OPENED IN SAFETY!
WHATEVER YOU SAY, SUPERBOY! GOOD LUCK!
PRESENTLY, IN A MOUNTAINOUS REGION OUT OF TOWN...
THE BOX IS COMPLETELY SEALED, WITH NO HINGES OR DRAWERS! SO I'LL CREATE A LID BY SLICING OPEN THE TOP OF IT!
ZZZTT
THEN, AS SUPERBOY RIPS THE "LID" OFF...
GOOD GRIEF! THERE ARE A NUMBER OF THINGS INSIDE! A SCROLL... A HELMET... AND THREE WEAPON-LIKE OBJECTS! MAYBE THE SCROLL CAN EXPLAIN WHAT THIS IS ALL ABOUT!
IT'S IN KRYPTONESE TOO! I'LL TRANSLATE IT INTO ENGLISH!
WARNING! THE CONTENTS OF THIS BOX ARE WEAPONS DEVELOPED BY ADVANCED KRYPTONESE SCIENCE! WE OF KRYPTON CONSIDER THEM TOO DANGEROUS TO KEEP. WE HAVE THEREFORE SEALED THEM IN A CONTAINER, PLACED THE CONTAINER IN A SATELLITE ROCKET AND LAUNCHED IT INTO OUTER SPACE, WHERE THE WEAPONS CAN NEVER MENACE OUR PLANET! (SIGNED) JOR-EL
5

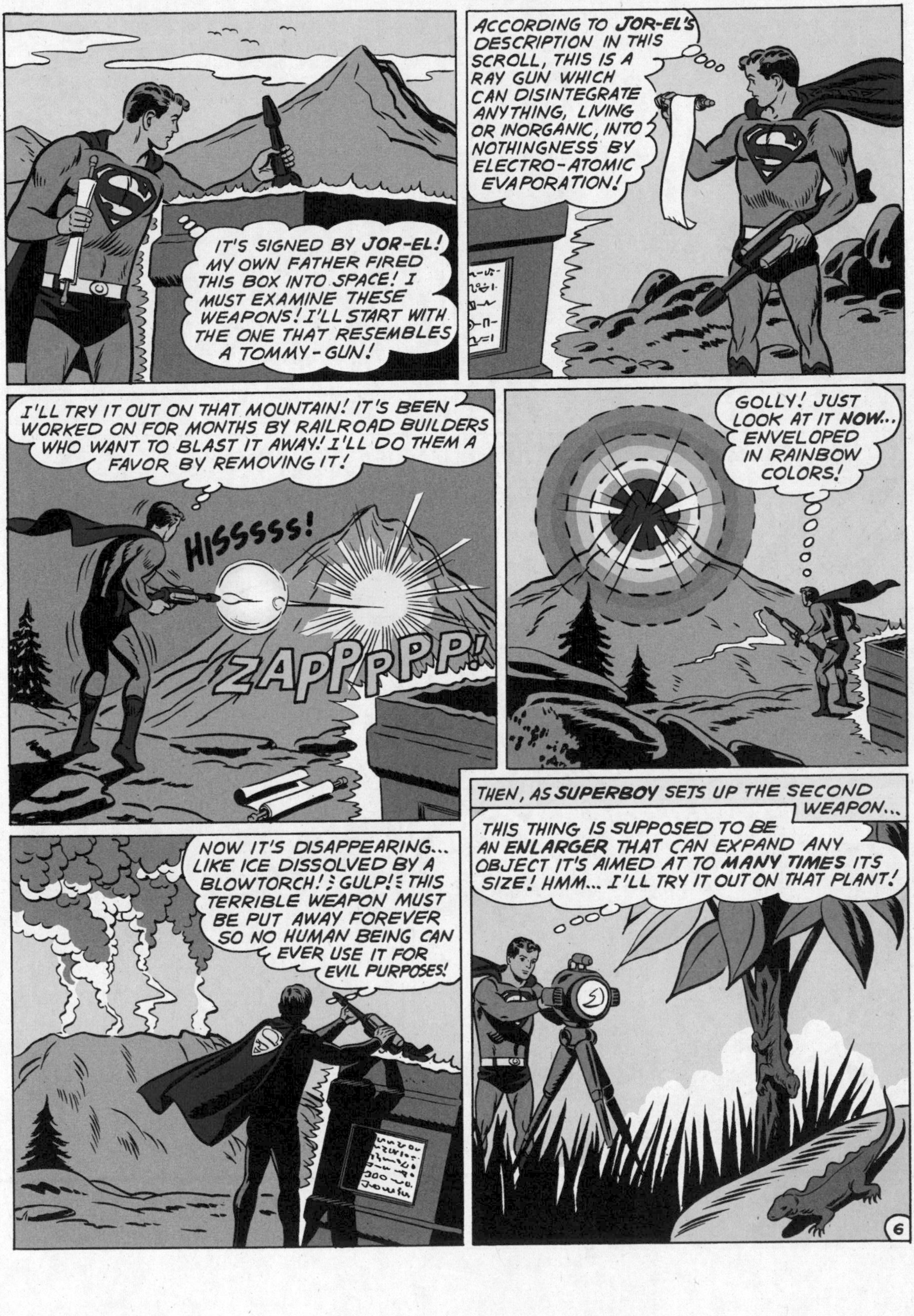
IT'S SIGNED BY JOR-EL! MY OWN FATHER FIRED THIS BOX INTO SPACE! I MUST EXAMINE THESE WEAPONS! I'LL START WITH THE ONE THAT RESEMBLES A TOMMY-GUN!
ACCORDING TO JOR-EL'S DESCRIPTION IN THIS SCROLL, THIS IS A RAY GUN WHICH CAN DISINTEGRATE ANYTHING, LIVING OR INORGANIC, INTO NOTHINGNESS BY ELECTRO-ATOMIC EVAPORATION!
I'LL TRY IT OUT ON THAT MOUNTAIN! IT'S BEEN WORKED ON FOR MONTHS BY RAILROAD BUILDERS WHO WANT TO BLAST IT AWAY! I'LL DO THEM A FAVOR BY REMOVING IT!
HISSSSS!
ZAPPPPPP!
GOLLY! JUST LOOK AT IT NOW... ENVELOPED IN RAINBOW COLORS!
NOW IT'S DISAPPEARING... LIKE ICE DISSOLVED BY A BLOWTORCH! GULP! THIS TERRIBLE WEAPON MUST BE PUT AWAY FOREVER SO NO HUMAN BEING CAN EVER USE IT FOR EVIL PURPOSES!
THEN, AS SUPERBOY SETS UP THE SECOND WEAPON...
THIS THING IS SUPPOSED TO BE AN ENLARGER THAT CAN EXPAND ANY OBJECT IT'S AIMED AT TO MANY TIMES ITS SIZE! HMM... I'LL TRY IT OUT ON THAT PLANT!
6

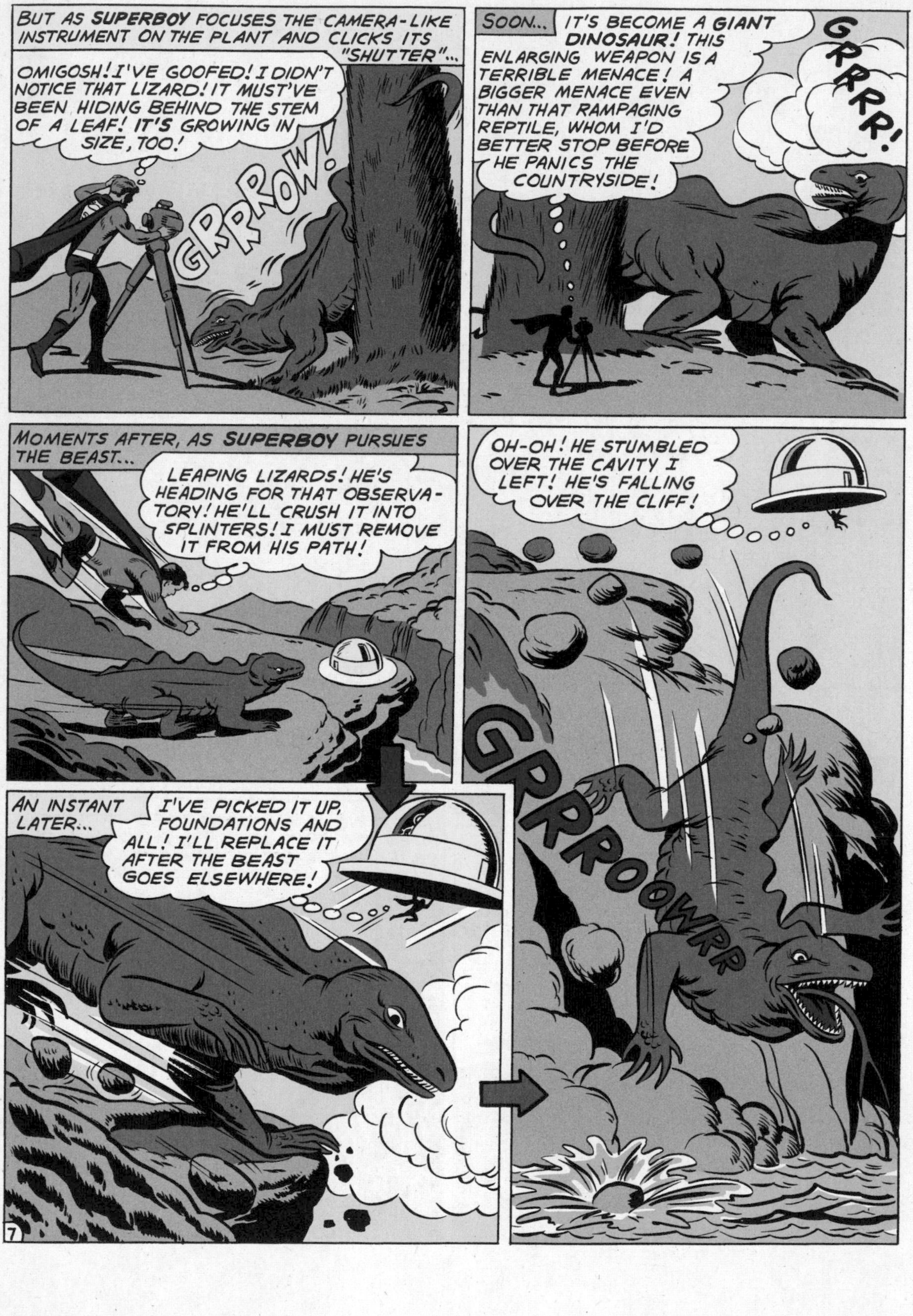
BUT AS SUPERBOY FOCUSES THE CAMERA-LIKE INSTRUMENT ON THE PLANT AND CLICKS ITS "SHUTTER"...
OMIGOSH! I'VE GOOFED! I DIDN'T NOTICE THAT LIZARD! IT MUST'VE BEEN HIDING BEHIND THE STEM OF A LEAF! IT'S GROWING IN SIZE, TOO!
GRPROW!
SOON...
IT'S BECOME A GIANT DINOSAUR! THIS ENLARGING WEAPON IS A TERRIBLE MENACE! A BIGGER MENACE EVEN THAN THAT RAMPAGING REPTILE, WHOM I'D BETTER STOP BEFORE HE PANICS THE COUNTRYSIDE!
GRRRR!
MOMENTS AFTER, AS SUPERBOY PURSUES THE BEAST...
LEAPING LIZARDS! HE'S HEADING FOR THAT OBSERVATORY! HE'LL CRUSH IT INTO SPLINTERS! I MUST REMOVE IT FROM HIS PATH!
AN INSTANT LATER...
I'VE PICKED IT UP, FOUNDATIONS AND ALL! I'LL REPLACE IT AFTER THE BEAST GOES ELSEWHERE!
7
OH-OH! HE STUMBLED OVER THE CAVITY I LEFT! HE'S FALLING OVER THE CLIFF!
GRRROOWRR

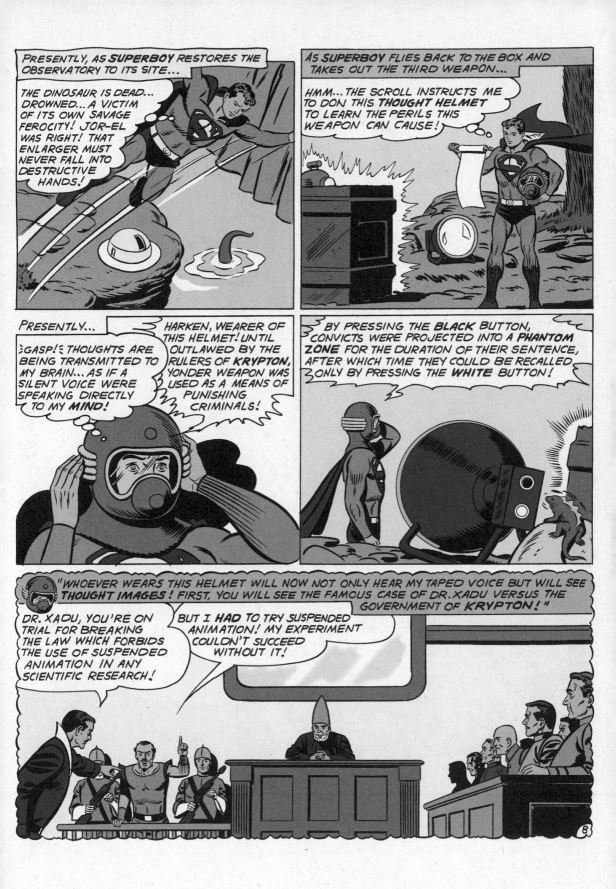

PRESENTLY, AS **SUPERBOY** RESTORES THE OBSERVATORY TO ITS SITE...

THE DINOSAUR IS DEAD... DROWNED... A VICTIM OF ITS OWN SAVAGE FEROCITY! JOR-EL WAS RIGHT! THAT ENLARGER MUST NEVER FALL INTO DESTRUCTIVE HANDS!

AS SUPERBOY FLIES BACK TO THE BOX AND TAKES OUT THE THIRD WEAPON...

HMM... THE SCROLL INSTRUCTS ME TO DON THIS **THOUGHT HELMET** TO LEARN THE PERILS THIS WEAPON CAN CAUSE!

PRESENTLY...

≥GASP!≤ THOUGHTS ARE BEING TRANSMITTED TO MY BRAIN.... AS IF A SILENT VOICE WERE SPEAKING DIRECTLY TO MY **MIND**!

HARKEN, WEARER OF THIS HELMET! UNTIL OUTLAWED BY THE RULERS OF **KRYPTON**, YONDER WEAPON WAS USED AS A MEANS OF PUNISHING CRIMINALS!

BY PRESSING THE **BLACK** BUTTON, CONVICTS WERE PROJECTED INTO A **PHANTOM ZONE** FOR THE DURATION OF THEIR SENTENCE, AFTER WHICH TIME THEY COULD BE RECALLED ONLY BY PRESSING THE **WHITE** BUTTON!

"WHOEVER WEARS THIS HELMET WILL NOW NOT ONLY HEAR MY TAPED VOICE BUT WILL SEE **THOUGHT IMAGES**! FIRST, YOU WILL SEE THE FAMOUS CASE OF DR. XADU VERSUS THE GOVERNMENT OF **KRYPTON**!"

DR. XADU, YOU'RE ON TRIAL FOR BREAKING THE LAW WHICH FORBIDS THE USE OF SUSPENDED ANIMATION IN ANY SCIENTIFIC RESEARCH!

BUT I **HAD** TO TRY SUSPENDED ANIMATION! MY EXPERIMENT COULDN'T SUCCEED WITHOUT IT!

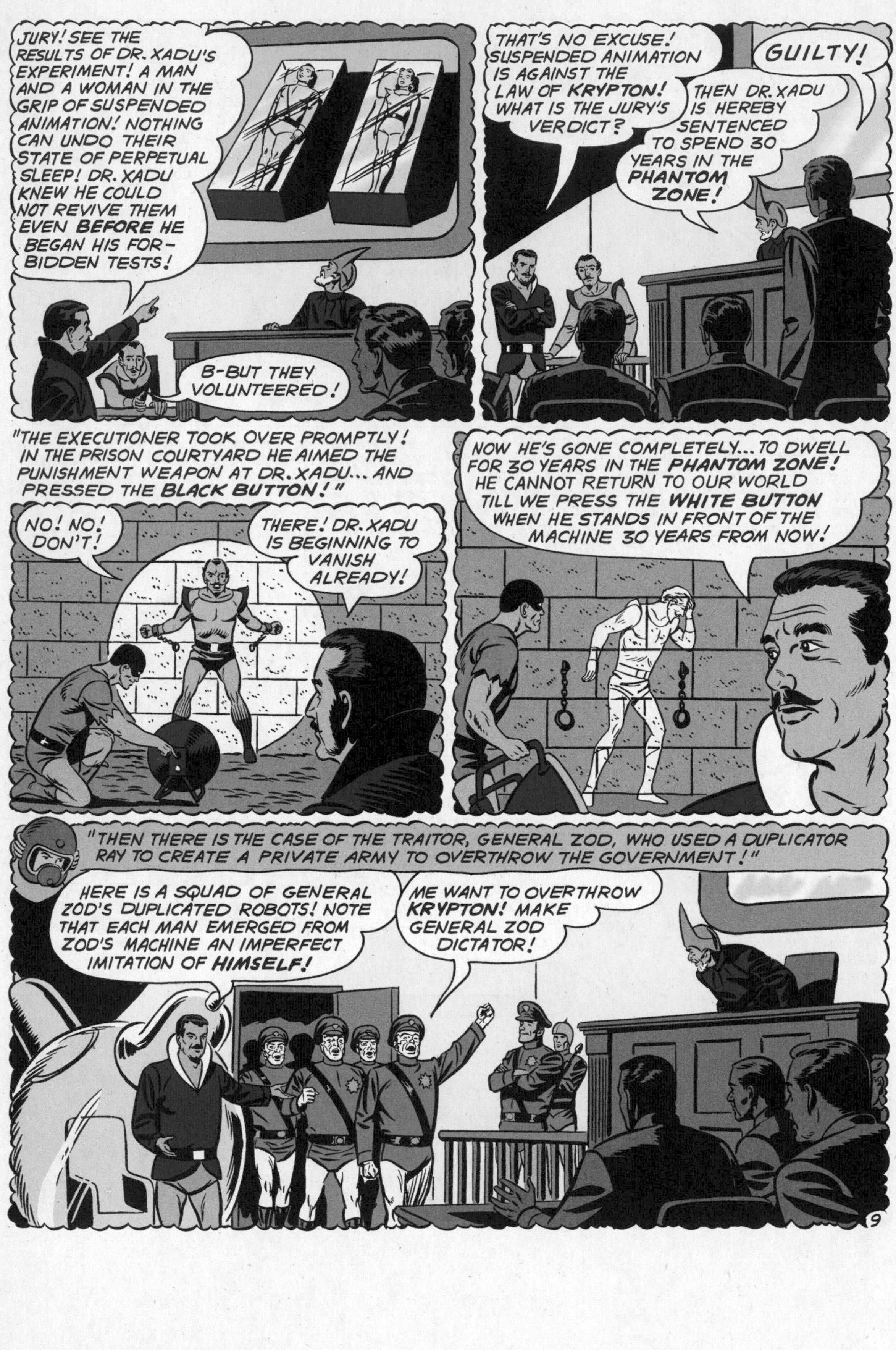
JURY! SEE THE RESULTS OF DR. XADU'S EXPERIMENT! A MAN AND A WOMAN IN THE GRIP OF SUSPENDED ANIMATION! NOTHING CAN UNDO THEIR STATE OF PERPETUAL SLEEP! DR. XADU KNEW HE COULD NOT REVIVE THEM EVEN BEFORE HE BEGAN HIS FOR-BIDDEN TESTS!
B-BUT THEY VOLUNTEERED!
THAT'S NO EXCUSE! SUSPENDED ANIMATION IS AGAINST THE LAW OF KRYPTON! WHAT IS THE JURY'S VERDICT?
GUILTY!
THEN DR. XADU IS HEREBY SENTENCED TO SPEND 30 YEARS IN THE PHANTOM ZONE!
"THE EXECUTIONER TOOK OVER PROMPTLY! IN THE PRISON COURTYARD HE AIMED THE PUNISHMENT WEAPON AT DR. XADU... AND PRESSED THE BLACK BUTTON!"
NO! NO! DON'T!
THERE! DR. XADU IS BEGINNING TO VANISH ALREADY!
NOW HE'S GONE COMPLETELY... TO DWELL FOR 30 YEARS IN THE PHANTOM ZONE! HE CANNOT RETURN TO OUR WORLD TILL WE PRESS THE WHITE BUTTON WHEN HE STANDS IN FRONT OF THE MACHINE 30 YEARS FROM NOW!
"THEN THERE IS THE CASE OF THE TRAITOR, GENERAL ZOD, WHO USED A DUPLICATOR RAY TO CREATE A PRIVATE ARMY TO OVERTHROW THE GOVERNMENT!"
HERE IS A SQUAD OF GENERAL ZOD'S DUPLICATED ROBOTS! NOTE THAT EACH MAN EMERGED FROM ZOD'S MACHINE AN IMPERFECT IMITATION OF HIMSELF!
ME WANT TO OVERTHROW KRYPTON! MAKE GENERAL ZOD DICTATOR!
9

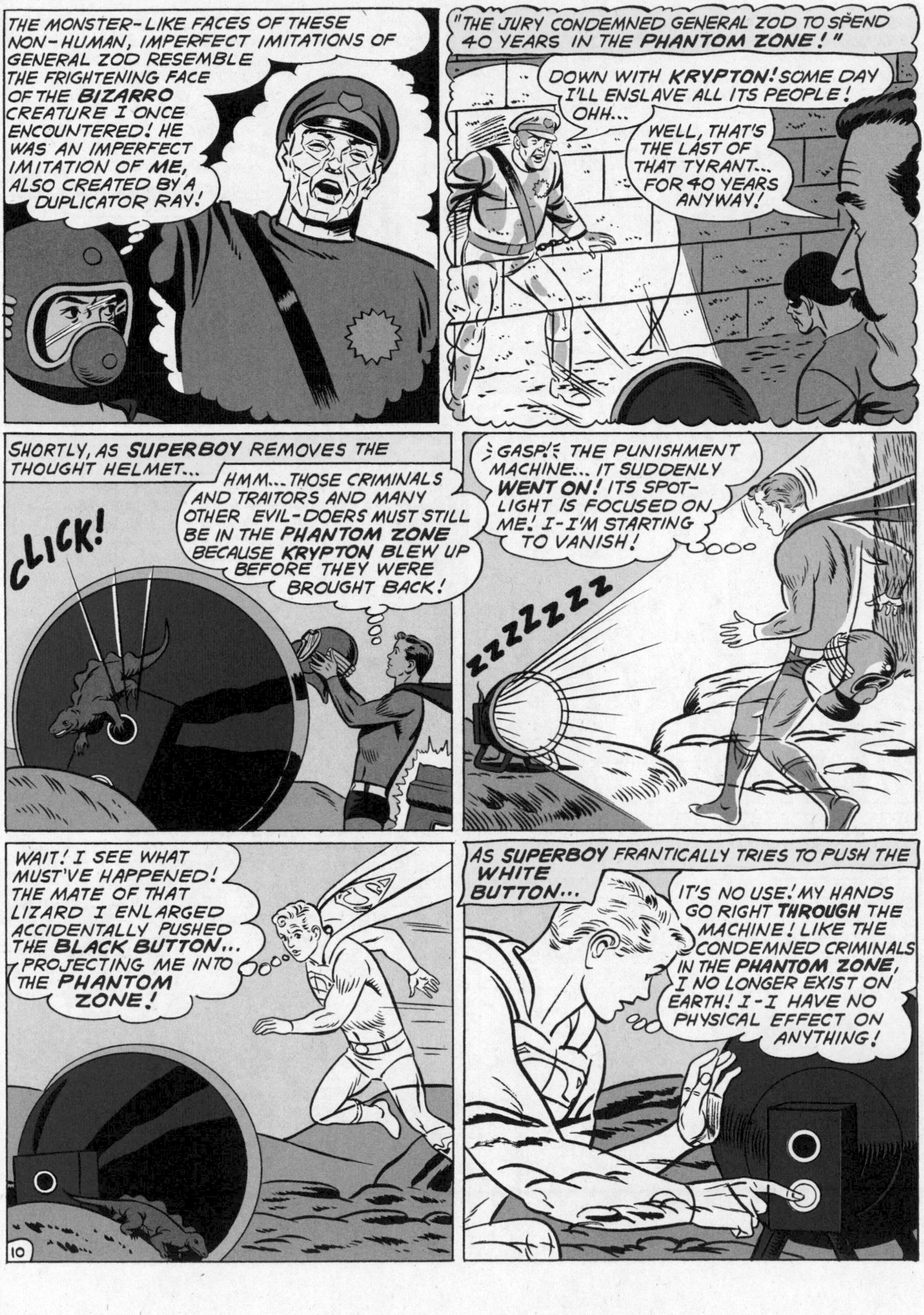
THE MONSTER-LIKE FACES OF THESE NON-HUMAN, IMPERFECT IMITATIONS OF GENERAL ZOD RESEMBLE THE FRIGHTENING FACE OF THE BIZARRO CREATURE I ONCE ENCOUNTERED! HE WAS AN IMPERFECT IMITATION OF ME, ALSO CREATED BY A DUPLICATOR RAY!
"THE JURY CONDEMNED GENERAL ZOD TO SPEND 40 YEARS IN THE PHANTOM ZONE!"
DOWN WITH KRYPTON! SOME DAY I'LL ENSLAVE ALL ITS PEOPLE! OHH...
WELL, THAT'S THE LAST OF THAT TYRANT... FOR 40 YEARS ANYWAY!
SHORTLY, AS SUPERBOY REMOVES THE THOUGHT HELMET...
HMM... THOSE CRIMINALS AND TRAITORS AND MANY OTHER EVIL-DOERS MUST STILL BE IN THE PHANTOM ZONE BECAUSE KRYPTON BLEW UP BEFORE THEY WERE BROUGHT BACK!
CLICK!
GASP! THE PUNISHMENT MACHINE... IT SUDDENLY WENT ON! ITS SPOT-LIGHT IS FOCUSED ON ME! I-I'M STARTING TO VANISH!
ZZZZZZZ
WAIT! I SEE WHAT MUST'VE HAPPENED! THE MATE OF THAT LIZARD I ENLARGED ACCIDENTALLY PUSHED THE BLACK BUTTON... PROJECTING ME INTO THE PHANTOM ZONE!
10
AS SUPERBOY FRANTICALLY TRIES TO PUSH THE WHITE BUTTON...
IT'S NO USE! MY HANDS GO RIGHT THROUGH THE MACHINE! LIKE THE CONDEMNED CRIMINALS IN THE PHANTOM ZONE, I NO LONGER EXIST ON EARTH! I-I HAVE NO PHYSICAL EFFECT ON ANYTHING!

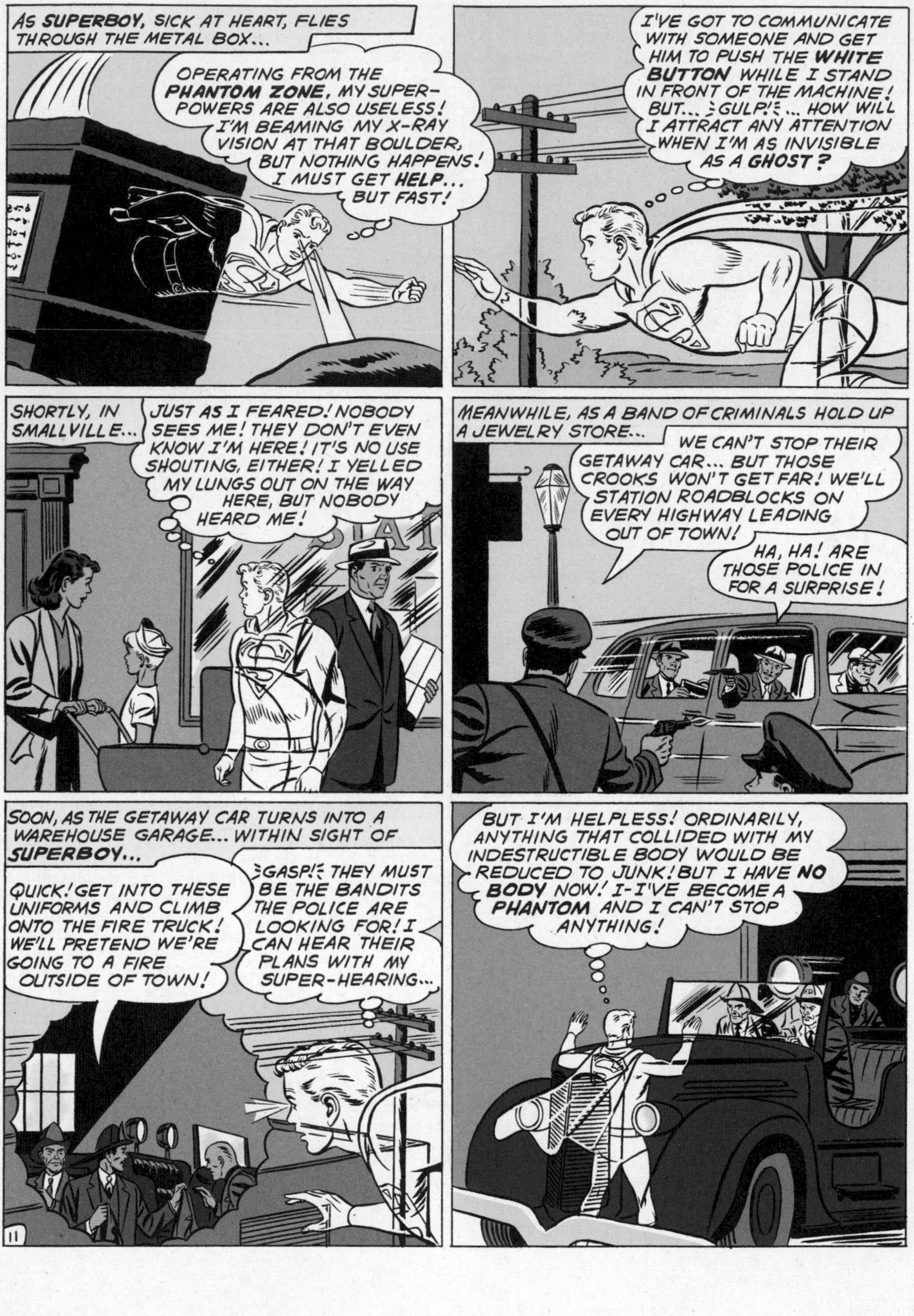
AS SUPERBOY, SICK AT HEART, FLIES THROUGH THE METAL BOX...
OPERATING FROM THE PHANTOM ZONE, MY SUPER-POWERS ARE ALSO USELESS! I'M BEAMING MY X-RAY VISION AT THAT BOULDER, BUT NOTHING HAPPENS! I MUST GET HELP... BUT FAST!
I'VE GOT TO COMMUNICATE WITH SOMEONE AND GET HIM TO PUSH THE WHITE BUTTON WHILE I STAND IN FRONT OF THE MACHINE! BUT... GULP! ... HOW WILL I ATTRACT ANY ATTENTION WHEN I'M AS INVISIBLE AS A GHOST?
SHORTLY, IN SMALLVILLE...
JUST AS I FEARED! NOBODY SEES ME! THEY DON'T EVEN KNOW I'M HERE! IT'S NO USE SHOUTING, EITHER! I YELLED MY LUNGS OUT ON THE WAY HERE, BUT NOBODY HEARD ME!
MEANWHILE, AS A BAND OF CRIMINALS HOLD UP A JEWELRY STORE...
WE CAN'T STOP THEIR GETAWAY CAR... BUT THOSE CROOKS WON'T GET FAR! WE'LL STATION ROADBLOCKS ON EVERY HIGHWAY LEADING OUT OF TOWN!
HA, HA! ARE THOSE POLICE IN FOR A SURPRISE!
SOON, AS THE GETAWAY CAR TURNS INTO A WAREHOUSE GARAGE... WITHIN SIGHT OF SUPERBOY...
QUICK! GET INTO THESE UNIFORMS AND CLIMB ONTO THE FIRE TRUCK! WE'LL PRETEND WE'RE GOING TO A FIRE OUTSIDE OF TOWN!
GASP! THEY MUST BE THE BANDITS THE POLICE ARE LOOKING FOR! I CAN HEAR THEIR PLANS WITH MY SUPER-HEARING...
11
BUT I'M HELPLESS! ORDINARILY, ANYTHING THAT COLLIDED WITH MY INDESTRUCTIBLE BODY WOULD BE REDUCED TO JUNK! BUT I HAVE NO BODY NOW! I-I'VE BECOME A PHANTOM AND I CAN'T STOP ANYTHING!

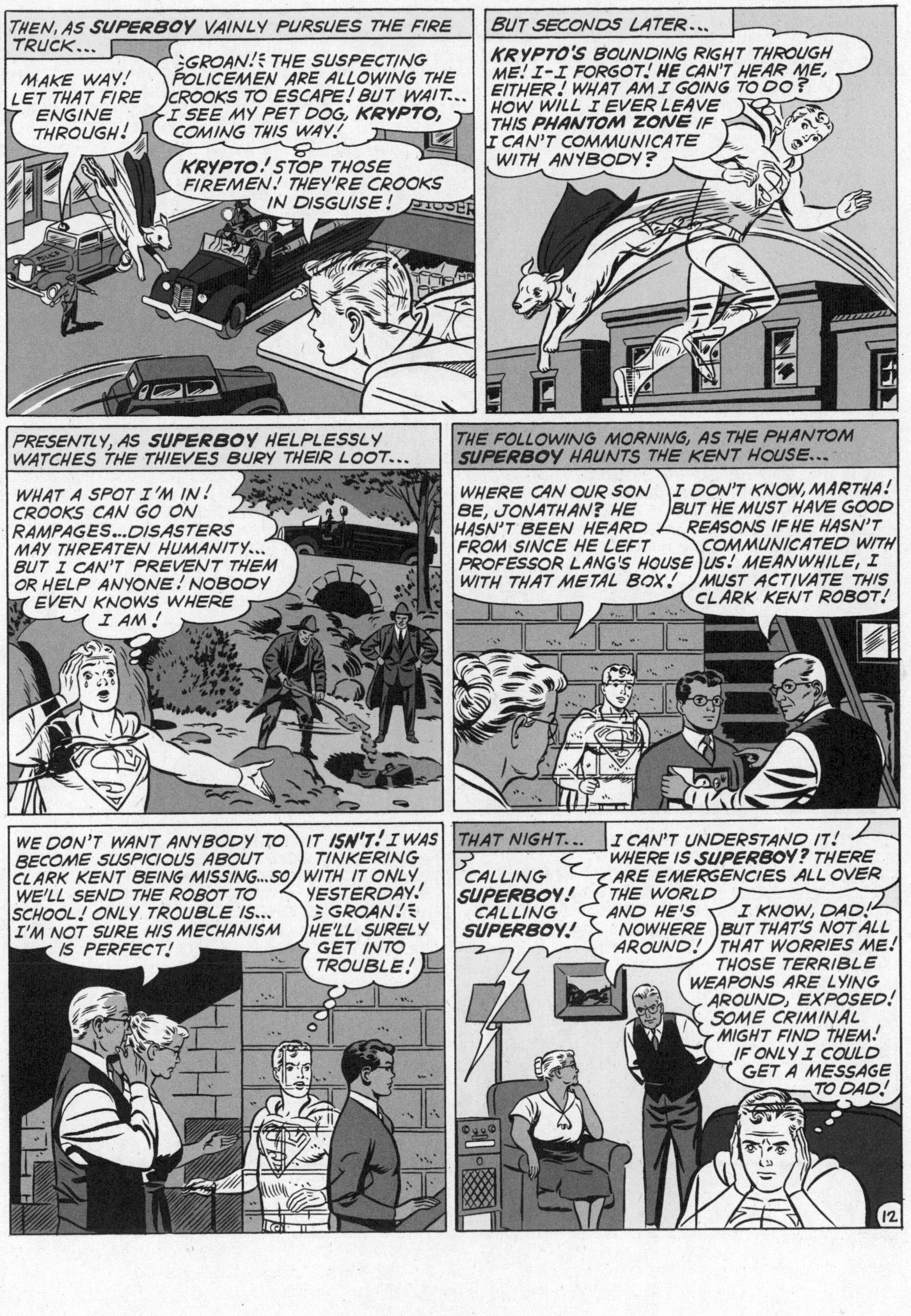
THEN, AS SUPERBOY VAINLY PURSUES THE FIRE TRUCK...
MAKE WAY! LET THAT FIRE ENGINE THROUGH!
GROAN! THE SUSPECTING POLICEMEN ARE ALLOWING THE CROOKS TO ESCAPE! BUT WAIT... I SEE MY PET DOG, KRYPTO, COMING THIS WAY!
KRYPTO! STOP THOSE FIREMEN! THEY'RE CROOKS IN DISGUISE!
BUT SECONDS LATER...
KRYPTO'S BOUNDING RIGHT THROUGH ME! I-I FORGOT! HE CAN'T HEAR ME, EITHER! WHAT AM I GOING TO DO? HOW WILL I EVER LEAVE THIS PHANTOM ZONE IF I CAN'T COMMUNICATE WITH ANYBODY?
PRESENTLY, AS SUPERBOY HELPLESSLY WATCHES THE THIEVES BURY THEIR LOOT...
WHAT A SPOT I'M IN! CROOKS CAN GO ON RAMPAGES...DISASTERS MAY THREATEN HUMANITY... BUT I CAN'T PREVENT THEM OR HELP ANYONE! NOBODY EVEN KNOWS WHERE I AM!
THE FOLLOWING MORNING, AS THE PHANTOM SUPERBOY HAUNTS THE KENT HOUSE...
WHERE CAN OUR SON BE, JONATHAN? HE HASN'T BEEN HEARD FROM SINCE HE LEFT PROFESSOR LANG'S HOUSE WITH THAT METAL BOX!
I DON'T KNOW, MARTHA! BUT HE MUST HAVE GOOD REASONS IF HE HASN'T COMMUNICATED WITH US! MEANWHILE, I MUST ACTIVATE THIS CLARK KENT ROBOT!
WE DON'T WANT ANYBODY TO BECOME SUSPICIOUS ABOUT CLARK KENT BEING MISSING...SO WE'LL SEND THE ROBOT TO SCHOOL! ONLY TROUBLE IS... I'M NOT SURE HIS MECHANISM IS PERFECT!
IT ISN'T! I WAS TINKERING WITH IT ONLY YESTERDAY! GROAN! HE'LL SURELY GET INTO TROUBLE!
THAT NIGHT...
CALLING SUPERBOY! CALLING SUPERBOY!
I CAN'T UNDERSTAND IT! WHERE IS SUPERBOY? THERE ARE EMERGENCIES ALL OVER THE WORLD AND HE'S NOWHERE AROUND!
I KNOW, DAD! BUT THAT'S NOT ALL THAT WORRIES ME! THOSE TERRIBLE WEAPONS ARE LYING AROUND, EXPOSED! SOME CRIMINAL MIGHT FIND THEM! IF ONLY I COULD GET A MESSAGE TO DAD!
12

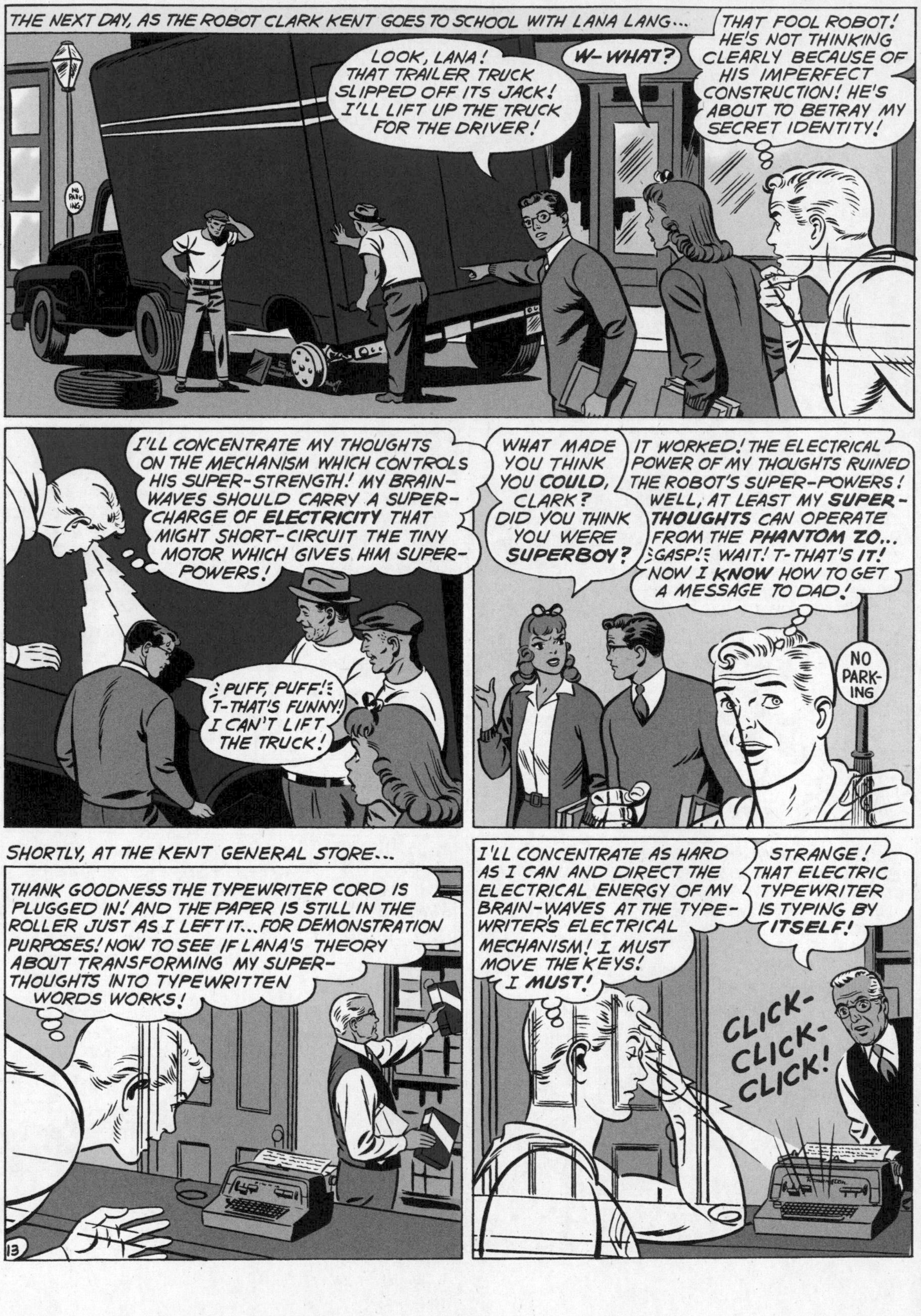
THE NEXT DAY, AS THE ROBOT CLARK KENT GOES TO SCHOOL WITH LANA LANG...
LOOK, LANA! THAT TRAILER TRUCK SLIPPED OFF ITS JACK! I'LL LIFT UP THE TRUCK FOR THE DRIVER!
W-WHAT?
THAT FOOL ROBOT! HE'S NOT THINKING CLEARLY BECAUSE OF HIS IMPERFECT CONSTRUCTION! HE'S ABOUT TO BETRAY MY SECRET IDENTITY!
NO PARKING
I'LL CONCENTRATE MY THOUGHTS ON THE MECHANISM WHICH CONTROLS HIS SUPER-STRENGTH! MY BRAIN-WAVES SHOULD CARRY A SUPER-CHARGE OF ELECTRICITY THAT MIGHT SHORT-CIRCUIT THE TINY MOTOR WHICH GIVES HIM SUPER-POWERS!
PUFF, PUFF! T-THAT'S FUNNY! I CAN'T LIFT THE TRUCK!
WHAT MADE YOU THINK YOU COULD, CLARK? DID YOU THINK YOU WERE SUPERBOY?
IT WORKED! THE ELECTRICAL POWER OF MY THOUGHTS RUINED THE ROBOT'S SUPER-POWERS! WELL, AT LEAST MY SUPER-THOUGHTS CAN OPERATE FROM THE PHANTOM ZO... GASP! WAIT! T-THAT'S IT! NOW I KNOW HOW TO GET A MESSAGE TO DAD!
NO PARKING
SHORTLY, AT THE KENT GENERAL STORE...
THANK GOODNESS THE TYPEWRITER CORD IS PLUGGED IN! AND THE PAPER IS STILL IN THE ROLLER JUST AS I LEFT IT... FOR DEMONSTRATION PURPOSES! NOW TO SEE IF LANA'S THEORY ABOUT TRANSFORMING MY SUPER-THOUGHTS INTO TYPEWRITTEN WORDS WORKS!
13
I'LL CONCENTRATE AS HARD AS I CAN AND DIRECT THE ELECTRICAL ENERGY OF MY BRAIN-WAVES AT THE TYPE-WRITER'S ELECTRICAL MECHANISM! I MUST MOVE THE KEYS! I MUST!
STRANGE! THAT ELECTRIC TYPEWRITER IS TYPING BY ITSELF!
CLICK-CLICK-CLICK!

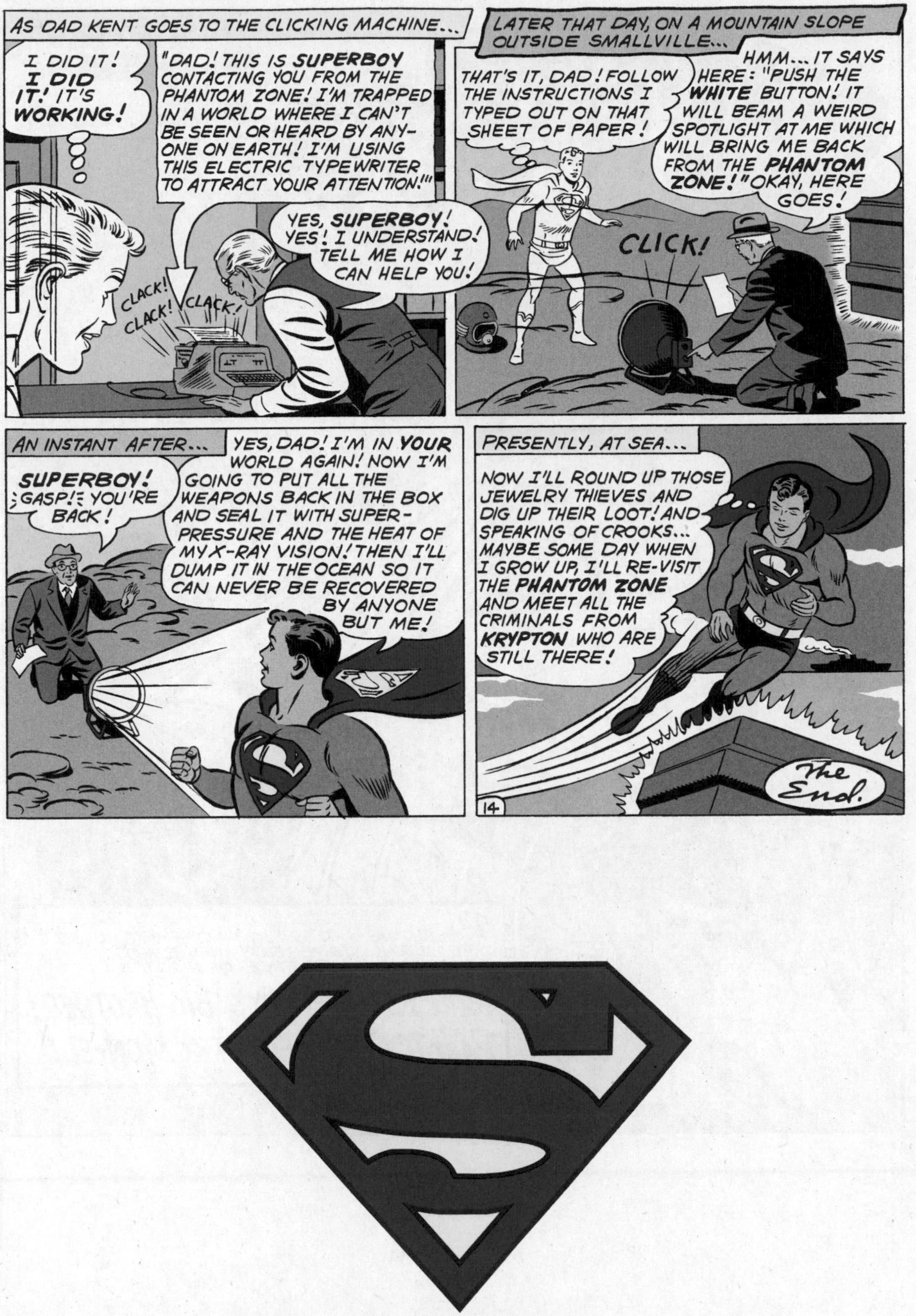
AS DAD KENT GOES TO THE CLICKING MACHINE...
I DID IT! I DID IT! IT'S WORKING!
"DAD! THIS IS SUPERBOY CONTACTING YOU FROM THE PHANTOM ZONE! I'M TRAPPED IN A WORLD WHERE I CAN'T BE SEEN OR HEARD BY ANYONE ON EARTH! I'M USING THIS ELECTRIC TYPEWRITER TO ATTRACT YOUR ATTENTION!"
YES, SUPERBOY! YES! I UNDERSTAND! TELL ME HOW I CAN HELP YOU!
CLACK! CLACK! CLACK!
LATER THAT DAY, ON A MOUNTAIN SLOPE OUTSIDE SMALLVILLE...
THAT'S IT, DAD! FOLLOW THE INSTRUCTIONS I TYPED OUT ON THAT SHEET OF PAPER!
HMM... IT SAYS HERE: "PUSH THE WHITE BUTTON! IT WILL BEAM A WEIRD SPOTLIGHT AT ME WHICH WILL BRING ME BACK FROM THE PHANTOM ZONE!" OKAY, HERE GOES!
CLICK!
AN INSTANT AFTER...
SUPERBOY! GASP! YOU'RE BACK!
YES, DAD! I'M IN YOUR WORLD AGAIN! NOW I'M GOING TO PUT ALL THE WEAPONS BACK IN THE BOX AND SEAL IT WITH SUPER-PRESSURE AND THE HEAT OF MY X-RAY VISION! THEN I'LL DUMP IT IN THE OCEAN SO IT CAN NEVER BE RECOVERED BY ANYONE BUT ME!
PRESENTLY, AT SEA...
NOW I'LL ROUND UP THOSE JEWELRY THIEVES AND DIG UP THEIR LOOT! AND SPEAKING OF CROOKS... MAYBE SOME DAY WHEN I GROW UP, I'LL RE-VISIT THE PHANTOM ZONE AND MEET ALL THE CRIMINALS FROM KRYPTON WHO ARE STILL THERE!
14
The End.

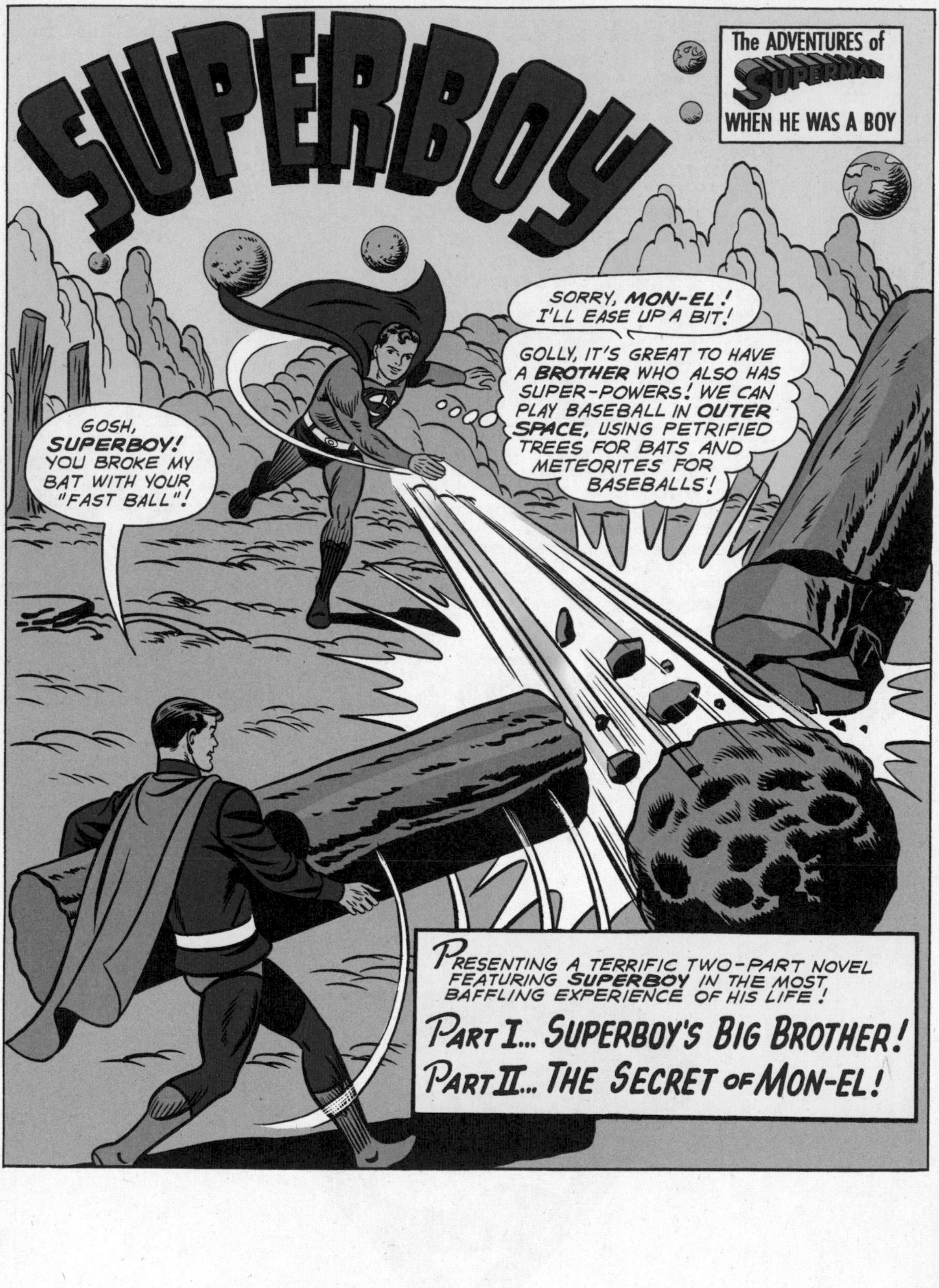
SUPERBOY
The ADVENTURES of SUPERMAN WHEN HE WAS A BOY
SORRY, MON-EL! I'LL EASE UP A BIT!
GOLLY, IT'S GREAT TO HAVE A BROTHER WHO ALSO HAS SUPER-POWERS! WE CAN PLAY BASEBALL IN OUTER SPACE, USING PETRIFIED TREES FOR BATS AND METEORITES FOR BASEBALLS!
GOSH, SUPERBOY! YOU BROKE MY BAT WITH YOUR "FAST BALL"!
PRESENTING A TERRIFIC TWO-PART NOVEL FEATURING SUPERBOY IN THE MOST BAFFLING EXPERIENCE OF HIS LIFE!
PART I... SUPERBOY'S BIG BROTHER!
PART II... THE SECRET OF MON-EL!

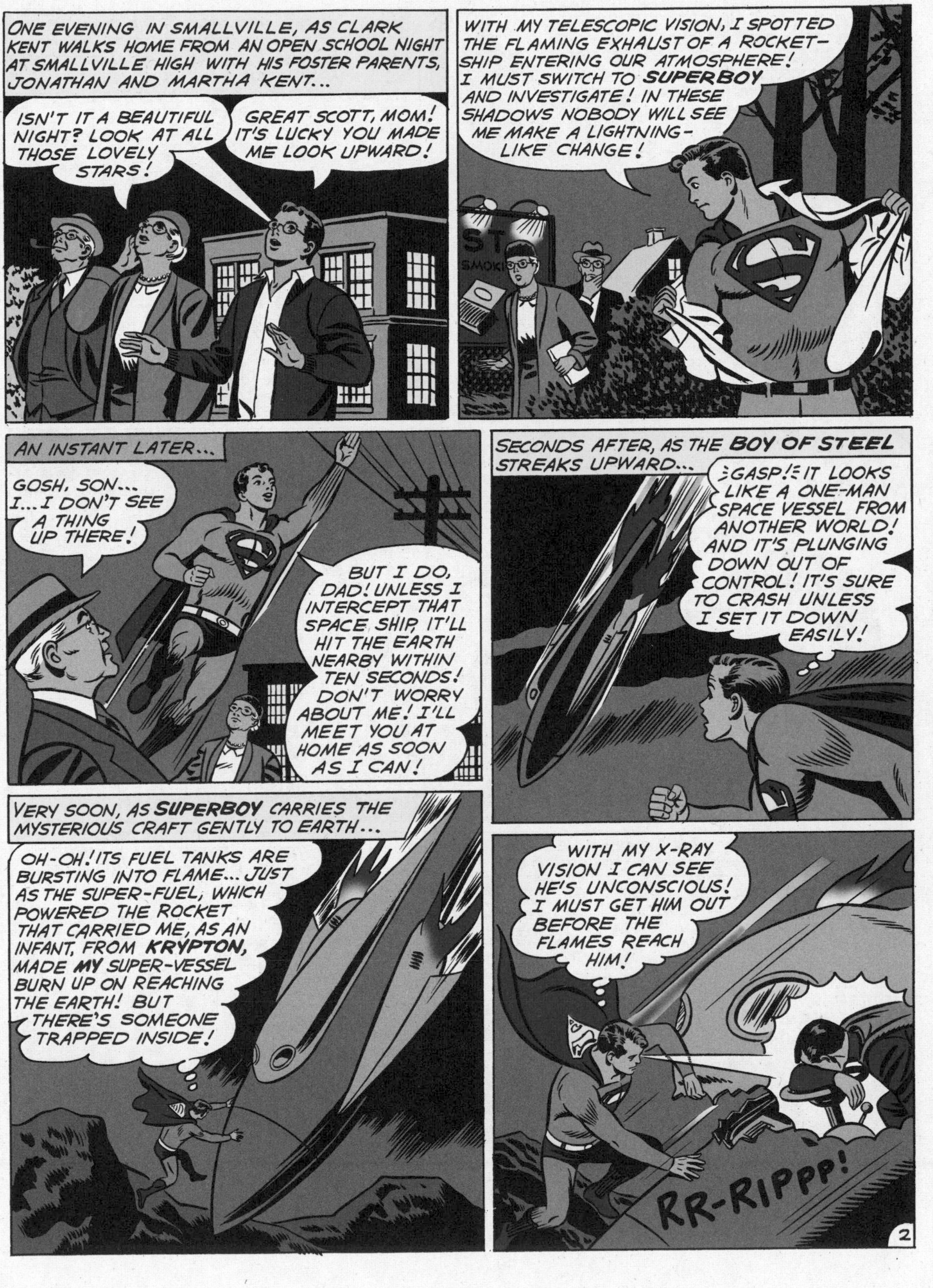
ONE EVENING IN SMALLVILLE, AS CLARK KENT WALKS HOME FROM AN OPEN SCHOOL NIGHT AT SMALLVILLE HIGH WITH HIS FOSTER PARENTS, JONATHAN AND MARTHA KENT...
ISN'T IT A BEAUTIFUL NIGHT? LOOK AT ALL THOSE LOVELY STARS!
GREAT SCOTT, MOM! IT'S LUCKY YOU MADE ME LOOK UPWARD!
WITH MY TELESCOPIC VISION, I SPOTTED THE FLAMING EXHAUST OF A ROCKET-SHIP ENTERING OUR ATMOSPHERE! I MUST SWITCH TO SUPERBOY AND INVESTIGATE! IN THESE SHADOWS NOBODY WILL SEE ME MAKE A LIGHTNING-LIKE CHANGE!
AN INSTANT LATER...
GOSH, SON... I... I DON'T SEE A THING UP THERE!
BUT I DO, DAD! UNLESS I INTERCEPT THAT SPACE SHIP, IT'LL HIT THE EARTH NEARBY WITHIN TEN SECONDS! DON'T WORRY ABOUT ME! I'LL MEET YOU AT HOME AS SOON AS I CAN!
SECONDS AFTER, AS THE BOY OF STEEL STREAKS UPWARD...
GASP! IT LOOKS LIKE A ONE-MAN SPACE VESSEL FROM ANOTHER WORLD! AND IT'S PLUNGING DOWN OUT OF CONTROL! IT'S SURE TO CRASH UNLESS I SET IT DOWN EASILY!
VERY SOON, AS SUPERBOY CARRIES THE MYSTERIOUS CRAFT GENTLY TO EARTH...
OH-OH! ITS FUEL TANKS ARE BURSTING INTO FLAME... JUST AS THE SUPER-FUEL, WHICH POWERED THE ROCKET THAT CARRIED ME, AS AN INFANT, FROM KRYPTON, MADE MY SUPER-VESSEL BURN UP ON REACHING THE EARTH! BUT THERE'S SOMEONE TRAPPED INSIDE!
WITH MY X-RAY VISION I CAN SEE HE'S UNCONSCIOUS! I MUST GET HIM OUT BEFORE THE FLAMES REACH HIM!
RR-RIPPP!
2

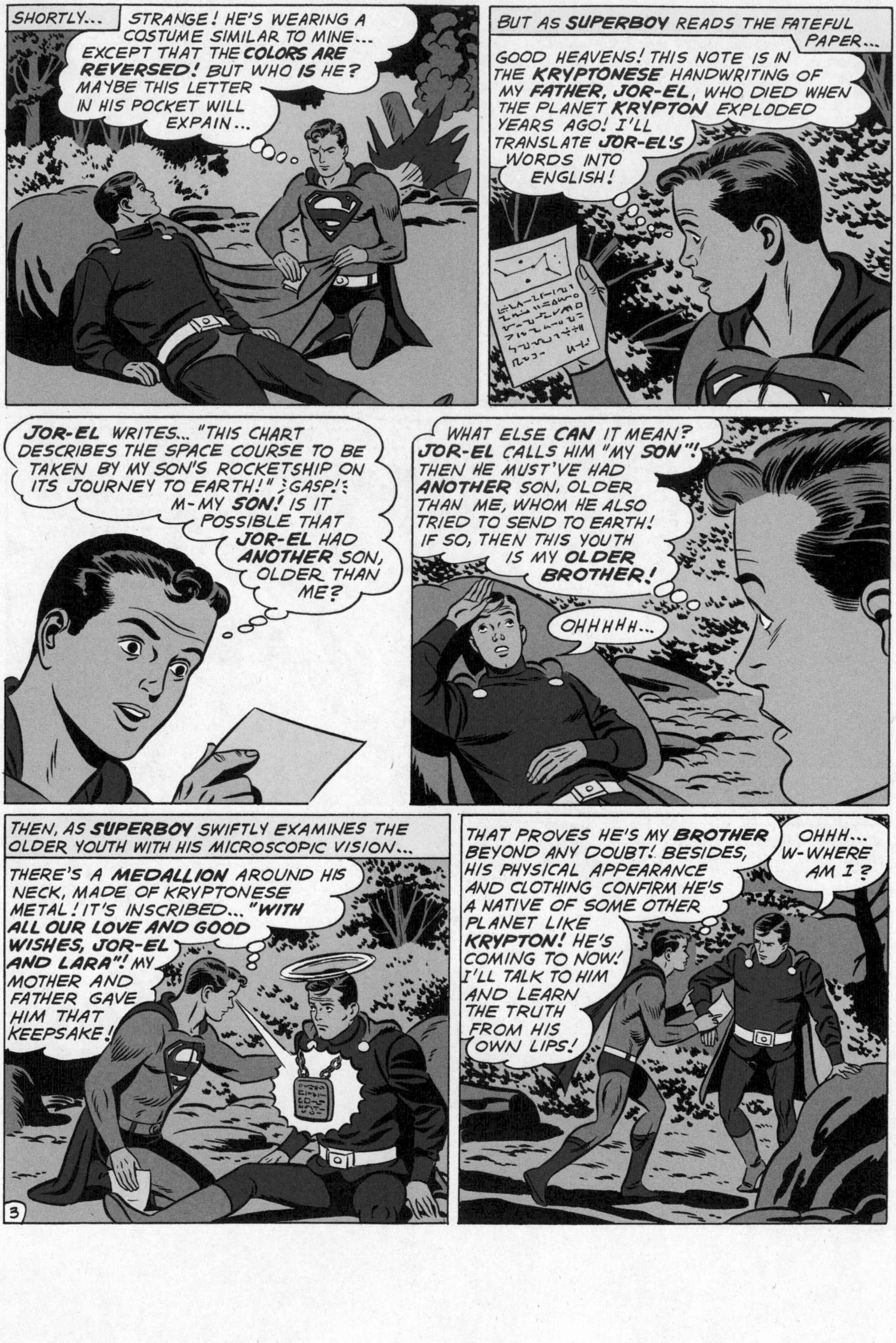

SHORTLY...
STRANGE! HE'S WEARING A COSTUME SIMILAR TO MINE... EXCEPT THAT THE COLORS ARE REVERSED! BUT WHO IS HE? MAYBE THIS LETTER IN HIS POCKET WILL EXPAIN...
BUT AS SUPERBOY READS THE FATEFUL PAPER...
GOOD HEAVENS! THIS NOTE IS IN THE KRYPTONESE HANDWRITING OF MY FATHER, JOR-EL, WHO DIED WHEN THE PLANET KRYPTON EXPLODED YEARS AGO! I'LL TRANSLATE JOR-EL'S WORDS INTO ENGLISH!
JOR-EL WRITES... "THIS CHART DESCRIBES THE SPACE COURSE TO BE TAKEN BY MY SON'S ROCKETSHIP ON ITS JOURNEY TO EARTH!" GASP! M-MY SON! IS IT POSSIBLE THAT JOR-EL HAD ANOTHER SON, OLDER THAN ME?
WHAT ELSE CAN IT MEAN? JOR-EL CALLS HIM "MY SON"! THEN HE MUST'VE HAD ANOTHER SON, OLDER THAN ME, WHOM HE ALSO TRIED TO SEND TO EARTH! IF SO, THEN THIS YOUTH IS MY OLDER BROTHER!
OHHHHH...
THEN, AS SUPERBOY SWIFTLY EXAMINES THE OLDER YOUTH WITH HIS MICROSCOPIC VISION...
THERE'S A MEDALLION AROUND HIS NECK, MADE OF KRYPTONESE METAL! IT'S INSCRIBED... "WITH ALL OUR LOVE AND GOOD WISHES, JOR-EL AND LARA"! MY MOTHER AND FATHER GAVE HIM THAT KEEPSAKE!
3
THAT PROVES HE'S MY BROTHER BEYOND ANY DOUBT! BESIDES, HIS PHYSICAL APPEARANCE AND CLOTHING CONFIRM HE'S A NATIVE OF SOME OTHER PLANET LIKE KRYPTON! HE'S COMING TO NOW! I'LL TALK TO HIM AND LEARN THE TRUTH FROM HIS OWN LIPS!
OHHH... W-WHERE AM I?

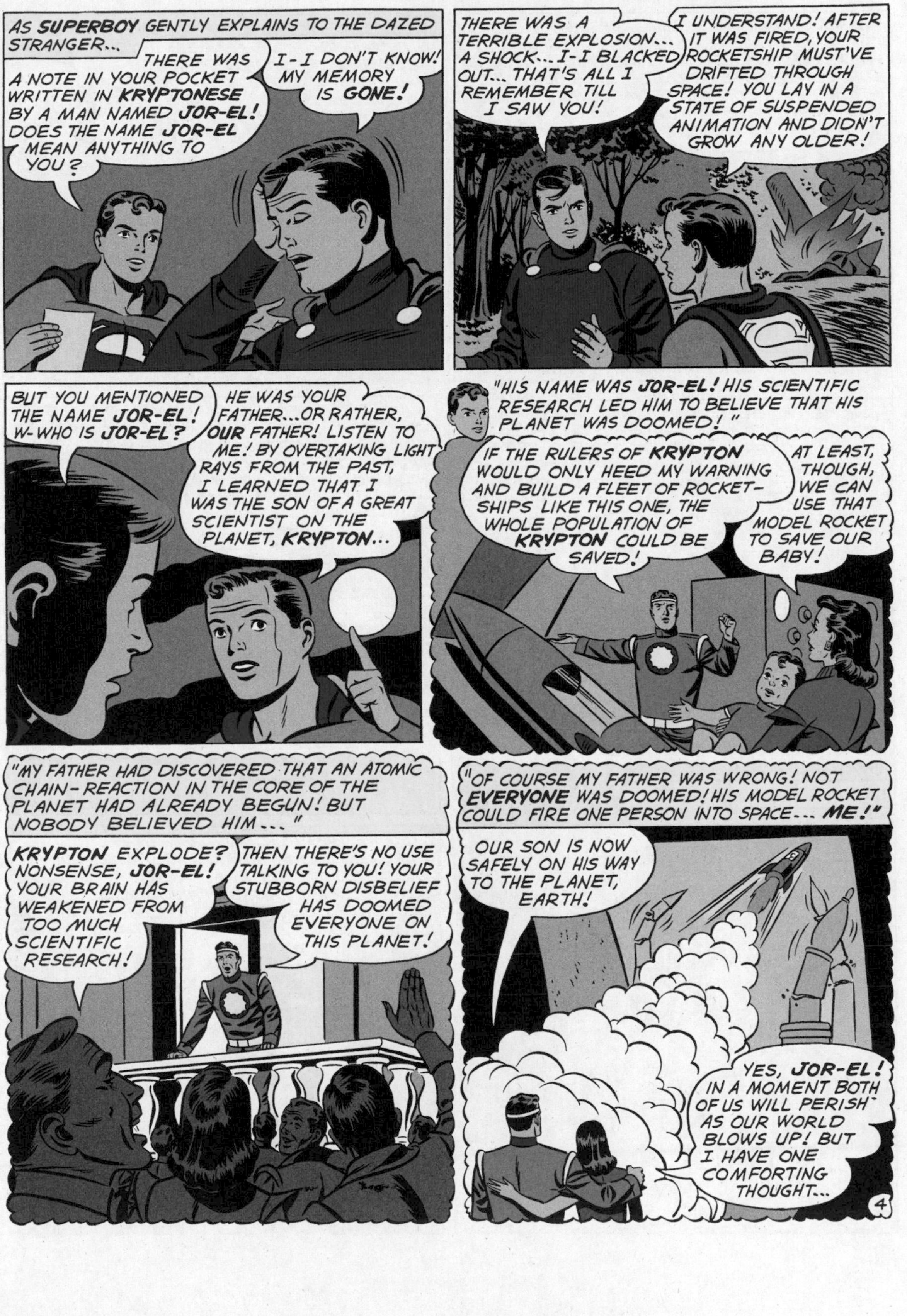
AS SUPERBOY GENTLY EXPLAINS TO THE DAZED STRANGER...
THERE WAS A NOTE IN YOUR POCKET WRITTEN IN KRYPTONESE BY A MAN NAMED JOR-EL! DOES THE NAME JOR-EL MEAN ANYTHING TO YOU?
I-I DON'T KNOW! MY MEMORY IS GONE!
THERE WAS A TERRIBLE EXPLOSION... A SHOCK... I-I BLACKED OUT... THAT'S ALL I REMEMBER TILL I SAW YOU!
I UNDERSTAND! AFTER IT WAS FIRED, YOUR ROCKETSHIP MUST'VE DRIFTED THROUGH SPACE! YOU LAY IN A STATE OF SUSPENDED ANIMATION AND DIDN'T GROW ANY OLDER!
BUT YOU MENTIONED THE NAME JOR-EL! W-WHO IS JOR-EL?
HE WAS YOUR FATHER... OR RATHER, OUR FATHER! LISTEN TO ME! BY OVERTAKING LIGHT RAYS FROM THE PAST, I LEARNED THAT I WAS THE SON OF A GREAT SCIENTIST ON THE PLANET, KRYPTON...
"HIS NAME WAS JOR-EL! HIS SCIENTIFIC RESEARCH LED HIM TO BELIEVE THAT HIS PLANET WAS DOOMED!"
IF THE RULERS OF KRYPTON WOULD ONLY HEED MY WARNING AND BUILD A FLEET OF ROCKET-SHIPS LIKE THIS ONE, THE WHOLE POPULATION OF KRYPTON COULD BE SAVED!
AT LEAST, THOUGH, WE CAN USE THAT MODEL ROCKET TO SAVE OUR BABY!
"MY FATHER HAD DISCOVERED THAT AN ATOMIC CHAIN-REACTION IN THE CORE OF THE PLANET HAD ALREADY BEGUN! BUT NOBODY BELIEVED HIM..."
KRYPTON EXPLODE? NONSENSE, JOR-EL! YOUR BRAIN HAS WEAKENED FROM TOO MUCH SCIENTIFIC RESEARCH!
THEN THERE'S NO USE TALKING TO YOU! YOUR STUBBORN DISBELIEF HAS DOOMED EVERYONE ON THIS PLANET!
"OF COURSE MY FATHER WAS WRONG! NOT EVERYONE WAS DOOMED! HIS MODEL ROCKET COULD FIRE ONE PERSON INTO SPACE... ME!"
OUR SON IS NOW SAFELY ON HIS WAY TO THE PLANET, EARTH!
YES, JOR-EL! IN A MOMENT BOTH OF US WILL PERISH AS OUR WORLD BLOWS UP! BUT I HAVE ONE COMFORTING THOUGHT...
4

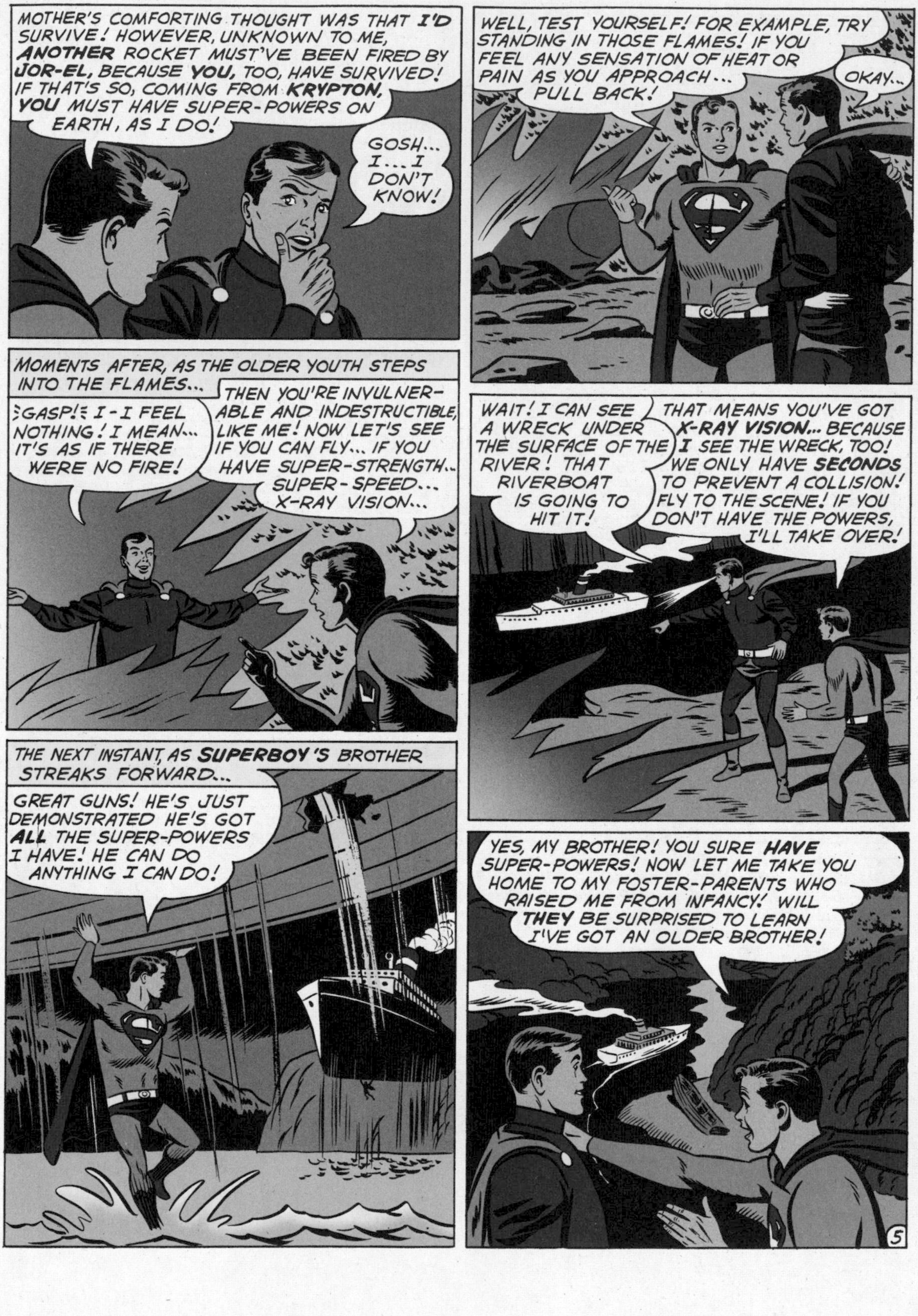
MOTHER'S COMFORTING THOUGHT WAS THAT I'D SURVIVE! HOWEVER, UNKNOWN TO ME, ANOTHER ROCKET MUST'VE BEEN FIRED BY JOR-EL, BECAUSE YOU, TOO, HAVE SURVIVED! IF THAT'S SO, COMING FROM KRYPTON, YOU MUST HAVE SUPER-POWERS ON EARTH, AS I DO!
GOSH... I... I DON'T KNOW!
WELL, TEST YOURSELF! FOR EXAMPLE, TRY STANDING IN THOSE FLAMES! IF YOU FEEL ANY SENSATION OF HEAT OR PAIN AS YOU APPROACH... PULL BACK!
OKAY...
MOMENTS AFTER, AS THE OLDER YOUTH STEPS INTO THE FLAMES...
GASP! I-I FEEL NOTHING! I MEAN... IT'S AS IF THERE WERE NO FIRE!
THEN YOU'RE INVULNERABLE AND INDESTRUCTIBLE, LIKE ME! NOW LET'S SEE IF YOU CAN FLY... IF YOU HAVE SUPER-STRENGTH... SUPER-SPEED... X-RAY VISION...
WAIT! I CAN SEE A WRECK UNDER THE SURFACE OF THE RIVER! THAT RIVERBOAT IS GOING TO HIT IT!
THAT MEANS YOU'VE GOT X-RAY VISION... BECAUSE I SEE THE WRECK, TOO! WE ONLY HAVE SECONDS TO PREVENT A COLLISION! FLY TO THE SCENE! IF YOU DON'T HAVE THE POWERS, I'LL TAKE OVER!
THE NEXT INSTANT, AS SUPERBOY'S BROTHER STREAKS FORWARD...
GREAT GUNS! HE'S JUST DEMONSTRATED HE'S GOT ALL THE SUPER-POWERS I HAVE! HE CAN DO ANYTHING I CAN DO!
YES, MY BROTHER! YOU SURE HAVE SUPER-POWERS! NOW LET ME TAKE YOU HOME TO MY FOSTER-PARENTS WHO RAISED ME FROM INFANCY! WILL THEY BE SURPRISED TO LEARN I'VE GOT AN OLDER BROTHER!
5

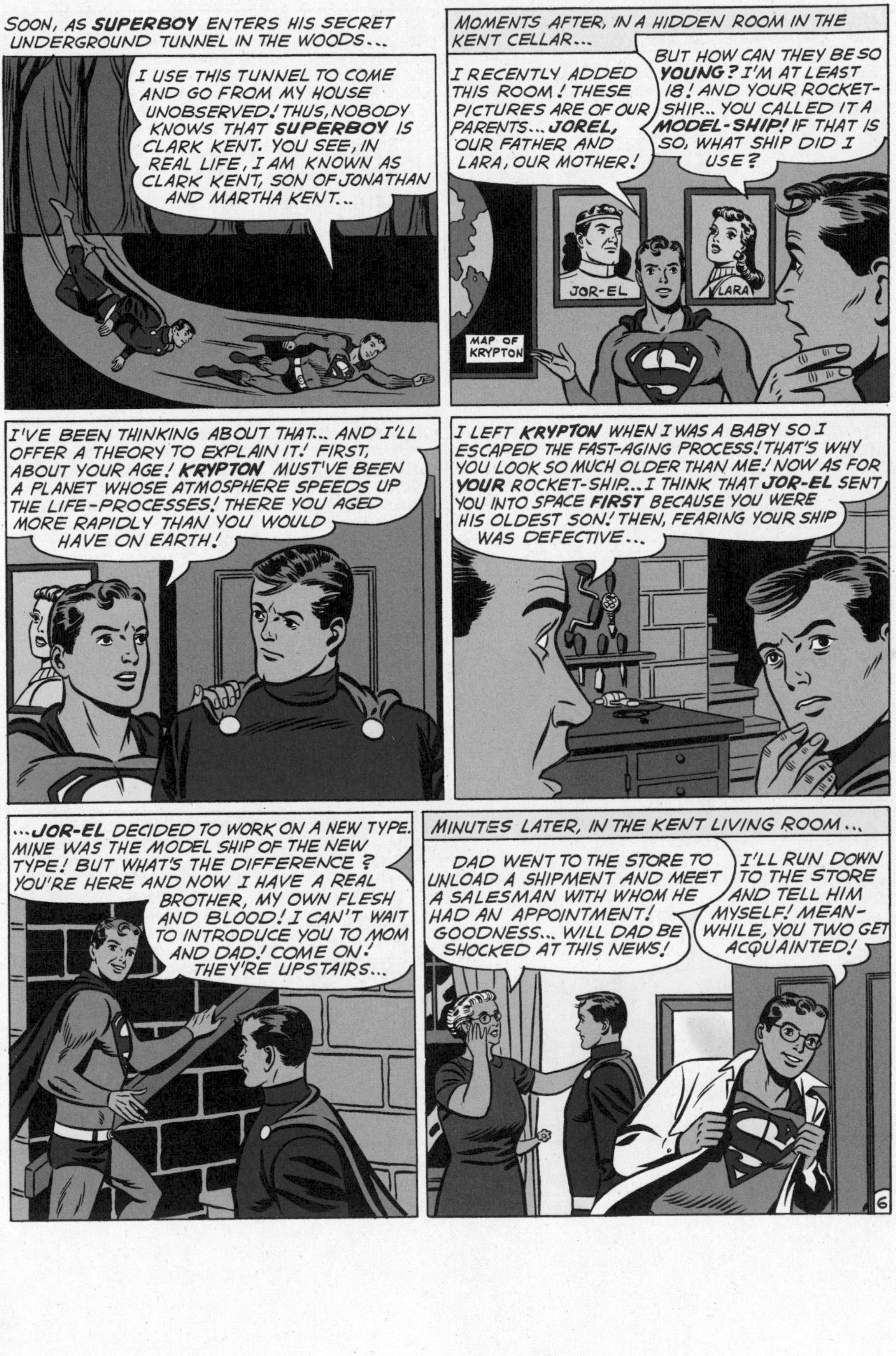
SOON, AS SUPERBOY ENTERS HIS SECRET UNDERGROUND TUNNEL IN THE WOODS...
I USE THIS TUNNEL TO COME AND GO FROM MY HOUSE UNOBSERVED! THUS, NOBODY KNOWS THAT SUPERBOY IS CLARK KENT. YOU SEE, IN REAL LIFE, I AM KNOWN AS CLARK KENT, SON OF JONATHAN AND MARTHA KENT...
MOMENTS AFTER, IN A HIDDEN ROOM IN THE KENT CELLAR...
I RECENTLY ADDED THIS ROOM! THESE PICTURES ARE OF OUR PARENTS... JOREL, OUR FATHER AND LARA, OUR MOTHER!
BUT HOW CAN THEY BE SO YOUNG? I'M AT LEAST 18! AND YOUR ROCKET-SHIP... YOU CALLED IT A MODEL-SHIP! IF THAT IS SO, WHAT SHIP DID I USE?
JOR-EL
LARA
MAP OF KRYPTON
I'VE BEEN THINKING ABOUT THAT... AND I'LL OFFER A THEORY TO EXPLAIN IT! FIRST, ABOUT YOUR AGE! KRYPTON MUST'VE BEEN A PLANET WHOSE ATMOSPHERE SPEEDS UP THE LIFE-PROCESSES! THERE YOU AGED MORE RAPIDLY THAN YOU WOULD HAVE ON EARTH!
I LEFT KRYPTON WHEN I WAS A BABY SO I ESCAPED THE FAST-AGING PROCESS! THAT'S WHY YOU LOOK SO MUCH OLDER THAN ME! NOW AS FOR YOUR ROCKET-SHIP... I THINK THAT JOR-EL SENT YOU INTO SPACE FIRST BECAUSE YOU WERE HIS OLDEST SON! THEN, FEARING YOUR SHIP WAS DEFECTIVE...
...JOR-EL DECIDED TO WORK ON A NEW TYPE. MINE WAS THE MODEL SHIP OF THE NEW TYPE! BUT WHAT'S THE DIFFERENCE? YOU'RE HERE AND NOW I HAVE A REAL BROTHER, MY OWN FLESH AND BLOOD! I CAN'T WAIT TO INTRODUCE YOU TO MOM AND DAD! COME ON! THEY'RE UPSTAIRS...
MINUTES LATER, IN THE KENT LIVING ROOM...
DAD WENT TO THE STORE TO UNLOAD A SHIPMENT AND MEET A SALESMAN WITH WHOM HE HAD AN APPOINTMENT! GOODNESS... WILL DAD BE SHOCKED AT THIS NEWS!
I'LL RUN DOWN TO THE STORE AND TELL HIM MYSELF! MEAN-WHILE, YOU TWO GET ACQUAINTED!
6

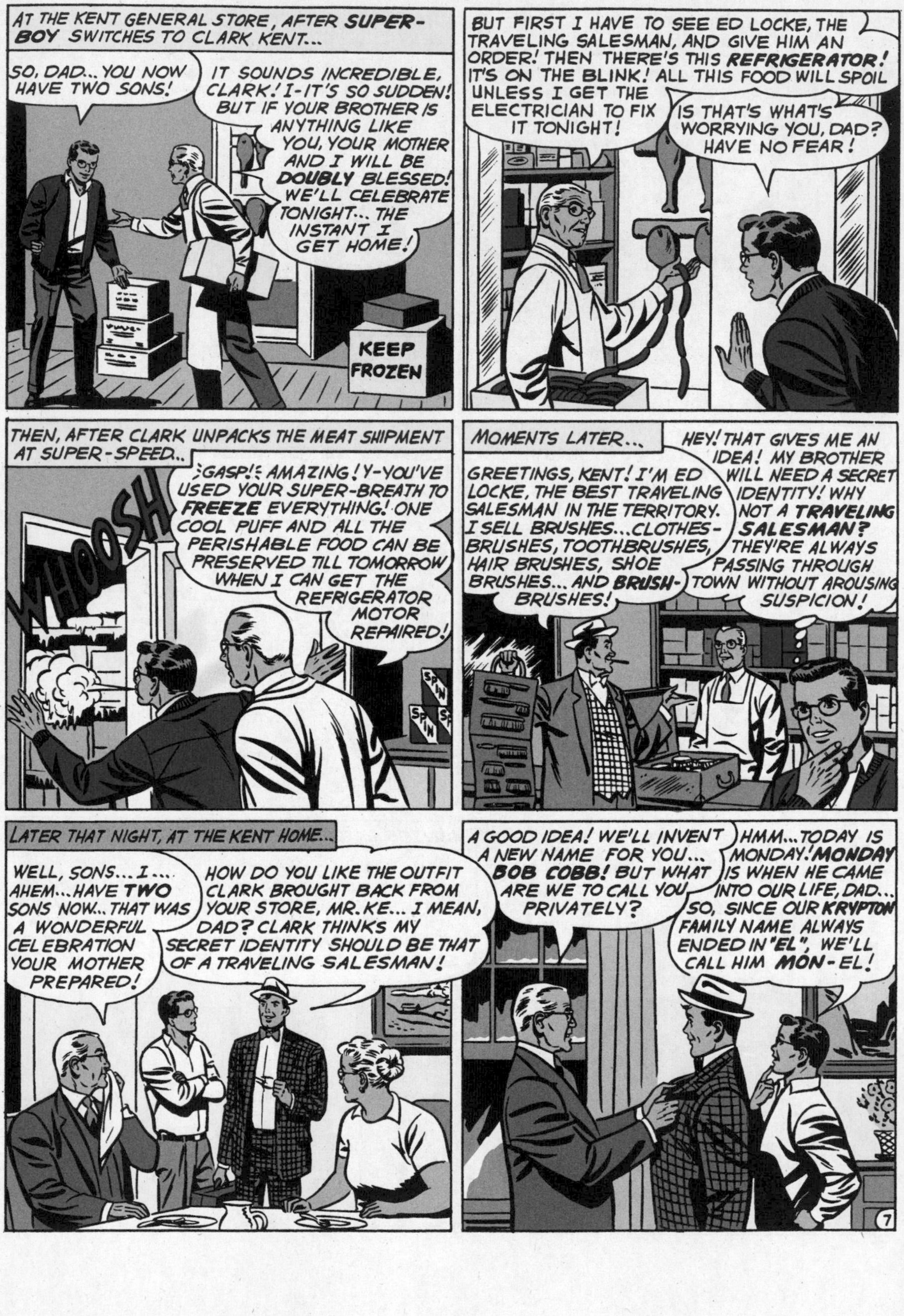
AT THE KENT GENERAL STORE, AFTER SUPERBOY SWITCHES TO CLARK KENT...
SO, DAD... YOU NOW HAVE TWO SONS!
IT SOUNDS INCREDIBLE, CLARK! I-IT'S SO SUDDEN! BUT IF YOUR BROTHER IS ANYTHING LIKE YOU, YOUR MOTHER AND I WILL BE DOUBLY BLESSED! WE'LL CELEBRATE TONIGHT... THE INSTANT I GET HOME!
KEEP FROZEN
BUT FIRST I HAVE TO SEE ED LOCKE, THE TRAVELING SALESMAN, AND GIVE HIM AN ORDER! THEN THERE'S THIS REFRIGERATOR! IT'S ON THE BLINK! ALL THIS FOOD WILL SPOIL UNLESS I GET THE ELECTRICIAN TO FIX IT TONIGHT!
IS THAT'S WHAT'S WORRYING YOU, DAD? HAVE NO FEAR!
THEN, AFTER CLARK UNPACKS THE MEAT SHIPMENT AT SUPER-SPEED..
WHOOSH
GASP! AMAZING! Y-YOU'VE USED YOUR SUPER-BREATH TO FREEZE EVERYTHING! ONE COOL PUFF AND ALL THE PERISHABLE FOOD CAN BE PRESERVED TILL TOMORROW WHEN I CAN GET THE REFRIGERATOR MOTOR REPAIRED!
SPIN
MOMENTS LATER...
GREETINGS, KENT! I'M ED LOCKE, THE BEST TRAVELING SALESMAN IN THE TERRITORY. I SELL BRUSHES... CLOTHES-BRUSHES, TOOTHBRUSHES, HAIR BRUSHES, SHOE BRUSHES... AND BRUSH-BRUSHES!
HEY! THAT GIVES ME AN IDEA! MY BROTHER WILL NEED A SECRET IDENTITY! WHY NOT A TRAVELING SALESMAN? THEY'RE ALWAYS PASSING THROUGH TOWN WITHOUT AROUSING SUSPICION!
LATER THAT NIGHT, AT THE KENT HOME...
WELL, SONS... I... AHEM... HAVE TWO SONS NOW.. THAT WAS A WONDERFUL CELEBRATION YOUR MOTHER PREPARED!
HOW DO YOU LIKE THE OUTFIT CLARK BROUGHT BACK FROM YOUR STORE, MR. KE... I MEAN, DAD? CLARK THINKS MY SECRET IDENTITY SHOULD BE THAT OF A TRAVELING SALESMAN!
A GOOD IDEA! WE'LL INVENT A NEW NAME FOR YOU... BOB COBB! BUT WHAT ARE WE TO CALL YOU PRIVATELY?
HMM... TODAY IS MONDAY! MONDAY IS WHEN HE CAME INTO OUR LIFE, DAD... SO, SINCE OUR KRYPTON FAMILY NAME ALWAYS ENDED IN "EL", WE'LL CALL HIM MON-EL!
7

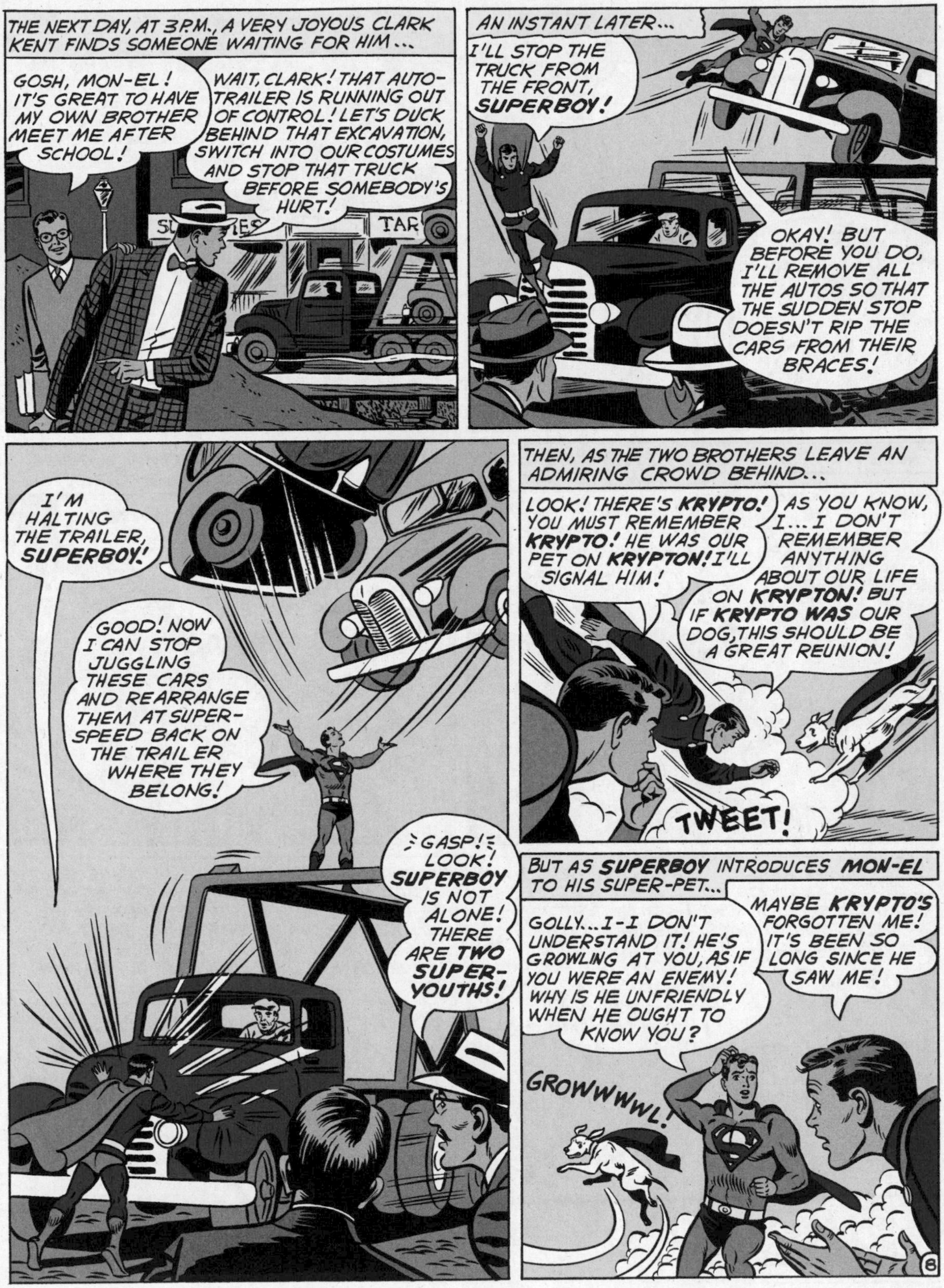

THE NEXT DAY, AT 3 P.M., A VERY JOYOUS CLARK KENT FINDS SOMEONE WAITING FOR HIM...
GOSH, MON-EL! IT'S GREAT TO HAVE MY OWN BROTHER MEET ME AFTER SCHOOL!
WAIT, CLARK! THAT AUTO-TRAILER IS RUNNING OUT OF CONTROL! LET'S DUCK BEHIND THAT EXCAVATION, SWITCH INTO OUR COSTUMES AND STOP THAT TRUCK BEFORE SOMEBODY'S HURT!
AN INSTANT LATER...
I'LL STOP THE TRUCK FROM THE FRONT, SUPERBOY!
OKAY! BUT BEFORE YOU DO, I'LL REMOVE ALL THE AUTOS SO THAT THE SUDDEN STOP DOESN'T RIP THE CARS FROM THEIR BRACES!
I'M HALTING THE TRAILER, SUPERBOY!
GOOD! NOW I CAN STOP JUGGLING THESE CARS AND REARRANGE THEM AT SUPER-SPEED BACK ON THE TRAILER WHERE THEY BELONG!
GASP! LOOK! SUPERBOY IS NOT ALONE! THERE ARE TWO SUPER-YOUTHS!
THEN, AS THE TWO BROTHERS LEAVE AN ADMIRING CROWD BEHIND...
LOOK! THERE'S KRYPTO! YOU MUST REMEMBER KRYPTO! HE WAS OUR PET ON KRYPTON! I'LL SIGNAL HIM!
AS YOU KNOW, I... I DON'T REMEMBER ANYTHING ABOUT OUR LIFE ON KRYPTON! BUT IF KRYPTO WAS OUR DOG, THIS SHOULD BE A GREAT REUNION!
TWEET!
BUT AS SUPERBOY INTRODUCES MON-EL TO HIS SUPER-PET...
GOLLY... I-I DON'T UNDERSTAND IT! HE'S GROWLING AT YOU, AS IF YOU WERE AN ENEMY! WHY IS HE UNFRIENDLY WHEN HE OUGHT TO KNOW YOU?
MAYBE KRYPTO'S FORGOTTEN ME! IT'S BEEN SO LONG SINCE HE SAW ME!
GROWWWWL!
8

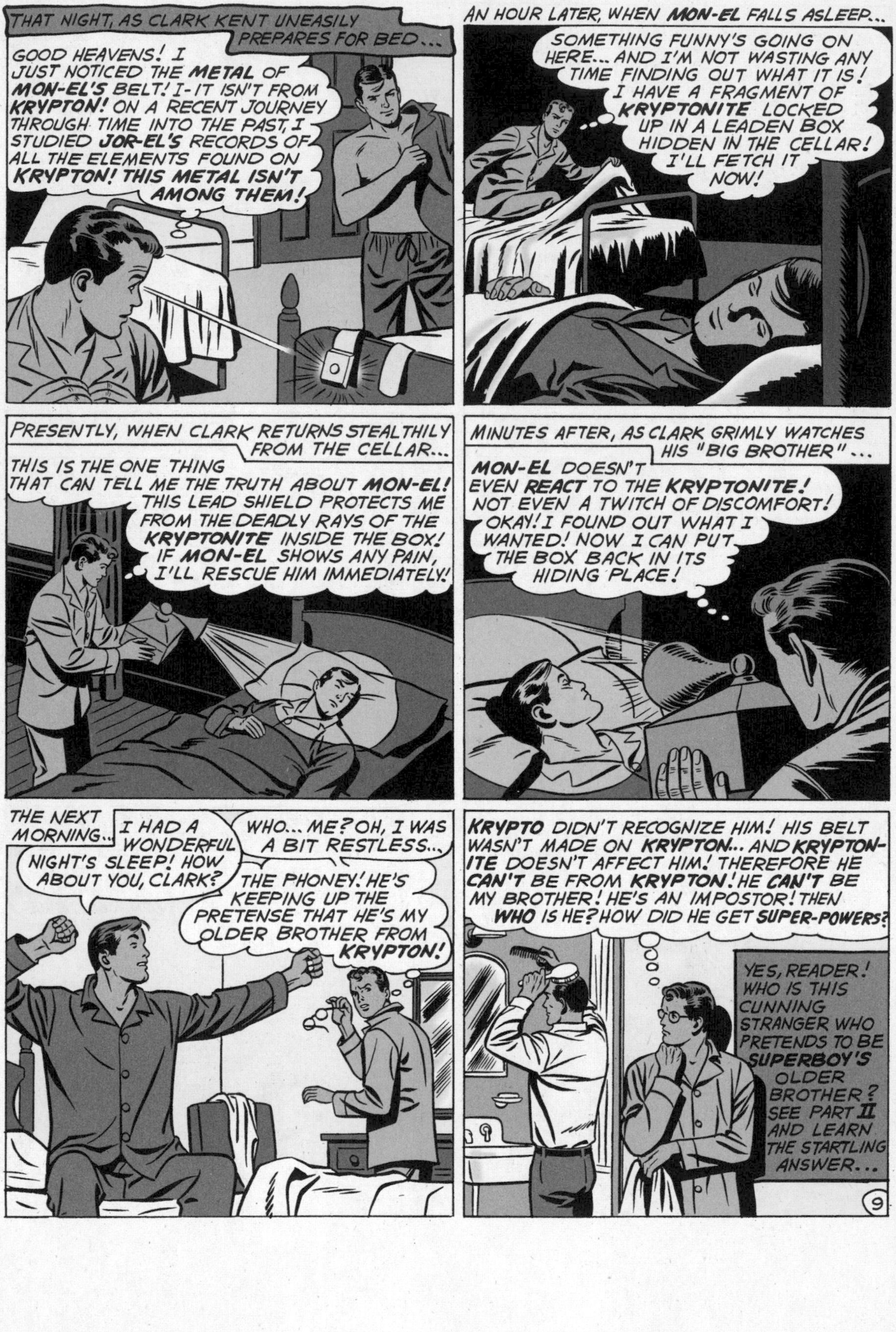
THAT NIGHT, AS CLARK KENT UNEASILY PREPARES FOR BED...
GOOD HEAVENS! I JUST NOTICED THE METAL OF MON-EL'S BELT! I-IT ISN'T FROM KRYPTON! ON A RECENT JOURNEY THROUGH TIME INTO THE PAST, I STUDIED JOR-EL'S RECORDS OF ALL THE ELEMENTS FOUND ON KRYPTON! THIS METAL ISN'T AMONG THEM!
AN HOUR LATER, WHEN MON-EL FALLS ASLEEP...
SOMETHING FUNNY'S GOING ON HERE... AND I'M NOT WASTING ANY TIME FINDING OUT WHAT IT IS! I HAVE A FRAGMENT OF KRYPTONITE LOCKED UP IN A LEADEN BOX HIDDEN IN THE CELLAR! I'LL FETCH IT NOW!
PRESENTLY, WHEN CLARK RETURNS STEALTHILY FROM THE CELLAR...
THIS IS THE ONE THING THAT CAN TELL ME THE TRUTH ABOUT MON-EL! THIS LEAD SHIELD PROTECTS ME FROM THE DEADLY RAYS OF THE KRYPTONITE INSIDE THE BOX! IF MON-EL SHOWS ANY PAIN, I'LL RESCUE HIM IMMEDIATELY!
MINUTES AFTER, AS CLARK GRIMLY WATCHES HIS "BIG BROTHER"...
MON-EL DOESN'T EVEN REACT TO THE KRYPTONITE! NOT EVEN A TWITCH OF DISCOMFORT! OKAY! I FOUND OUT WHAT I WANTED! NOW I CAN PUT THE BOX BACK IN ITS HIDING PLACE!
THE NEXT MORNING...
I HAD A WONDERFUL NIGHT'S SLEEP! HOW ABOUT YOU, CLARK?
WHO... ME? OH, I WAS A BIT RESTLESS...
THE PHONEY! HE'S KEEPING UP THE PRETENSE THAT HE'S MY OLDER BROTHER FROM KRYPTON!
KRYPTO DIDN'T RECOGNIZE HIM! HIS BELT WASN'T MADE ON KRYPTON... AND KRYPTONITE DOESN'T AFFECT HIM! THEREFORE HE CAN'T BE FROM KRYPTON! HE CAN'T BE MY BROTHER! HE'S AN IMPOSTOR! THEN WHO IS HE? HOW DID HE GET SUPER-POWERS?
YES, READER! WHO IS THIS CUNNING STRANGER WHO PRETENDS TO BE SUPERBOY'S OLDER BROTHER? SEE PART II AND LEARN THE STARTLING ANSWER...
9

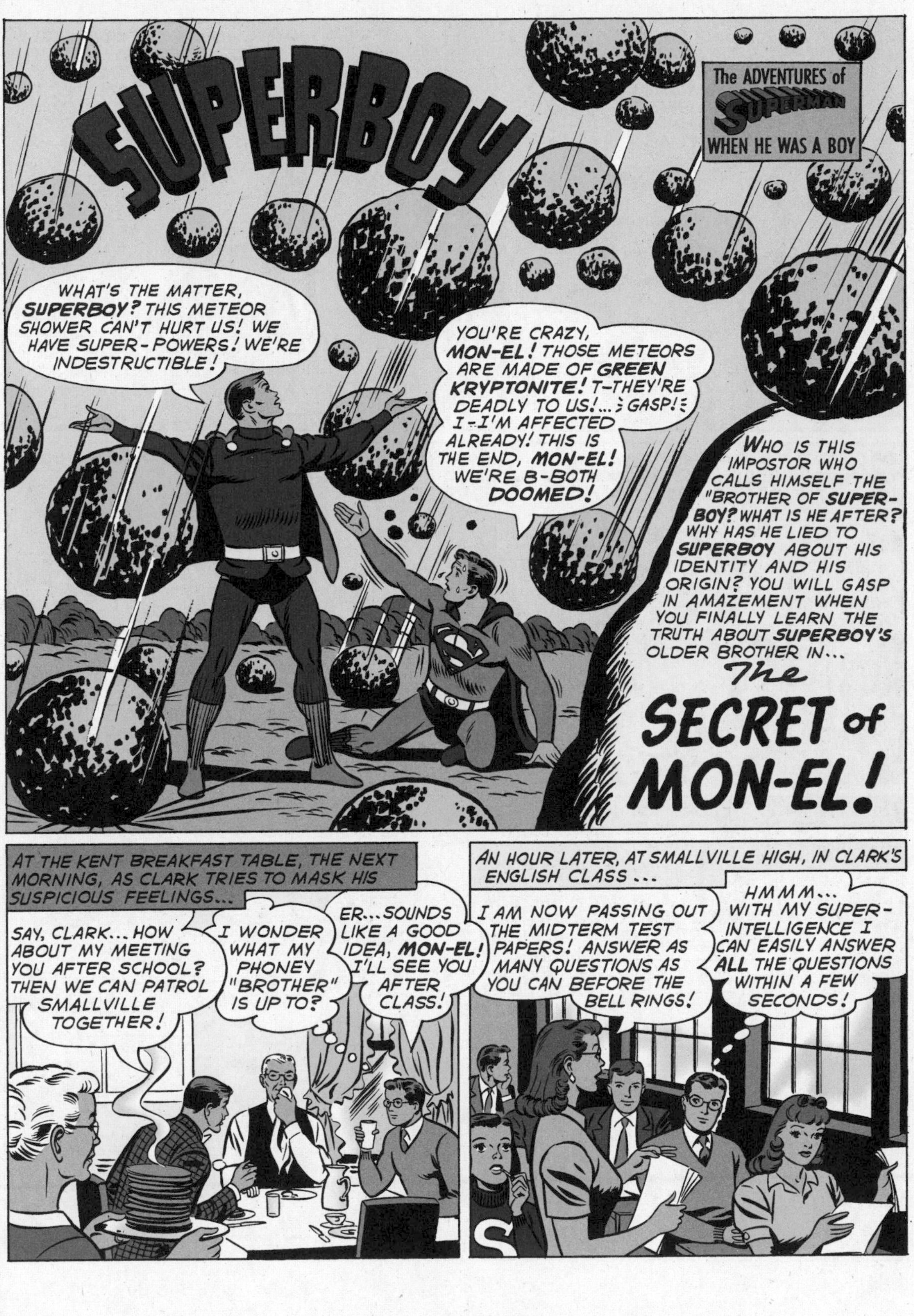

SUPERBOY
The ADVENTURES of SUPERMAN WHEN HE WAS A BOY
WHAT'S THE MATTER, SUPERBOY? THIS METEOR SHOWER CAN'T HURT US! WE HAVE SUPER-POWERS! WE'RE INDESTRUCTIBLE!
YOU'RE CRAZY, MON-EL! THOSE METEORS ARE MADE OF GREEN KRYPTONITE! T-THEY'RE DEADLY TO US!... GASP! I-I'M AFFECTED ALREADY! THIS IS THE END, MON-EL! WE'RE B-BOTH DOOMED!
WHO IS THIS IMPOSTOR WHO CALLS HIMSELF THE "BROTHER OF SUPERBOY? WHAT IS HE AFTER? WHY HAS HE LIED TO SUPERBOY ABOUT HIS IDENTITY AND HIS ORIGIN? YOU WILL GASP IN AMAZEMENT WHEN YOU FINALLY LEARN THE TRUTH ABOUT SUPERBOY'S OLDER BROTHER IN...
The SECRET of MON-EL!
AT THE KENT BREAKFAST TABLE, THE NEXT MORNING, AS CLARK TRIES TO MASK HIS SUSPICIOUS FEELINGS...
SAY, CLARK... HOW ABOUT MY MEETING YOU AFTER SCHOOL? THEN WE CAN PATROL SMALLVILLE TOGETHER!
I WONDER WHAT MY PHONEY "BROTHER" IS UP TO?
ER... SOUNDS LIKE A GOOD IDEA, MON-EL! I'LL SEE YOU AFTER CLASS!
AN HOUR LATER, AT SMALLVILLE HIGH, IN CLARK'S ENGLISH CLASS...
I AM NOW PASSING OUT THE MIDTERM TEST PAPERS! ANSWER AS MANY QUESTIONS AS YOU CAN BEFORE THE BELL RINGS!
HMMM... WITH MY SUPER-INTELLIGENCE I CAN EASILY ANSWER ALL THE QUESTIONS WITHIN A FEW SECONDS!

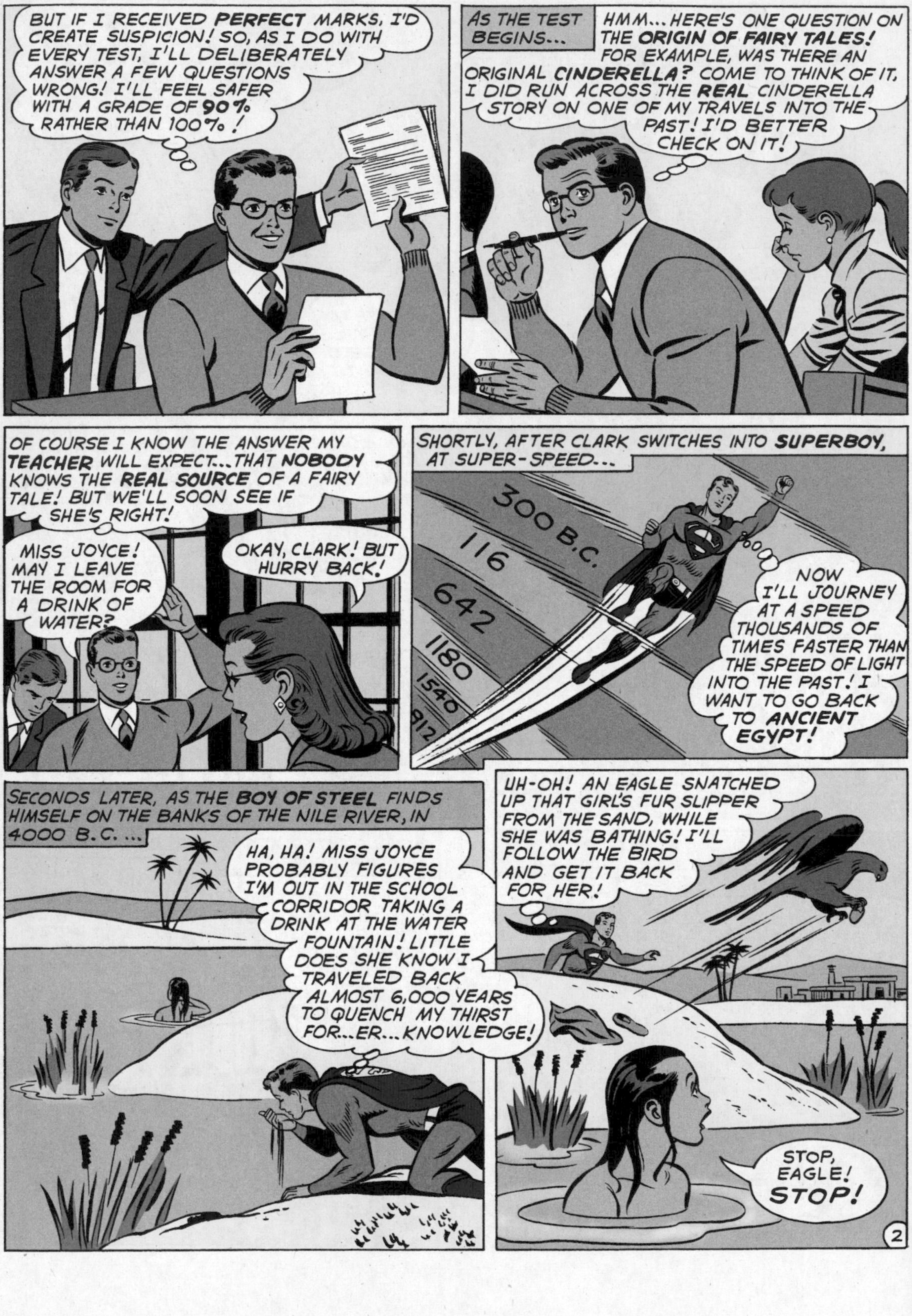
BUT IF I RECEIVED PERFECT MARKS, I'D CREATE SUSPICION! SO, AS I DO WITH EVERY TEST, I'LL DELIBERATELY ANSWER A FEW QUESTIONS WRONG! I'LL FEEL SAFER WITH A GRADE OF 90% RATHER THAN 100%!
AS THE TEST BEGINS...
HMM... HERE'S ONE QUESTION ON THE ORIGIN OF FAIRY TALES! FOR EXAMPLE, WAS THERE AN ORIGINAL CINDERELLA? COME TO THINK OF IT, I DID RUN ACROSS THE REAL CINDERELLA STORY ON ONE OF MY TRAVELS INTO THE PAST! I'D BETTER CHECK ON IT!
OF COURSE I KNOW THE ANSWER MY TEACHER WILL EXPECT...THAT NOBODY KNOWS THE REAL SOURCE OF A FAIRY TALE! BUT WE'LL SOON SEE IF SHE'S RIGHT!
MISS JOYCE! MAY I LEAVE THE ROOM FOR A DRINK OF WATER?
OKAY, CLARK! BUT HURRY BACK!
SHORTLY, AFTER CLARK SWITCHES INTO SUPERBOY, AT SUPER-SPEED...
300 B.C.
116
642
1180
1540
1812
NOW I'LL JOURNEY AT A SPEED THOUSANDS OF TIMES FASTER THAN THE SPEED OF LIGHT INTO THE PAST! I WANT TO GO BACK TO ANCIENT EGYPT!
SECONDS LATER, AS THE BOY OF STEEL FINDS HIMSELF ON THE BANKS OF THE NILE RIVER, IN 4000 B.C. ...
HA, HA! MISS JOYCE PROBABLY FIGURES I'M OUT IN THE SCHOOL CORRIDOR TAKING A DRINK AT THE WATER FOUNTAIN! LITTLE DOES SHE KNOW I TRAVELED BACK ALMOST 6,000 YEARS TO QUENCH MY THIRST FOR...ER...KNOWLEDGE!
UH-OH! AN EAGLE SNATCHED UP THAT GIRL'S FUR SLIPPER FROM THE SAND, WHILE SHE WAS BATHING! I'LL FOLLOW THE BIRD AND GET IT BACK FOR HER!
STOP, EAGLE! STOP!
2

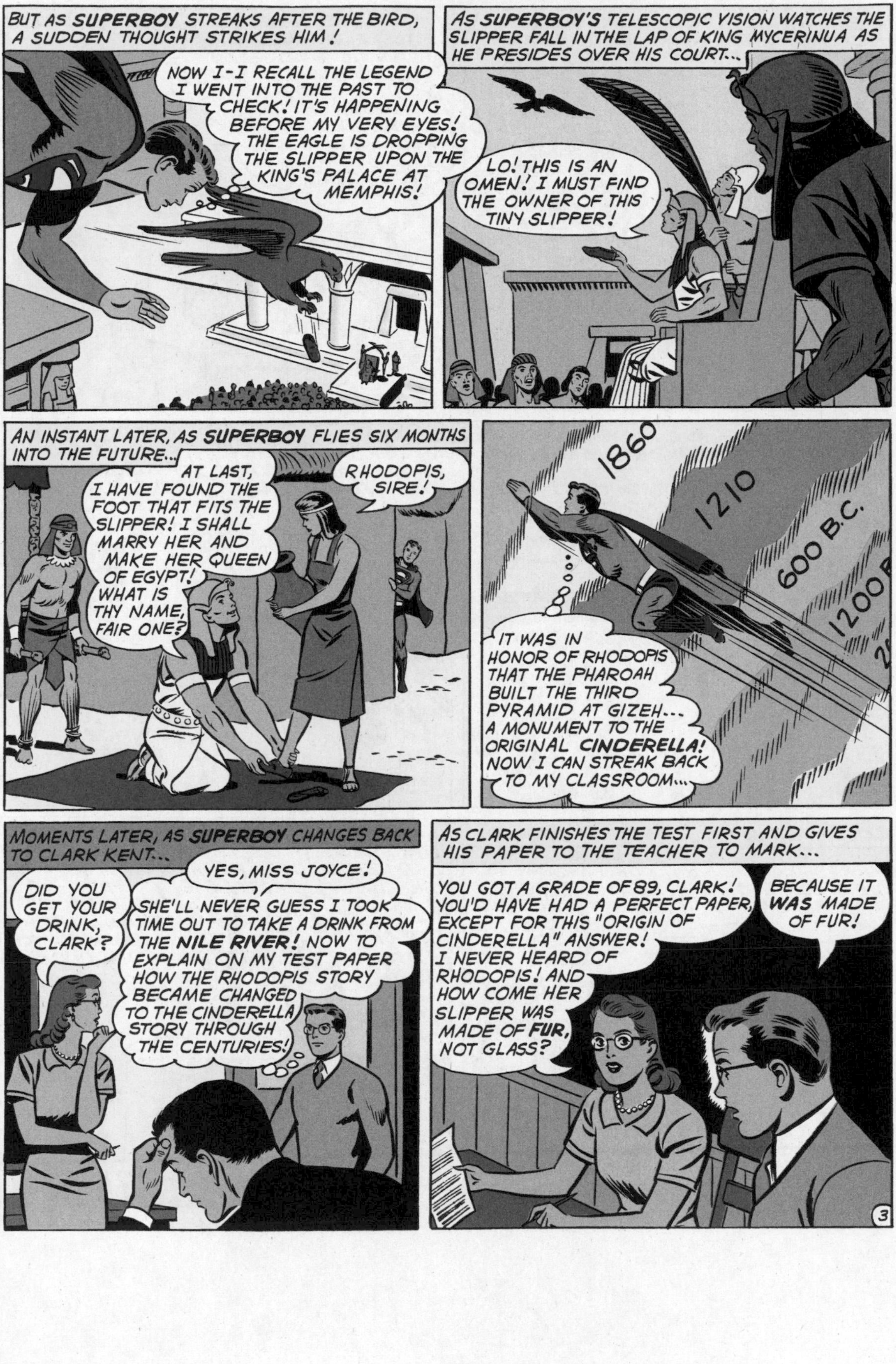
BUT AS SUPERBOY STREAKS AFTER THE BIRD, A SUDDEN THOUGHT STRIKES HIM!
NOW I-I RECALL THE LEGEND I WENT INTO THE PAST TO CHECK! IT'S HAPPENING BEFORE MY VERY EYES! THE EAGLE IS DROPPING THE SLIPPER UPON THE KING'S PALACE AT MEMPHIS!
AS SUPERBOY'S TELESCOPIC VISION WATCHES THE SLIPPER FALL IN THE LAP OF KING MYCERINUA AS HE PRESIDES OVER HIS COURT...
LO! THIS IS AN OMEN! I MUST FIND THE OWNER OF THIS TINY SLIPPER!
AN INSTANT LATER, AS SUPERBOY FLIES SIX MONTHS INTO THE FUTURE...
AT LAST, I HAVE FOUND THE FOOT THAT FITS THE SLIPPER! I SHALL MARRY HER AND MAKE HER QUEEN OF EGYPT! WHAT IS THY NAME, FAIR ONE?
RHODOPIS, SIRE!
1860
1210
600 B.C.
IT WAS IN HONOR OF RHODOPIS THAT THE PHAROAH BUILT THE THIRD PYRAMID AT GIZEH... A MONUMENT TO THE ORIGINAL CINDERELLA! NOW I CAN STREAK BACK TO MY CLASSROOM...
MOMENTS LATER, AS SUPERBOY CHANGES BACK TO CLARK KENT...
DID YOU GET YOUR DRINK, CLARK?
YES, MISS JOYCE!
SHE'LL NEVER GUESS I TOOK TIME OUT TO TAKE A DRINK FROM THE NILE RIVER! NOW TO EXPLAIN ON MY TEST PAPER HOW THE RHODOPIS STORY BECAME CHANGED TO THE CINDERELLA STORY THROUGH THE CENTURIES!
AS CLARK FINISHES THE TEST FIRST AND GIVES HIS PAPER TO THE TEACHER TO MARK...
YOU GOT A GRADE OF 89, CLARK! YOU'D HAVE HAD A PERFECT PAPER, EXCEPT FOR THIS "ORIGIN OF CINDERELLA" ANSWER! I NEVER HEARD OF RHODOPIS! AND HOW COME HER SLIPPER WAS MADE OF FUR, NOT GLASS?
BECAUSE IT WAS MADE OF FUR!
3

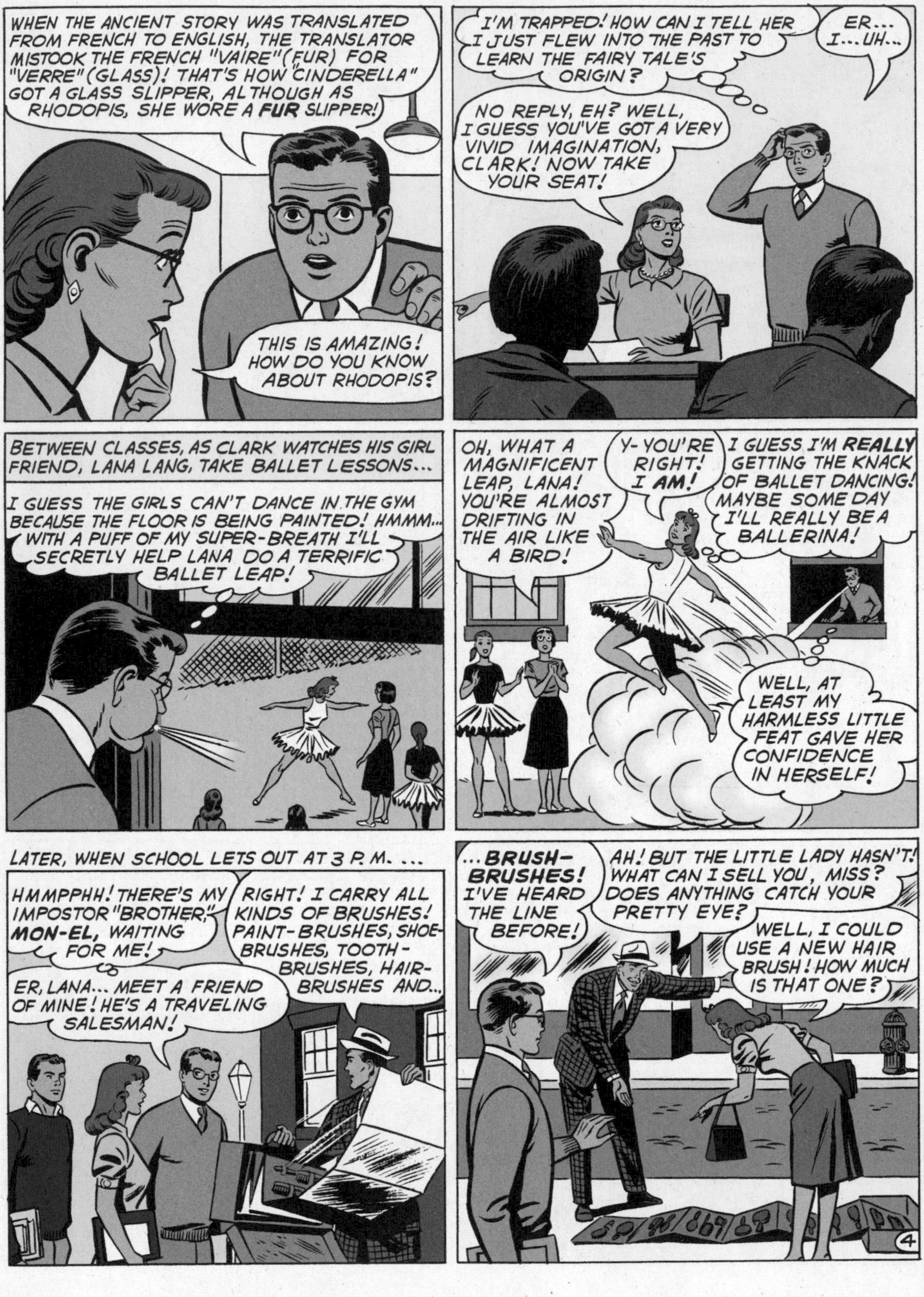
WHEN THE ANCIENT STORY WAS TRANSLATED FROM FRENCH TO ENGLISH, THE TRANSLATOR MISTOOK THE FRENCH "VAIRE" (FUR) FOR "VERRE" (GLASS)! THAT'S HOW "CINDERELLA" GOT A GLASS SLIPPER, ALTHOUGH AS RHODOPIS, SHE WORE A **FUR** SLIPPER!
THIS IS AMAZING! HOW DO YOU KNOW ABOUT RHODOPIS?
I'M TRAPPED! HOW CAN I TELL HER I JUST FLEW INTO THE PAST TO LEARN THE FAIRY TALE'S ORIGIN?
ER... I...UH...
NO REPLY, EH? WELL, I GUESS YOU'VE GOT A VERY VIVID IMAGINATION, CLARK! NOW TAKE YOUR SEAT!
BETWEEN CLASSES, AS CLARK WATCHES HIS GIRL FRIEND, LANA LANG, TAKE BALLET LESSONS...
I GUESS THE GIRLS CAN'T DANCE IN THE GYM BECAUSE THE FLOOR IS BEING PAINTED! HMMM... WITH A PUFF OF MY SUPER-BREATH I'LL SECRETLY HELP LANA DO A TERRIFIC BALLET LEAP!
OH, WHAT A MAGNIFICENT LEAP, LANA! YOU'RE ALMOST DRIFTING IN THE AIR LIKE A BIRD!
Y-YOU'RE RIGHT! I **AM**!
I GUESS I'M **REALLY** GETTING THE KNACK OF BALLET DANCING! MAYBE SOME DAY I'LL REALLY BE A BALLERINA!
WELL, AT LEAST MY HARMLESS LITTLE FEAT GAVE HER CONFIDENCE IN HERSELF!
LATER, WHEN SCHOOL LETS OUT AT 3 P.M. ...
HMMPPHH! THERE'S MY IMPOSTOR "BROTHER," **MON-EL**, WAITING FOR ME!
ER, LANA... MEET A FRIEND OF MINE! HE'S A TRAVELING SALESMAN!
RIGHT! I CARRY ALL KINDS OF BRUSHES! PAINT-BRUSHES, SHOE-BRUSHES, TOOTH-BRUSHES, HAIR-BRUSHES AND...
...**BRUSH-BRUSHES!** I'VE HEARD THE LINE BEFORE!
AH! BUT THE LITTLE LADY HASN'T! WHAT CAN I SELL YOU, MISS? DOES ANYTHING CATCH YOUR PRETTY EYE?
WELL, I COULD USE A NEW HAIR BRUSH! HOW MUCH IS THAT ONE?
4

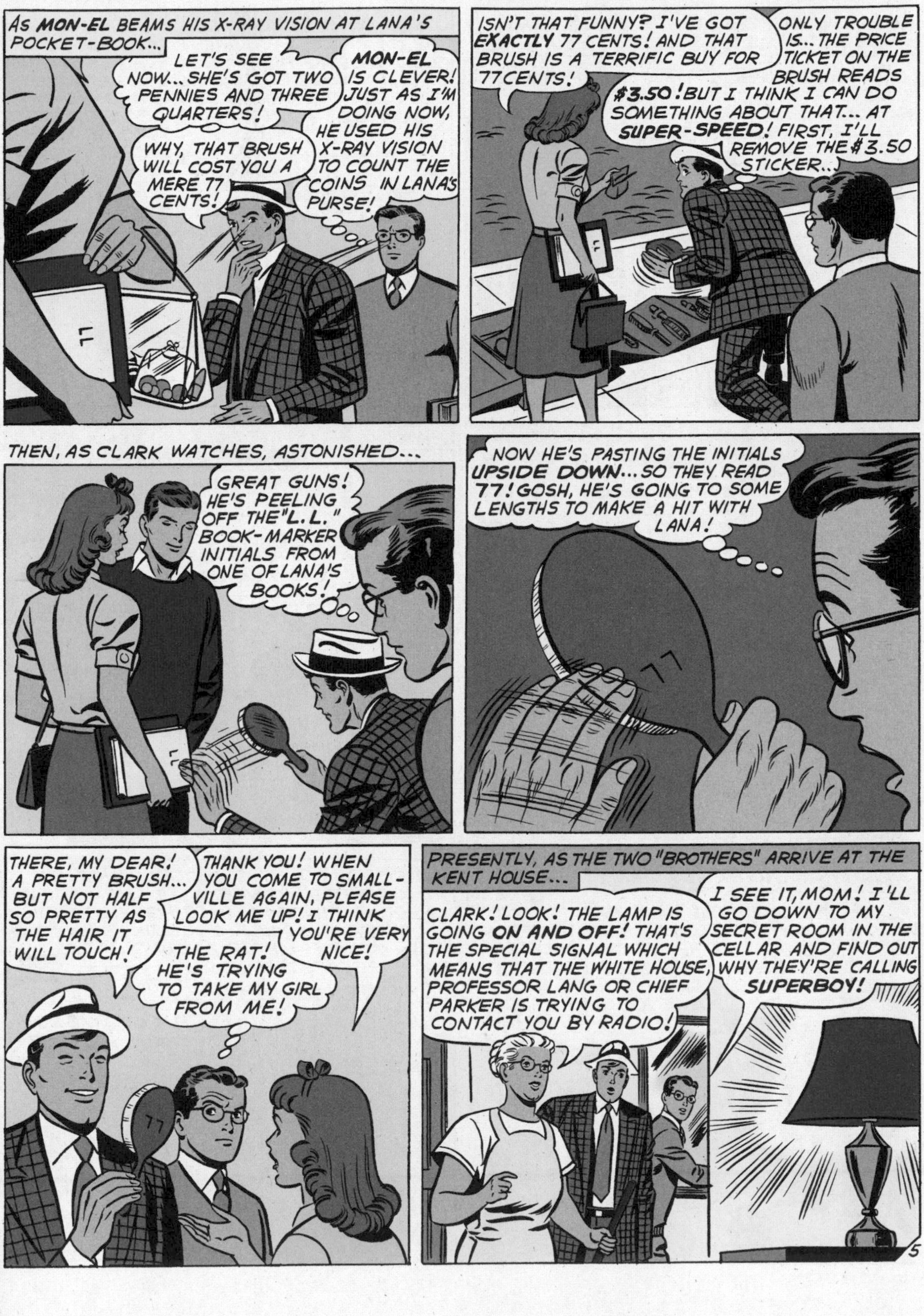

AS MON-EL BEAMS HIS X-RAY VISION AT LANA'S POCKET-BOOK...
LET'S SEE NOW... SHE'S GOT TWO PENNIES AND THREE QUARTERS!
WHY, THAT BRUSH WILL COST YOU A MERE 77 CENTS!
MON-EL IS CLEVER! JUST AS I'M DOING NOW, HE USED HIS X-RAY VISION TO COUNT THE COINS IN LANA'S PURSE!
ISN'T THAT FUNNY? I'VE GOT EXACTLY 77 CENTS! AND THAT BRUSH IS A TERRIFIC BUY FOR 77 CENTS!
ONLY TROUBLE IS... THE PRICE TICKET ON THE BRUSH READS $3.50! BUT I THINK I CAN DO SOMETHING ABOUT THAT... AT SUPER-SPEED! FIRST, I'LL REMOVE THE $3.50 STICKER...
THEN, AS CLARK WATCHES, ASTONISHED...
GREAT GUNS! HE'S PEELING OFF THE "L. L." BOOK-MARKER INITIALS FROM ONE OF LANA'S BOOKS!
NOW HE'S PASTING THE INITIALS UPSIDE DOWN... SO THEY READ 77! GOSH, HE'S GOING TO SOME LENGTHS TO MAKE A HIT WITH LANA!
THERE, MY DEAR! A PRETTY BRUSH... BUT NOT HALF SO PRETTY AS THE HAIR IT WILL TOUCH!
THANK YOU! WHEN YOU COME TO SMALL-VILLE AGAIN, PLEASE LOOK ME UP! I THINK YOU'RE VERY NICE!
THE RAT! HE'S TRYING TO TAKE MY GIRL FROM ME!
PRESENTLY, AS THE TWO "BROTHERS" ARRIVE AT THE KENT HOUSE...
CLARK! LOOK! THE LAMP IS GOING ON AND OFF! THAT'S THE SPECIAL SIGNAL WHICH MEANS THAT THE WHITE HOUSE, PROFESSOR LANG OR CHIEF PARKER IS TRYING TO CONTACT YOU BY RADIO!
I SEE IT, MOM! I'LL GO DOWN TO MY SECRET ROOM IN THE CELLAR AND FIND OUT WHY THEY'RE CALLING SUPERBOY!
5

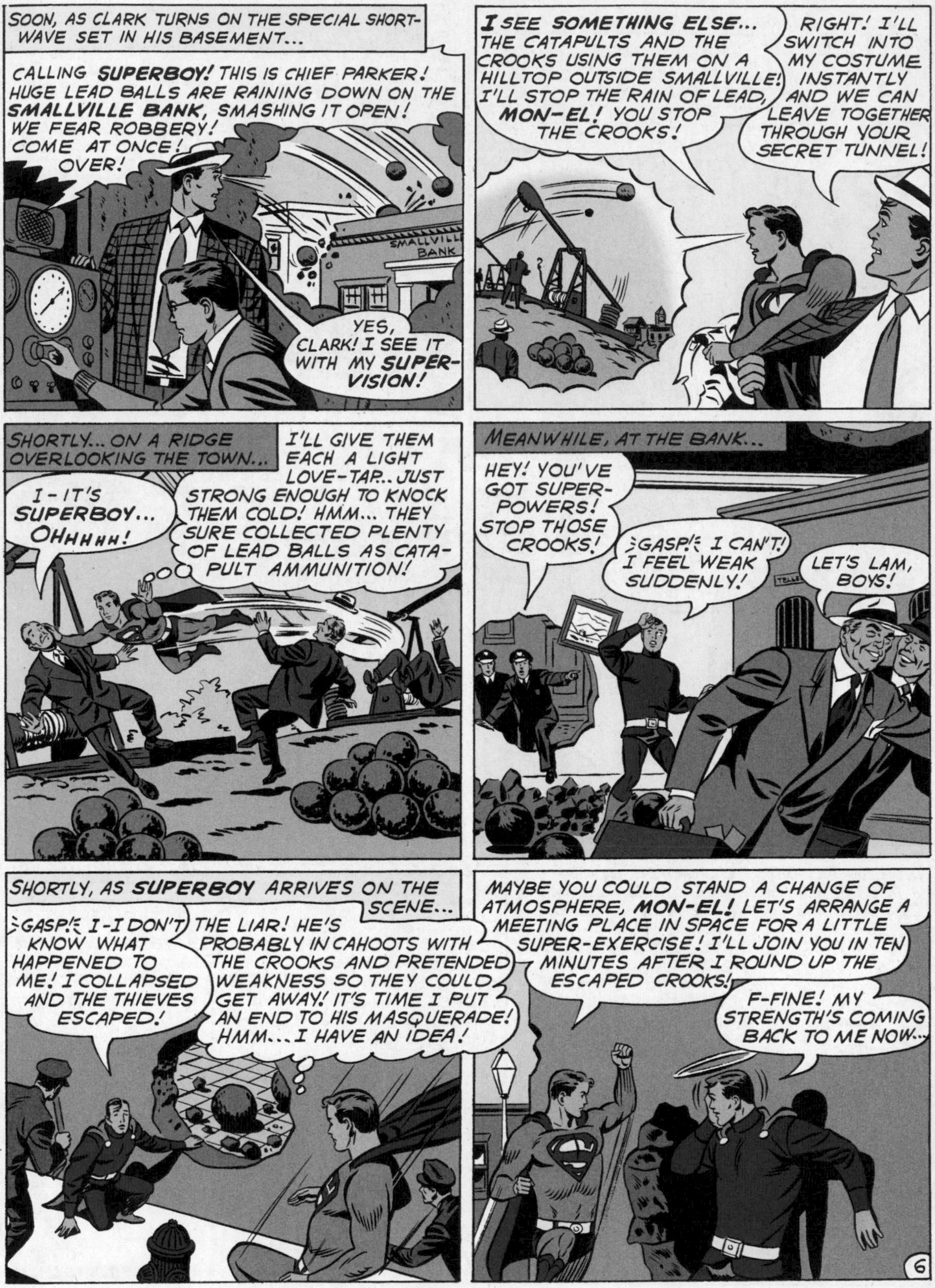
SOON, AS CLARK TURNS ON THE SPECIAL SHORT-WAVE SET IN HIS BASEMENT...
CALLING SUPERBOY! THIS IS CHIEF PARKER! HUGE LEAD BALLS ARE RAINING DOWN ON THE SMALLVILLE BANK, SMASHING IT OPEN! WE FEAR ROBBERY! COME AT ONCE! OVER!
SMALLVILLE BANK
YES, CLARK! I SEE IT WITH MY SUPER-VISION!
I SEE SOMETHING ELSE... THE CATAPULTS AND THE CROOKS USING THEM ON A HILLTOP OUTSIDE SMALLVILLE! I'LL STOP THE RAIN OF LEAD, MON-EL! YOU STOP THE CROOKS!
RIGHT! I'LL SWITCH INTO MY COSTUME INSTANTLY AND WE CAN LEAVE TOGETHER THROUGH YOUR SECRET TUNNEL!
SHORTLY... ON A RIDGE OVERLOOKING THE TOWN...
I'LL GIVE THEM EACH A LIGHT LOVE-TAP... JUST STRONG ENOUGH TO KNOCK THEM COLD! HMM... THEY SURE COLLECTED PLENTY OF LEAD BALLS AS CATAPULT AMMUNITION!
I-IT'S SUPERBOY... OHHHHH!
MEANWHILE, AT THE BANK...
HEY! YOU'VE GOT SUPER-POWERS! STOP THOSE CROOKS!
GASP! I CAN'T! I FEEL WEAK SUDDENLY!
LET'S LAM, BOYS!
SHORTLY, AS SUPERBOY ARRIVES ON THE SCENE...
GASP! I-I DON'T KNOW WHAT HAPPENED TO ME! I COLLAPSED AND THE THIEVES ESCAPED!
THE LIAR! HE'S PROBABLY IN CAHOOTS WITH THE CROOKS AND PRETENDED WEAKNESS SO THEY COULD GET AWAY! IT'S TIME I PUT AN END TO HIS MASQUERADE! HMM... I HAVE AN IDEA!
MAYBE YOU COULD STAND A CHANGE OF ATMOSPHERE, MON-EL! LET'S ARRANGE A MEETING PLACE IN SPACE FOR A LITTLE SUPER-EXERCISE! I'LL JOIN YOU IN TEN MINUTES AFTER I ROUND UP THE ESCAPED CROOKS!
F-FINE! MY STRENGTH'S COMING BACK TO ME NOW...
6

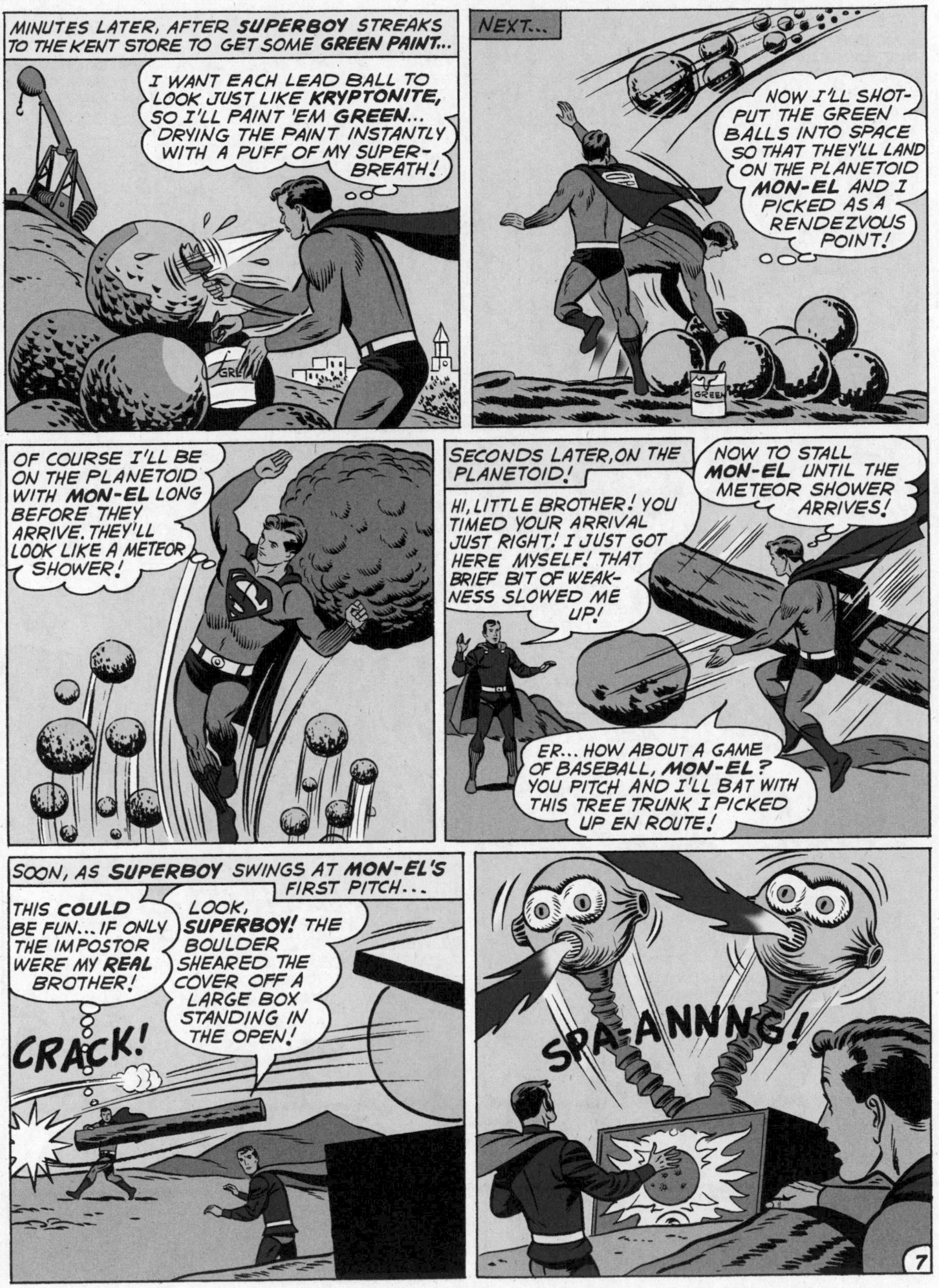

MINUTES LATER, AFTER SUPERBOY STREAKS TO THE KENT STORE TO GET SOME GREEN PAINT...
I WANT EACH LEAD BALL TO LOOK JUST LIKE KRYPTONITE, SO I'LL PAINT 'EM GREEN... DRYING THE PAINT INSTANTLY WITH A PUFF OF MY SUPER-BREATH!
NEXT...
NOW I'LL SHOT-PUT THE GREEN BALLS INTO SPACE SO THAT THEY'LL LAND ON THE PLANETOID MON-EL AND I PICKED AS A RENDEZVOUS POINT!
GREEN
OF COURSE I'LL BE ON THE PLANETOID WITH MON-EL LONG BEFORE THEY ARRIVE. THEY'LL LOOK LIKE A METEOR SHOWER!
SECONDS LATER, ON THE PLANETOID!
NOW TO STALL MON-EL UNTIL THE METEOR SHOWER ARRIVES!
HI, LITTLE BROTHER! YOU TIMED YOUR ARRIVAL JUST RIGHT! I JUST GOT HERE MYSELF! THAT BRIEF BIT OF WEAKNESS SLOWED ME UP!
ER... HOW ABOUT A GAME OF BASEBALL, MON-EL? YOU PITCH AND I'LL BAT WITH THIS TREE TRUNK I PICKED UP EN ROUTE!
SOON, AS SUPERBOY SWINGS AT MON-EL'S FIRST PITCH...
THIS COULD BE FUN... IF ONLY THE IMPOSTOR WERE MY REAL BROTHER!
LOOK, SUPERBOY! THE BOULDER SHEARED THE COVER OFF A LARGE BOX STANDING IN THE OPEN!
CRACK!
SPA-ANNNG!
7

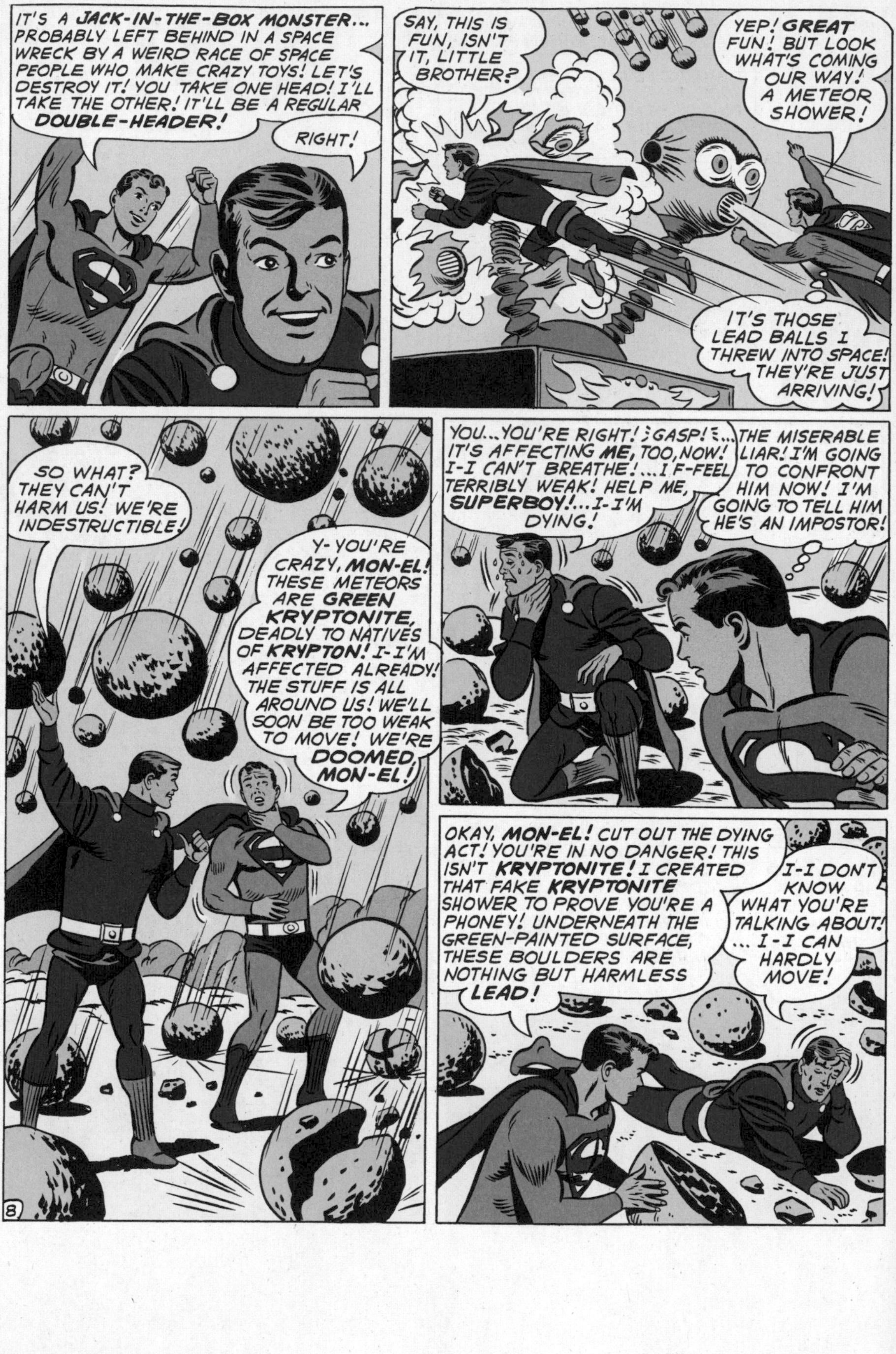
IT'S A JACK-IN-THE-BOX MONSTER... PROBABLY LEFT BEHIND IN A SPACE WRECK BY A WEIRD RACE OF SPACE PEOPLE WHO MAKE CRAZY TOYS! LET'S DESTROY IT! YOU TAKE ONE HEAD! I'LL TAKE THE OTHER! IT'LL BE A REGULAR DOUBLE-HEADER!
RIGHT!
SAY, THIS IS FUN, ISN'T IT, LITTLE BROTHER?
YEP! GREAT FUN! BUT LOOK WHAT'S COMING OUR WAY! A METEOR SHOWER!
IT'S THOSE LEAD BALLS I THREW INTO SPACE! THEY'RE JUST ARRIVING!
SO WHAT? THEY CAN'T HARM US! WE'RE INDESTRUCTIBLE!
Y-YOU'RE CRAZY, MON-EL! THESE METEORS ARE GREEN KRYPTONITE, DEADLY TO NATIVES OF KRYPTON! I-I'M AFFECTED ALREADY! THE STUFF IS ALL AROUND US! WE'LL SOON BE TOO WEAK TO MOVE! WE'RE DOOMED, MON-EL!
8
YOU...YOU'RE RIGHT! GASP! ... IT'S AFFECTING ME, TOO, NOW! I-I CAN'T BREATHE! ...I F-FEEL TERRIBLY WEAK! HELP ME, SUPERBOY! ...I-I'M DYING!
THE MISERABLE LIAR! I'M GOING TO CONFRONT HIM NOW! I'M GOING TO TELL HIM HE'S AN IMPOSTOR!
OKAY, MON-EL! CUT OUT THE DYING ACT! YOU'RE IN NO DANGER! THIS ISN'T KRYPTONITE! I CREATED THAT FAKE KRYPTONITE SHOWER TO PROVE YOU'RE A PHONEY! UNDERNEATH THE GREEN-PAINTED SURFACE, THESE BOULDERS ARE NOTHING BUT HARMLESS LEAD!
I-I DON'T KNOW WHAT YOU'RE TALKING ABOUT! ... I-I CAN HARDLY MOVE!

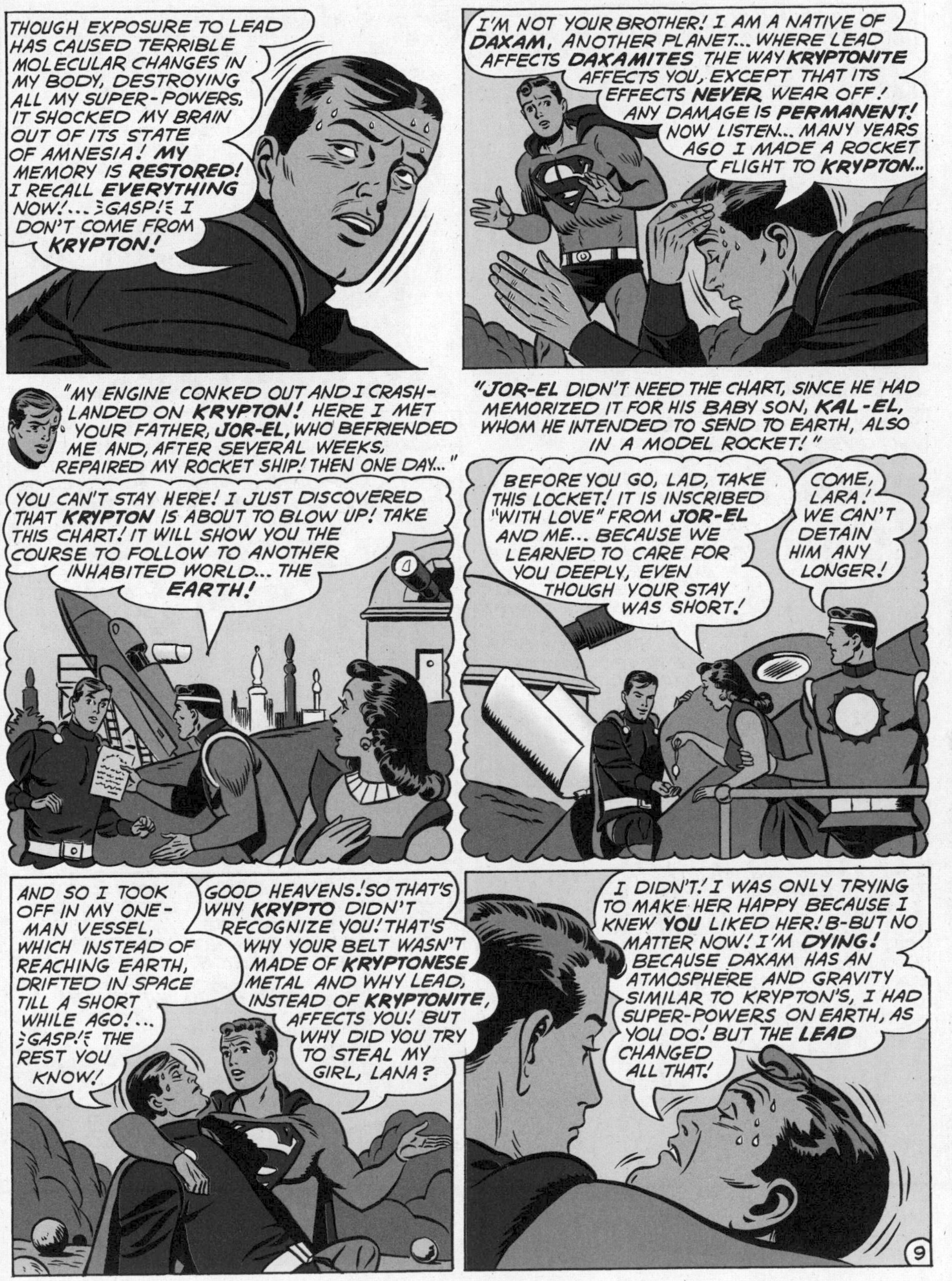
THOUGH EXPOSURE TO LEAD HAS CAUSED TERRIBLE MOLECULAR CHANGES IN MY BODY, DESTROYING ALL MY SUPER-POWERS, IT SHOCKED MY BRAIN OUT OF ITS STATE OF AMNESIA! MY MEMORY IS RESTORED! I RECALL EVERYTHING NOW!... GASP! I DON'T COME FROM KRYPTON!
I'M NOT YOUR BROTHER! I AM A NATIVE OF DAXAM, ANOTHER PLANET... WHERE LEAD AFFECTS DAXAMITES THE WAY KRYPTONITE AFFECTS YOU, EXCEPT THAT ITS EFFECTS NEVER WEAR OFF! ANY DAMAGE IS PERMANENT! NOW LISTEN... MANY YEARS AGO I MADE A ROCKET FLIGHT TO KRYPTON...
"MY ENGINE CONKED OUT AND I CRASH-LANDED ON KRYPTON! HERE I MET YOUR FATHER, JOR-EL, WHO BEFRIENDED ME AND, AFTER SEVERAL WEEKS, REPAIRED MY ROCKET SHIP! THEN ONE DAY..."
YOU CAN'T STAY HERE! I JUST DISCOVERED THAT KRYPTON IS ABOUT TO BLOW UP! TAKE THIS CHART! IT WILL SHOW YOU THE COURSE TO FOLLOW TO ANOTHER INHABITED WORLD... THE EARTH!
"JOR-EL DIDN'T NEED THE CHART, SINCE HE HAD MEMORIZED IT FOR HIS BABY SON, KAL-EL, WHOM HE INTENDED TO SEND TO EARTH, ALSO IN A MODEL ROCKET!"
BEFORE YOU GO, LAD, TAKE THIS LOCKET! IT IS INSCRIBED "WITH LOVE" FROM JOR-EL AND ME... BECAUSE WE LEARNED TO CARE FOR YOU DEEPLY, EVEN THOUGH YOUR STAY WAS SHORT!
COME, LARA! WE CAN'T DETAIN HIM ANY LONGER!
AND SO I TOOK OFF IN MY ONE-MAN VESSEL, WHICH INSTEAD OF REACHING EARTH, DRIFTED IN SPACE TILL A SHORT WHILE AGO!... GASP! THE REST YOU KNOW!
GOOD HEAVENS! SO THAT'S WHY KRYPTO DIDN'T RECOGNIZE YOU! THAT'S WHY YOUR BELT WASN'T MADE OF KRYPTONESE METAL AND WHY LEAD, INSTEAD OF KRYPTONITE, AFFECTS YOU! BUT WHY DID YOU TRY TO STEAL MY GIRL, LANA?
I DIDN'T! I WAS ONLY TRYING TO MAKE HER HAPPY BECAUSE I KNEW YOU LIKED HER! B-BUT NO MATTER NOW! I'M DYING! BECAUSE DAXAM HAS AN ATMOSPHERE AND GRAVITY SIMILAR TO KRYPTON'S, I HAD SUPER-POWERS ON EARTH, AS YOU DO! BUT THE LEAD CHANGED ALL THAT!
9

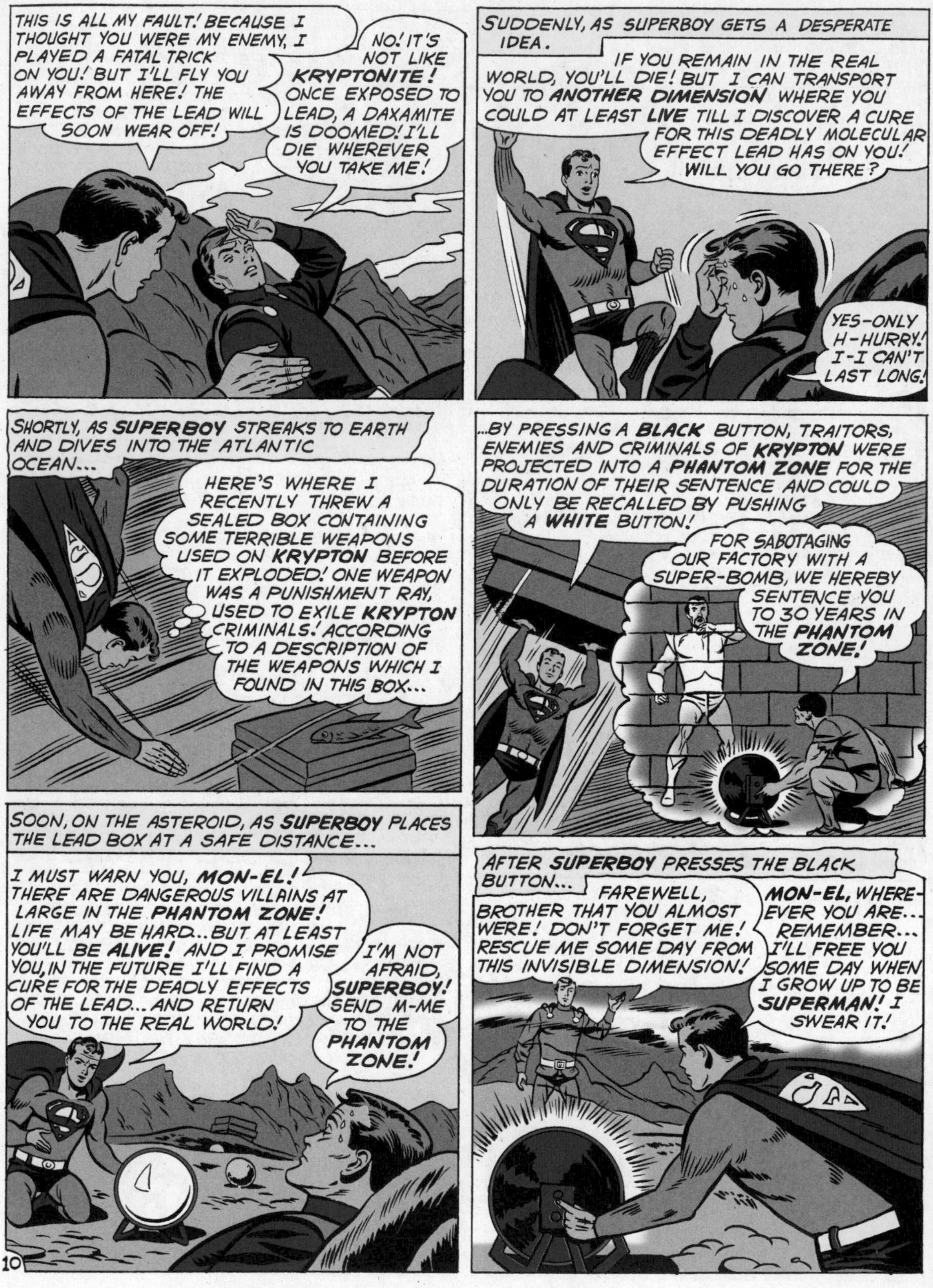
THIS IS ALL MY FAULT! BECAUSE I THOUGHT YOU WERE MY ENEMY, I PLAYED A FATAL TRICK ON YOU! BUT I'LL FLY YOU AWAY FROM HERE! THE EFFECTS OF THE LEAD WILL SOON WEAR OFF!
NO! IT'S NOT LIKE KRYPTONITE! ONCE EXPOSED TO LEAD, A DAXAMITE IS DOOMED! I'LL DIE WHEREVER YOU TAKE ME!
SUDDENLY, AS SUPERBOY GETS A DESPERATE IDEA.
IF YOU REMAIN IN THE REAL WORLD, YOU'LL DIE! BUT I CAN TRANSPORT YOU TO ANOTHER DIMENSION WHERE YOU COULD AT LEAST LIVE TILL I DISCOVER A CURE FOR THIS DEADLY MOLECULAR EFFECT LEAD HAS ON YOU! WILL YOU GO THERE?
YES-ONLY H-HURRY! I-I CAN'T LAST LONG!
SHORTLY, AS SUPERBOY STREAKS TO EARTH AND DIVES INTO THE ATLANTIC OCEAN...
HERE'S WHERE I RECENTLY THREW A SEALED BOX CONTAINING SOME TERRIBLE WEAPONS USED ON KRYPTON BEFORE IT EXPLODED! ONE WEAPON WAS A PUNISHMENT RAY, USED TO EXILE KRYPTON CRIMINALS! ACCORDING TO A DESCRIPTION OF THE WEAPONS WHICH I FOUND IN THIS BOX...
...BY PRESSING A BLACK BUTTON, TRAITORS, ENEMIES AND CRIMINALS OF KRYPTON WERE PROJECTED INTO A PHANTOM ZONE FOR THE DURATION OF THEIR SENTENCE AND COULD ONLY BE RECALLED BY PUSHING A WHITE BUTTON!
FOR SABOTAGING OUR FACTORY WITH A SUPER-BOMB, WE HEREBY SENTENCE YOU TO 30 YEARS IN THE PHANTOM ZONE!
SOON, ON THE ASTEROID, AS SUPERBOY PLACES THE LEAD BOX AT A SAFE DISTANCE...
I MUST WARN YOU, MON-EL! THERE ARE DANGEROUS VILLAINS AT LARGE IN THE PHANTOM ZONE! LIFE MAY BE HARD...BUT AT LEAST YOU'LL BE ALIVE! AND I PROMISE YOU, IN THE FUTURE I'LL FIND A CURE FOR THE DEADLY EFFECTS OF THE LEAD... AND RETURN YOU TO THE REAL WORLD!
I'M NOT AFRAID, SUPERBOY! SEND M-ME TO THE PHANTOM ZONE!
10
AFTER SUPERBOY PRESSES THE BLACK BUTTON...
FAREWELL, BROTHER THAT YOU ALMOST WERE! DON'T FORGET ME! RESCUE ME SOME DAY FROM THIS INVISIBLE DIMENSION!
MON-EL, WHEREVER YOU ARE... REMEMBER... I'LL FREE YOU SOME DAY WHEN I GROW UP TO BE SUPERMAN! I SWEAR IT!

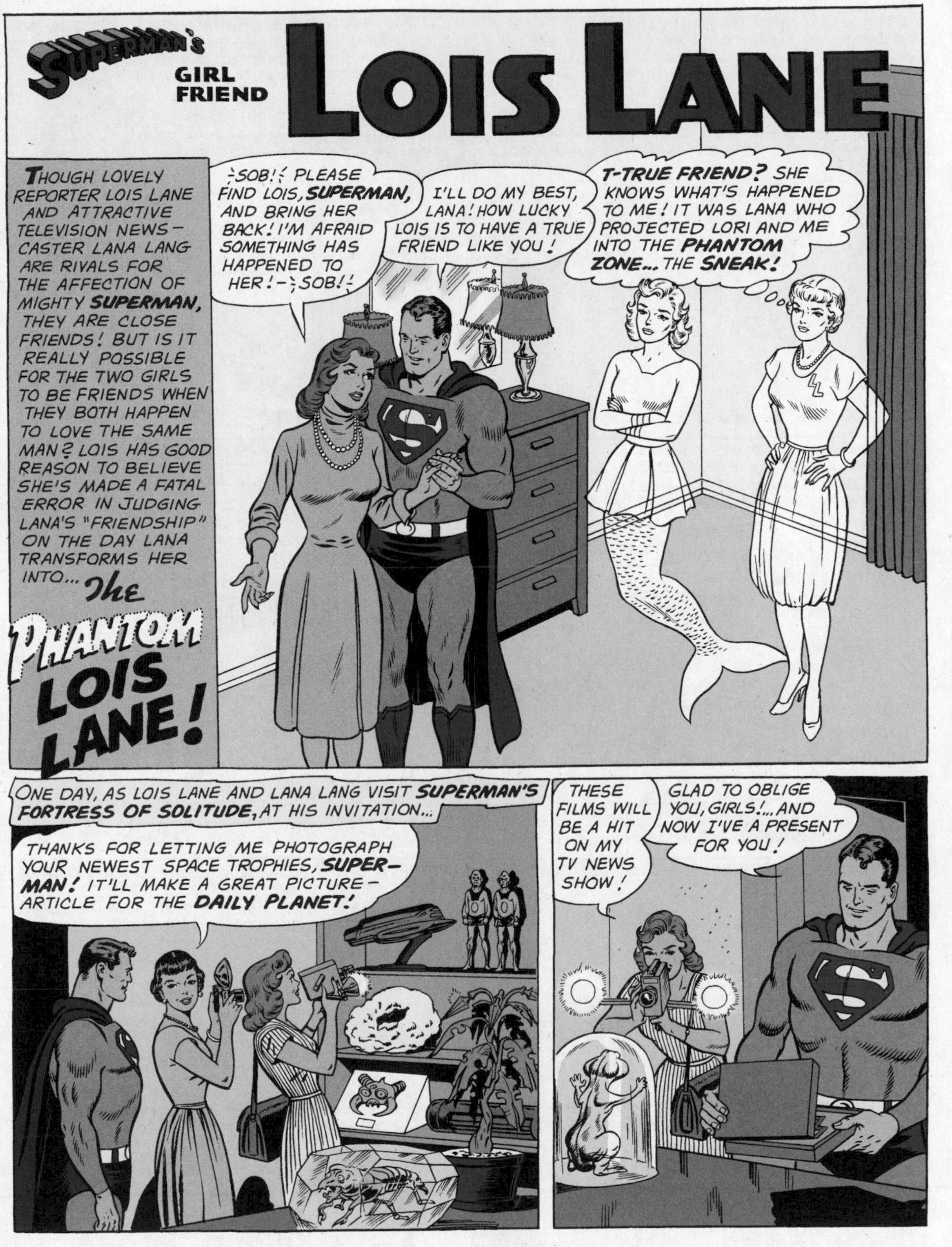
SUPERMAN'S GIRL FRIEND LOIS LANE
THOUGH LOVELY REPORTER LOIS LANE AND ATTRACTIVE TELEVISION NEWS-CASTER LANA LANG ARE RIVALS FOR THE AFFECTION OF MIGHTY SUPERMAN, THEY ARE CLOSE FRIENDS! BUT IS IT REALLY POSSIBLE FOR THE TWO GIRLS TO BE FRIENDS WHEN THEY BOTH HAPPEN TO LOVE THE SAME MAN? LOIS HAS GOOD REASON TO BELIEVE SHE'S MADE A FATAL ERROR IN JUDGING LANA'S "FRIENDSHIP" ON THE DAY LANA TRANSFORMS HER INTO... The PHANTOM LOIS LANE!
-SOB!- PLEASE FIND LOIS, SUPERMAN, AND BRING HER BACK! I'M AFRAID SOMETHING HAS HAPPENED TO HER! -SOB!-
I'LL DO MY BEST, LANA! HOW LUCKY LOIS IS TO HAVE A TRUE FRIEND LIKE YOU!
T-TRUE FRIEND? SHE KNOWS WHAT'S HAPPENED TO ME! IT WAS LANA WHO PROJECTED LORI AND ME INTO THE PHANTOM ZONE... THE SNEAK!
ONE DAY, AS LOIS LANE AND LANA LANG VISIT SUPERMAN'S FORTRESS OF SOLITUDE, AT HIS INVITATION...
THANKS FOR LETTING ME PHOTOGRAPH YOUR NEWEST SPACE TROPHIES, SUPER-MAN! IT'LL MAKE A GREAT PICTURE-ARTICLE FOR THE DAILY PLANET!
THESE FILMS WILL BE A HIT ON MY TV NEWS SHOW!
GLAD TO OBLIGE YOU, GIRLS!... AND NOW I'VE A PRESENT FOR YOU!

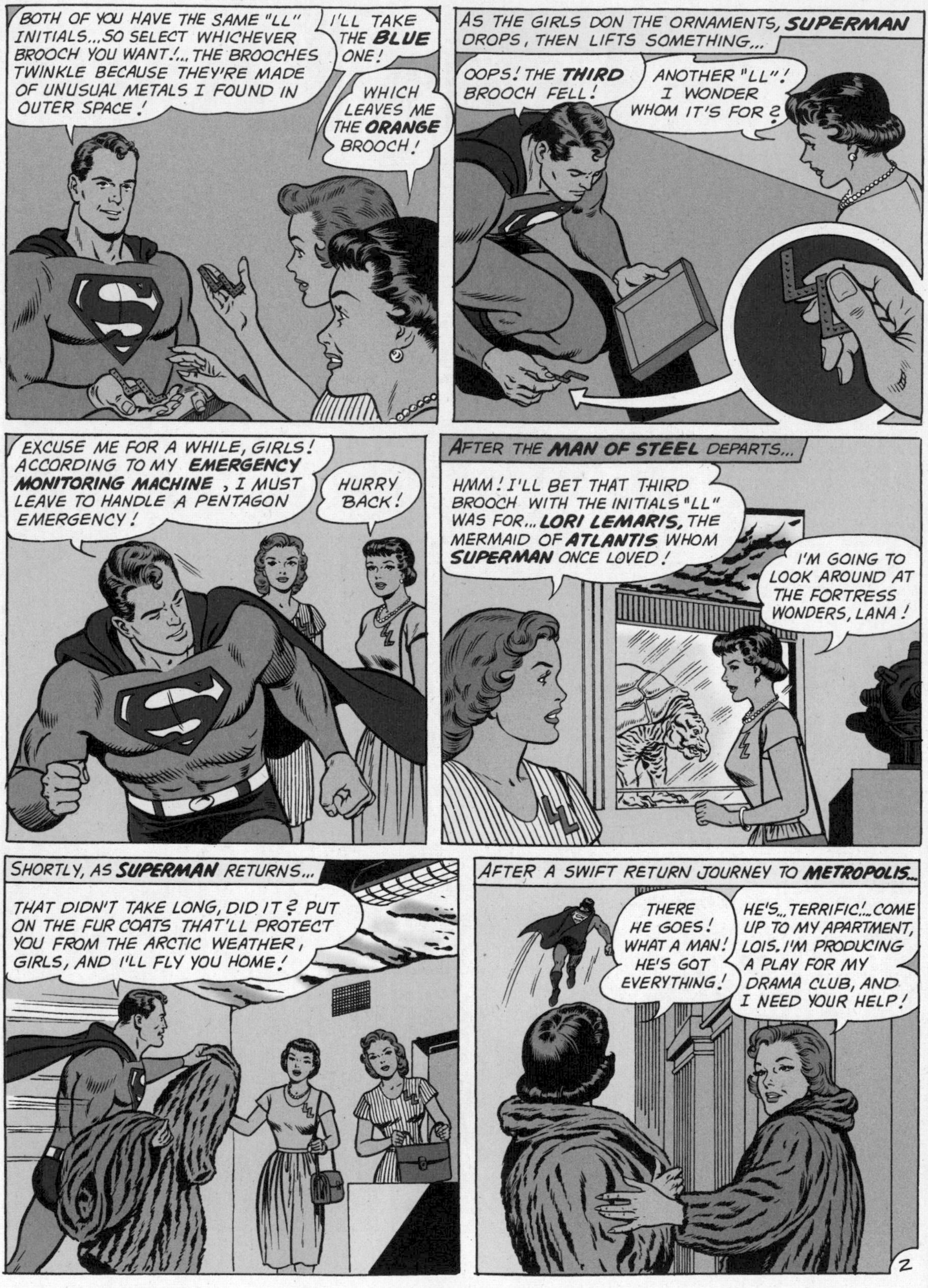

BOTH OF YOU HAVE THE SAME "LL" INITIALS...SO SELECT WHICHEVER BROOCH YOU WANT!... THE BROOCHES TWINKLE BECAUSE THEY'RE MADE OF UNUSUAL METALS I FOUND IN OUTER SPACE!
I'LL TAKE THE BLUE ONE!
WHICH LEAVES ME THE ORANGE BROOCH!
AS THE GIRLS DON THE ORNAMENTS, SUPERMAN DROPS, THEN LIFTS SOMETHING...
OOPS! THE THIRD BROOCH FELL!
ANOTHER "LL"! I WONDER WHOM IT'S FOR?
EXCUSE ME FOR A WHILE, GIRLS! ACCORDING TO MY EMERGENCY MONITORING MACHINE, I MUST LEAVE TO HANDLE A PENTAGON EMERGENCY!
HURRY BACK!
AFTER THE MAN OF STEEL DEPARTS...
HMM! I'LL BET THAT THIRD BROOCH WITH THE INITIALS "LL" WAS FOR... LORI LEMARIS, THE MERMAID OF ATLANTIS WHOM SUPERMAN ONCE LOVED!
I'M GOING TO LOOK AROUND AT THE FORTRESS WONDERS, LANA!
SHORTLY, AS SUPERMAN RETURNS...
THAT DIDN'T TAKE LONG, DID IT? PUT ON THE FUR COATS THAT'LL PROTECT YOU FROM THE ARCTIC WEATHER, GIRLS, AND I'LL FLY YOU HOME!
AFTER A SWIFT RETURN JOURNEY TO METROPOLIS...
THERE HE GOES! WHAT A MAN! HE'S GOT EVERYTHING!
HE'S... TERRIFIC!... COME UP TO MY APARTMENT, LOIS. I'M PRODUCING A PLAY FOR MY DRAMA CLUB, AND I NEED YOUR HELP!
2

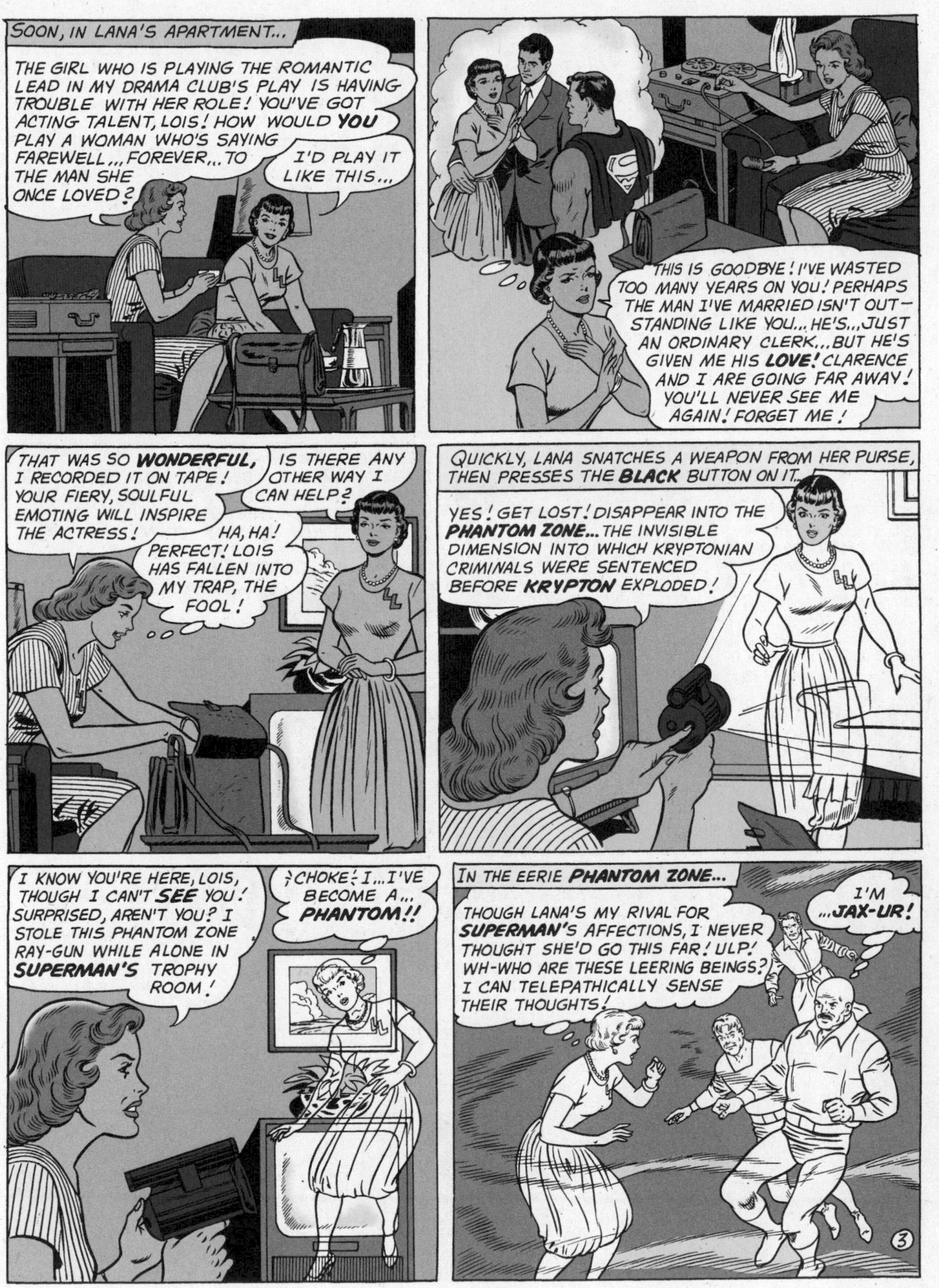
SOON, IN LANA'S APARTMENT...
THE GIRL WHO IS PLAYING THE ROMANTIC LEAD IN MY DRAMA CLUB'S PLAY IS HAVING TROUBLE WITH HER ROLE! YOU'VE GOT ACTING TALENT, LOIS! HOW WOULD YOU PLAY A WOMAN WHO'S SAYING FAREWELL... FOREVER... TO THE MAN SHE ONCE LOVED?
I'D PLAY IT LIKE THIS...
THIS IS GOODBYE! I'VE WASTED TOO MANY YEARS ON YOU! PERHAPS THE MAN I'VE MARRIED ISN'T OUT-STANDING LIKE YOU... HE'S... JUST AN ORDINARY CLERK... BUT HE'S GIVEN ME HIS LOVE! CLARENCE AND I ARE GOING FAR AWAY! YOU'LL NEVER SEE ME AGAIN! FORGET ME!
THAT WAS SO WONDERFUL, I RECORDED IT ON TAPE! YOUR FIERY, SOULFUL EMOTING WILL INSPIRE THE ACTRESS!
IS THERE ANY OTHER WAY I CAN HELP?
HA, HA! PERFECT! LOIS HAS FALLEN INTO MY TRAP, THE FOOL!
QUICKLY, LANA SNATCHES A WEAPON FROM HER PURSE, THEN PRESSES THE BLACK BUTTON ON IT...
YES! GET LOST! DISAPPEAR INTO THE PHANTOM ZONE... THE INVISIBLE DIMENSION INTO WHICH KRYPTONIAN CRIMINALS WERE SENTENCED BEFORE KRYPTON EXPLODED!
I KNOW YOU'RE HERE, LOIS, THOUGH I CAN'T SEE YOU! SURPRISED, AREN'T YOU? I STOLE THIS PHANTOM ZONE RAY-GUN WHILE ALONE IN SUPERMAN'S TROPHY ROOM!
-CHOKE- I... I'VE BECOME A... PHANTOM!!
IN THE EERIE PHANTOM ZONE...
THOUGH LANA'S MY RIVAL FOR SUPERMAN'S AFFECTIONS, I NEVER THOUGHT SHE'D GO THIS FAR! ULP! WH-WHO ARE THESE LEERING BEINGS? I CAN TELEPATHICALLY SENSE THEIR THOUGHTS!
I'M ...JAX-UR!
3

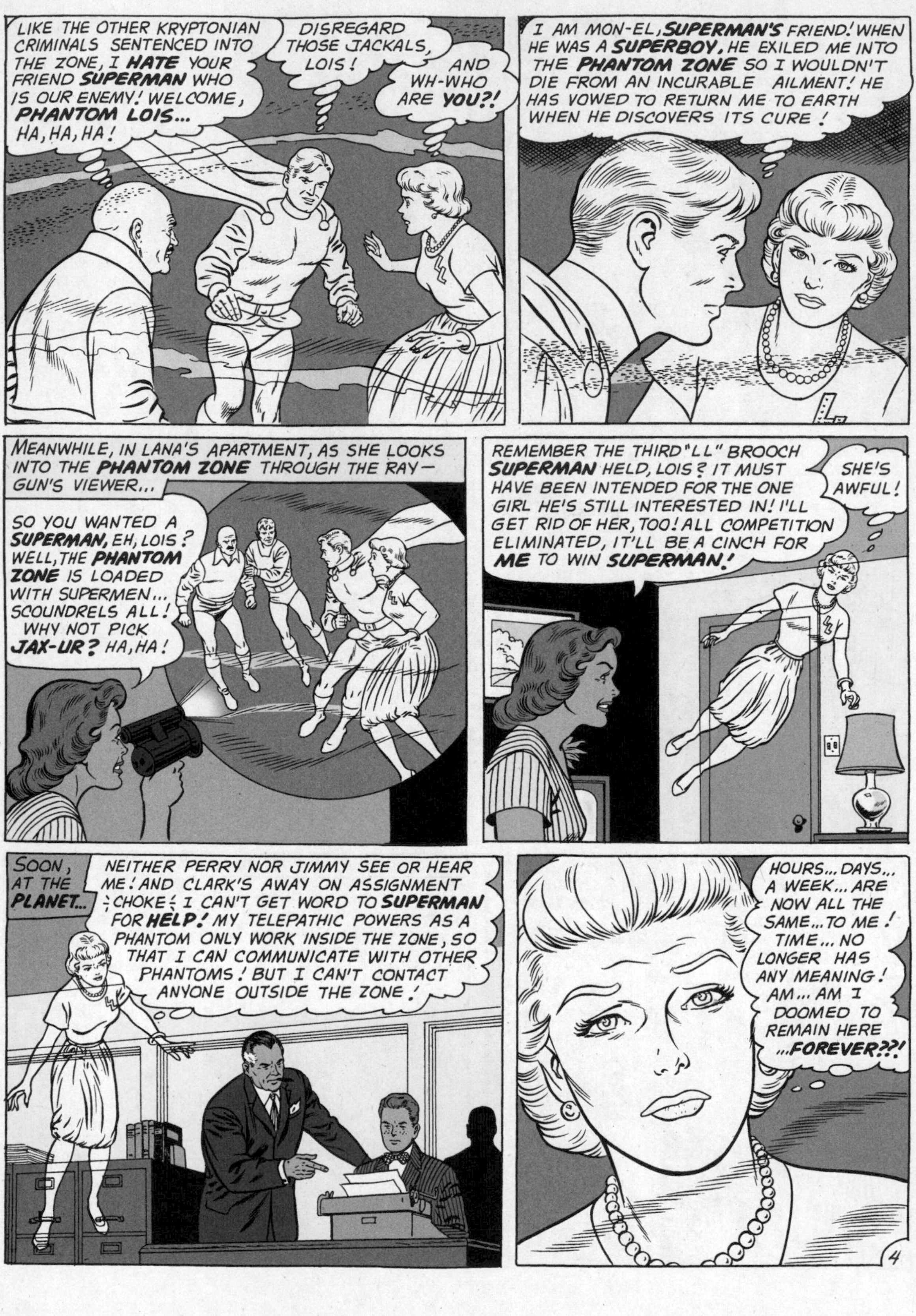
LIKE THE OTHER KRYPTONIAN CRIMINALS SENTENCED INTO THE ZONE, I HATE YOUR FRIEND SUPERMAN WHO IS OUR ENEMY! WELCOME, PHANTOM LOIS... HA, HA, HA!
DISREGARD THOSE JACKALS, LOIS!
AND WH-WHO ARE YOU?!
I AM MON-EL, SUPERMAN'S FRIEND! WHEN HE WAS A SUPERBOY, HE EXILED ME INTO THE PHANTOM ZONE SO I WOULDN'T DIE FROM AN INCURABLE AILMENT! HE HAS VOWED TO RETURN ME TO EARTH WHEN HE DISCOVERS ITS CURE!
MEANWHILE, IN LANA'S APARTMENT, AS SHE LOOKS INTO THE PHANTOM ZONE THROUGH THE RAY-GUN'S VIEWER...
SO YOU WANTED A SUPERMAN, EH, LOIS? WELL, THE PHANTOM ZONE IS LOADED WITH SUPERMEN... SCOUNDRELS ALL! WHY NOT PICK JAX-UR? HA, HA!
REMEMBER THE THIRD "LL" BROOCH SUPERMAN HELD, LOIS? IT MUST HAVE BEEN INTENDED FOR THE ONE GIRL HE'S STILL INTERESTED IN! I'LL GET RID OF HER, TOO! ALL COMPETITION ELIMINATED, IT'LL BE A CINCH FOR ME TO WIN SUPERMAN!
SHE'S AWFUL!
SOON, AT THE PLANET...
NEITHER PERRY NOR JIMMY SEE OR HEAR ME! AND CLARK'S AWAY ON ASSIGNMENT -CHOKE- I CAN'T GET WORD TO SUPERMAN FOR HELP! MY TELEPATHIC POWERS AS A PHANTOM ONLY WORK INSIDE THE ZONE, SO THAT I CAN COMMUNICATE WITH OTHER PHANTOMS! BUT I CAN'T CONTACT ANYONE OUTSIDE THE ZONE!
HOURS... DAYS... A WEEK... ARE NOW ALL THE SAME... TO ME! TIME... NO LONGER HAS ANY MEANING! AM... AM I DOOMED TO REMAIN HERE ...FOREVER??!
4

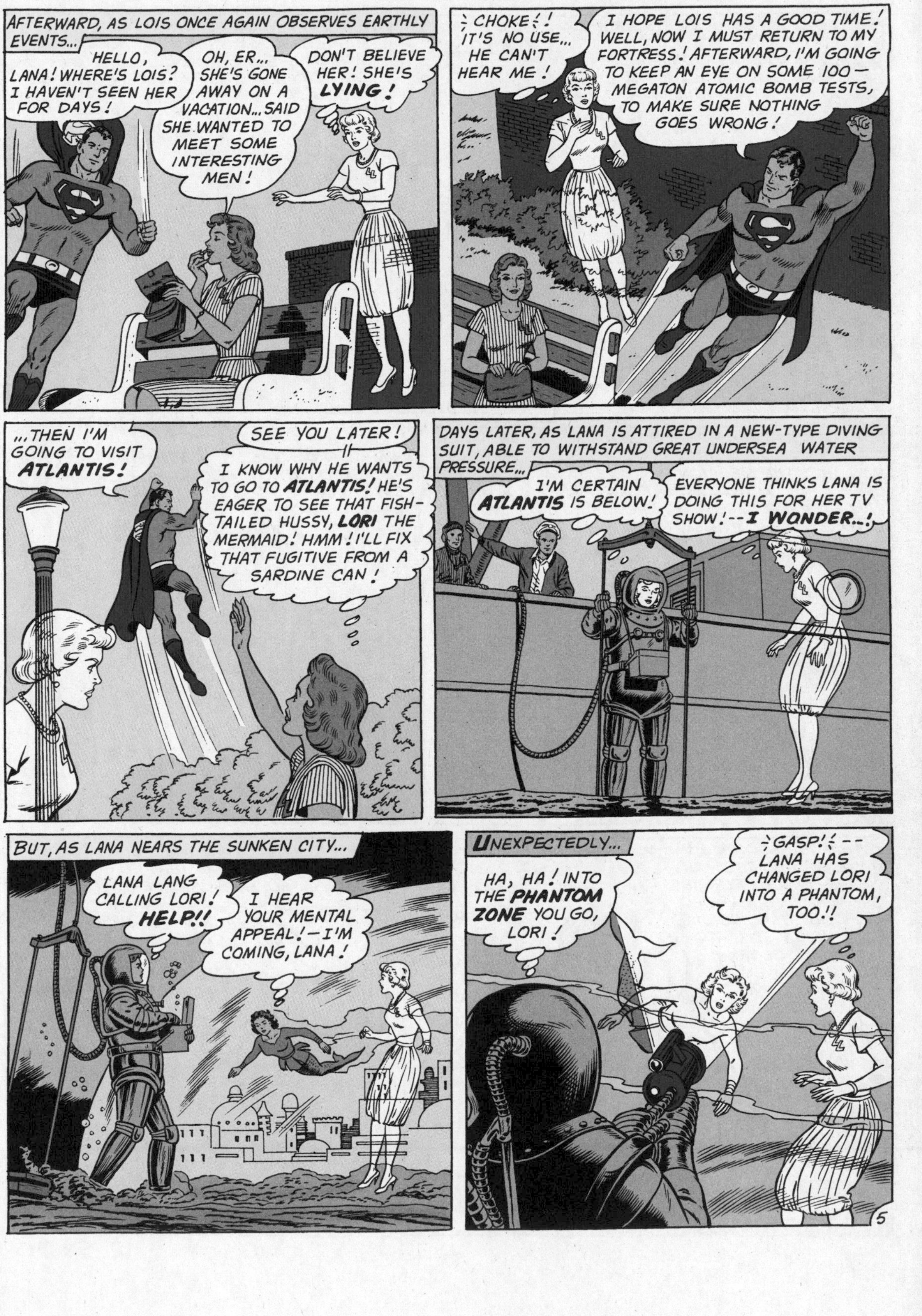
AFTERWARD, AS LOIS ONCE AGAIN OBSERVES EARTHLY EVENTS...
HELLO, LANA! WHERE'S LOIS? I HAVEN'T SEEN HER FOR DAYS!
OH, ER... SHE'S GONE AWAY ON A VACATION... SAID SHE WANTED TO MEET SOME INTERESTING MEN!
DON'T BELIEVE HER! SHE'S LYING!
-CHOKE!- IT'S NO USE... HE CAN'T HEAR ME!
I HOPE LOIS HAS A GOOD TIME! WELL, NOW I MUST RETURN TO MY FORTRESS! AFTERWARD, I'M GOING TO KEEP AN EYE ON SOME 100-MEGATON ATOMIC BOMB TESTS, TO MAKE SURE NOTHING GOES WRONG!
...THEN I'M GOING TO VISIT ATLANTIS!
SEE YOU LATER!
I KNOW WHY HE WANTS TO GO TO ATLANTIS! HE'S EAGER TO SEE THAT FISH-TAILED HUSSY, LORI THE MERMAID! HMM! I'LL FIX THAT FUGITIVE FROM A SARDINE CAN!
DAYS LATER, AS LANA IS ATTIRED IN A NEW-TYPE DIVING SUIT, ABLE TO WITHSTAND GREAT UNDERSEA WATER PRESSURE...
I'M CERTAIN ATLANTIS IS BELOW!
EVERYONE THINKS LANA IS DOING THIS FOR HER TV SHOW!--I WONDER...!
BUT, AS LANA NEARS THE SUNKEN CITY...
LANA LANG CALLING LORI! HELP!!
I HEAR YOUR MENTAL APPEAL!-I'M COMING, LANA!
UNEXPECTEDLY...
HA, HA! INTO THE PHANTOM ZONE YOU GO, LORI!
-GASP!- -- LANA HAS CHANGED LORI INTO A PHANTOM, TOO!!
5

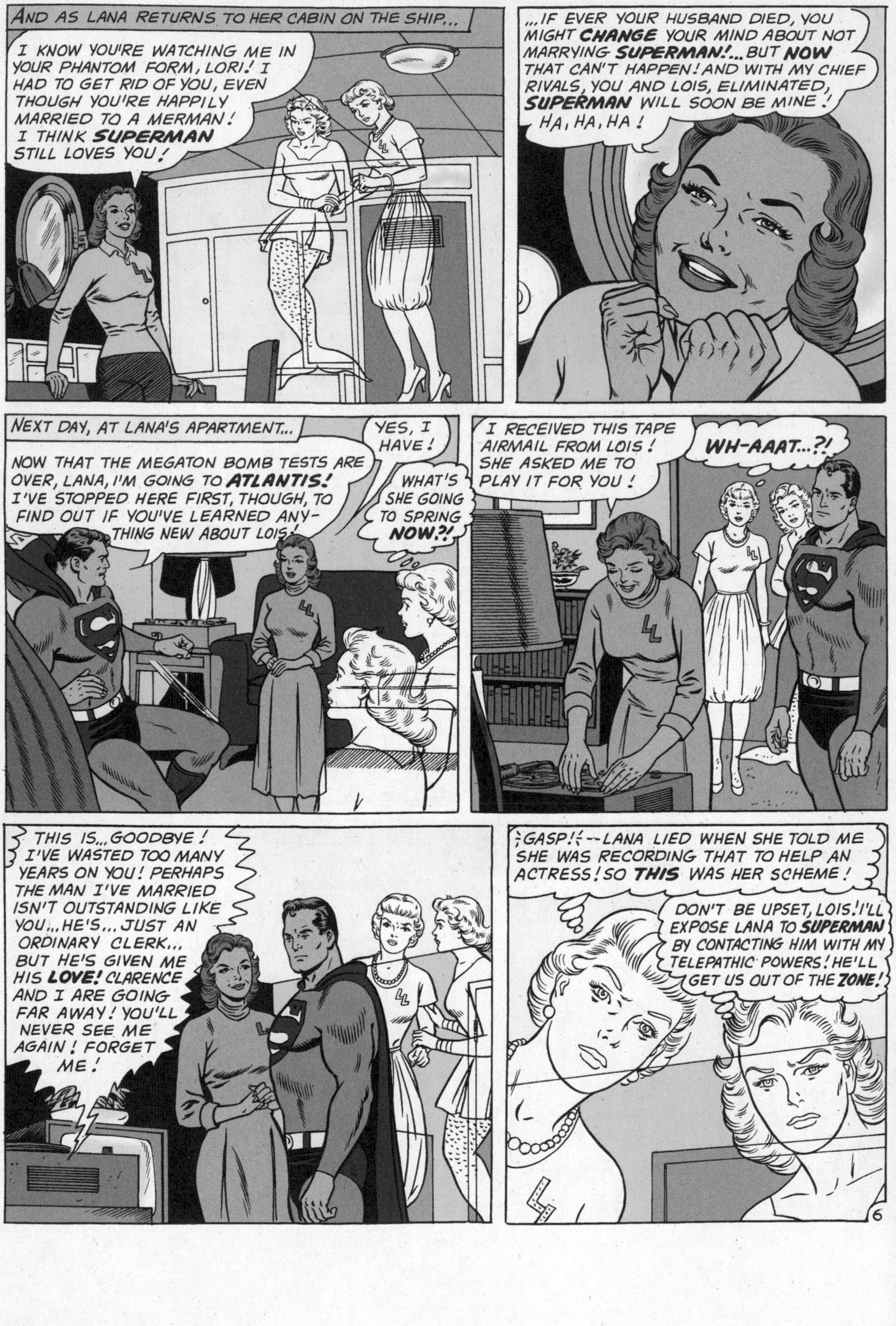
AND AS LANA RETURNS TO HER CABIN ON THE SHIP...
I KNOW YOU'RE WATCHING ME IN YOUR PHANTOM FORM, LORI! I HAD TO GET RID OF YOU, EVEN THOUGH YOU'RE HAPPILY MARRIED TO A MERMAN! I THINK SUPERMAN STILL LOVES YOU!
...IF EVER YOUR HUSBAND DIED, YOU MIGHT CHANGE YOUR MIND ABOUT NOT MARRYING SUPERMAN!... BUT NOW THAT CAN'T HAPPEN! AND WITH MY CHIEF RIVALS, YOU AND LOIS, ELIMINATED, SUPERMAN WILL SOON BE MINE! HA, HA, HA!
NEXT DAY, AT LANA'S APARTMENT...
NOW THAT THE MEGATON BOMB TESTS ARE OVER, LANA, I'M GOING TO ATLANTIS! I'VE STOPPED HERE FIRST, THOUGH, TO FIND OUT IF YOU'VE LEARNED ANY-THING NEW ABOUT LOIS!
YES, I HAVE!
WHAT'S SHE GOING TO SPRING NOW?!
I RECEIVED THIS TAPE AIRMAIL FROM LOIS! SHE ASKED ME TO PLAY IT FOR YOU!
WH-AAAT...?!
THIS IS... GOODBYE! I'VE WASTED TOO MANY YEARS ON YOU! PERHAPS THE MAN I'VE MARRIED ISN'T OUTSTANDING LIKE YOU... HE'S... JUST AN ORDINARY CLERK... BUT HE'S GIVEN ME HIS LOVE! CLARENCE AND I ARE GOING FAR AWAY! YOU'LL NEVER SEE ME AGAIN! FORGET ME!
GASP! --LANA LIED WHEN SHE TOLD ME SHE WAS RECORDING THAT TO HELP AN ACTRESS! SO THIS WAS HER SCHEME!
DON'T BE UPSET, LOIS! I'LL EXPOSE LANA TO SUPERMAN BY CONTACTING HIM WITH MY TELEPATHIC POWERS! HE'LL GET US OUT OF THE ZONE!
6

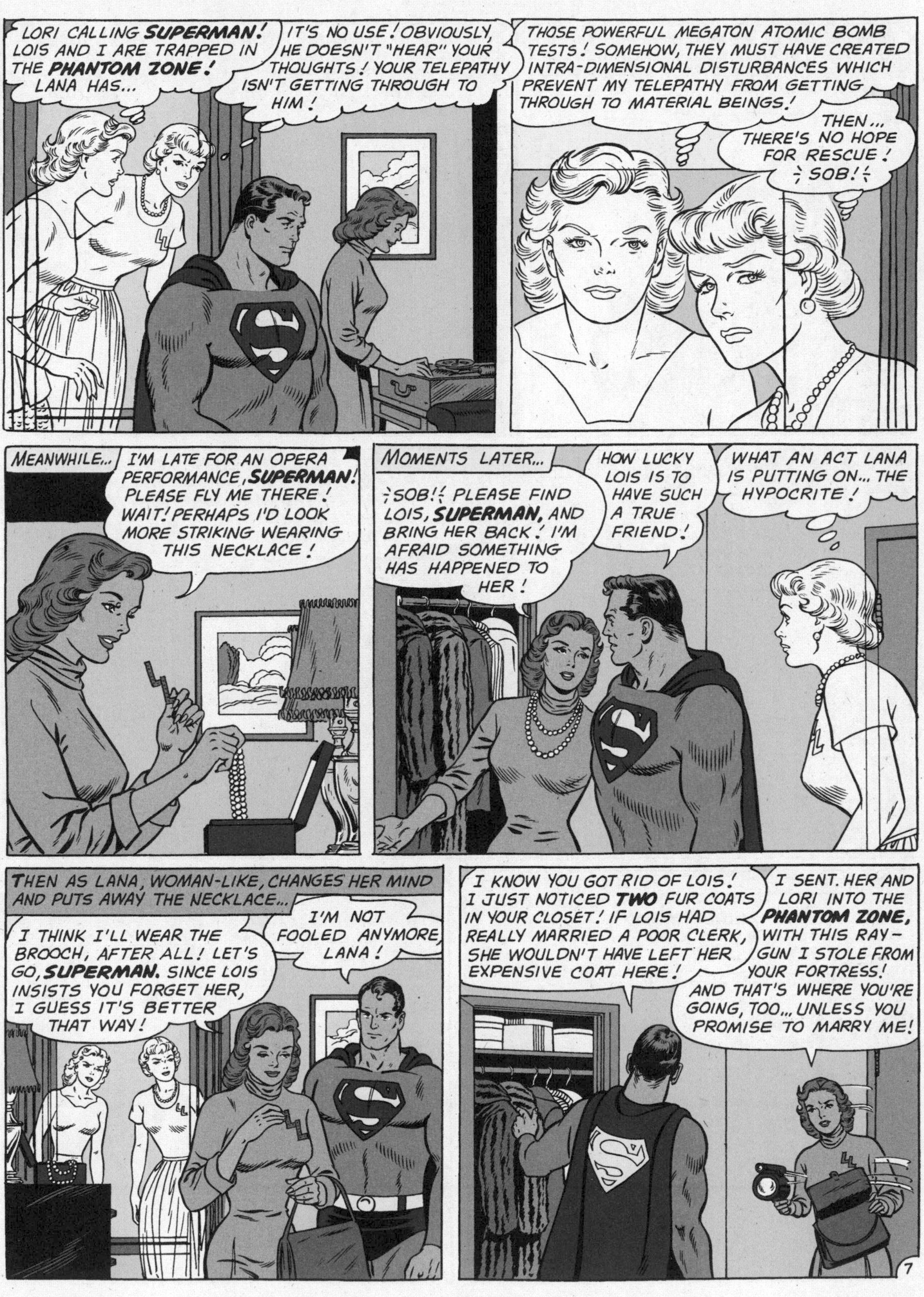
LORI CALLING SUPERMAN! LOIS AND I ARE TRAPPED IN THE PHANTOM ZONE! LANA HAS...
IT'S NO USE! OBVIOUSLY, HE DOESN'T "HEAR" YOUR THOUGHTS! YOUR TELEPATHY ISN'T GETTING THROUGH TO HIM!
THOSE POWERFUL MEGATON ATOMIC BOMB TESTS! SOMEHOW, THEY MUST HAVE CREATED INTRA-DIMENSIONAL DISTURBANCES WHICH PREVENT MY TELEPATHY FROM GETTING THROUGH TO MATERIAL BEINGS!
THEN... THERE'S NO HOPE FOR RESCUE! SOB!
MEANWHILE...
I'M LATE FOR AN OPERA PERFORMANCE, SUPERMAN! PLEASE FLY ME THERE! WAIT! PERHAPS I'D LOOK MORE STRIKING WEARING THIS NECKLACE!
MOMENTS LATER...
SOB!! PLEASE FIND LOIS, SUPERMAN, AND BRING HER BACK! I'M AFRAID SOMETHING HAS HAPPENED TO HER!
HOW LUCKY LOIS IS TO HAVE SUCH A TRUE FRIEND!
WHAT AN ACT LANA IS PUTTING ON... THE HYPOCRITE!
THEN AS LANA, WOMAN-LIKE, CHANGES HER MIND AND PUTS AWAY THE NECKLACE...
I THINK I'LL WEAR THE BROOCH, AFTER ALL! LET'S GO, SUPERMAN. SINCE LOIS INSISTS YOU FORGET HER, I GUESS IT'S BETTER THAT WAY!
I'M NOT FOOLED ANYMORE, LANA!
I KNOW YOU GOT RID OF LOIS! I JUST NOTICED TWO FUR COATS IN YOUR CLOSET! IF LOIS HAD REALLY MARRIED A POOR CLERK, SHE WOULDN'T HAVE LEFT HER EXPENSIVE COAT HERE!
I SENT HER AND LORI INTO THE PHANTOM ZONE, WITH THIS RAY-GUN I STOLE FROM YOUR FORTRESS! AND THAT'S WHERE YOU'RE GOING, TOO... UNLESS YOU PROMISE TO MARRY ME!
7

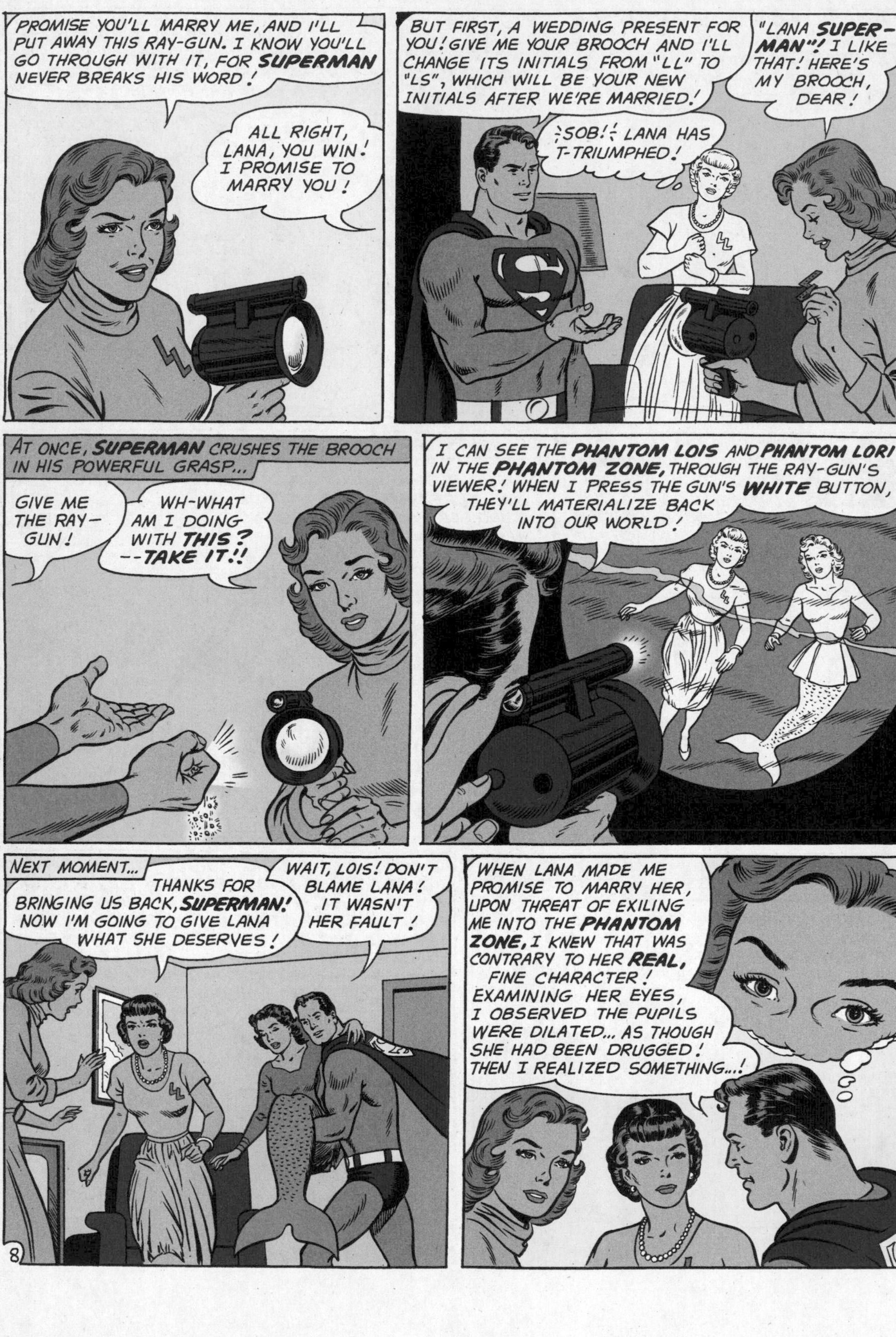
PROMISE YOU'LL MARRY ME, AND I'LL PUT AWAY THIS RAY-GUN. I KNOW YOU'LL GO THROUGH WITH IT, FOR SUPERMAN NEVER BREAKS HIS WORD!
ALL RIGHT, LANA, YOU WIN! I PROMISE TO MARRY YOU!
BUT FIRST, A WEDDING PRESENT FOR YOU! GIVE ME YOUR BROOCH AND I'LL CHANGE ITS INITIALS FROM "LL" TO "LS", WHICH WILL BE YOUR NEW INITIALS AFTER WE'RE MARRIED!
"LANA SUPERMAN"! I LIKE THAT! HERE'S MY BROOCH, DEAR!
SOB! LANA HAS T-TRIUMPHED!
AT ONCE, SUPERMAN CRUSHES THE BROOCH IN HIS POWERFUL GRASP...
GIVE ME THE RAY-GUN!
WH-WHAT AM I DOING WITH THIS? --TAKE IT!!
I CAN SEE THE PHANTOM LOIS AND PHANTOM LORI IN THE PHANTOM ZONE, THROUGH THE RAY-GUN'S VIEWER! WHEN I PRESS THE GUN'S WHITE BUTTON, THEY'LL MATERIALIZE BACK INTO OUR WORLD!
NEXT MOMENT...
THANKS FOR BRINGING US BACK, SUPERMAN! NOW I'M GOING TO GIVE LANA WHAT SHE DESERVES!
WAIT, LOIS! DON'T BLAME LANA! IT WASN'T HER FAULT!
8
WHEN LANA MADE ME PROMISE TO MARRY HER, UPON THREAT OF EXILING ME INTO THE PHANTOM ZONE, I KNEW THAT WAS CONTRARY TO HER REAL, FINE CHARACTER! EXAMINING HER EYES, I OBSERVED THE PUPILS WERE DILATED... AS THOUGH SHE HAD BEEN DRUGGED! THEN I REALIZED SOMETHING...!

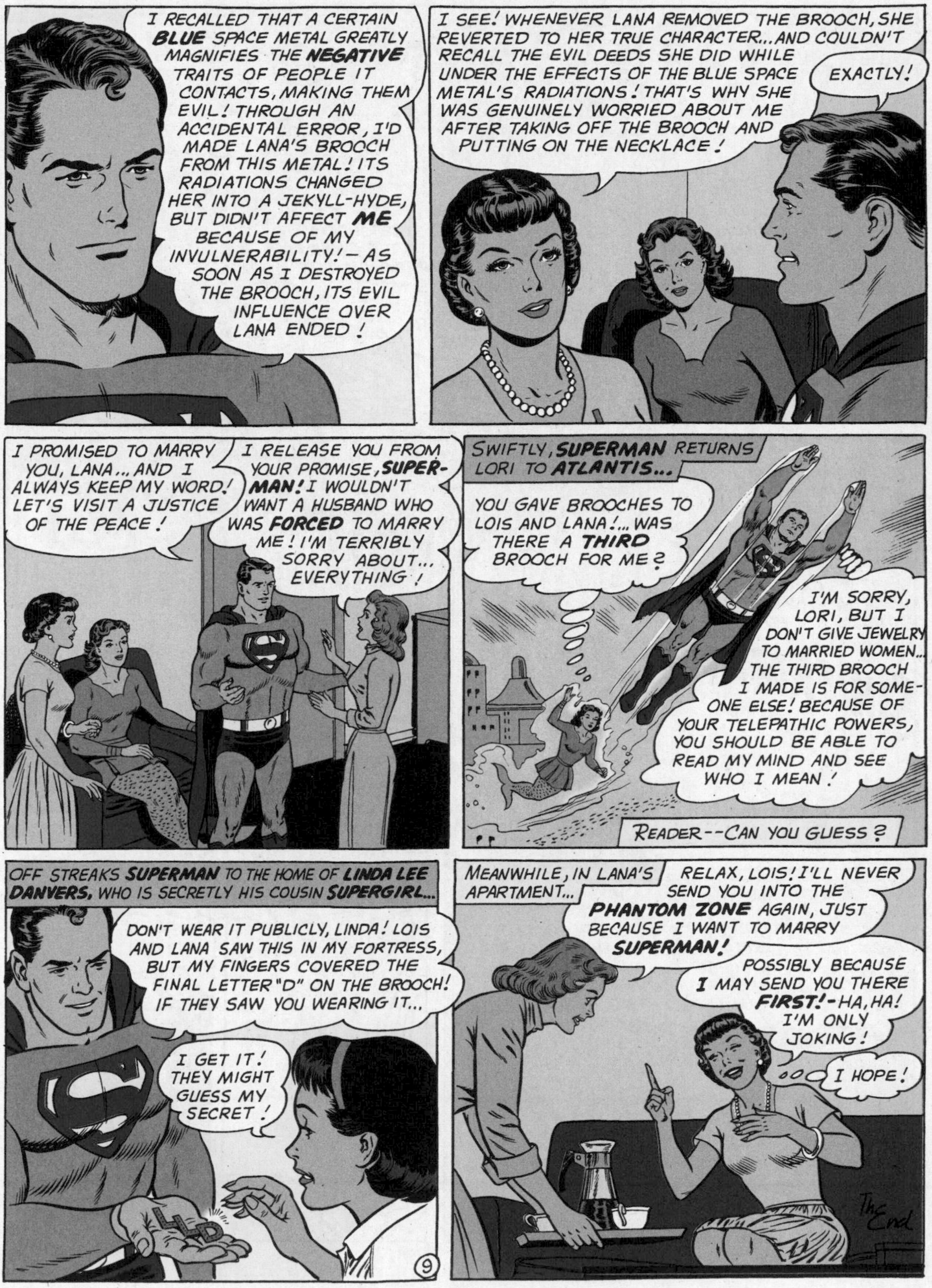
I RECALLED THAT A CERTAIN **BLUE** SPACE METAL GREATLY MAGNIFIES THE **NEGATIVE** TRAITS OF PEOPLE IT CONTACTS, MAKING THEM EVIL! THROUGH AN ACCIDENTAL ERROR, I'D MADE LANA'S BROOCH FROM THIS METAL! ITS RADIATIONS CHANGED HER INTO A JEKYLL-HYDE, BUT DIDN'T AFFECT **ME** BECAUSE OF MY INVULNERABILITY!-- AS SOON AS I DESTROYED THE BROOCH, ITS EVIL INFLUENCE OVER LANA ENDED!
I SEE! WHENEVER LANA REMOVED THE BROOCH, SHE REVERTED TO HER TRUE CHARACTER... AND COULDN'T RECALL THE EVIL DEEDS SHE DID WHILE UNDER THE EFFECTS OF THE BLUE SPACE METAL'S RADIATIONS! THAT'S WHY SHE WAS GENUINELY WORRIED ABOUT ME AFTER TAKING OFF THE BROOCH AND PUTTING ON THE NECKLACE!
EXACTLY!
I PROMISED TO MARRY YOU, LANA... AND I ALWAYS KEEP MY WORD! LET'S VISIT A JUSTICE OF THE PEACE!
I RELEASE YOU FROM YOUR PROMISE, **SUPERMAN!** I WOULDN'T WANT A HUSBAND WHO WAS **FORCED** TO MARRY ME! I'M TERRIBLY SORRY ABOUT... EVERYTHING!
SWIFTLY, **SUPERMAN** RETURNS LORI TO **ATLANTIS**...
YOU GAVE BROOCHES TO LOIS AND LANA!... WAS THERE A **THIRD** BROOCH FOR ME?
I'M SORRY, LORI, BUT I DON'T GIVE JEWELRY TO MARRIED WOMEN... THE THIRD BROOCH I MADE IS FOR SOMEONE ELSE! BECAUSE OF YOUR TELEPATHIC POWERS, YOU SHOULD BE ABLE TO READ MY MIND AND SEE WHO I MEAN!
READER--CAN YOU GUESS?
OFF STREAKS **SUPERMAN** TO THE HOME OF **LINDA LEE DANVERS**, WHO IS SECRETLY HIS COUSIN **SUPERGIRL**...
DON'T WEAR IT PUBLICLY, LINDA! LOIS AND LANA SAW THIS IN MY FORTRESS, BUT MY FINGERS COVERED THE FINAL LETTER "D" ON THE BROOCH! IF THEY SAW YOU WEARING IT...
I GET IT! THEY MIGHT GUESS MY SECRET!
LLD
9
MEANWHILE, IN LANA'S APARTMENT...
RELAX, LOIS! I'LL NEVER SEND YOU INTO THE **PHANTOM ZONE** AGAIN, JUST BECAUSE I WANT TO MARRY **SUPERMAN!**
POSSIBLY BECAUSE **I** MAY SEND YOU THERE **FIRST!**-HA, HA! I'M ONLY JOKING!
I HOPE!
The End

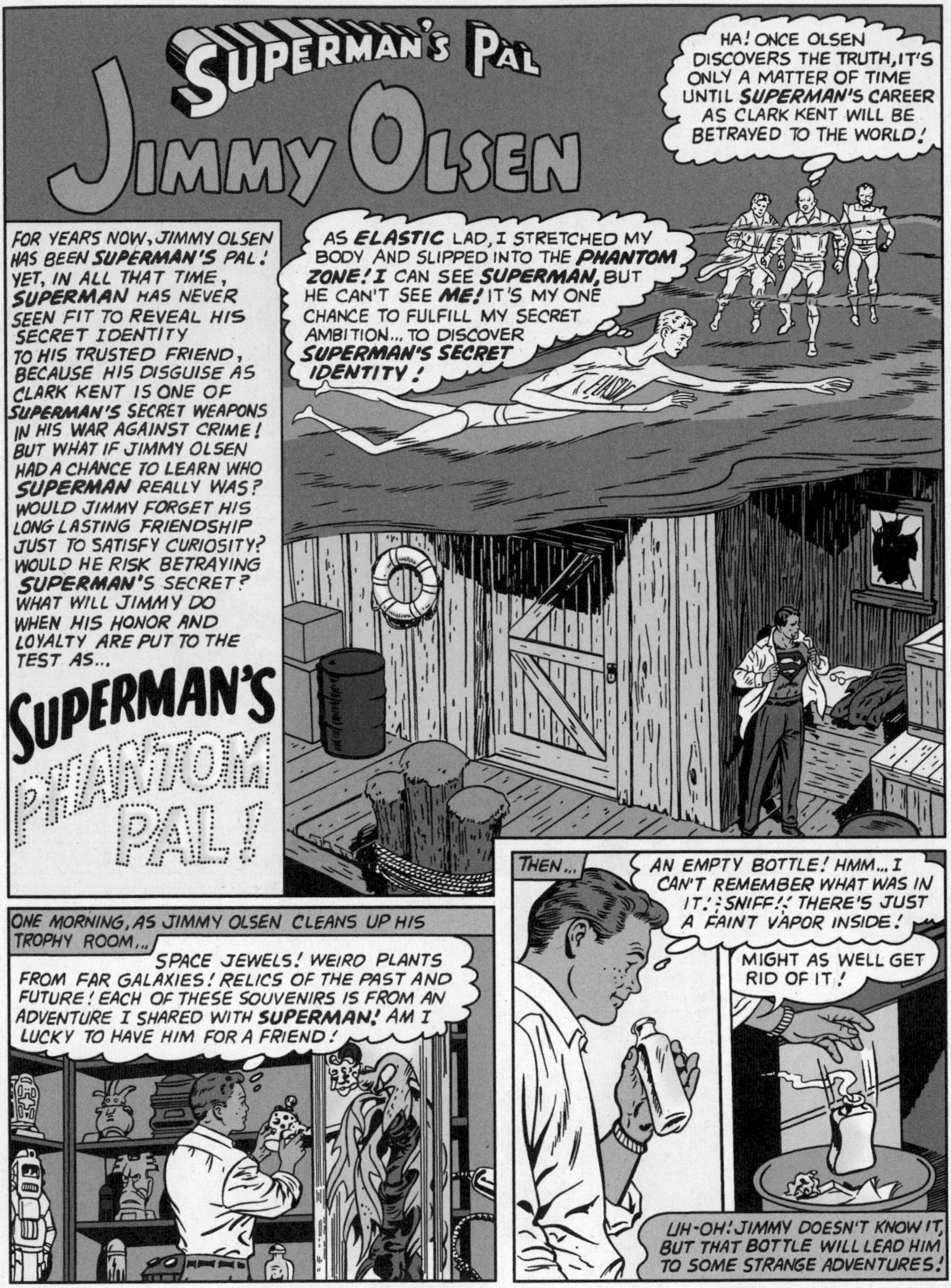
SUPERMAN'S PAL JIMMY OLSEN
HA! ONCE OLSEN DISCOVERS THE TRUTH, IT'S ONLY A MATTER OF TIME UNTIL SUPERMAN'S CAREER AS CLARK KENT WILL BE BETRAYED TO THE WORLD!
FOR YEARS NOW, JIMMY OLSEN HAS BEEN SUPERMAN'S PAL! YET, IN ALL THAT TIME, SUPERMAN HAS NEVER SEEN FIT TO REVEAL HIS SECRET IDENTITY TO HIS TRUSTED FRIEND, BECAUSE HIS DISGUISE AS CLARK KENT IS ONE OF SUPERMAN'S SECRET WEAPONS IN HIS WAR AGAINST CRIME! BUT WHAT IF JIMMY OLSEN HAD A CHANCE TO LEARN WHO SUPERMAN REALLY WAS? WOULD JIMMY FORGET HIS LONG LASTING FRIENDSHIP JUST TO SATISFY CURIOSITY? WOULD HE RISK BETRAYING SUPERMAN'S SECRET? WHAT WILL JIMMY DO WHEN HIS HONOR AND LOYALTY ARE PUT TO THE TEST AS...
SUPERMAN'S PHANTOM PAL!
AS ELASTIC LAD, I STRETCHED MY BODY AND SLIPPED INTO THE PHANTOM ZONE! I CAN SEE SUPERMAN, BUT HE CAN'T SEE ME! IT'S MY ONE CHANCE TO FULFILL MY SECRET AMBITION... TO DISCOVER SUPERMAN'S SECRET IDENTITY!
ONE MORNING, AS JIMMY OLSEN CLEANS UP HIS TROPHY ROOM...
SPACE JEWELS! WEIRD PLANTS FROM FAR GALAXIES! RELICS OF THE PAST AND FUTURE! EACH OF THESE SOUVENIRS IS FROM AN ADVENTURE I SHARED WITH SUPERMAN! AM I LUCKY TO HAVE HIM FOR A FRIEND!
THEN...
AN EMPTY BOTTLE! HMM... I CAN'T REMEMBER WHAT WAS IN IT! SNIFF! THERE'S JUST A FAINT VAPOR INSIDE!
MIGHT AS WELL GET RID OF IT!
UH-OH! JIMMY DOESN'T KNOW IT, BUT THAT BOTTLE WILL LEAD HIM TO SOME STRANGE ADVENTURES!

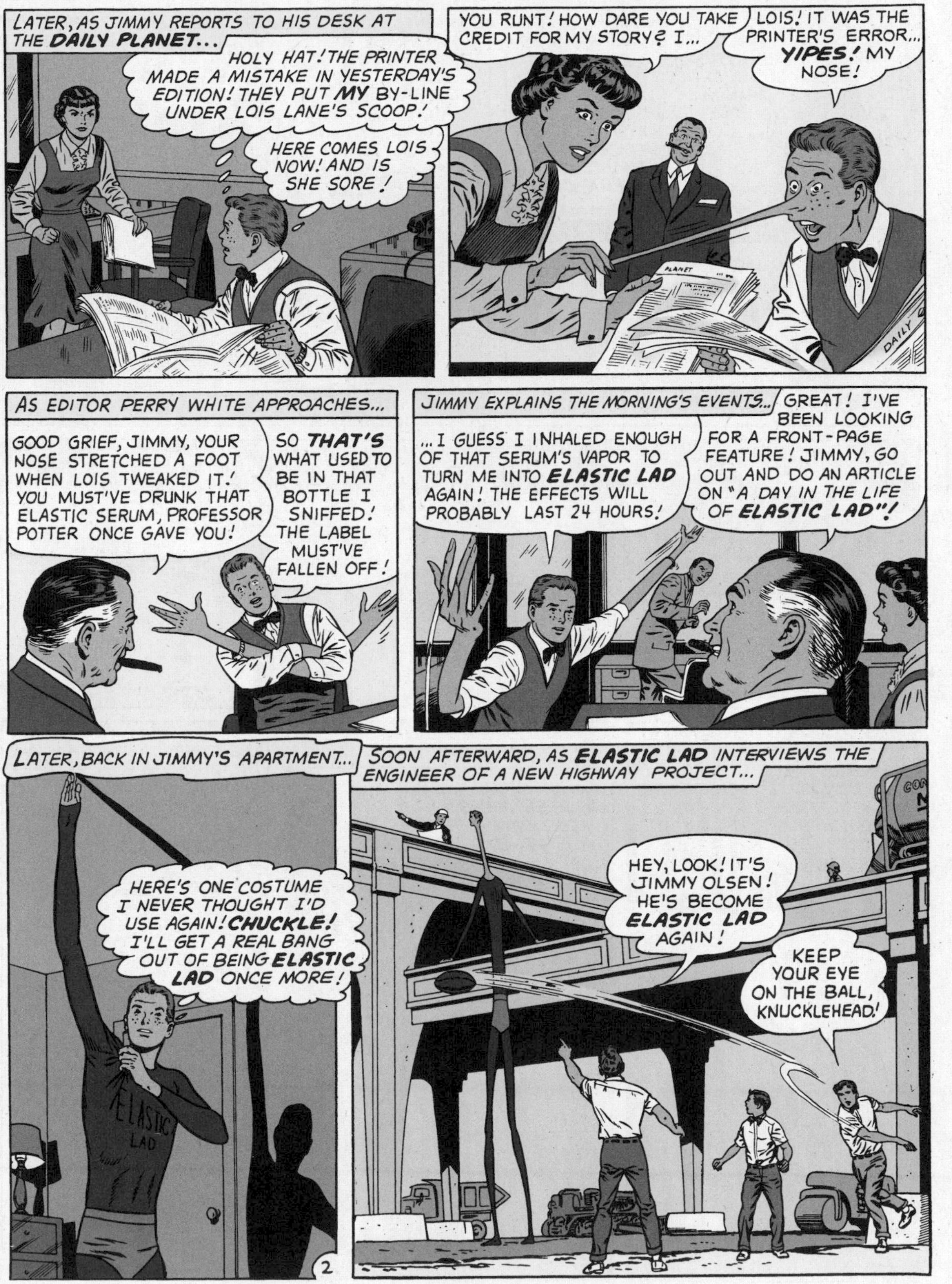

LATER, AS JIMMY REPORTS TO HIS DESK AT THE DAILY PLANET...
HOLY HAT! THE PRINTER MADE A MISTAKE IN YESTERDAY'S EDITION! THEY PUT MY BY-LINE UNDER LOIS LANE'S SCOOP!
HERE COMES LOIS NOW! AND IS SHE SORE!
YOU RUNT! HOW DARE YOU TAKE CREDIT FOR MY STORY? I...
LOIS! IT WAS THE PRINTER'S ERROR... YIPES! MY NOSE!
PLANET
DAILY
AS EDITOR PERRY WHITE APPROACHES...
GOOD GRIEF, JIMMY, YOUR NOSE STRETCHED A FOOT WHEN LOIS TWEAKED IT! YOU MUST'VE DRUNK THAT ELASTIC SERUM, PROFESSOR POTTER ONCE GAVE YOU!
SO THAT'S WHAT USED TO BE IN THAT BOTTLE I SNIFFED! THE LABEL MUST'VE FALLEN OFF!
JIMMY EXPLAINS THE MORNING'S EVENTS...
...I GUESS I INHALED ENOUGH OF THAT SERUM'S VAPOR TO TURN ME INTO ELASTIC LAD AGAIN! THE EFFECTS WILL PROBABLY LAST 24 HOURS!
GREAT! I'VE BEEN LOOKING FOR A FRONT-PAGE FEATURE! JIMMY, GO OUT AND DO AN ARTICLE ON "A DAY IN THE LIFE OF ELASTIC LAD"!
LATER, BACK IN JIMMY'S APARTMENT...
HERE'S ONE COSTUME I NEVER THOUGHT I'D USE AGAIN! CHUCKLE! I'LL GET A REAL BANG OUT OF BEING ELASTIC LAD ONCE MORE!
ELASTIC LAD
2
SOON AFTERWARD, AS ELASTIC LAD INTERVIEWS THE ENGINEER OF A NEW HIGHWAY PROJECT...
HEY, LOOK! IT'S JIMMY OLSEN! HE'S BECOME ELASTIC LAD AGAIN!
KEEP YOUR EYE ON THE BALL, KNUCKLEHEAD!

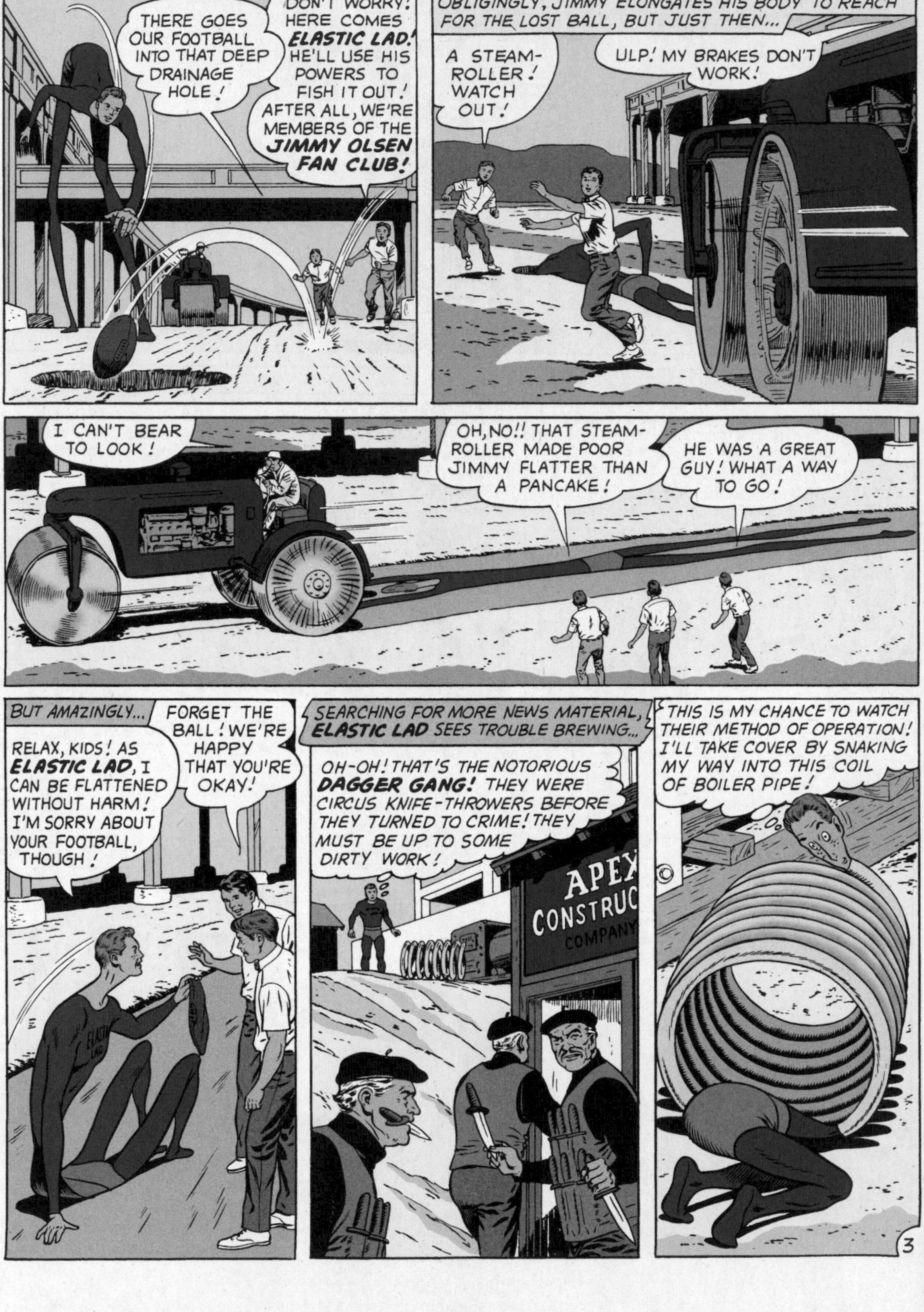
THERE GOES OUR FOOTBALL INTO THAT DEEP DRAINAGE HOLE!
DON'T WORRY! HERE COMES ELASTIC LAD! HE'LL USE HIS POWERS TO FISH IT OUT! AFTER ALL, WE'RE MEMBERS OF THE JIMMY OLSEN FAN CLUB!
OBLIGINGLY, JIMMY ELONGATES HIS BODY TO REACH FOR THE LOST BALL, BUT JUST THEN...
A STEAM-ROLLER! WATCH OUT!
ULP! MY BRAKES DON'T WORK!
I CAN'T BEAR TO LOOK!
OH, NO!! THAT STEAM-ROLLER MADE POOR JIMMY FLATTER THAN A PANCAKE!
HE WAS A GREAT GUY! WHAT A WAY TO GO!
BUT AMAZINGLY...
RELAX, KIDS! AS ELASTIC LAD, I CAN BE FLATTENED WITHOUT HARM! I'M SORRY ABOUT YOUR FOOTBALL, THOUGH!
FORGET THE BALL! WE'RE HAPPY THAT YOU'RE OKAY!
ELASTIC LAD
SEARCHING FOR MORE NEWS MATERIAL, ELASTIC LAD SEES TROUBLE BREWING...
OH-OH! THAT'S THE NOTORIOUS DAGGER GANG! THEY WERE CIRCUS KNIFE-THROWERS BEFORE THEY TURNED TO CRIME! THEY MUST BE UP TO SOME DIRTY WORK!
APEX CONSTRUC COMPANY
THIS IS MY CHANCE TO WATCH THEIR METHOD OF OPERATION! I'LL TAKE COVER BY SNAKING MY WAY INTO THIS COIL OF BOILER PIPE!
3

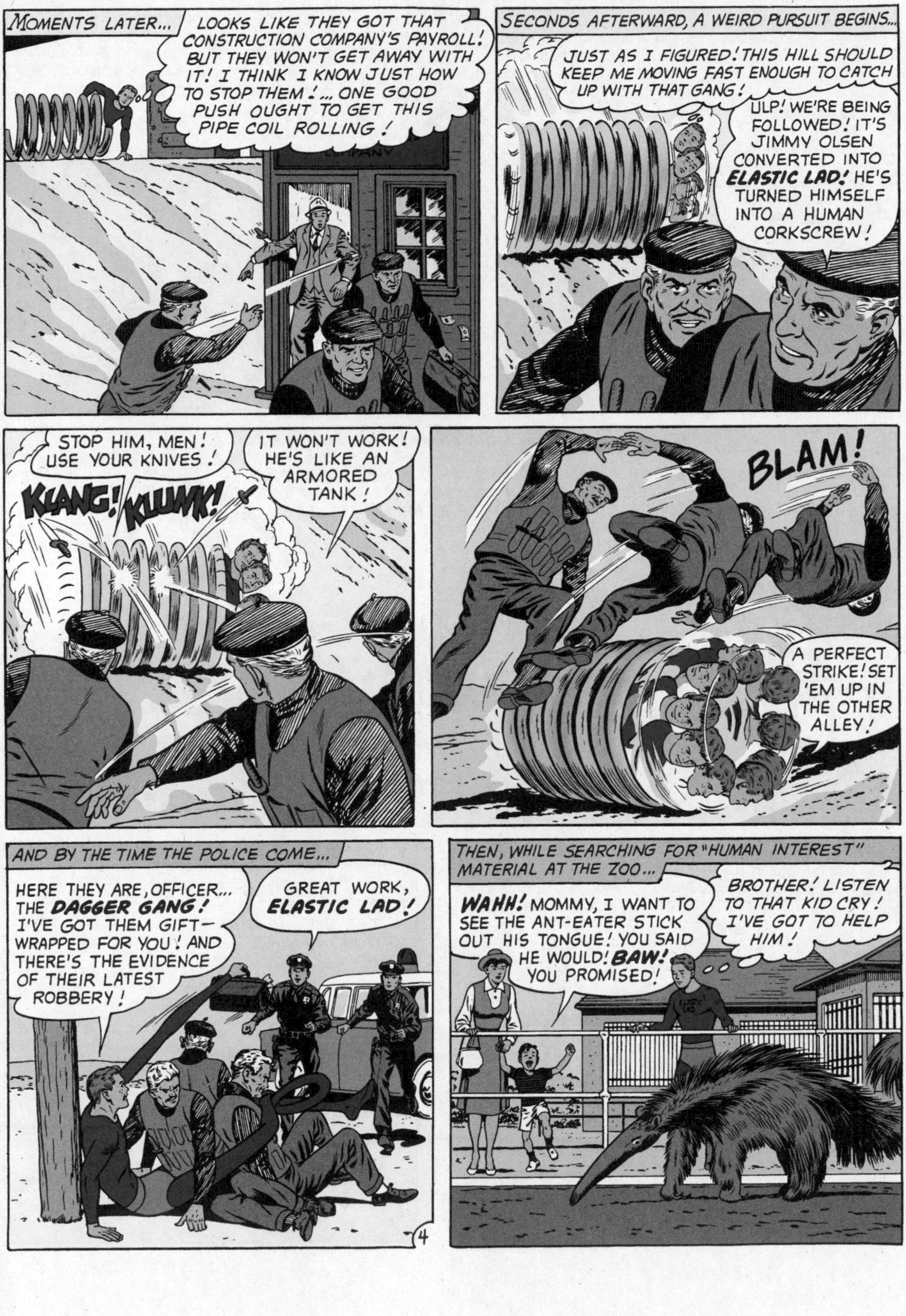
MOMENTS LATER...
LOOKS LIKE THEY GOT THAT CONSTRUCTION COMPANY'S PAYROLL! BUT THEY WON'T GET AWAY WITH IT! I THINK I KNOW JUST HOW TO STOP THEM! ... ONE GOOD PUSH OUGHT TO GET THIS PIPE COIL ROLLING!
SECONDS AFTERWARD, A WEIRD PURSUIT BEGINS...
JUST AS I FIGURED! THIS HILL SHOULD KEEP ME MOVING FAST ENOUGH TO CATCH UP WITH THAT GANG!
ULP! WE'RE BEING FOLLOWED! IT'S JIMMY OLSEN CONVERTED INTO ELASTIC LAD! HE'S TURNED HIMSELF INTO A HUMAN CORKSCREW!
STOP HIM, MEN! USE YOUR KNIVES!
IT WON'T WORK! HE'S LIKE AN ARMORED TANK!
KLANG! KLUNK!
BLAM!
A PERFECT STRIKE! SET 'EM UP IN THE OTHER ALLEY!
AND BY THE TIME THE POLICE COME...
HERE THEY ARE, OFFICER... THE DAGGER GANG! I'VE GOT THEM GIFT-WRAPPED FOR YOU! AND THERE'S THE EVIDENCE OF THEIR LATEST ROBBERY!
GREAT WORK, ELASTIC LAD!
4
THEN, WHILE SEARCHING FOR "HUMAN INTEREST" MATERIAL AT THE ZOO...
WAHH! MOMMY, I WANT TO SEE THE ANT-EATER STICK OUT HIS TONGUE! YOU SAID HE WOULD! BAW! YOU PROMISED!
BROTHER! LISTEN TO THAT KID CRY! I'VE GOT TO HELP HIM!

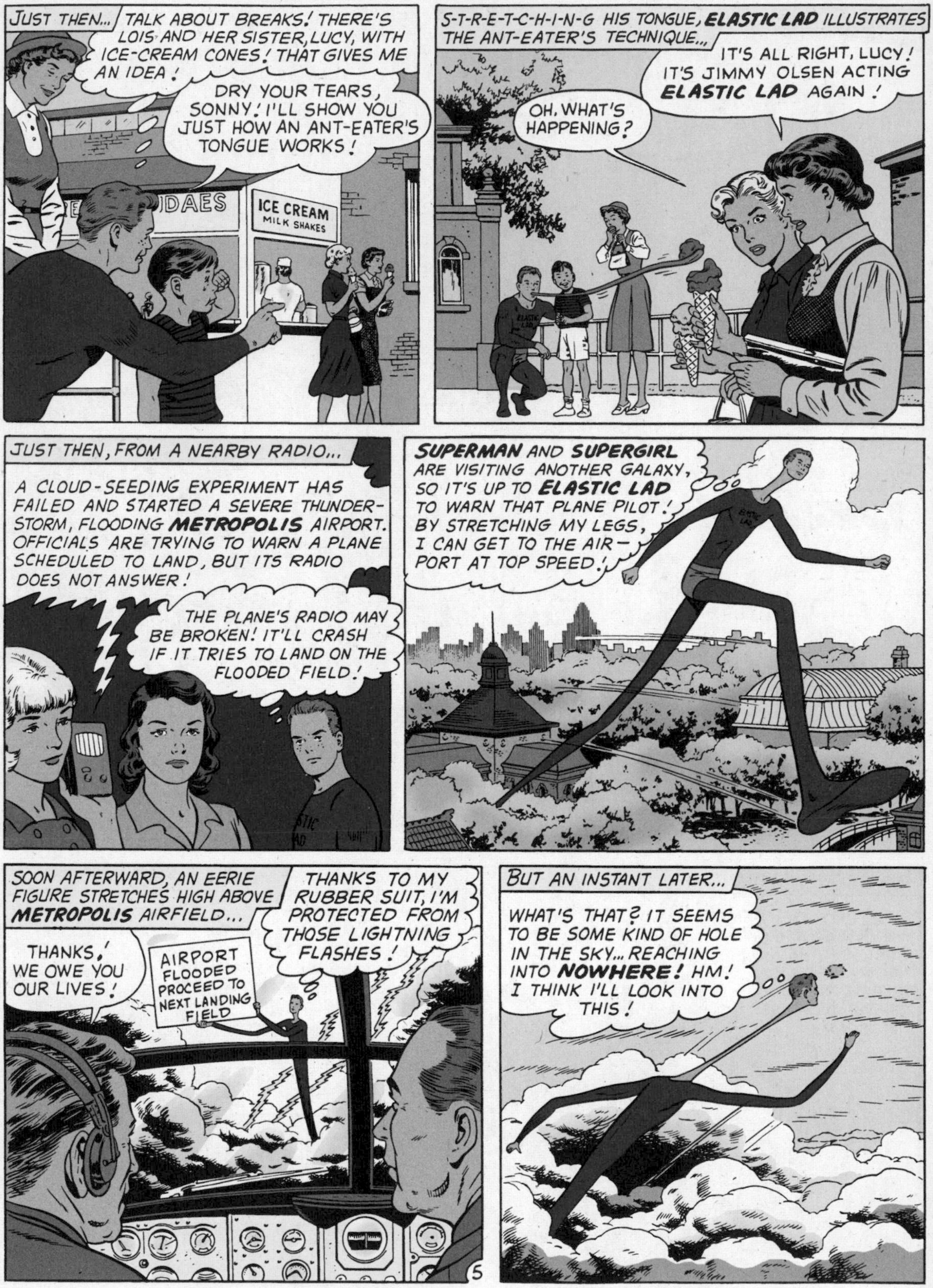
JUST THEN...
TALK ABOUT BREAKS! THERE'S LOIS AND HER SISTER, LUCY, WITH ICE-CREAM CONES! THAT GIVES ME AN IDEA!
DRY YOUR TEARS, SONNY! I'LL SHOW YOU JUST HOW AN ANT-EATER'S TONGUE WORKS!
DAES
ICE CREAM
MILK SHAKES
S-T-R-E-T-C-H-I-N-G HIS TONGUE, ELASTIC LAD ILLUSTRATES THE ANT-EATER'S TECHNIQUE...
IT'S ALL RIGHT, LUCY! IT'S JIMMY OLSEN ACTING ELASTIC LAD AGAIN!
OH, WHAT'S HAPPENING?
JUST THEN, FROM A NEARBY RADIO...
A CLOUD-SEEDING EXPERIMENT HAS FAILED AND STARTED A SEVERE THUNDER-STORM, FLOODING METROPOLIS AIRPORT. OFFICIALS ARE TRYING TO WARN A PLANE SCHEDULED TO LAND, BUT ITS RADIO DOES NOT ANSWER!
THE PLANE'S RADIO MAY BE BROKEN! IT'LL CRASH IF IT TRIES TO LAND ON THE FLOODED FIELD!
SUPERMAN AND SUPERGIRL ARE VISITING ANOTHER GALAXY, SO IT'S UP TO ELASTIC LAD TO WARN THAT PLANE PILOT! BY STRETCHING MY LEGS, I CAN GET TO THE AIR-PORT AT TOP SPEED!
SOON AFTERWARD, AN EERIE FIGURE STRETCHES HIGH ABOVE METROPOLIS AIRFIELD...
THANKS TO MY RUBBER SUIT, I'M PROTECTED FROM THOSE LIGHTNING FLASHES!
THANKS! WE OWE YOU OUR LIVES!
AIRPORT FLOODED PROCEED TO NEXT LANDING FIELD
5
BUT AN INSTANT LATER...
WHAT'S THAT? IT SEEMS TO BE SOME KIND OF HOLE IN THE SKY... REACHING INTO NOWHERE! HM! I THINK I'LL LOOK INTO THIS!

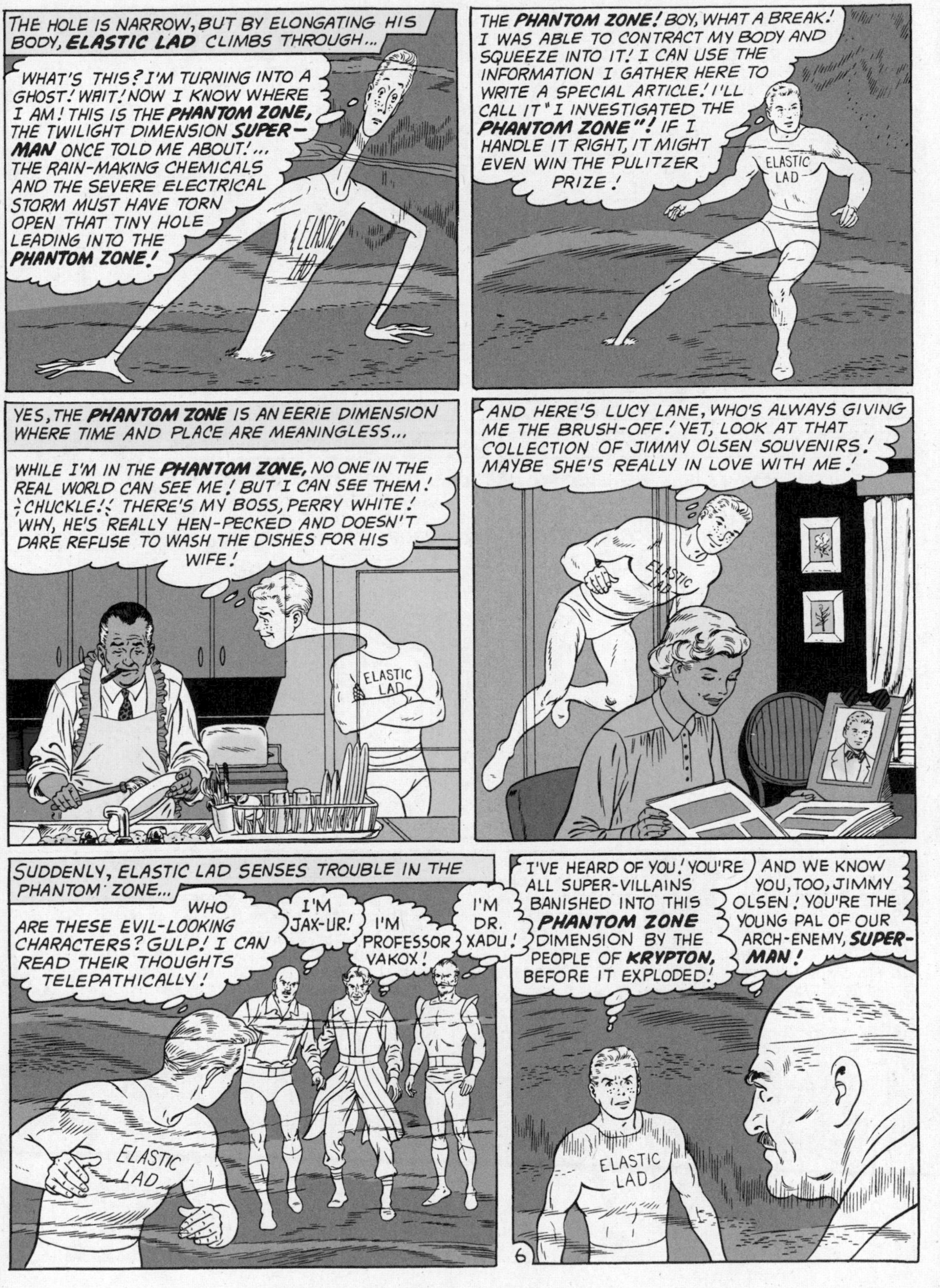
THE HOLE IS NARROW, BUT BY ELONGATING HIS BODY, ELASTIC LAD CLIMBS THROUGH...
WHAT'S THIS? I'M TURNING INTO A GHOST! WAIT! NOW I KNOW WHERE I AM! THIS IS THE PHANTOM ZONE, THE TWILIGHT DIMENSION SUPERMAN ONCE TOLD ME ABOUT!... THE RAIN-MAKING CHEMICALS AND THE SEVERE ELECTRICAL STORM MUST HAVE TORN OPEN THAT TINY HOLE LEADING INTO THE PHANTOM ZONE!
ELASTIC LAD
THE PHANTOM ZONE! BOY, WHAT A BREAK! I WAS ABLE TO CONTRACT MY BODY AND SQUEEZE INTO IT! I CAN USE THE INFORMATION I GATHER HERE TO WRITE A SPECIAL ARTICLE! I'LL CALL IT "I INVESTIGATED THE PHANTOM ZONE"! IF I HANDLE IT RIGHT, IT MIGHT EVEN WIN THE PULITZER PRIZE!
ELASTIC LAD
YES, THE PHANTOM ZONE IS AN EERIE DIMENSION WHERE TIME AND PLACE ARE MEANINGLESS...
WHILE I'M IN THE PHANTOM ZONE, NO ONE IN THE REAL WORLD CAN SEE ME! BUT I CAN SEE THEM! CHUCKLE! THERE'S MY BOSS, PERRY WHITE! WHY, HE'S REALLY HEN-PECKED AND DOESN'T DARE REFUSE TO WASH THE DISHES FOR HIS WIFE!
ELASTIC LAD
AND HERE'S LUCY LANE, WHO'S ALWAYS GIVING ME THE BRUSH-OFF! YET, LOOK AT THAT COLLECTION OF JIMMY OLSEN SOUVENIRS! MAYBE SHE'S REALLY IN LOVE WITH ME!
ELASTIC LAD
SUDDENLY, ELASTIC LAD SENSES TROUBLE IN THE PHANTOM ZONE...
WHO ARE THESE EVIL-LOOKING CHARACTERS? GULP! I CAN READ THEIR THOUGHTS TELEPATHICALLY!
I'M JAX-UR!
I'M PROFESSOR VAKOX!
I'M DR. XADU!
ELASTIC LAD
I'VE HEARD OF YOU! YOU'RE ALL SUPER-VILLAINS BANISHED INTO THIS PHANTOM ZONE DIMENSION BY THE PEOPLE OF KRYPTON, BEFORE IT EXPLODED!
AND WE KNOW YOU, TOO, JIMMY OLSEN! YOU'RE THE YOUNG PAL OF OUR ARCH-ENEMY, SUPERMAN!
ELASTIC LAD
6

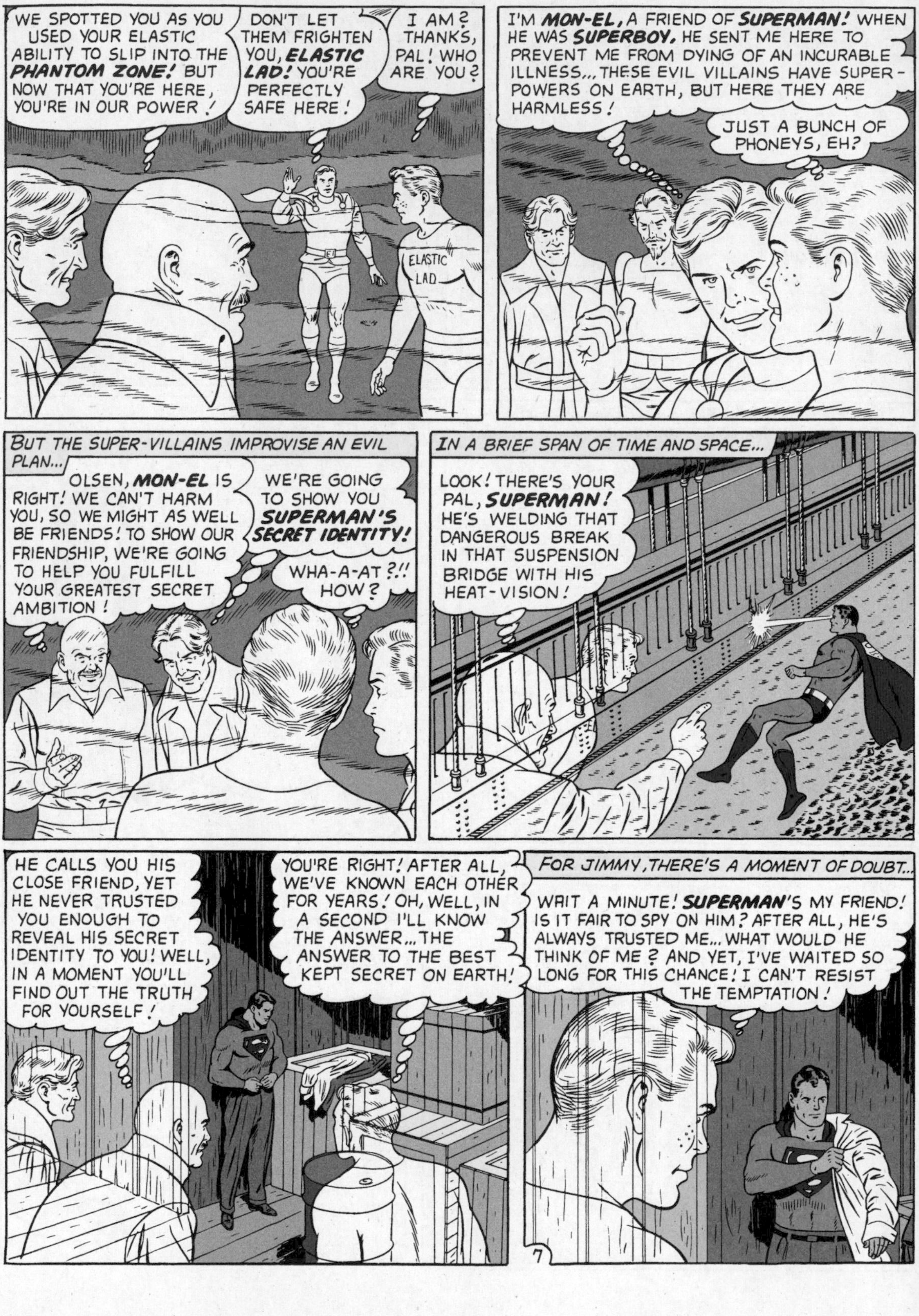
WE SPOTTED YOU AS YOU USED YOUR ELASTIC ABILITY TO SLIP INTO THE PHANTOM ZONE! BUT NOW THAT YOU'RE HERE, YOU'RE IN OUR POWER!
DON'T LET THEM FRIGHTEN YOU, ELASTIC LAD! YOU'RE PERFECTLY SAFE HERE!
I AM? THANKS, PAL! WHO ARE YOU?
ELASTIC LAD
I'M MON-EL, A FRIEND OF SUPERMAN! WHEN HE WAS SUPERBOY, HE SENT ME HERE TO PREVENT ME FROM DYING OF AN INCURABLE ILLNESS... THESE EVIL VILLAINS HAVE SUPER-POWERS ON EARTH, BUT HERE THEY ARE HARMLESS!
JUST A BUNCH OF PHONEYS, EH?
BUT THE SUPER-VILLAINS IMPROVISE AN EVIL PLAN...
OLSEN, MON-EL IS RIGHT! WE CAN'T HARM YOU, SO WE MIGHT AS WELL BE FRIENDS! TO SHOW OUR FRIENDSHIP, WE'RE GOING TO HELP YOU FULFILL YOUR GREATEST SECRET AMBITION!
WE'RE GOING TO SHOW YOU SUPERMAN'S SECRET IDENTITY!
WHA-A-AT?!! HOW?
IN A BRIEF SPAN OF TIME AND SPACE...
LOOK! THERE'S YOUR PAL, SUPERMAN! HE'S WELDING THAT DANGEROUS BREAK IN THAT SUSPENSION BRIDGE WITH HIS HEAT-VISION!
HE CALLS YOU HIS CLOSE FRIEND, YET HE NEVER TRUSTED YOU ENOUGH TO REVEAL HIS SECRET IDENTITY TO YOU! WELL, IN A MOMENT YOU'LL FIND OUT THE TRUTH FOR YOURSELF!
YOU'RE RIGHT! AFTER ALL, WE'VE KNOWN EACH OTHER FOR YEARS! OH, WELL, IN A SECOND I'LL KNOW THE ANSWER... THE ANSWER TO THE BEST KEPT SECRET ON EARTH!
FOR JIMMY, THERE'S A MOMENT OF DOUBT...
WAIT A MINUTE! SUPERMAN'S MY FRIEND! IS IT FAIR TO SPY ON HIM? AFTER ALL, HE'S ALWAYS TRUSTED ME... WHAT WOULD HE THINK OF ME? AND YET, I'VE WAITED SO LONG FOR THIS CHANCE! I CAN'T RESIST THE TEMPTATION!
7

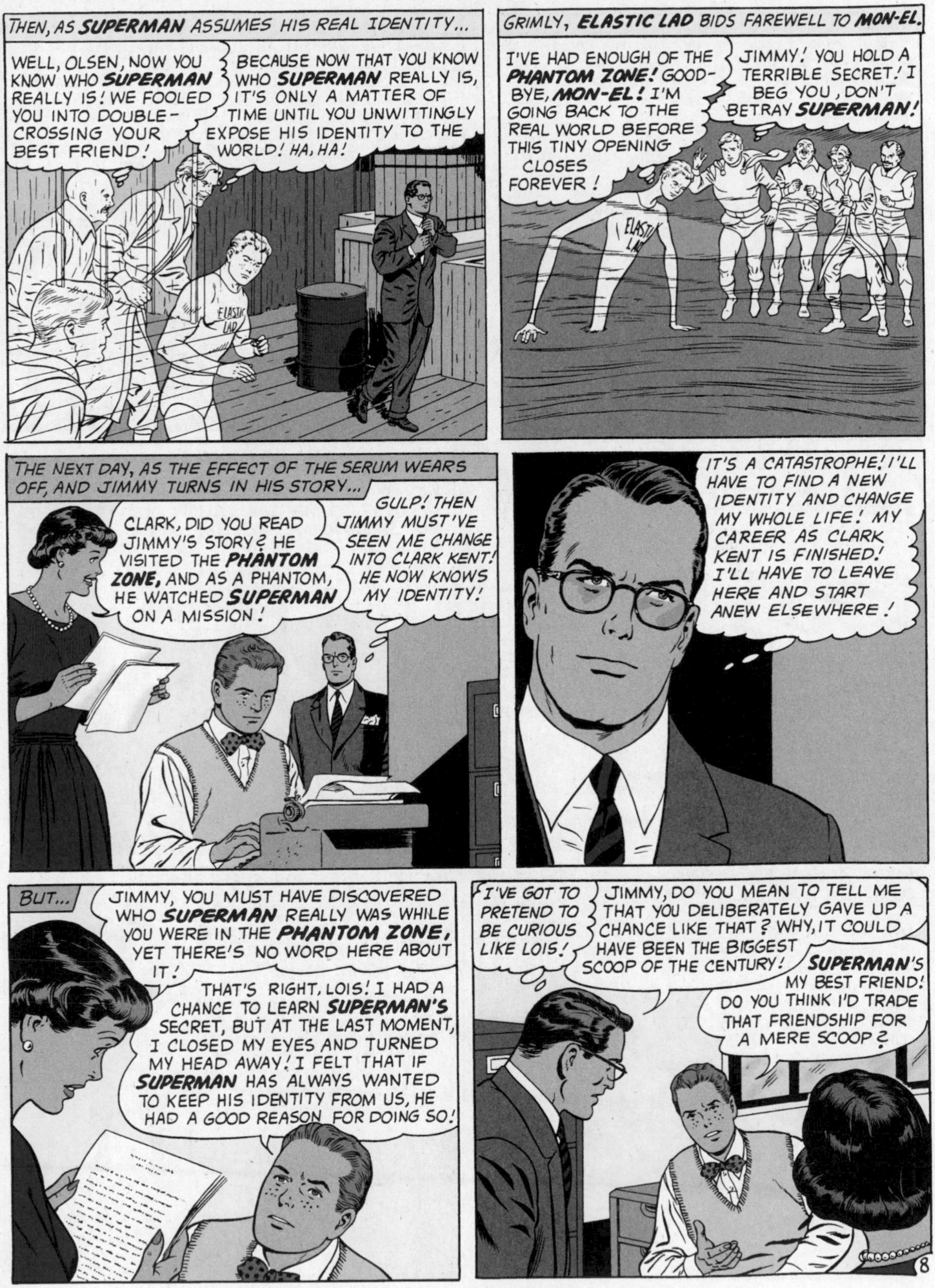
THEN, AS SUPERMAN ASSUMES HIS REAL IDENTITY...
WELL, OLSEN, NOW YOU KNOW WHO SUPERMAN REALLY IS! WE FOOLED YOU INTO DOUBLE-CROSSING YOUR BEST FRIEND!
BECAUSE NOW THAT YOU KNOW WHO SUPERMAN REALLY IS, IT'S ONLY A MATTER OF TIME UNTIL YOU UNWITTINGLY EXPOSE HIS IDENTITY TO THE WORLD! HA, HA!
GRIMLY, ELASTIC LAD BIDS FAREWELL TO MON-EL.
I'VE HAD ENOUGH OF THE PHANTOM ZONE! GOOD-BYE, MON-EL! I'M GOING BACK TO THE REAL WORLD BEFORE THIS TINY OPENING CLOSES FOREVER!
JIMMY! YOU HOLD A TERRIBLE SECRET! I BEG YOU, DON'T BETRAY SUPERMAN!
THE NEXT DAY, AS THE EFFECT OF THE SERUM WEARS OFF, AND JIMMY TURNS IN HIS STORY...
CLARK, DID YOU READ JIMMY'S STORY? HE VISITED THE PHANTOM ZONE, AND AS A PHANTOM, HE WATCHED SUPERMAN ON A MISSION!
GULP! THEN JIMMY MUST'VE SEEN ME CHANGE INTO CLARK KENT! HE NOW KNOWS MY IDENTITY!
IT'S A CATASTROPHE! I'LL HAVE TO FIND A NEW IDENTITY AND CHANGE MY WHOLE LIFE! MY CAREER AS CLARK KENT IS FINISHED! I'LL HAVE TO LEAVE HERE AND START ANEW ELSEWHERE!
BUT...
JIMMY, YOU MUST HAVE DISCOVERED WHO SUPERMAN REALLY WAS WHILE YOU WERE IN THE PHANTOM ZONE, YET THERE'S NO WORD HERE ABOUT IT!
THAT'S RIGHT, LOIS! I HAD A CHANCE TO LEARN SUPERMAN'S SECRET, BUT AT THE LAST MOMENT, I CLOSED MY EYES AND TURNED MY HEAD AWAY! I FELT THAT IF SUPERMAN HAS ALWAYS WANTED TO KEEP HIS IDENTITY FROM US, HE HAD A GOOD REASON FOR DOING SO!
I'VE GOT TO PRETEND TO BE CURIOUS LIKE LOIS!
JIMMY, DO YOU MEAN TO TELL ME THAT YOU DELIBERATELY GAVE UP A CHANCE LIKE THAT? WHY, IT COULD HAVE BEEN THE BIGGEST SCOOP OF THE CENTURY!
SUPERMAN'S MY BEST FRIEND! DO YOU THINK I'D TRADE THAT FRIENDSHIP FOR A MERE SCOOP?
8

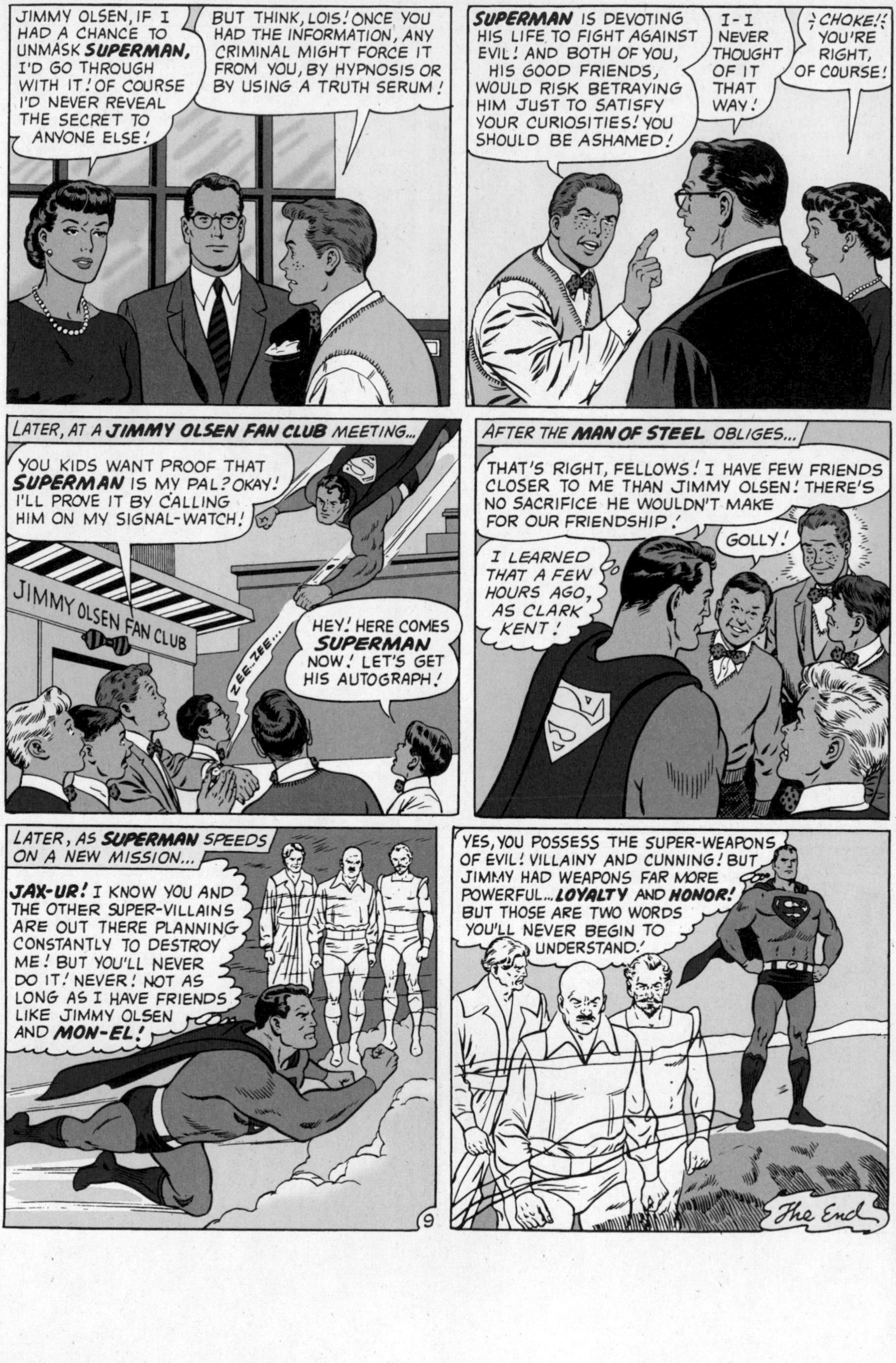
JIMMY OLSEN, IF I HAD A CHANCE TO UNMASK SUPERMAN, I'D GO THROUGH WITH IT! OF COURSE I'D NEVER REVEAL THE SECRET TO ANYONE ELSE!
BUT THINK, LOIS! ONCE YOU HAD THE INFORMATION, ANY CRIMINAL MIGHT FORCE IT FROM YOU, BY HYPNOSIS OR BY USING A TRUTH SERUM!
SUPERMAN IS DEVOTING HIS LIFE TO FIGHT AGAINST EVIL! AND BOTH OF YOU, HIS GOOD FRIENDS, WOULD RISK BETRAYING HIM JUST TO SATISFY YOUR CURIOSITIES! YOU SHOULD BE ASHAMED!
I-I NEVER THOUGHT OF IT THAT WAY!
CHOKE! YOU'RE RIGHT, OF COURSE!
LATER, AT A JIMMY OLSEN FAN CLUB MEETING...
YOU KIDS WANT PROOF THAT SUPERMAN IS MY PAL? OKAY! I'LL PROVE IT BY CALLING HIM ON MY SIGNAL-WATCH!
JIMMY OLSEN FAN CLUB
ZEE...ZEE...
HEY! HERE COMES SUPERMAN NOW! LET'S GET HIS AUTOGRAPH!
AFTER THE MAN OF STEEL OBLIGES...
THAT'S RIGHT, FELLOWS! I HAVE FEW FRIENDS CLOSER TO ME THAN JIMMY OLSEN! THERE'S NO SACRIFICE HE WOULDN'T MAKE FOR OUR FRIENDSHIP!
I LEARNED THAT A FEW HOURS AGO, AS CLARK KENT!
GOLLY!
LATER, AS SUPERMAN SPEEDS ON A NEW MISSION...
JAX-UR! I KNOW YOU AND THE OTHER SUPER-VILLAINS ARE OUT THERE PLANNING CONSTANTLY TO DESTROY ME! BUT YOU'LL NEVER DO IT! NEVER! NOT AS LONG AS I HAVE FRIENDS LIKE JIMMY OLSEN AND MON-EL!
9
YES, YOU POSSESS THE SUPER-WEAPONS OF EVIL! VILLAINY AND CUNNING! BUT JIMMY HAD WEAPONS FAR MORE POWERFUL... LOYALTY AND HONOR! BUT THOSE ARE TWO WORDS YOU'LL NEVER BEGIN TO UNDERSTAND!
The End

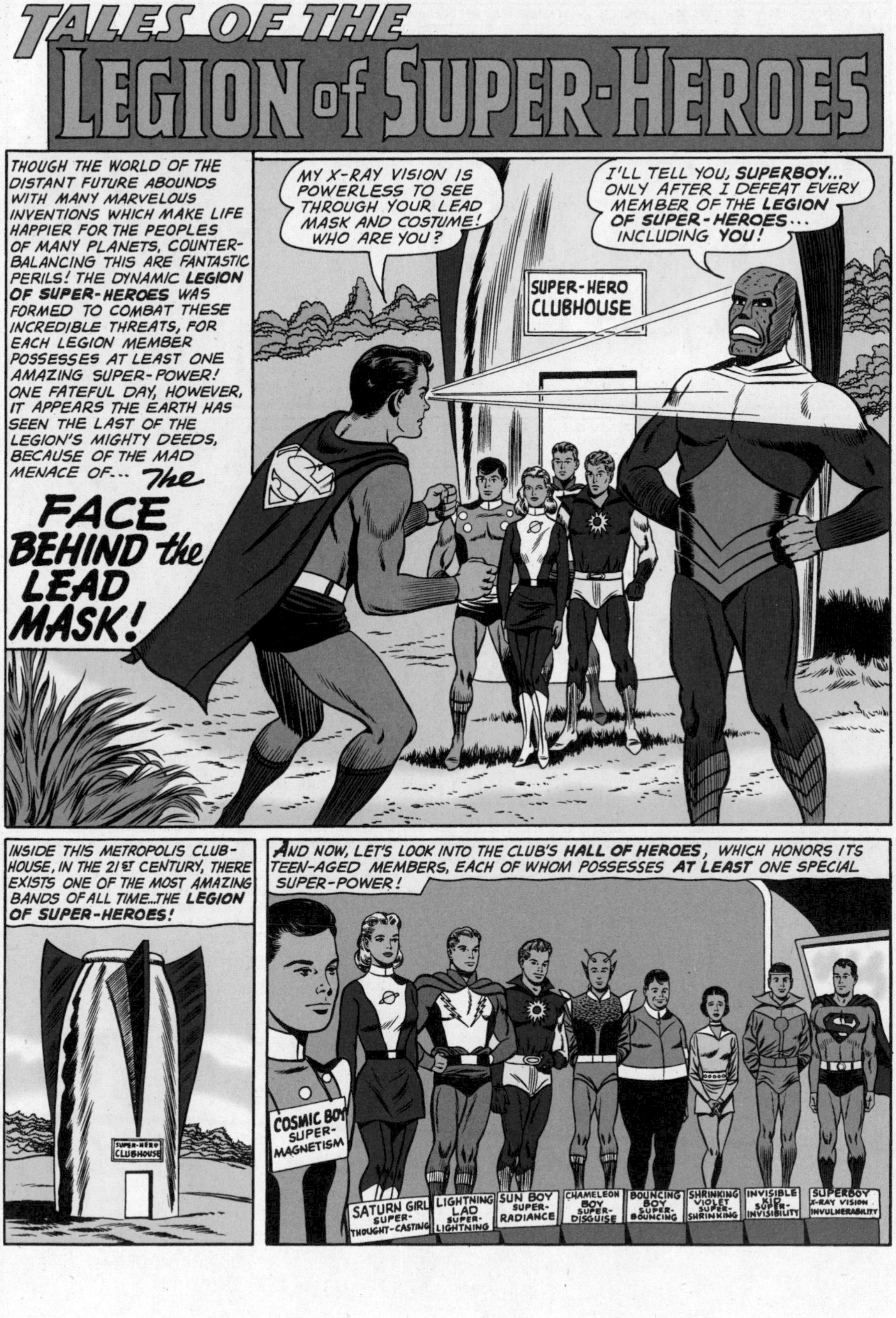
TALES OF THE
LEGION of SUPER-HEROES
THOUGH THE WORLD OF THE DISTANT FUTURE ABOUNDS WITH MANY MARVELOUS INVENTIONS WHICH MAKE LIFE HAPPIER FOR THE PEOPLES OF MANY PLANETS, COUNTER-BALANCING THIS ARE FANTASTIC PERILS! THE DYNAMIC LEGION OF SUPER-HEROES WAS FORMED TO COMBAT THESE INCREDIBLE THREATS, FOR EACH LEGION MEMBER POSSESSES AT LEAST ONE AMAZING SUPER-POWER! ONE FATEFUL DAY, HOWEVER, IT APPEARS THE EARTH HAS SEEN THE LAST OF THE LEGION'S MIGHTY DEEDS, BECAUSE OF THE MAD MENACE OF... The
FACE BEHIND the LEAD MASK!
MY X-RAY VISION IS POWERLESS TO SEE THROUGH YOUR LEAD MASK AND COSTUME! WHO ARE YOU?
I'LL TELL YOU, SUPERBOY... ONLY AFTER I DEFEAT EVERY MEMBER OF THE LEGION OF SUPER-HEROES... INCLUDING YOU!
SUPER-HERO CLUBHOUSE
INSIDE THIS METROPOLIS CLUB-HOUSE, IN THE 21ST CENTURY, THERE EXISTS ONE OF THE MOST AMAZING BANDS OF ALL TIME...THE LEGION OF SUPER-HEROES!
SUPER-HERO CLUBHOUSE
AND NOW, LET'S LOOK INTO THE CLUB'S HALL OF HEROES, WHICH HONORS ITS TEEN-AGED MEMBERS, EACH OF WHOM POSSESSES AT LEAST ONE SPECIAL SUPER-POWER!
COSMIC BOY SUPER-MAGNETISM
SATURN GIRL SUPER-THOUGHT-CASTING
LIGHTNING LAD SUPER-LIGHTNING
SUN BOY SUPER-RADIANCE
CHAMELEON BOY SUPER-DISGUISE
BOUNCING BOY SUPER-BOUNCING
SHRINKING VIOLET SUPER-SHRINKING
INVISIBLE KID SUPER-INVISIBILITY
SUPERBOY X-RAY VISION INVULNERABILITY

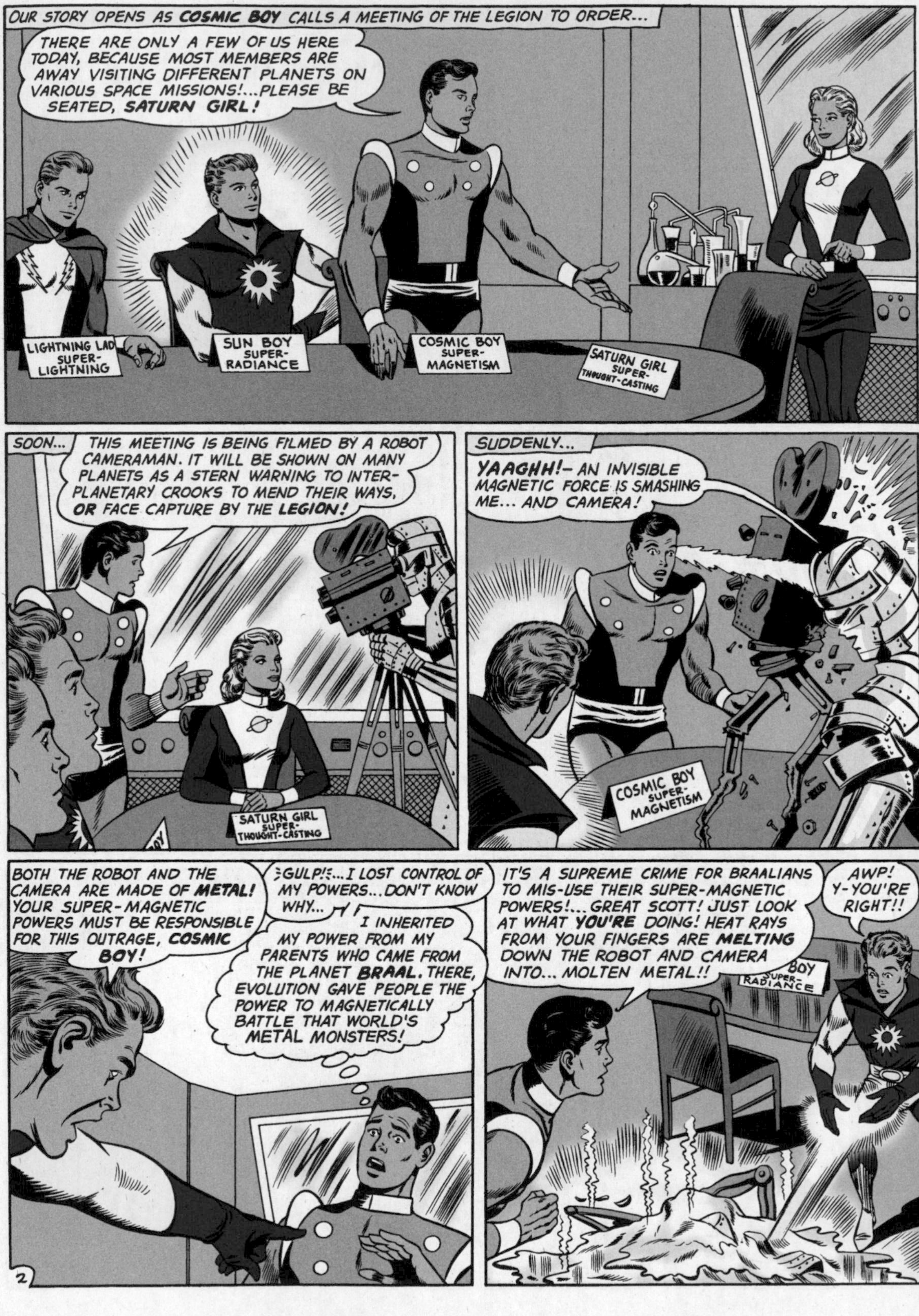
OUR STORY OPENS AS COSMIC BOY CALLS A MEETING OF THE LEGION TO ORDER...
THERE ARE ONLY A FEW OF US HERE TODAY, BECAUSE MOST MEMBERS ARE AWAY VISITING DIFFERENT PLANETS ON VARIOUS SPACE MISSIONS!...PLEASE BE SEATED, SATURN GIRL!
LIGHTNING LAD SUPER-LIGHTNING
SUN BOY SUPER-RADIANCE
COSMIC BOY SUPER-MAGNETISM
SATURN GIRL SUPER-THOUGHT-CASTING
SOON...
THIS MEETING IS BEING FILMED BY A ROBOT CAMERAMAN. IT WILL BE SHOWN ON MANY PLANETS AS A STERN WARNING TO INTER-PLANETARY CROOKS TO MEND THEIR WAYS, OR FACE CAPTURE BY THE LEGION!
SATURN GIRL SUPER-THOUGHT-CASTING
SUDDENLY...
YAAGHH!-- AN INVISIBLE MAGNETIC FORCE IS SMASHING ME... AND CAMERA!
COSMIC BOY SUPER-MAGNETISM
BOTH THE ROBOT AND THE CAMERA ARE MADE OF METAL! YOUR SUPER-MAGNETIC POWERS MUST BE RESPONSIBLE FOR THIS OUTRAGE, COSMIC BOY!
GULP!...I LOST CONTROL OF MY POWERS...DON'T KNOW WHY...
I INHERITED MY POWER FROM MY PARENTS WHO CAME FROM THE PLANET BRAAL. THERE, EVOLUTION GAVE PEOPLE THE POWER TO MAGNETICALLY BATTLE THAT WORLD'S METAL MONSTERS!
IT'S A SUPREME CRIME FOR BRAALIANS TO MIS-USE THEIR SUPER-MAGNETIC POWERS!... GREAT SCOTT! JUST LOOK AT WHAT YOU'RE DOING! HEAT RAYS FROM YOUR FINGERS ARE MELTING DOWN THE ROBOT AND CAMERA INTO... MOLTEN METAL!!
AWP! Y-YOU'RE RIGHT!!
2

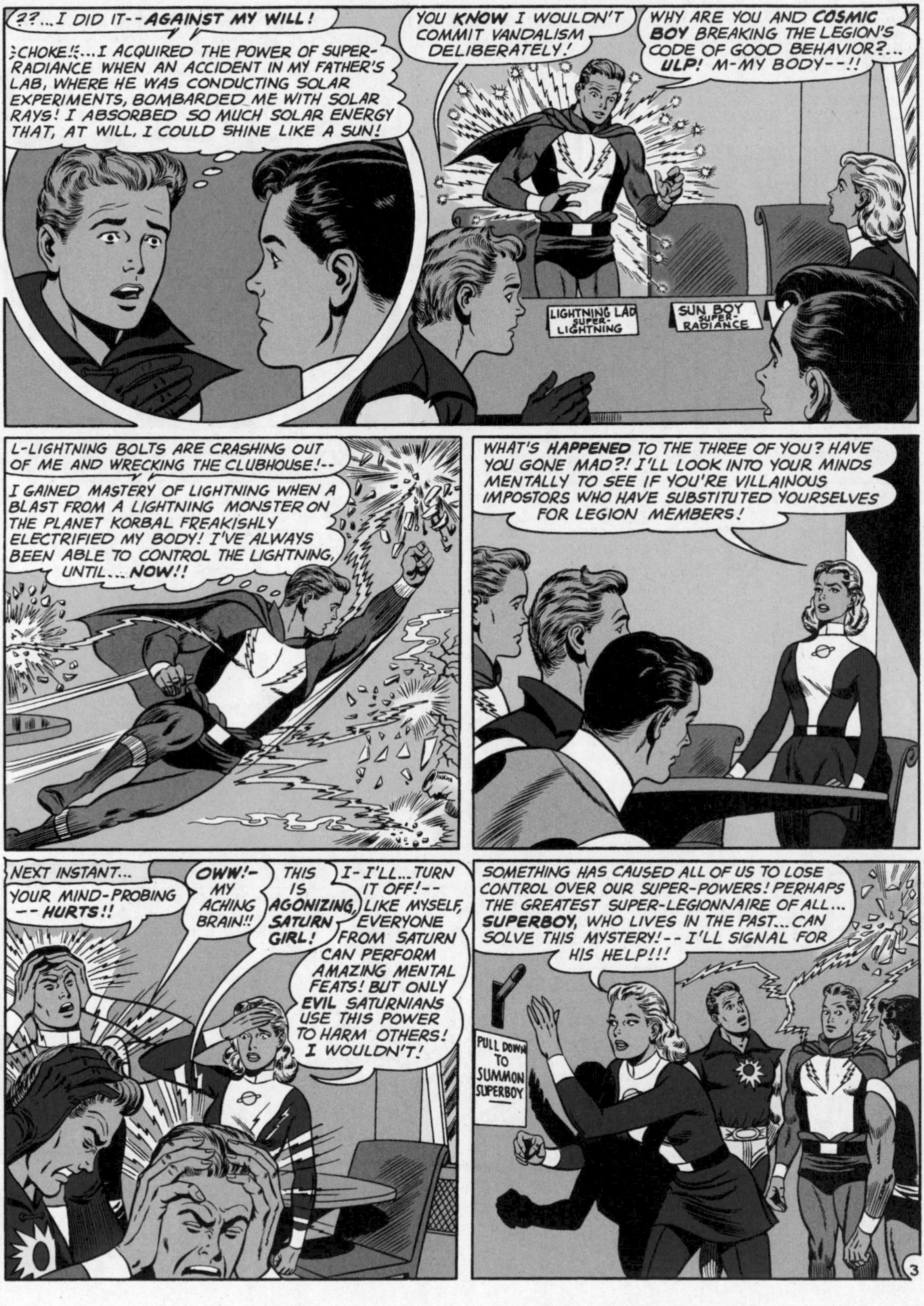
??... I DID IT-- AGAINST MY WILL!
CHOKE!... I ACQUIRED THE POWER OF SUPER-RADIANCE WHEN AN ACCIDENT IN MY FATHER'S LAB, WHERE HE WAS CONDUCTING SOLAR EXPERIMENTS, BOMBARDED ME WITH SOLAR RAYS! I ABSORBED SO MUCH SOLAR ENERGY THAT, AT WILL, I COULD SHINE LIKE A SUN!
YOU KNOW I WOULDN'T COMMIT VANDALISM DELIBERATELY!
WHY ARE YOU AND COSMIC BOY BREAKING THE LEGION'S CODE OF GOOD BEHAVIOR?... ULP! M-MY BODY--!!
LIGHTNING LAD SUPER-LIGHTNING
SUN BOY SUPER-RADIANCE
L-LIGHTNING BOLTS ARE CRASHING OUT OF ME AND WRECKING THE CLUBHOUSE!--
I GAINED MASTERY OF LIGHTNING WHEN A BLAST FROM A LIGHTNING MONSTER ON THE PLANET KORBAL FREAKISHLY ELECTRIFIED MY BODY! I'VE ALWAYS BEEN ABLE TO CONTROL THE LIGHTNING, UNTIL... NOW!!
WHAT'S HAPPENED TO THE THREE OF YOU? HAVE YOU GONE MAD?! I'LL LOOK INTO YOUR MINDS MENTALLY TO SEE IF YOU'RE VILLAINOUS IMPOSTORS WHO HAVE SUBSTITUTED YOURSELVES FOR LEGION MEMBERS!
NEXT INSTANT...
YOUR MIND-PROBING -- HURTS!!
OWW!- MY ACHING BRAIN!!
THIS IS AGONIZING, SATURN GIRL!
I- I'LL... TURN IT OFF!-- LIKE MYSELF, EVERYONE FROM SATURN CAN PERFORM AMAZING MENTAL FEATS! BUT ONLY EVIL SATURNIANS USE THIS POWER TO HARM OTHERS! I WOULDN'T!
SOMETHING HAS CAUSED ALL OF US TO LOSE CONTROL OVER OUR SUPER-POWERS! PERHAPS THE GREATEST SUPER-LEGIONNAIRE OF ALL... SUPERBOY, WHO LIVES IN THE PAST... CAN SOLVE THIS MYSTERY!-- I'LL SIGNAL FOR HIS HELP!!!
PULL DOWN TO SUMMON SUPERBOY
3

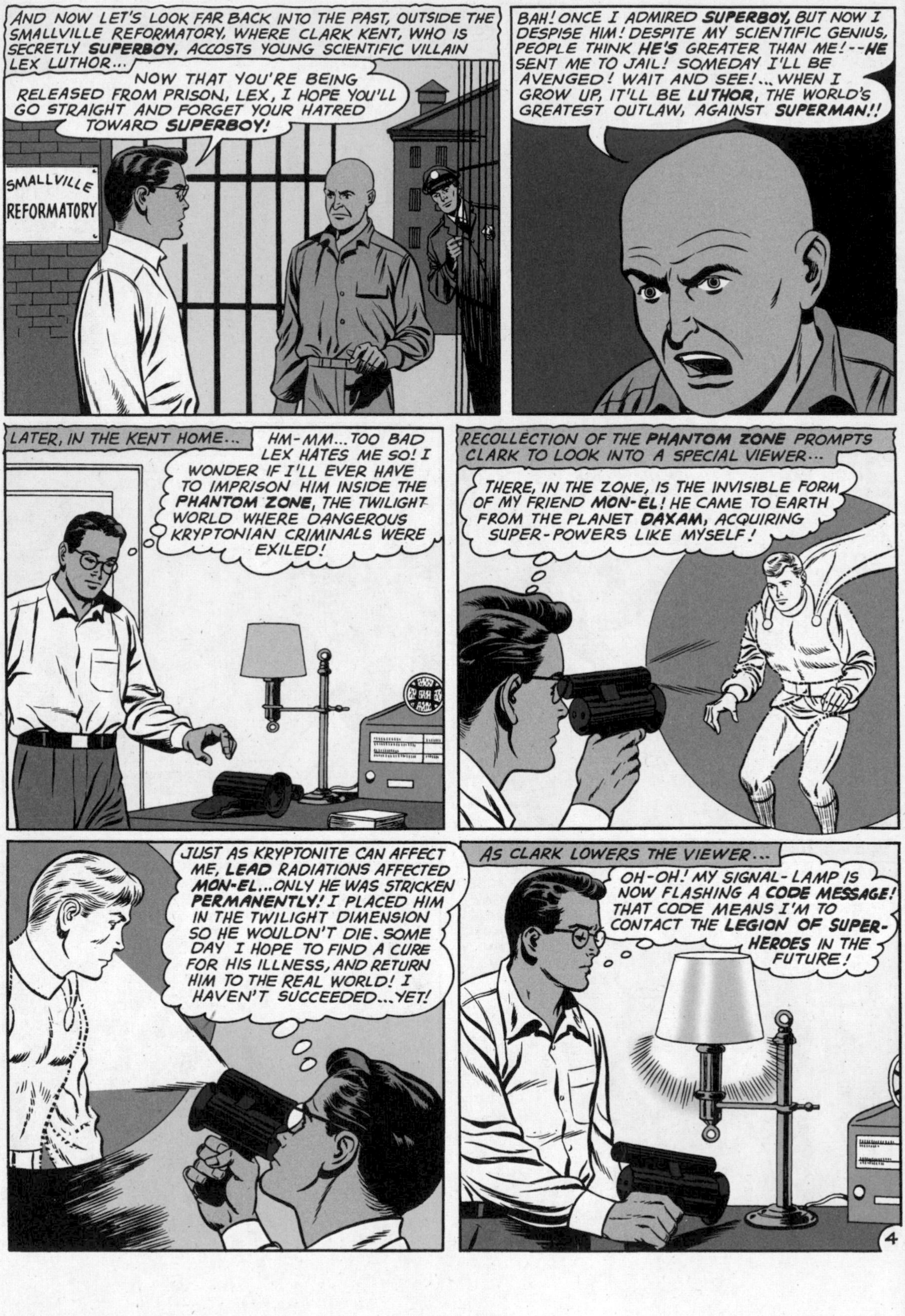
AND NOW LET'S LOOK FAR BACK INTO THE PAST, OUTSIDE THE SMALLVILLE REFORMATORY, WHERE CLARK KENT, WHO IS SECRETLY SUPERBOY, ACCOSTS YOUNG SCIENTIFIC VILLAIN LEX LUTHOR...
NOW THAT YOU'RE BEING RELEASED FROM PRISON, LEX, I HOPE YOU'LL GO STRAIGHT AND FORGET YOUR HATRED TOWARD SUPERBOY!
SMALLVILLE REFORMATORY
BAH! ONCE I ADMIRED SUPERBOY, BUT NOW I DESPISE HIM! DESPITE MY SCIENTIFIC GENIUS, PEOPLE THINK HE'S GREATER THAN ME! --HE SENT ME TO JAIL! SOMEDAY I'LL BE AVENGED! WAIT AND SEE!... WHEN I GROW UP, IT'LL BE LUTHOR, THE WORLD'S GREATEST OUTLAW, AGAINST SUPERMAN!!
LATER, IN THE KENT HOME...
HM-MM... TOO BAD LEX HATES ME SO! I WONDER IF I'LL EVER HAVE TO IMPRISON HIM INSIDE THE PHANTOM ZONE, THE TWILIGHT WORLD WHERE DANGEROUS KRYPTONIAN CRIMINALS WERE EXILED!
RECOLLECTION OF THE PHANTOM ZONE PROMPTS CLARK TO LOOK INTO A SPECIAL VIEWER...
THERE, IN THE ZONE, IS THE INVISIBLE FORM OF MY FRIEND MON-EL! HE CAME TO EARTH FROM THE PLANET DAXAM, ACQUIRING SUPER-POWERS LIKE MYSELF!
JUST AS KRYPTONITE CAN AFFECT ME, LEAD RADIATIONS AFFECTED MON-EL... ONLY HE WAS STRICKEN PERMANENTLY! I PLACED HIM IN THE TWILIGHT DIMENSION SO HE WOULDN'T DIE. SOME DAY I HOPE TO FIND A CURE FOR HIS ILLNESS, AND RETURN HIM TO THE REAL WORLD! I HAVEN'T SUCCEEDED... YET!
AS CLARK LOWERS THE VIEWER...
OH-OH! MY SIGNAL-LAMP IS NOW FLASHING A CODE MESSAGE! THAT CODE MEANS I'M TO CONTACT THE LEGION OF SUPER-HEROES IN THE FUTURE!
4

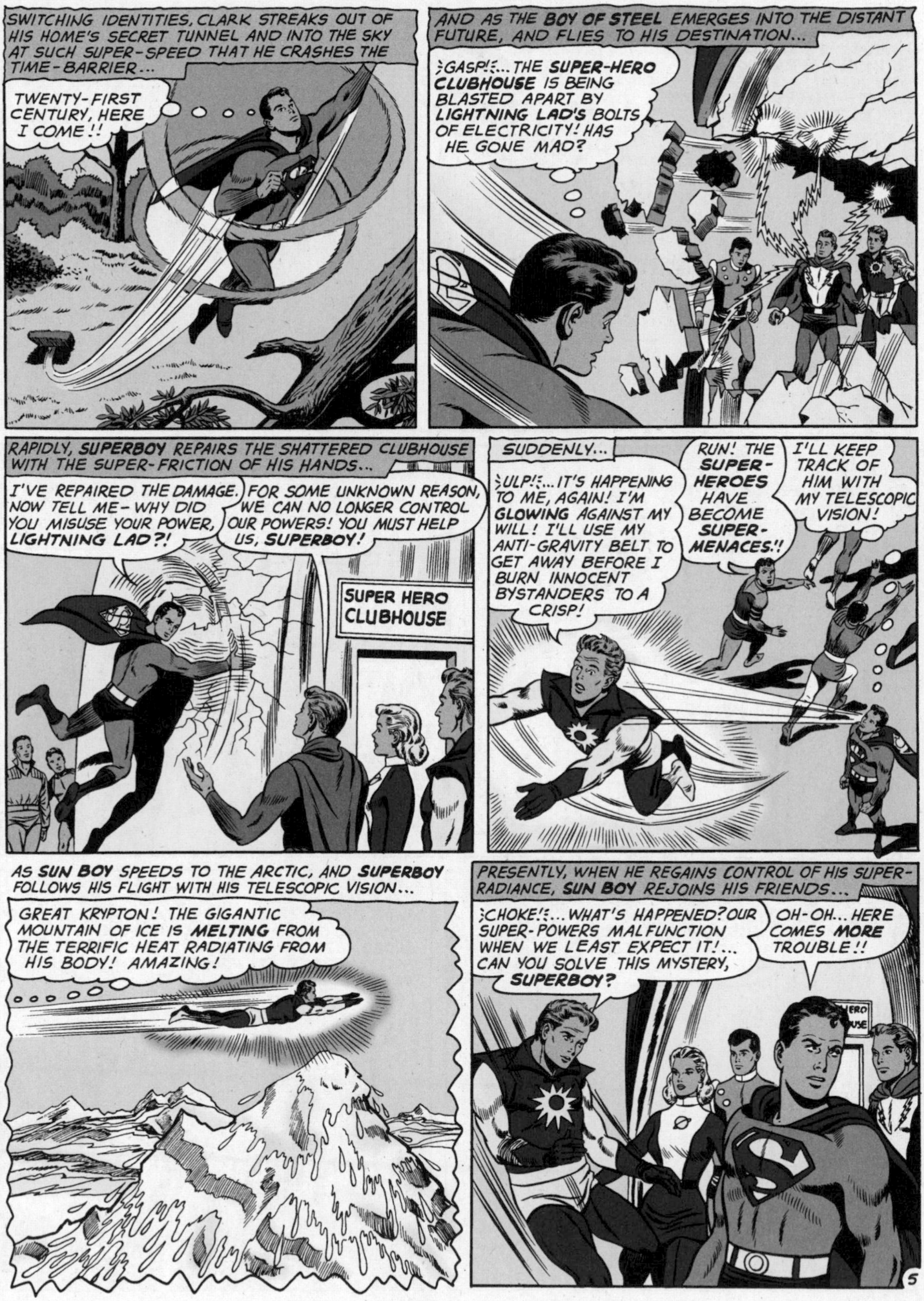

SWITCHING IDENTITIES, CLARK STREAKS OUT OF HIS HOME'S SECRET TUNNEL AND INTO THE SKY AT SUCH SUPER-SPEED THAT HE CRASHES THE TIME-BARRIER...
TWENTY-FIRST CENTURY, HERE I COME!!
AND AS THE BOY OF STEEL EMERGES INTO THE DISTANT FUTURE, AND FLIES TO HIS DESTINATION...
GASP!... THE SUPER-HERO CLUBHOUSE IS BEING BLASTED APART BY LIGHTNING LAD'S BOLTS OF ELECTRICITY! HAS HE GONE MAD?
RAPIDLY, SUPERBOY REPAIRS THE SHATTERED CLUBHOUSE WITH THE SUPER-FRICTION OF HIS HANDS...
I'VE REPAIRED THE DAMAGE. NOW TELL ME-- WHY DID YOU MISUSE YOUR POWER, LIGHTNING LAD?!
FOR SOME UNKNOWN REASON, WE CAN NO LONGER CONTROL OUR POWERS! YOU MUST HELP US, SUPERBOY!
SUPER HERO CLUBHOUSE
SUDDENLY...
ULP!... IT'S HAPPENING TO ME, AGAIN! I'M GLOWING AGAINST MY WILL! I'LL USE MY ANTI-GRAVITY BELT TO GET AWAY BEFORE I BURN INNOCENT BYSTANDERS TO A CRISP!
RUN! THE SUPER-HEROES HAVE BECOME SUPER-MENACES!!
I'LL KEEP TRACK OF HIM WITH MY TELESCOPIC VISION!
AS SUN BOY SPEEDS TO THE ARCTIC, AND SUPERBOY FOLLOWS HIS FLIGHT WITH HIS TELESCOPIC VISION...
GREAT KRYPTON! THE GIGANTIC MOUNTAIN OF ICE IS MELTING FROM THE TERRIFIC HEAT RADIATING FROM HIS BODY! AMAZING!
PRESENTLY, WHEN HE REGAINS CONTROL OF HIS SUPER-RADIANCE, SUN BOY REJOINS HIS FRIENDS...
CHOKE!... WHAT'S HAPPENED? OUR SUPER-POWERS MALFUNCTION WHEN WE LEAST EXPECT IT!... CAN YOU SOLVE THIS MYSTERY, SUPERBOY?
OH-OH... HERE COMES MORE TROUBLE!!
5

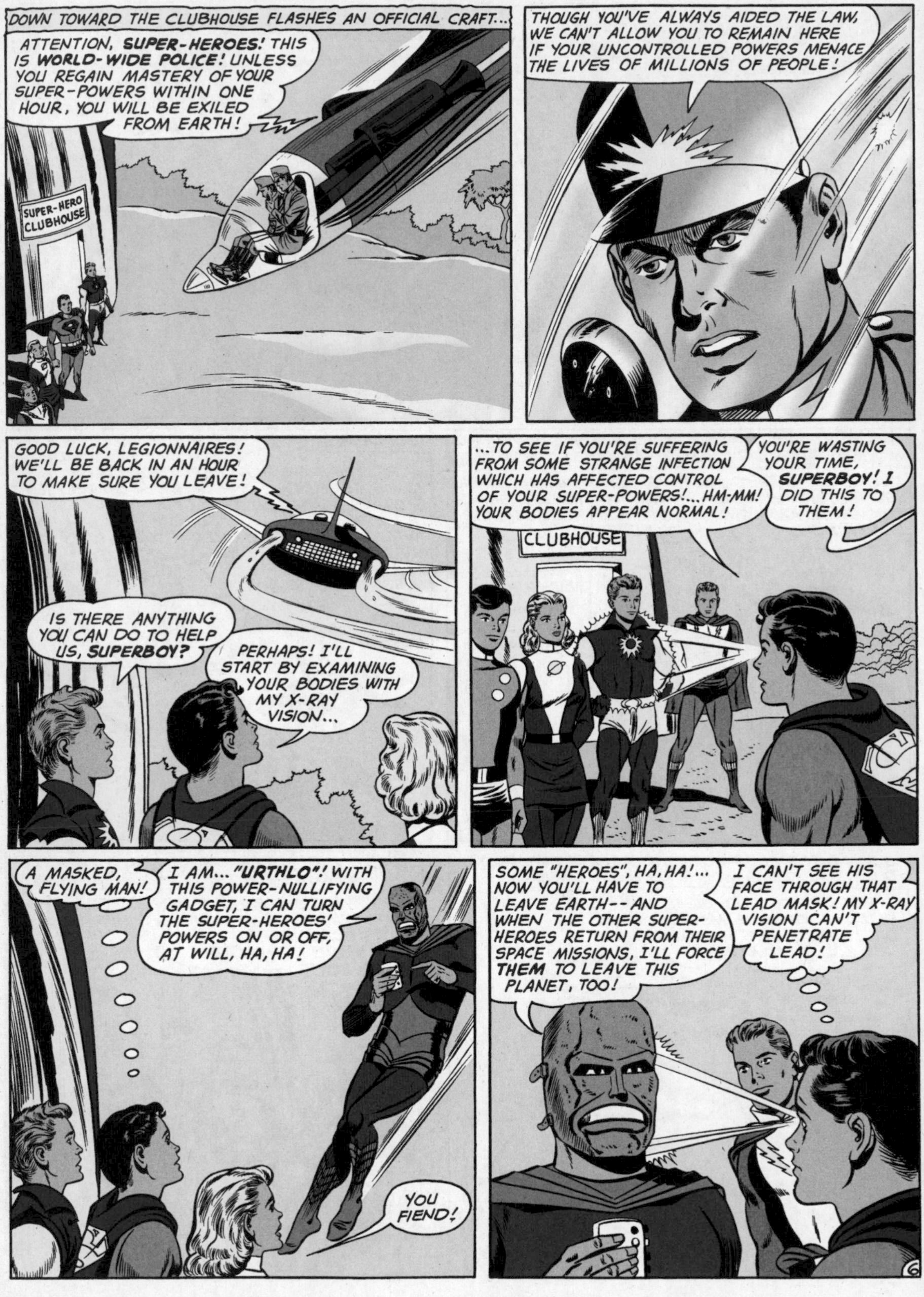
DOWN TOWARD THE CLUBHOUSE FLASHES AN OFFICIAL CRAFT...
ATTENTION, SUPER-HEROES! THIS IS WORLD-WIDE POLICE! UNLESS YOU REGAIN MASTERY OF YOUR SUPER-POWERS WITHIN ONE HOUR, YOU WILL BE EXILED FROM EARTH!
SUPER-HERO CLUBHOUSE
THOUGH YOU'VE ALWAYS AIDED THE LAW, WE CAN'T ALLOW YOU TO REMAIN HERE IF YOUR UNCONTROLLED POWERS MENACE THE LIVES OF MILLIONS OF PEOPLE!
GOOD LUCK, LEGIONNAIRES! WE'LL BE BACK IN AN HOUR TO MAKE SURE YOU LEAVE!
IS THERE ANYTHING YOU CAN DO TO HELP US, SUPERBOY?
PERHAPS! I'LL START BY EXAMINING YOUR BODIES WITH MY X-RAY VISION...
...TO SEE IF YOU'RE SUFFERING FROM SOME STRANGE INFECTION WHICH HAS AFFECTED CONTROL OF YOUR SUPER-POWERS!...HM-MM! YOUR BODIES APPEAR NORMAL!
YOU'RE WASTING YOUR TIME, SUPERBOY! I DID THIS TO THEM!
CLUBHOUSE
A MASKED, FLYING MAN!
I AM... "URTHLO"! WITH THIS POWER-NULLIFYING GADGET, I CAN TURN THE SUPER-HEROES' POWERS ON OR OFF, AT WILL, HA, HA!
YOU FIEND!
SOME "HEROES", HA, HA!... NOW YOU'LL HAVE TO LEAVE EARTH-- AND WHEN THE OTHER SUPER-HEROES RETURN FROM THEIR SPACE MISSIONS, I'LL FORCE THEM TO LEAVE THIS PLANET, TOO!
I CAN'T SEE HIS FACE THROUGH THAT LEAD MASK! MY X-RAY VISION CAN'T PENETRATE LEAD!
6

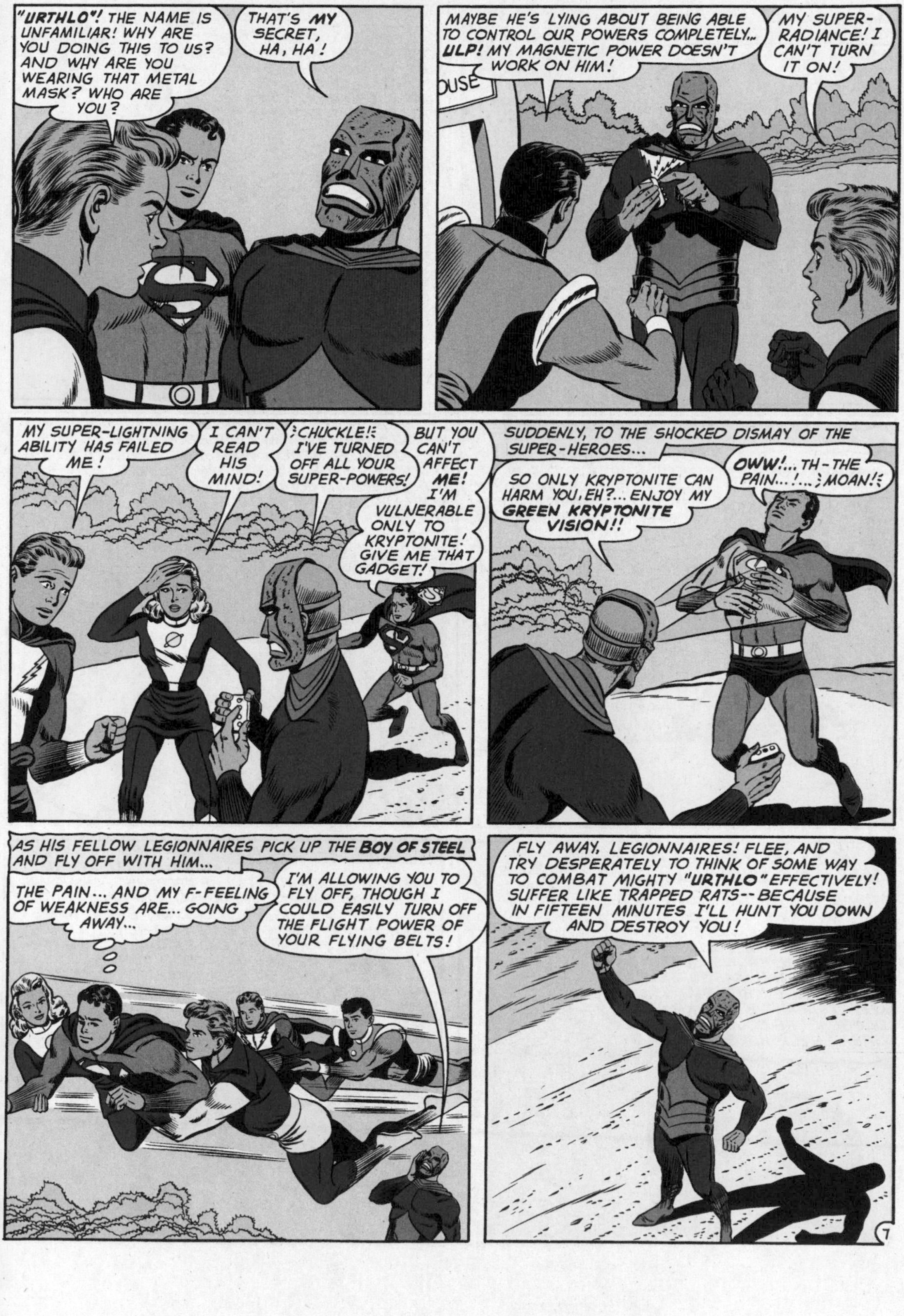
"URTHLO"! THE NAME IS UNFAMILIAR! WHY ARE YOU DOING THIS TO US? AND WHY ARE YOU WEARING THAT METAL MASK? WHO ARE YOU?
THAT'S MY SECRET, HA, HA!
MAYBE HE'S LYING ABOUT BEING ABLE TO CONTROL OUR POWERS COMPLETELY... ULP! MY MAGNETIC POWER DOESN'T WORK ON HIM!
MY SUPER-RADIANCE! I CAN'T TURN IT ON!
MY SUPER-LIGHTNING ABILITY HAS FAILED ME!
I CAN'T READ HIS MIND!
;CHUCKLE!; I'VE TURNED OFF ALL YOUR SUPER-POWERS!
BUT YOU CAN'T AFFECT ME! I'M VULNERABLE ONLY TO KRYPTONITE! GIVE ME THAT GADGET!
SUDDENLY, TO THE SHOCKED DISMAY OF THE SUPER-HEROES...
SO ONLY KRYPTONITE CAN HARM YOU, EH?... ENJOY MY GREEN KRYPTONITE VISION!!
OWW!... TH-THE PAIN...!...;MOAN!;
AS HIS FELLOW LEGIONNAIRES PICK UP THE BOY OF STEEL AND FLY OFF WITH HIM...
THE PAIN... AND MY F-FEELING OF WEAKNESS ARE... GOING AWAY...
I'M ALLOWING YOU TO FLY OFF, THOUGH I COULD EASILY TURN OFF THE FLIGHT POWER OF YOUR FLYING BELTS!
FLY AWAY, LEGIONNAIRES! FLEE, AND TRY DESPERATELY TO THINK OF SOME WAY TO COMBAT MIGHTY "URTHLO" EFFECTIVELY! SUFFER LIKE TRAPPED RATS-- BECAUSE IN FIFTEEN MINUTES I'LL HUNT YOU DOWN AND DESTROY YOU!
7

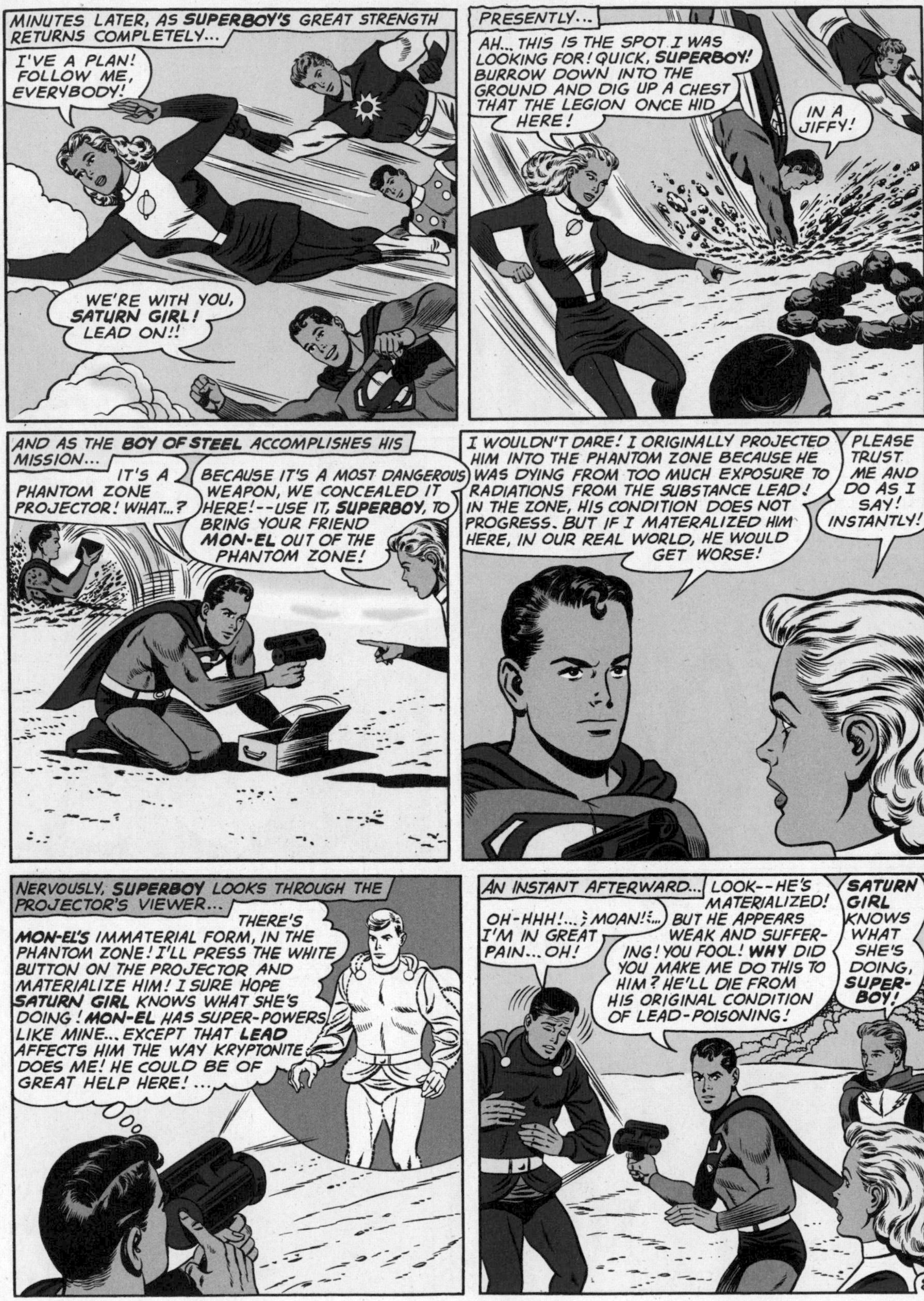
MINUTES LATER, AS SUPERBOY'S GREAT STRENGTH RETURNS COMPLETELY...
I'VE A PLAN! FOLLOW ME, EVERYBODY!
WE'RE WITH YOU, SATURN GIRL! LEAD ON!!
PRESENTLY...
AH... THIS IS THE SPOT I WAS LOOKING FOR! QUICK, SUPERBOY! BURROW DOWN INTO THE GROUND AND DIG UP A CHEST THAT THE LEGION ONCE HID HERE!
IN A JIFFY!
AND AS THE BOY OF STEEL ACCOMPLISHES HIS MISSION...
IT'S A PHANTOM ZONE PROJECTOR! WHAT...?
BECAUSE IT'S A MOST DANGEROUS WEAPON, WE CONCEALED IT HERE!--USE IT, SUPERBOY, TO BRING YOUR FRIEND MON-EL OUT OF THE PHANTOM ZONE!
I WOULDN'T DARE! I ORIGINALLY PROJECTED HIM INTO THE PHANTOM ZONE BECAUSE HE WAS DYING FROM TOO MUCH EXPOSURE TO RADIATIONS FROM THE SUBSTANCE LEAD! IN THE ZONE, HIS CONDITION DOES NOT PROGRESS. BUT IF I MATERALIZED HIM HERE, IN OUR REAL WORLD, HE WOULD GET WORSE!
PLEASE TRUST ME AND DO AS I SAY! INSTANTLY!
NERVOUSLY, SUPERBOY LOOKS THROUGH THE PROJECTOR'S VIEWER...
THERE'S MON-EL'S IMMATERIAL FORM, IN THE PHANTOM ZONE! I'LL PRESS THE WHITE BUTTON ON THE PROJECTOR AND MATERIALIZE HIM! I SURE HOPE SATURN GIRL KNOWS WHAT SHE'S DOING! MON-EL HAS SUPER-POWERS LIKE MINE... EXCEPT THAT LEAD AFFECTS HIM THE WAY KRYPTONITE DOES ME! HE COULD BE OF GREAT HELP HERE! ...
AN INSTANT AFTERWARD...
OH-HHH!... MOAN!... I'M IN GREAT PAIN... OH!
LOOK--HE'S MATERIALIZED! BUT HE APPEARS WEAK AND SUFFERING! YOU FOOL! WHY DID YOU MAKE ME DO THIS TO HIM? HE'LL DIE FROM HIS ORIGINAL CONDITION OF LEAD-POISONING!
SATURN GIRL KNOWS WHAT SHE'S DOING, SUPERBOY!
8

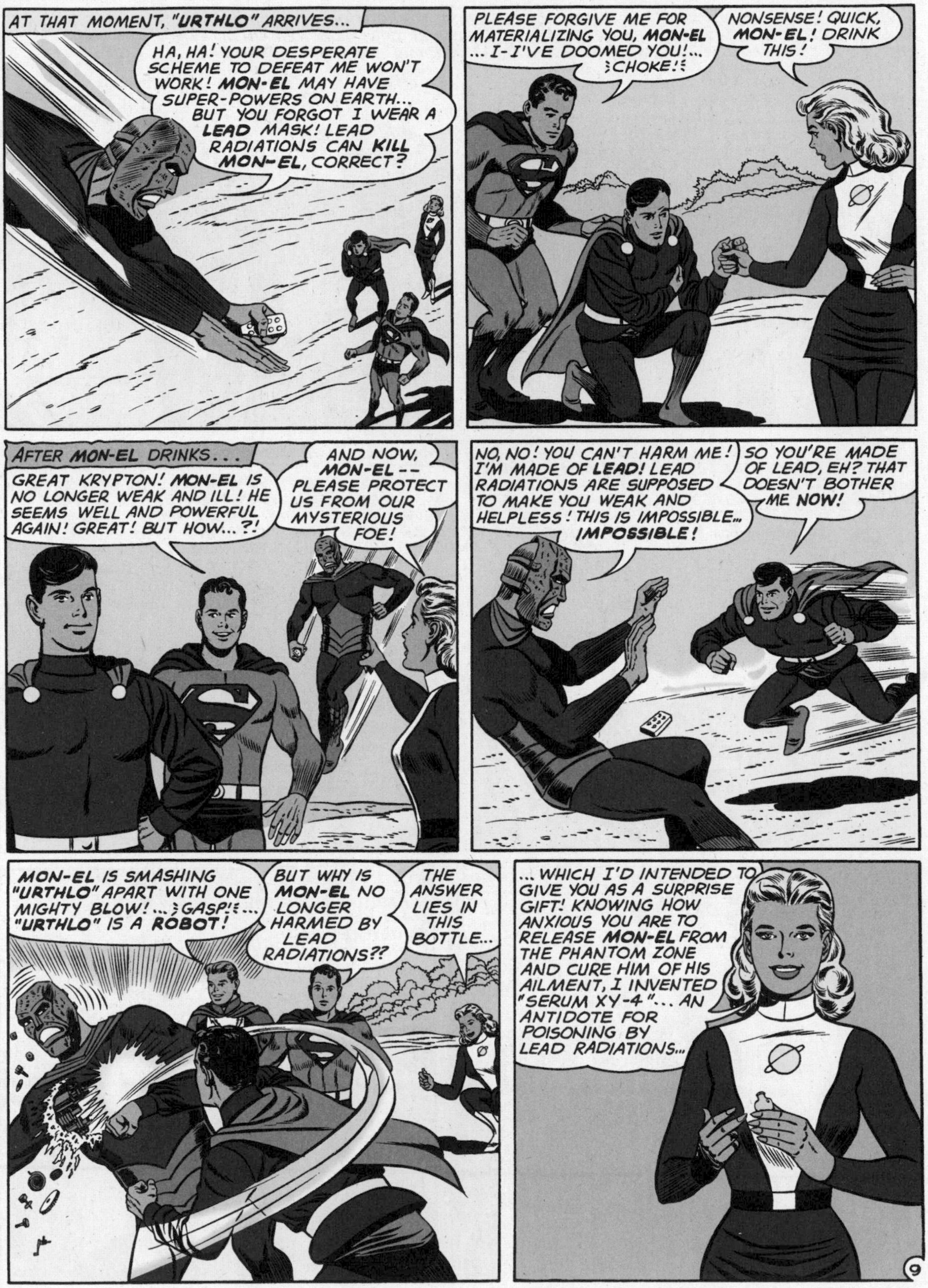
AT THAT MOMENT, "URTHLO" ARRIVES...
HA, HA! YOUR DESPERATE SCHEME TO DEFEAT ME WON'T WORK! MON-EL MAY HAVE SUPER-POWERS ON EARTH... BUT YOU FORGOT I WEAR A LEAD MASK! LEAD RADIATIONS CAN KILL MON-EL, CORRECT?
PLEASE FORGIVE ME FOR MATERIALIZING YOU, MON-EL ... I-I'VE DOOMED YOU!... CHOKE!
NONSENSE! QUICK, MON-EL! DRINK THIS!
AFTER MON-EL DRINKS...
GREAT KRYPTON! MON-EL IS NO LONGER WEAK AND ILL! HE SEEMS WELL AND POWERFUL AGAIN! GREAT! BUT HOW...?!
AND NOW, MON-EL -- PLEASE PROTECT US FROM OUR MYSTERIOUS FOE!
NO, NO! YOU CAN'T HARM ME! I'M MADE OF LEAD! LEAD RADIATIONS ARE SUPPOSED TO MAKE YOU WEAK AND HELPLESS! THIS IS IMPOSSIBLE... IMPOSSIBLE!
SO YOU'RE MADE OF LEAD, EH? THAT DOESN'T BOTHER ME NOW!
MON-EL IS SMASHING "URTHLO" APART WITH ONE MIGHTY BLOW!... GASP!... "URTHLO" IS A ROBOT!
BUT WHY IS MON-EL NO LONGER HARMED BY LEAD RADIATIONS??
THE ANSWER LIES IN THIS BOTTLE...
...WHICH I'D INTENDED TO GIVE YOU AS A SURPRISE GIFT! KNOWING HOW ANXIOUS YOU ARE TO RELEASE MON-EL FROM THE PHANTOM ZONE AND CURE HIM OF HIS AILMENT, I INVENTED "SERUM XY-4"... AN ANTIDOTE FOR POISONING BY LEAD RADIATIONS...
9

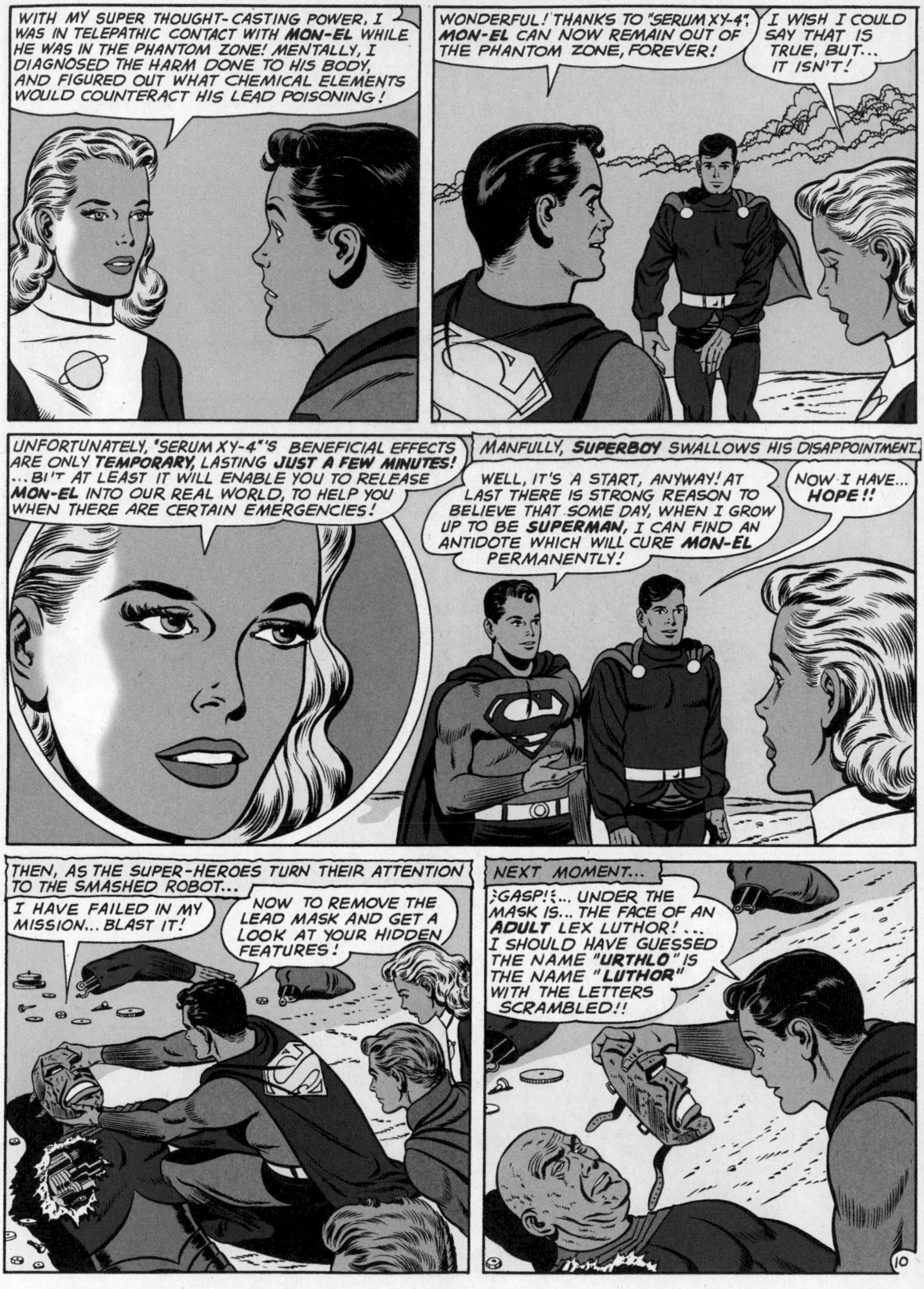
WITH MY SUPER THOUGHT-CASTING POWER, I WAS IN TELEPATHIC CONTACT WITH MON-EL WHILE HE WAS IN THE PHANTOM ZONE! MENTALLY, I DIAGNOSED THE HARM DONE TO HIS BODY, AND FIGURED OUT WHAT CHEMICAL ELEMENTS WOULD COUNTERACT HIS LEAD POISONING!
WONDERFUL! THANKS TO "SERUM XY-4", MON-EL CAN NOW REMAIN OUT OF THE PHANTOM ZONE, FOREVER!
I WISH I COULD SAY THAT IS TRUE, BUT... IT ISN'T!
UNFORTUNATELY, "SERUM XY-4"'S BENEFICIAL EFFECTS ARE ONLY TEMPORARY, LASTING JUST A FEW MINUTES! ...BUT AT LEAST IT WILL ENABLE YOU TO RELEASE MON-EL INTO OUR REAL WORLD, TO HELP YOU WHEN THERE ARE CERTAIN EMERGENCIES!
MANFULLY, SUPERBOY SWALLOWS HIS DISAPPOINTMENT...
WELL, IT'S A START, ANYWAY! AT LAST THERE IS STRONG REASON TO BELIEVE THAT SOME DAY, WHEN I GROW UP TO BE SUPERMAN, I CAN FIND AN ANTIDOTE WHICH WILL CURE MON-EL PERMANENTLY!
NOW I HAVE... HOPE!!
THEN, AS THE SUPER-HEROES TURN THEIR ATTENTION TO THE SMASHED ROBOT...
I HAVE FAILED IN MY MISSION... BLAST IT!
NOW TO REMOVE THE LEAD MASK AND GET A LOOK AT YOUR HIDDEN FEATURES!
NEXT MOMENT...
GASP!... UNDER THE MASK IS... THE FACE OF AN ADULT LEX LUTHOR!... I SHOULD HAVE GUESSED THE NAME "URTHLO" IS THE NAME "LUTHOR" WITH THE LETTERS SCRAMBLED!!
10

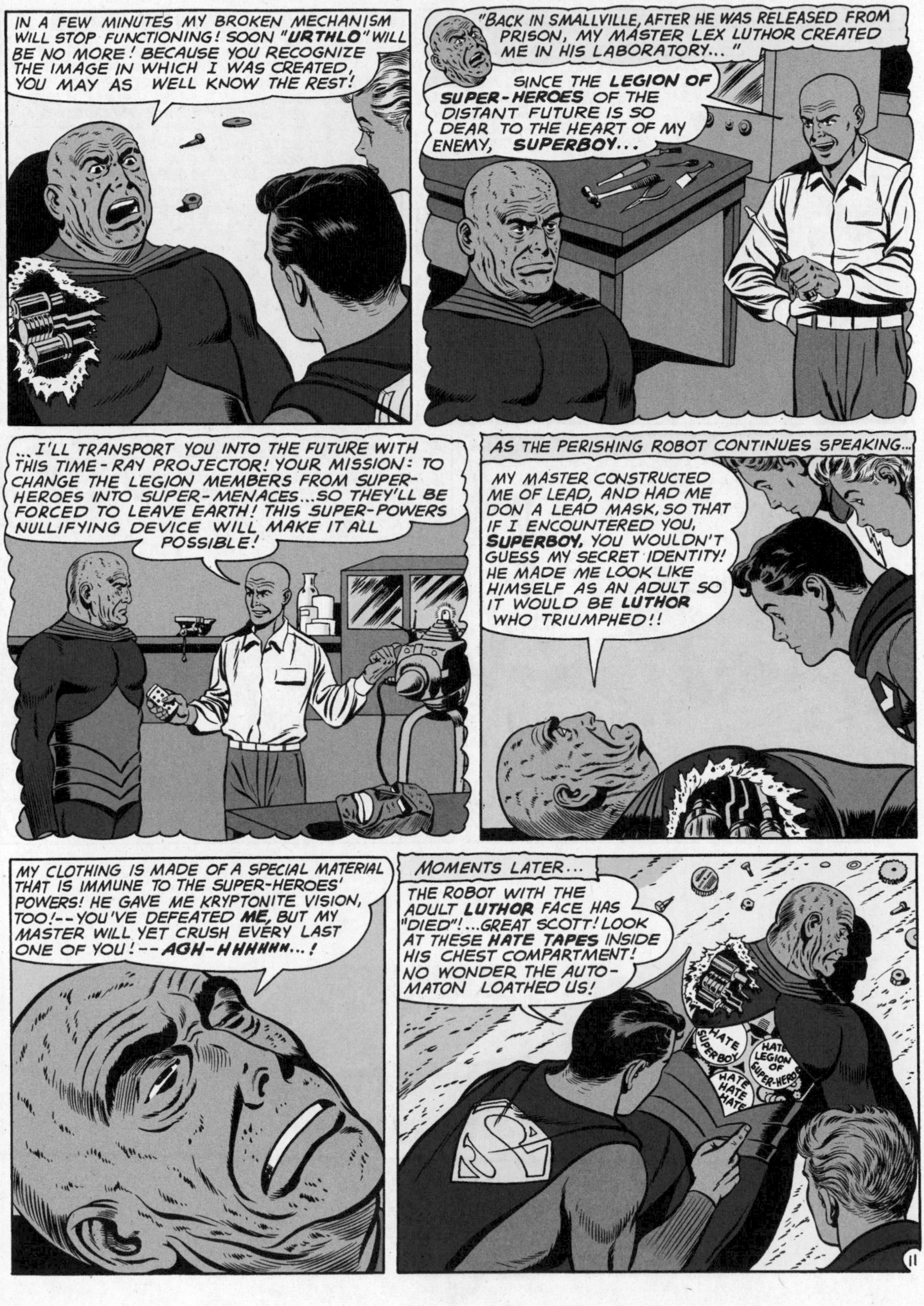
IN A FEW MINUTES MY BROKEN MECHANISM WILL STOP FUNCTIONING! SOON "URTHLO" WILL BE NO MORE! BECAUSE YOU RECOGNIZE THE IMAGE IN WHICH I WAS CREATED, YOU MAY AS WELL KNOW THE REST!
"BACK IN SMALLVILLE, AFTER HE WAS RELEASED FROM PRISON, MY MASTER LEX LUTHOR CREATED ME IN HIS LABORATORY..."
SINCE THE LEGION OF SUPER-HEROES OF THE DISTANT FUTURE IS SO DEAR TO THE HEART OF MY ENEMY, SUPERBOY...
...I'LL TRANSPORT YOU INTO THE FUTURE WITH THIS TIME-RAY PROJECTOR! YOUR MISSION: TO CHANGE THE LEGION MEMBERS FROM SUPER-HEROES INTO SUPER-MENACES...SO THEY'LL BE FORCED TO LEAVE EARTH! THIS SUPER-POWERS NULLIFYING DEVICE WILL MAKE IT ALL POSSIBLE!
AS THE PERISHING ROBOT CONTINUES SPEAKING...
MY MASTER CONSTRUCTED ME OF LEAD, AND HAD ME DON A LEAD MASK, SO THAT IF I ENCOUNTERED YOU, SUPERBOY, YOU WOULDN'T GUESS MY SECRET IDENTITY! HE MADE ME LOOK LIKE HIMSELF AS AN ADULT SO IT WOULD BE LUTHOR WHO TRIUMPHED!!
MY CLOTHING IS MADE OF A SPECIAL MATERIAL THAT IS IMMUNE TO THE SUPER-HEROES' POWERS! HE GAVE ME KRYPTONITE VISION, TOO!--YOU'VE DEFEATED ME, BUT MY MASTER WILL YET CRUSH EVERY LAST ONE OF YOU!--AGH-HHHHHH...!
MOMENTS LATER...
THE ROBOT WITH THE ADULT LUTHOR FACE HAS "DIED"!...GREAT SCOTT! LOOK AT THESE HATE TAPES INSIDE HIS CHEST COMPARTMENT! NO WONDER THE AUTO-MATON LOATHED US!
HATE SUPERBOY
HATE LEGION OF SUPER-HEROES
HATE HATE HATE
11

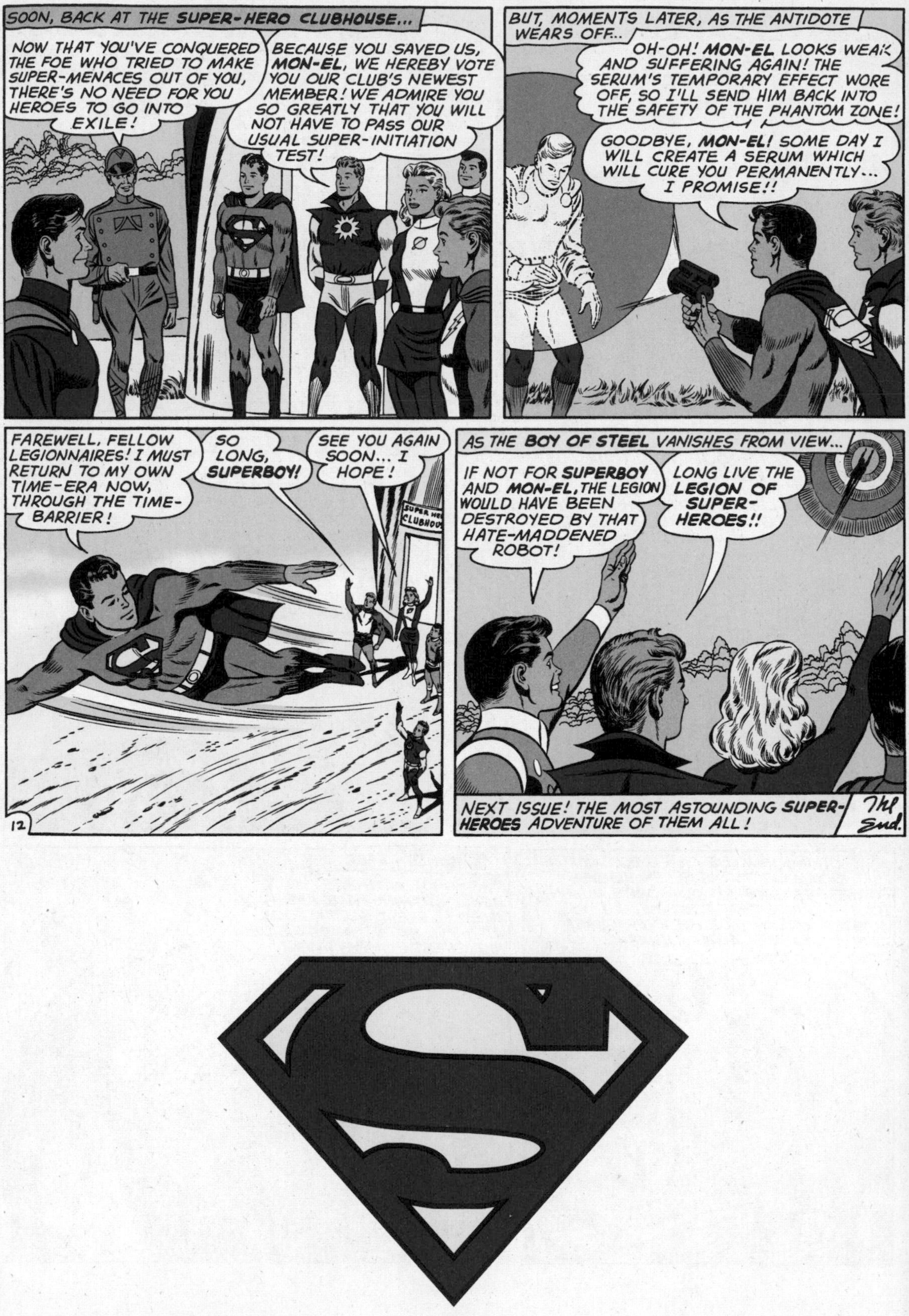

SOON, BACK AT THE SUPER-HERO CLUBHOUSE...
NOW THAT YOU'VE CONQUERED THE FOE WHO TRIED TO MAKE SUPER-MENACES OUT OF YOU, THERE'S NO NEED FOR YOU HEROES TO GO INTO EXILE!
BECAUSE YOU SAVED US, MON-EL, WE HEREBY VOTE YOU OUR CLUB'S NEWEST MEMBER! WE ADMIRE YOU SO GREATLY THAT YOU WILL NOT HAVE TO PASS OUR USUAL SUPER-INITIATION TEST!
BUT, MOMENTS LATER, AS THE ANTIDOTE WEARS OFF...
OH-OH! MON-EL LOOKS WEAK AND SUFFERING AGAIN! THE SERUM'S TEMPORARY EFFECT WORE OFF, SO I'LL SEND HIM BACK INTO THE SAFETY OF THE PHANTOM ZONE!
GOODBYE, MON-EL! SOME DAY I WILL CREATE A SERUM WHICH WILL CURE YOU PERMANENTLY... I PROMISE!!
FAREWELL, FELLOW LEGIONNAIRES! I MUST RETURN TO MY OWN TIME-ERA NOW, THROUGH THE TIME-BARRIER!
SO LONG, SUPERBOY!
SEE YOU AGAIN SOON... I HOPE!
SUPER HERO CLUBHOUS
12
AS THE BOY OF STEEL VANISHES FROM VIEW...
IF NOT FOR SUPERBOY AND MON-EL, THE LEGION WOULD HAVE BEEN DESTROYED BY THAT HATE-MADDENED ROBOT!
LONG LIVE THE LEGION OF SUPER-HEROES!!
NEXT ISSUE! THE MOST ASTOUNDING SUPER-HEROES ADVENTURE OF THEM ALL!
The End.

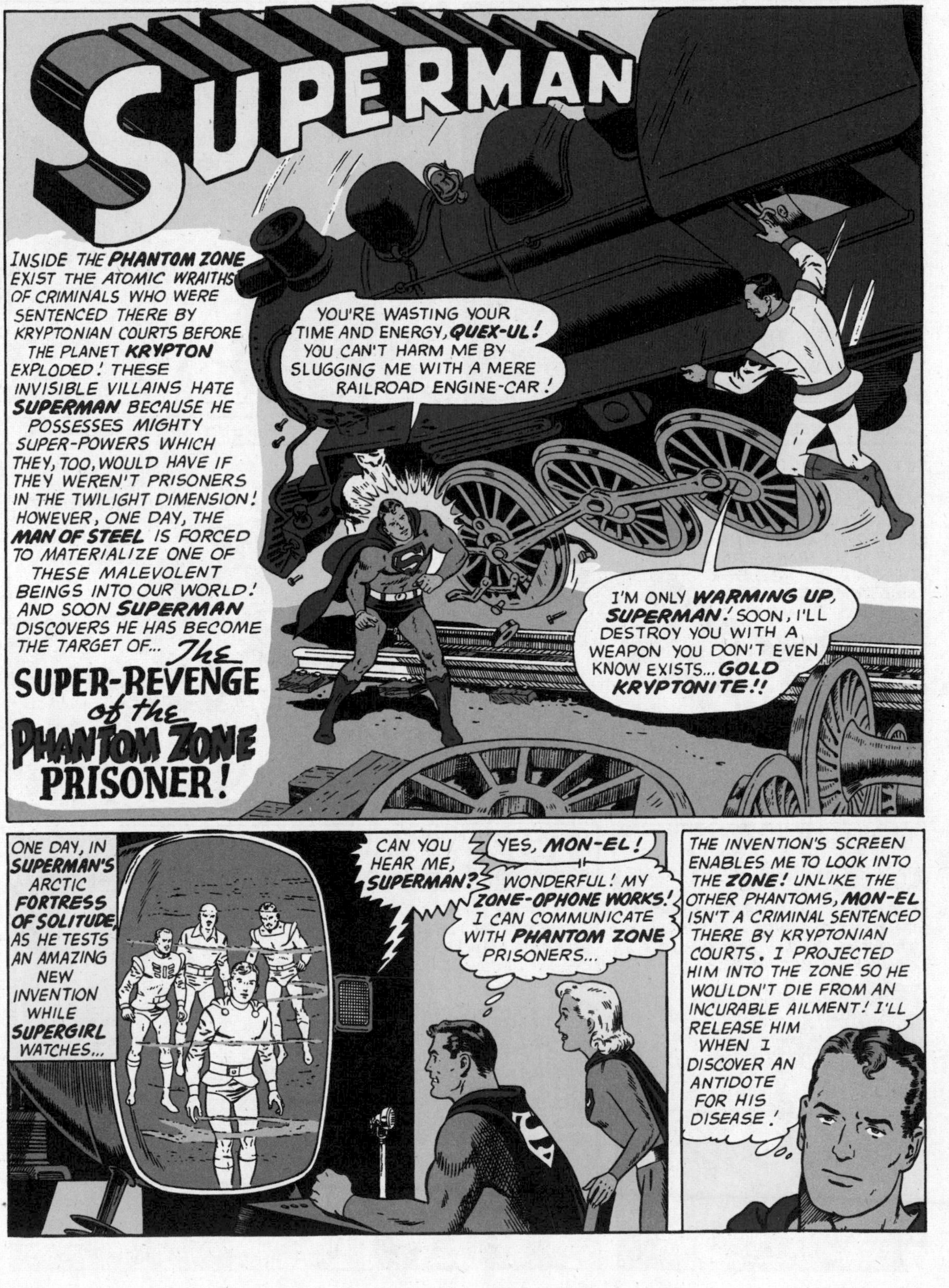
SUPERMAN
INSIDE THE PHANTOM ZONE EXIST THE ATOMIC WRAITHS OF CRIMINALS WHO WERE SENTENCED THERE BY KRYPTONIAN COURTS BEFORE THE PLANET KRYPTON EXPLODED! THESE INVISIBLE VILLAINS HATE SUPERMAN BECAUSE HE POSSESSES MIGHTY SUPER-POWERS WHICH THEY, TOO, WOULD HAVE IF THEY WEREN'T PRISONERS IN THE TWILIGHT DIMENSION! HOWEVER, ONE DAY, THE MAN OF STEEL IS FORCED TO MATERIALIZE ONE OF THESE MALEVOLENT BEINGS INTO OUR WORLD! AND SOON SUPERMAN DISCOVERS HE HAS BECOME THE TARGET OF...
The SUPER-REVENGE of the PHANTOM ZONE PRISONER!
YOU'RE WASTING YOUR TIME AND ENERGY, QUEX-UL! YOU CAN'T HARM ME BY SLUGGING ME WITH A MERE RAILROAD ENGINE-CAR!
I'M ONLY WARMING UP, SUPERMAN! SOON, I'LL DESTROY YOU WITH A WEAPON YOU DON'T EVEN KNOW EXISTS... GOLD KRYPTONITE!!
ONE DAY, IN SUPERMAN'S ARCTIC FORTRESS OF SOLITUDE, AS HE TESTS AN AMAZING NEW INVENTION WHILE SUPERGIRL WATCHES...
CAN YOU HEAR ME, SUPERMAN?
YES, MON-EL!
WONDERFUL! MY ZONE-OPHONE WORKS! I CAN COMMUNICATE WITH PHANTOM ZONE PRISONERS...
THE INVENTION'S SCREEN ENABLES ME TO LOOK INTO THE ZONE! UNLIKE THE OTHER PHANTOMS, MON-EL ISN'T A CRIMINAL SENTENCED THERE BY KRYPTONIAN COURTS. I PROJECTED HIM INTO THE ZONE SO HE WOULDN'T DIE FROM AN INCURABLE AILMENT! I'LL RELEASE HIM WHEN I DISCOVER AN ANTIDOTE FOR HIS DISEASE!

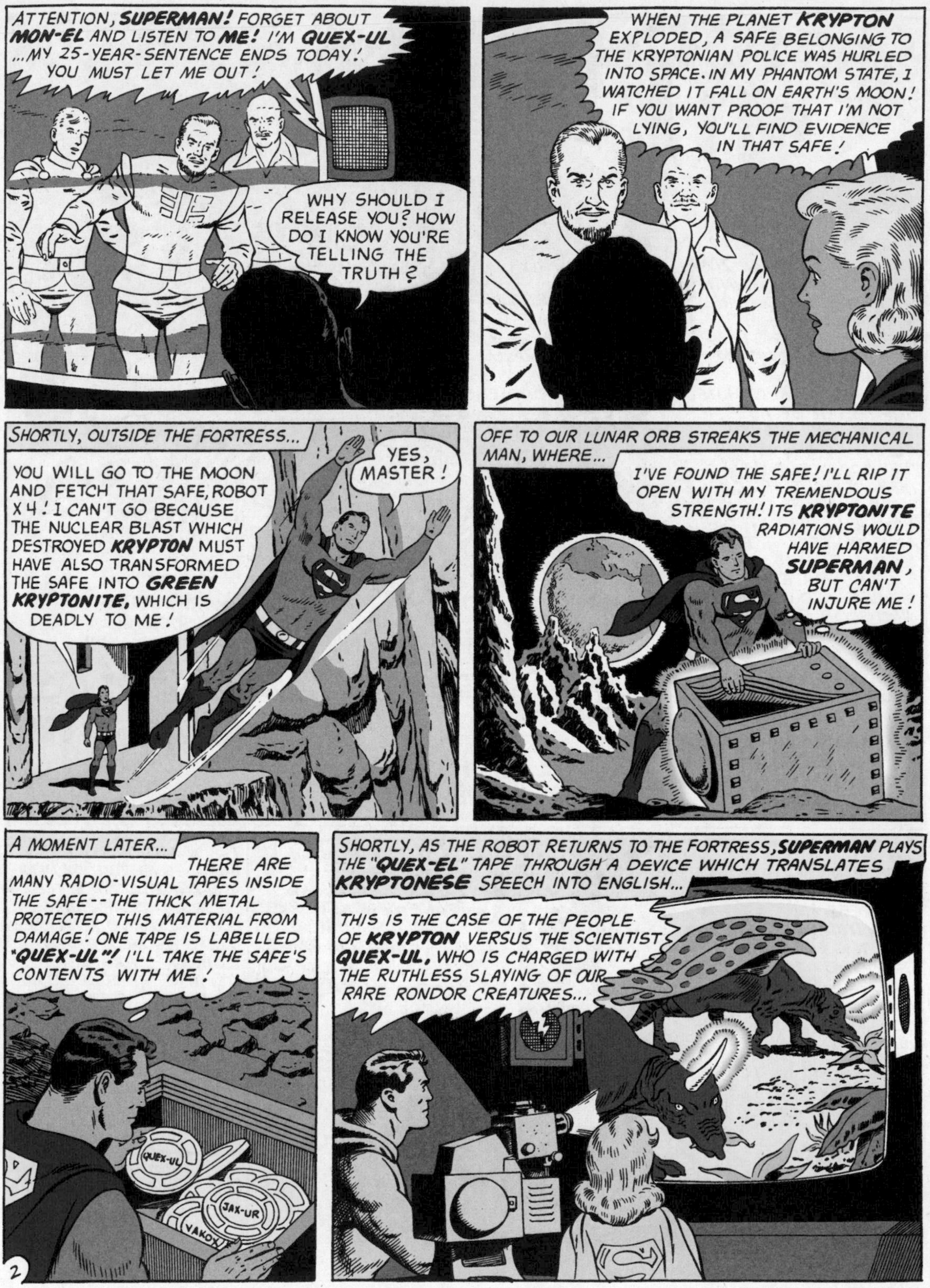
ATTENTION, SUPERMAN! FORGET ABOUT MON-EL AND LISTEN TO ME! I'M QUEX-UL ...MY 25-YEAR-SENTENCE ENDS TODAY! YOU MUST LET ME OUT!
WHY SHOULD I RELEASE YOU? HOW DO I KNOW YOU'RE TELLING THE TRUTH?
WHEN THE PLANET KRYPTON EXPLODED, A SAFE BELONGING TO THE KRYPTONIAN POLICE WAS HURLED INTO SPACE. IN MY PHANTOM STATE, I WATCHED IT FALL ON EARTH'S MOON! IF YOU WANT PROOF THAT I'M NOT LYING, YOU'LL FIND EVIDENCE IN THAT SAFE!
SHORTLY, OUTSIDE THE FORTRESS...
YOU WILL GO TO THE MOON AND FETCH THAT SAFE, ROBOT X4! I CAN'T GO BECAUSE THE NUCLEAR BLAST WHICH DESTROYED KRYPTON MUST HAVE ALSO TRANSFORMED THE SAFE INTO GREEN KRYPTONITE, WHICH IS DEADLY TO ME!
YES, MASTER!
OFF TO OUR LUNAR ORB STREAKS THE MECHANICAL MAN, WHERE...
I'VE FOUND THE SAFE! I'LL RIP IT OPEN WITH MY TREMENDOUS STRENGTH! ITS KRYPTONITE RADIATIONS WOULD HAVE HARMED SUPERMAN, BUT CAN'T INJURE ME!
A MOMENT LATER...
THERE ARE MANY RADIO-VISUAL TAPES INSIDE THE SAFE--THE THICK METAL PROTECTED THIS MATERIAL FROM DAMAGE! ONE TAPE IS LABELLED "QUEX-UL"! I'LL TAKE THE SAFE'S CONTENTS WITH ME!
QUEX-UL
JAX-UR
VAKOX
2
SHORTLY, AS THE ROBOT RETURNS TO THE FORTRESS, SUPERMAN PLAYS THE "QUEX-EL" TAPE THROUGH A DEVICE WHICH TRANSLATES KRYPTONESE SPEECH INTO ENGLISH...
THIS IS THE CASE OF THE PEOPLE OF KRYPTON VERSUS THE SCIENTIST QUEX-UL, WHO IS CHARGED WITH THE RUTHLESS SLAYING OF OUR RARE RONDOR CREATURES...

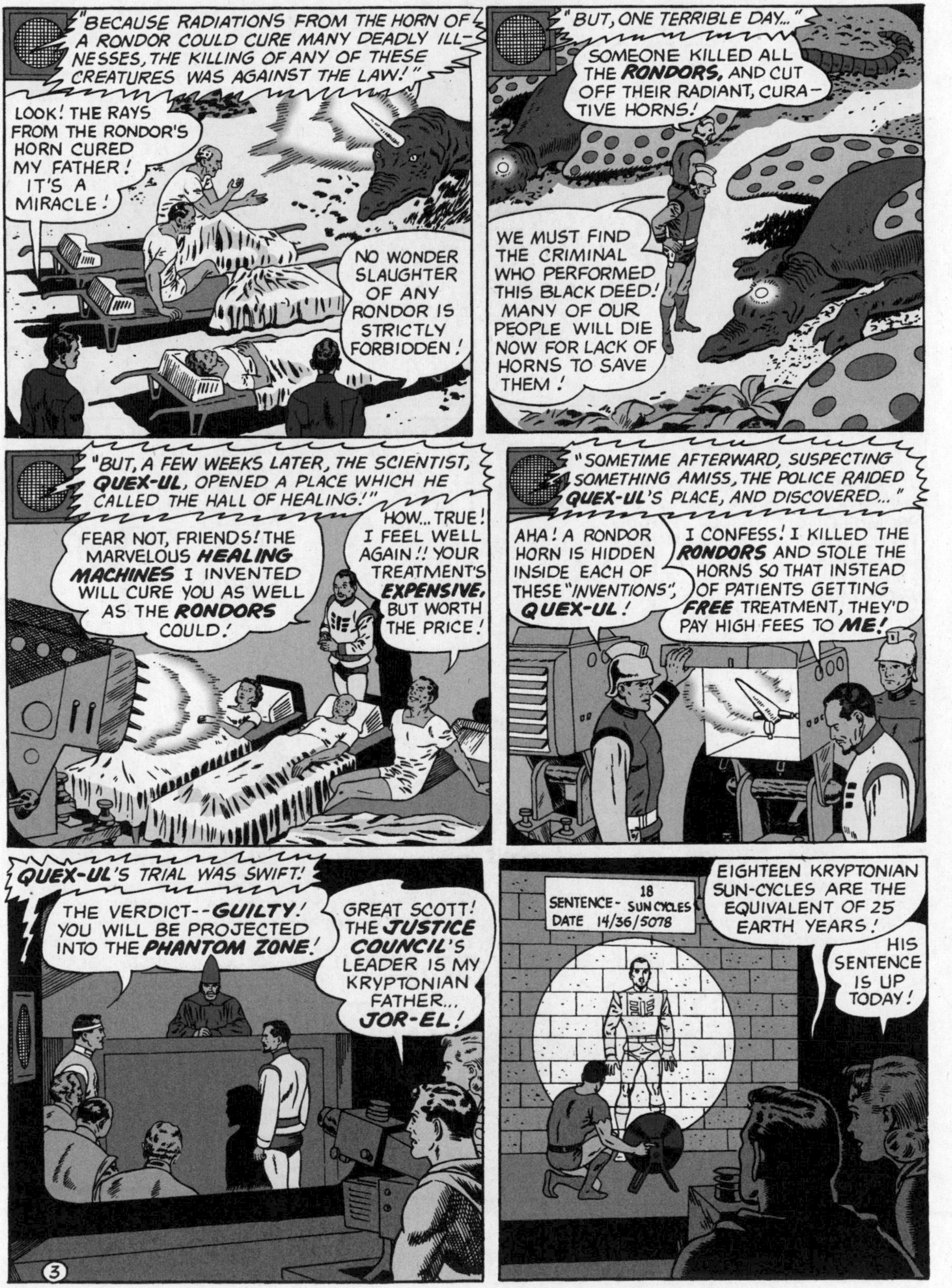
"BECAUSE RADIATIONS FROM THE HORN OF A RONDOR COULD CURE MANY DEADLY ILLNESSES, THE KILLING OF ANY OF THESE CREATURES WAS AGAINST THE LAW!"
LOOK! THE RAYS FROM THE RONDOR'S HORN CURED MY FATHER! IT'S A MIRACLE!
NO WONDER SLAUGHTER OF ANY RONDOR IS STRICTLY FORBIDDEN!
"BUT, ONE TERRIBLE DAY..."
SOMEONE KILLED ALL THE **RONDORS**, AND CUT OFF THEIR RADIANT, CURATIVE HORNS!
WE MUST FIND THE CRIMINAL WHO PERFORMED THIS BLACK DEED! MANY OF OUR PEOPLE WILL DIE NOW FOR LACK OF HORNS TO SAVE THEM!
"BUT, A FEW WEEKS LATER, THE SCIENTIST, **QUEX-UL**, OPENED A PLACE WHICH HE CALLED THE HALL OF HEALING!"
FEAR NOT, FRIENDS! THE MARVELOUS **HEALING MACHINES** I INVENTED WILL CURE YOU AS WELL AS THE **RONDORS** COULD!
HOW... TRUE! I FEEL WELL AGAIN!! YOUR TREATMENT'S **EXPENSIVE**, BUT WORTH THE PRICE!
"SOMETIME AFTERWARD, SUSPECTING SOMETHING AMISS, THE POLICE RAIDED **QUEX-UL**'S PLACE, AND DISCOVERED..."
AHA! A RONDOR HORN IS HIDDEN INSIDE EACH OF THESE "INVENTIONS", **QUEX-UL**!
I CONFESS! I KILLED THE **RONDORS** AND STOLE THE HORNS SO THAT INSTEAD OF PATIENTS GETTING **FREE** TREATMENT, THEY'D PAY HIGH FEES TO **ME!**
QUEX-UL'S TRIAL WAS SWIFT!
THE VERDICT--**GUILTY**! YOU WILL BE PROJECTED INTO THE **PHANTOM ZONE**!
GREAT SCOTT! THE **JUSTICE COUNCIL**'S LEADER IS MY KRYPTONIAN FATHER... **JOR-EL**!
SENTENCE- 18 SUN CYCLES
DATE 14/36/5078
EIGHTEEN KRYPTONIAN SUN-CYCLES ARE THE EQUIVALENT OF 25 EARTH YEARS!
HIS SENTENCE IS UP TODAY!

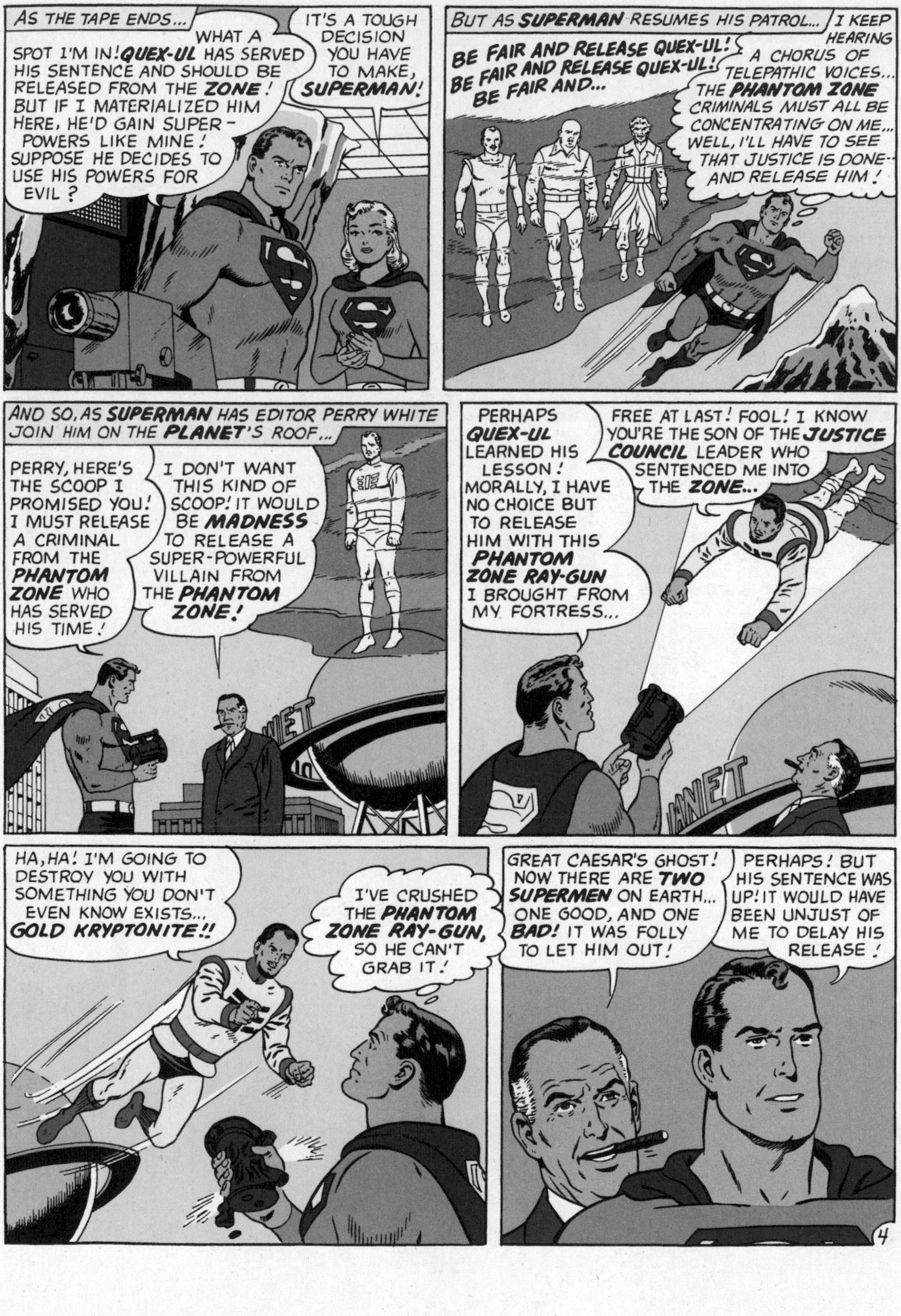
AS THE TAPE ENDS...
WHAT A SPOT I'M IN! QUEX-UL HAS SERVED HIS SENTENCE AND SHOULD BE RELEASED FROM THE ZONE! BUT IF I MATERIALIZED HIM HERE, HE'D GAIN SUPER-POWERS LIKE MINE! SUPPOSE HE DECIDES TO USE HIS POWERS FOR EVIL?
IT'S A TOUGH DECISION YOU HAVE TO MAKE, SUPERMAN!
BUT AS SUPERMAN RESUMES HIS PATROL...
BE FAIR AND RELEASE QUEX-UL! BE FAIR AND RELEASE QUEX-UL! BE FAIR AND...
I KEEP HEARING A CHORUS OF TELEPATHIC VOICES... THE PHANTOM ZONE CRIMINALS MUST ALL BE CONCENTRATING ON ME... WELL, I'LL HAVE TO SEE THAT JUSTICE IS DONE-- AND RELEASE HIM!
AND SO, AS SUPERMAN HAS EDITOR PERRY WHITE JOIN HIM ON THE PLANET'S ROOF...
PERRY, HERE'S THE SCOOP I PROMISED YOU! I MUST RELEASE A CRIMINAL FROM THE PHANTOM ZONE WHO HAS SERVED HIS TIME!
I DON'T WANT THIS KIND OF SCOOP! IT WOULD BE MADNESS TO RELEASE A SUPER-POWERFUL VILLAIN FROM THE PHANTOM ZONE!
PERHAPS QUEX-UL LEARNED HIS LESSON! MORALLY, I HAVE NO CHOICE BUT TO RELEASE HIM WITH THIS PHANTOM ZONE RAY-GUN I BROUGHT FROM MY FORTRESS...
FREE AT LAST! FOOL! I KNOW YOU'RE THE SON OF THE JUSTICE COUNCIL LEADER WHO SENTENCED ME INTO THE ZONE...
HA, HA! I'M GOING TO DESTROY YOU WITH SOMETHING YOU DON'T EVEN KNOW EXISTS... GOLD KRYPTONITE!!
I'VE CRUSHED THE PHANTOM ZONE RAY-GUN, SO HE CAN'T GRAB IT!
GREAT CAESAR'S GHOST! NOW THERE ARE TWO SUPERMEN ON EARTH... ONE GOOD, AND ONE BAD! IT WAS FOLLY TO LET HIM OUT!
PERHAPS! BUT HIS SENTENCE WAS UP! IT WOULD HAVE BEEN UNJUST OF ME TO DELAY HIS RELEASE!
4

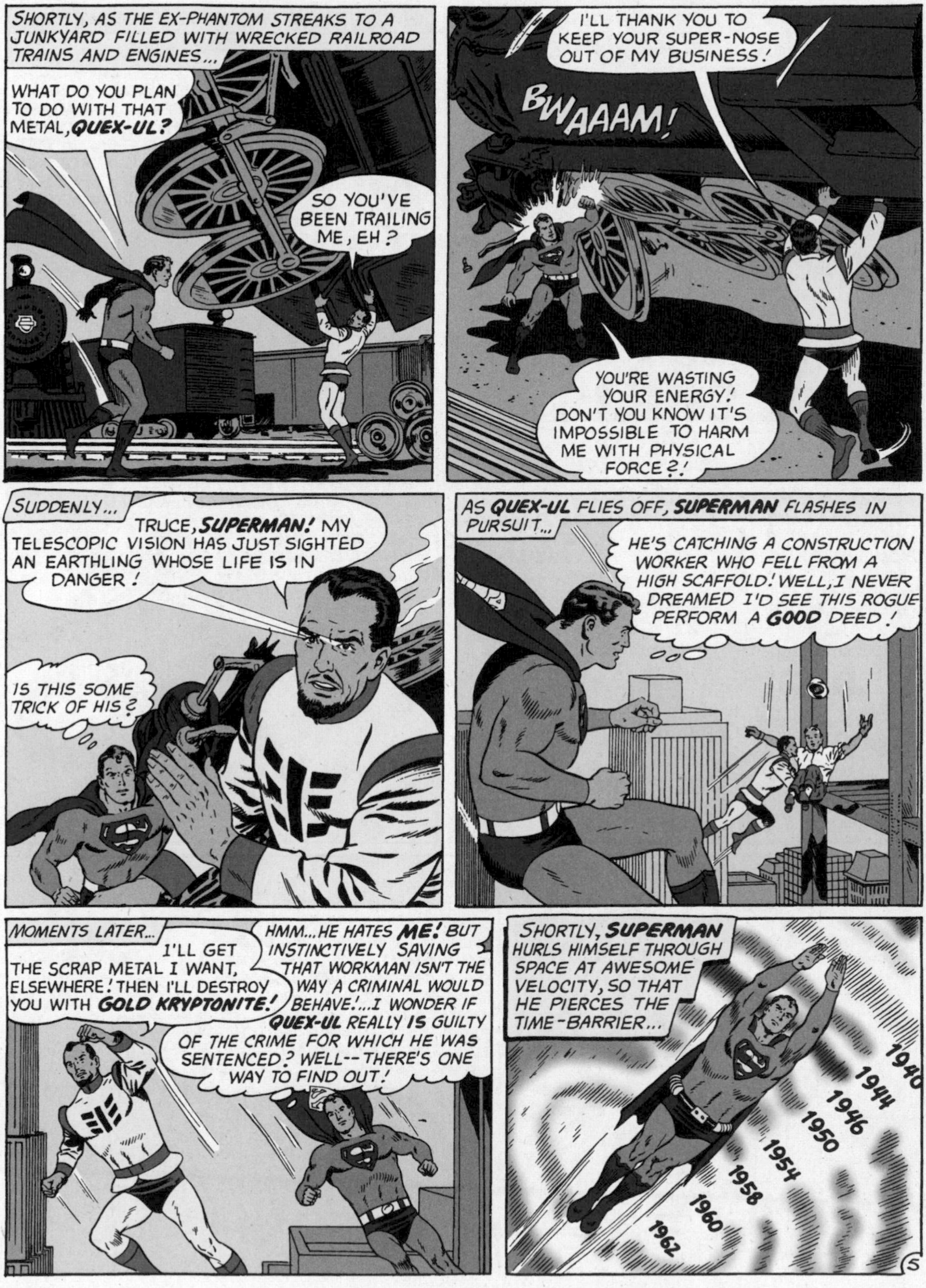
SHORTLY, AS THE EX-PHANTOM STREAKS TO A JUNKYARD FILLED WITH WRECKED RAILROAD TRAINS AND ENGINES...
WHAT DO YOU PLAN TO DO WITH THAT METAL, QUEX-UL?
SO YOU'VE BEEN TRAILING ME, EH?
I'LL THANK YOU TO KEEP YOUR SUPER-NOSE OUT OF MY BUSINESS!
BWAAAM!
YOU'RE WASTING YOUR ENERGY! DON'T YOU KNOW IT'S IMPOSSIBLE TO HARM ME WITH PHYSICAL FORCE?!
SUDDENLY...
TRUCE, SUPERMAN! MY TELESCOPIC VISION HAS JUST SIGHTED AN EARTHLING WHOSE LIFE IS IN DANGER!
IS THIS SOME TRICK OF HIS?
AS QUEX-UL FLIES OFF, SUPERMAN FLASHES IN PURSUIT...
HE'S CATCHING A CONSTRUCTION WORKER WHO FELL FROM A HIGH SCAFFOLD! WELL, I NEVER DREAMED I'D SEE THIS ROGUE PERFORM A GOOD DEED!
MOMENTS LATER...
I'LL GET THE SCRAP METAL I WANT, ELSEWHERE! THEN I'LL DESTROY YOU WITH GOLD KRYPTONITE!
HMM...HE HATES ME! BUT INSTINCTIVELY SAVING THAT WORKMAN ISN'T THE WAY A CRIMINAL WOULD BEHAVE!...I WONDER IF QUEX-UL REALLY IS GUILTY OF THE CRIME FOR WHICH HE WAS SENTENCED? WELL--THERE'S ONE WAY TO FIND OUT!
SHORTLY, SUPERMAN HURLS HIMSELF THROUGH SPACE AT AWESOME VELOCITY, SO THAT HE PIERCES THE TIME-BARRIER...
1940
1944
1946
1950
1954
1958
1960
1962
5

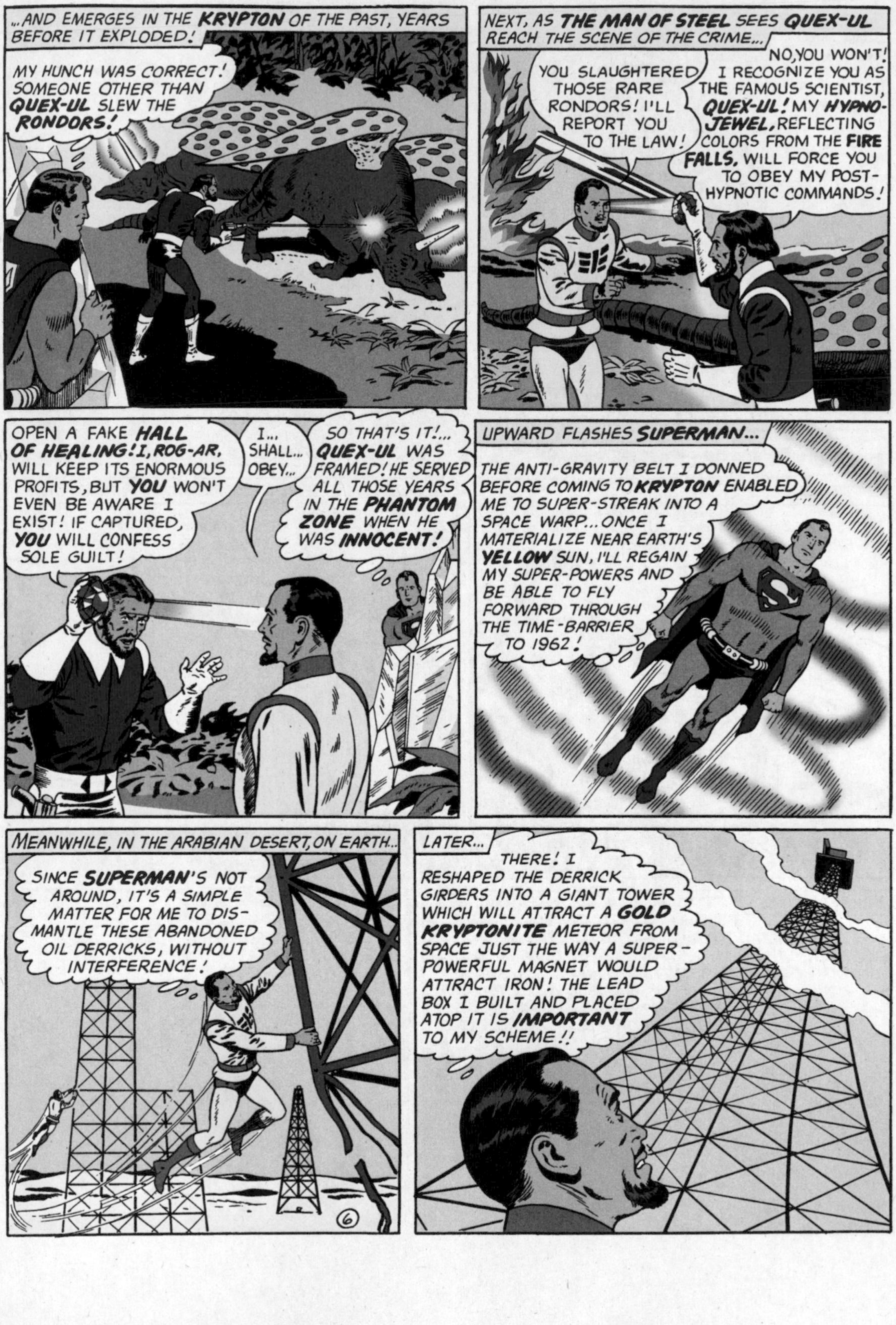
...AND EMERGES IN THE KRYPTON OF THE PAST, YEARS BEFORE IT EXPLODED!
MY HUNCH WAS CORRECT! SOMEONE OTHER THAN QUEX-UL SLEW THE RONDORS!
NEXT, AS THE MAN OF STEEL SEES QUEX-UL REACH THE SCENE OF THE CRIME...
YOU SLAUGHTERED THOSE RARE RONDORS! I'LL REPORT YOU TO THE LAW!
NO, YOU WON'T! I RECOGNIZE YOU AS THE FAMOUS SCIENTIST, QUEX-UL! MY HYPNO-JEWEL, REFLECTING COLORS FROM THE FIRE FALLS, WILL FORCE YOU TO OBEY MY POST-HYPNOTIC COMMANDS!
OPEN A FAKE HALL OF HEALING! I, ROG-AR, WILL KEEP ITS ENORMOUS PROFITS, BUT YOU WON'T EVEN BE AWARE I EXIST! IF CAPTURED, YOU WILL CONFESS SOLE GUILT!
I... SHALL... OBEY...
SO THAT'S IT!... QUEX-UL WAS FRAMED! HE SERVED ALL THOSE YEARS IN THE PHANTOM ZONE WHEN HE WAS INNOCENT!
UPWARD FLASHES SUPERMAN...
THE ANTI-GRAVITY BELT I DONNED BEFORE COMING TO KRYPTON ENABLED ME TO SUPER-STREAK INTO A SPACE WARP... ONCE I MATERIALIZE NEAR EARTH'S YELLOW SUN, I'LL REGAIN MY SUPER-POWERS AND BE ABLE TO FLY FORWARD THROUGH THE TIME-BARRIER TO 1962!
MEANWHILE, IN THE ARABIAN DESERT, ON EARTH...
SINCE SUPERMAN'S NOT AROUND, IT'S A SIMPLE MATTER FOR ME TO DISMANTLE THESE ABANDONED OIL DERRICKS, WITHOUT INTERFERENCE!
6
LATER...
THERE! I RESHAPED THE DERRICK GIRDERS INTO A GIANT TOWER WHICH WILL ATTRACT A GOLD KRYPTONITE METEOR FROM SPACE JUST THE WAY A SUPER-POWERFUL MAGNET WOULD ATTRACT IRON! THE LEAD BOX I BUILT AND PLACED ATOP IT IS IMPORTANT TO MY SCHEME!!

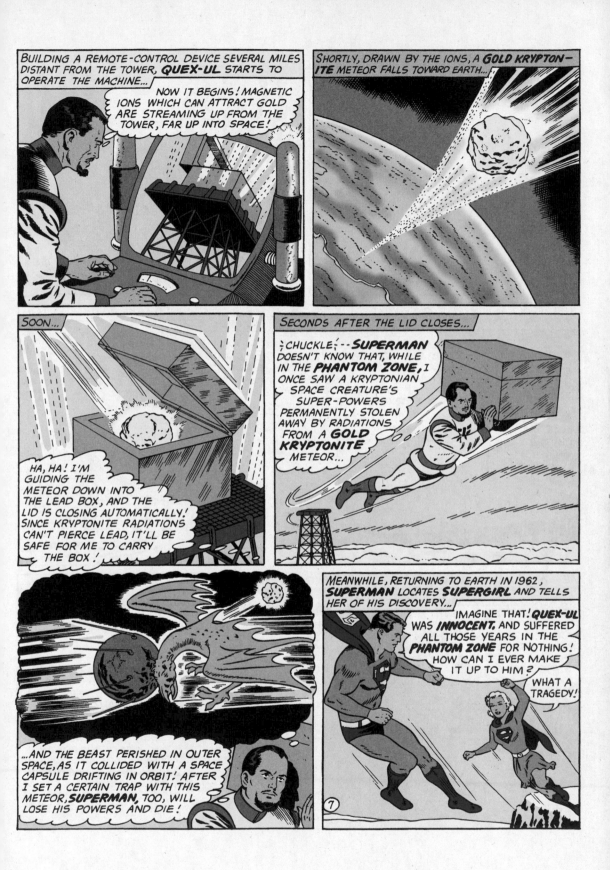

BUILDING A REMOTE-CONTROL DEVICE SEVERAL MILES DISTANT FROM THE TOWER, *QUEX-UL* STARTS TO OPERATE THE MACHINE...

NOW IT BEGINS! MAGNETIC IONS WHICH CAN ATTRACT GOLD ARE STREAMING UP FROM THE TOWER, FAR UP INTO SPACE!

SHORTLY, DRAWN BY THE IONS, A *GOLD KRYPTON-ITE* METEOR FALLS TOWARD EARTH...

SOON...

HA, HA! I'M GUIDING THE METEOR DOWN INTO THE LEAD BOX, AND THE LID IS CLOSING AUTOMATICALLY! SINCE KRYPTONITE RADIATIONS CAN'T PIERCE LEAD, IT'LL BE SAFE FOR ME TO CARRY THE BOX!

SECONDS AFTER THE LID CLOSES...

;-CHUCKLE;-- *SUPERMAN* DOESN'T KNOW THAT, WHILE IN THE *PHANTOM ZONE*, I ONCE SAW A KRYPTONIAN SPACE CREATURE'S SUPER-POWERS PERMANENTLY STOLEN AWAY BY RADIATIONS FROM A *GOLD KRYPTONITE* METEOR...

...AND THE BEAST PERISHED IN OUTER SPACE, AS IT COLLIDED WITH A SPACE CAPSULE DRIFTING IN ORBIT! AFTER I SET A CERTAIN TRAP WITH THIS METEOR, *SUPERMAN*, TOO, WILL LOSE HIS POWERS AND DIE!

MEANWHILE, RETURNING TO EARTH IN 1962, *SUPERMAN* LOCATES *SUPERGIRL* AND TELLS HER OF HIS DISCOVERY...

IMAGINE THAT! *QUEX-UL* WAS *INNOCENT*, AND SUFFERED ALL THOSE YEARS IN THE *PHANTOM ZONE* FOR NOTHING! HOW CAN I EVER MAKE IT UP TO HIM?

WHAT A TRAGEDY!

⑦

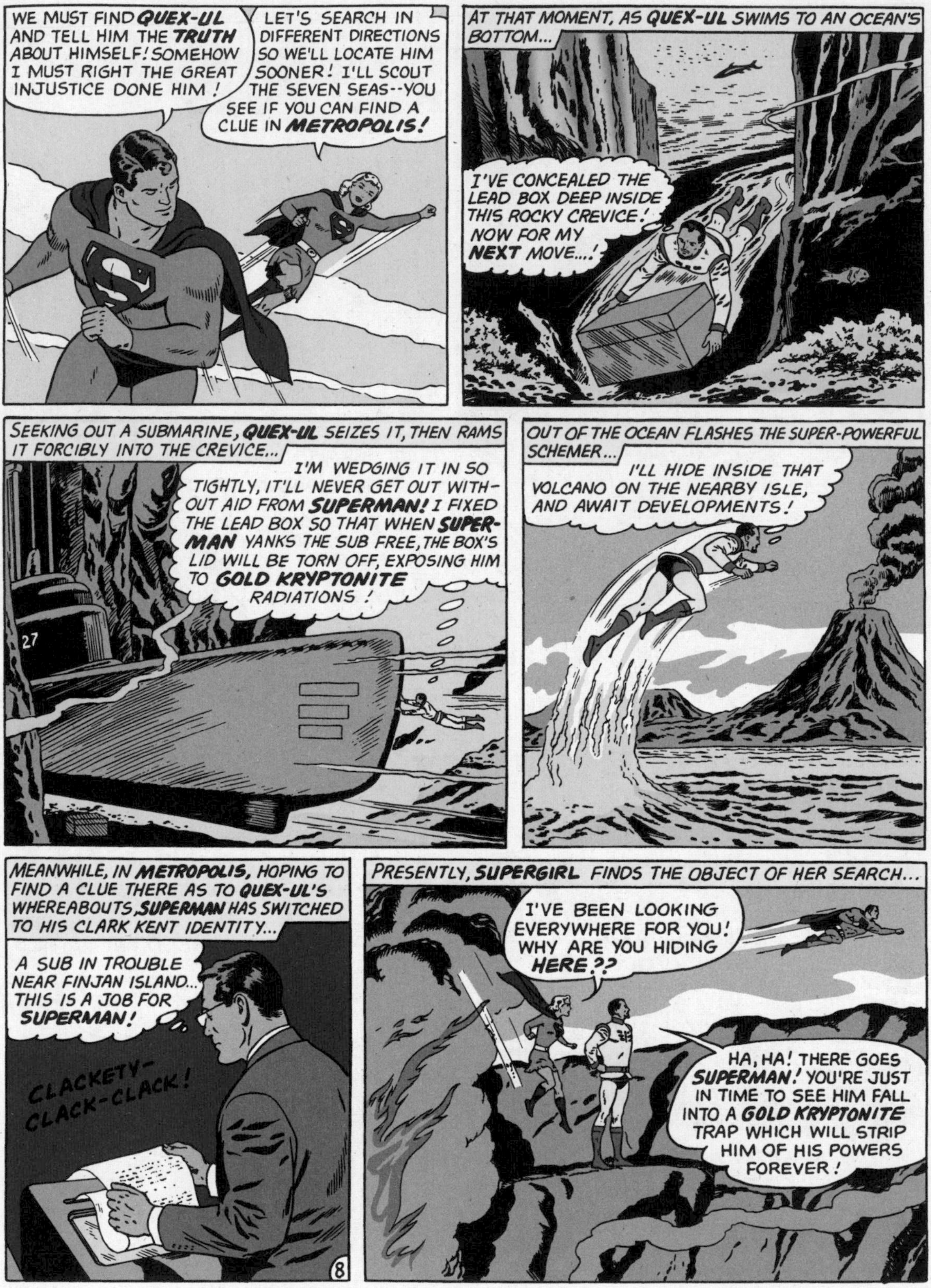

WE MUST FIND QUEX-UL AND TELL HIM THE TRUTH ABOUT HIMSELF! SOMEHOW I MUST RIGHT THE GREAT INJUSTICE DONE HIM!
LET'S SEARCH IN DIFFERENT DIRECTIONS SO WE'LL LOCATE HIM SOONER! I'LL SCOUT THE SEVEN SEAS--YOU SEE IF YOU CAN FIND A CLUE IN METROPOLIS!
AT THAT MOMENT, AS QUEX-UL SWIMS TO AN OCEAN'S BOTTOM...
I'VE CONCEALED THE LEAD BOX DEEP INSIDE THIS ROCKY CREVICE! NOW FOR MY NEXT MOVE...!
SEEKING OUT A SUBMARINE, QUEX-UL SEIZES IT, THEN RAMS IT FORCIBLY INTO THE CREVICE...
I'M WEDGING IT IN SO TIGHTLY, IT'LL NEVER GET OUT WITH-OUT AID FROM SUPERMAN! I FIXED THE LEAD BOX SO THAT WHEN SUPER-MAN YANKS THE SUB FREE, THE BOX'S LID WILL BE TORN OFF, EXPOSING HIM TO GOLD KRYPTONITE RADIATIONS!
27
OUT OF THE OCEAN FLASHES THE SUPER-POWERFUL SCHEMER...
I'LL HIDE INSIDE THAT VOLCANO ON THE NEARBY ISLE, AND AWAIT DEVELOPMENTS!
MEANWHILE, IN METROPOLIS, HOPING TO FIND A CLUE THERE AS TO QUEX-UL'S WHEREABOUTS, SUPERMAN HAS SWITCHED TO HIS CLARK KENT IDENTITY...
A SUB IN TROUBLE NEAR FINJAN ISLAND... THIS IS A JOB FOR SUPERMAN!
CLACKETY-CLACK-CLACK!
8
PRESENTLY, SUPERGIRL FINDS THE OBJECT OF HER SEARCH...
I'VE BEEN LOOKING EVERYWHERE FOR YOU! WHY ARE YOU HIDING HERE??
HA, HA! THERE GOES SUPERMAN! YOU'RE JUST IN TIME TO SEE HIM FALL INTO A GOLD KRYPTONITE TRAP WHICH WILL STRIP HIM OF HIS POWERS FOREVER!

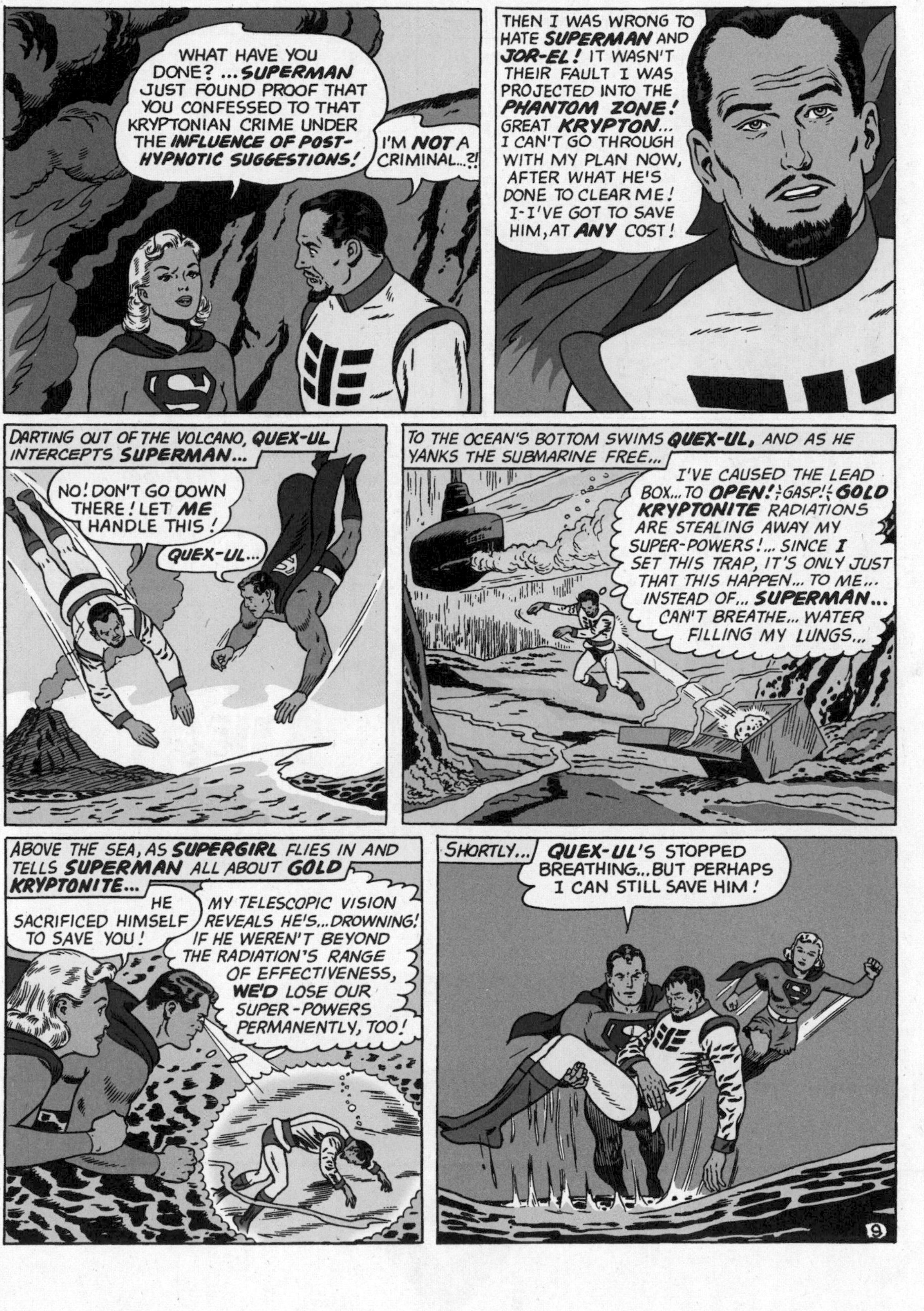

WHAT HAVE YOU DONE? ...SUPERMAN JUST FOUND PROOF THAT YOU CONFESSED TO THAT KRYPTONIAN CRIME UNDER THE INFLUENCE OF POST-HYPNOTIC SUGGESTIONS!
I'M NOT A CRIMINAL...?!
THEN I WAS WRONG TO HATE SUPERMAN AND JOR-EL! IT WASN'T THEIR FAULT I WAS PROJECTED INTO THE PHANTOM ZONE! GREAT KRYPTON... I CAN'T GO THROUGH WITH MY PLAN NOW, AFTER WHAT HE'S DONE TO CLEAR ME! I-I'VE GOT TO SAVE HIM, AT ANY COST!
DARTING OUT OF THE VOLCANO, QUEX-UL INTERCEPTS SUPERMAN...
NO! DON'T GO DOWN THERE! LET ME HANDLE THIS!
QUEX-UL...
TO THE OCEAN'S BOTTOM SWIMS QUEX-UL, AND AS HE YANKS THE SUBMARINE FREE...
I'VE CAUSED THE LEAD BOX... TO OPEN! GASP! GOLD KRYPTONITE RADIATIONS ARE STEALING AWAY MY SUPER-POWERS!... SINCE I SET THIS TRAP, IT'S ONLY JUST THAT THIS HAPPEN... TO ME... INSTEAD OF... SUPERMAN... CAN'T BREATHE... WATER FILLING MY LUNGS...
ABOVE THE SEA, AS SUPERGIRL FLIES IN AND TELLS SUPERMAN ALL ABOUT GOLD KRYPTONITE...
HE SACRIFICED HIMSELF TO SAVE YOU!
MY TELESCOPIC VISION REVEALS HE'S...DROWNING! IF HE WEREN'T BEYOND THE RADIATION'S RANGE OF EFFECTIVENESS, WE'D LOSE OUR SUPER-POWERS PERMANENTLY, TOO!
SHORTLY...
QUEX-UL'S STOPPED BREATHING...BUT PERHAPS I CAN STILL SAVE HIM!
9

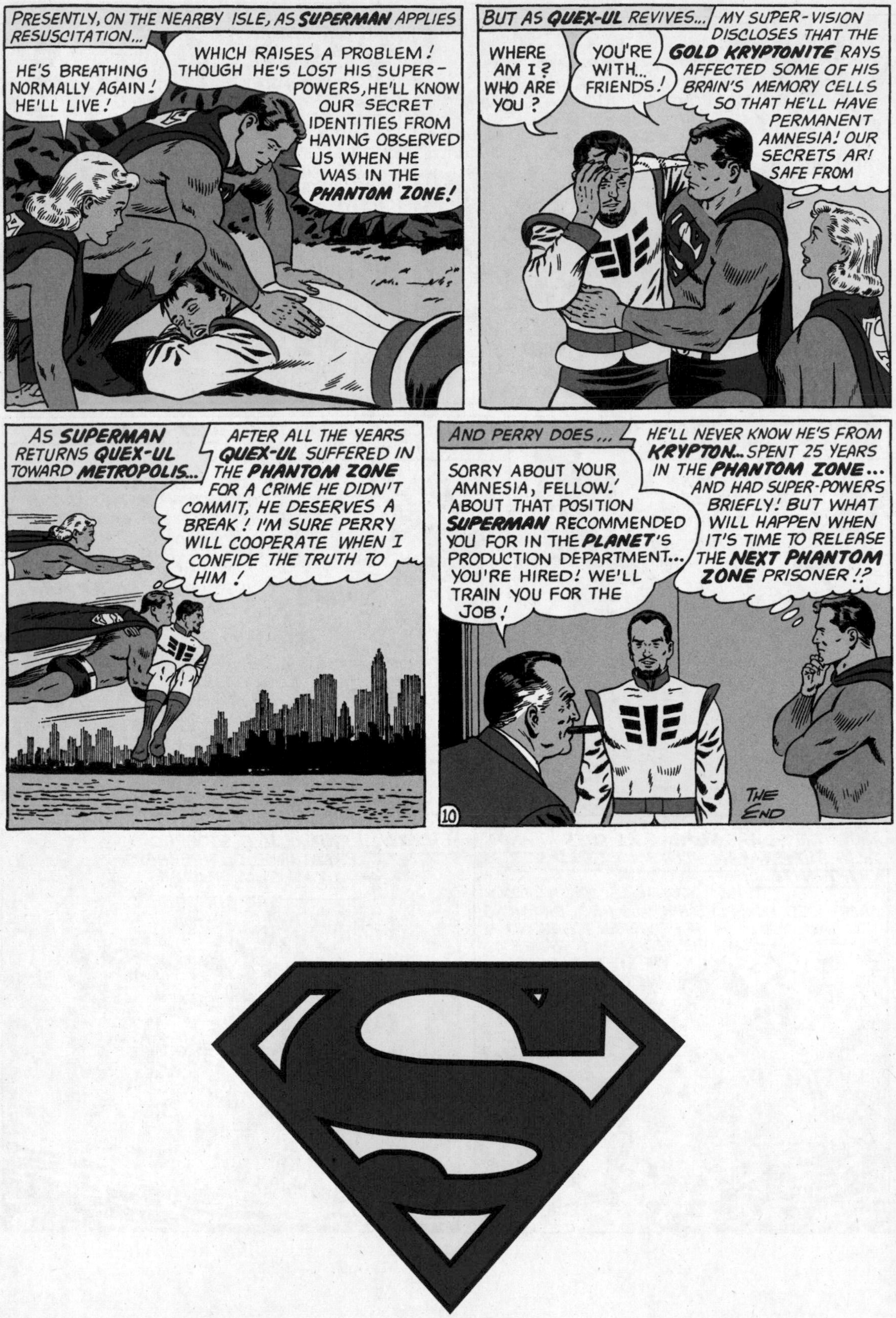

PRESENTLY, ON THE NEARBY ISLE, AS SUPERMAN APPLIES RESUSCITATION...
HE'S BREATHING NORMALLY AGAIN! HE'LL LIVE!
WHICH RAISES A PROBLEM! THOUGH HE'S LOST HIS SUPER-POWERS, HE'LL KNOW OUR SECRET IDENTITIES FROM HAVING OBSERVED US WHEN HE WAS IN THE PHANTOM ZONE!
BUT AS QUEX-UL REVIVES...
WHERE AM I? WHO ARE YOU?
YOU'RE WITH... FRIENDS!
MY SUPER-VISION DISCLOSES THAT THE GOLD KRYPTONITE RAYS AFFECTED SOME OF HIS BRAIN'S MEMORY CELLS SO THAT HE'LL HAVE PERMANENT AMNESIA! OUR SECRETS AR! SAFE FROM
AS SUPERMAN RETURNS QUEX-UL TOWARD METROPOLIS...
AFTER ALL THE YEARS QUEX-UL SUFFERED IN THE PHANTOM ZONE FOR A CRIME HE DIDN'T COMMIT, HE DESERVES A BREAK! I'M SURE PERRY WILL COOPERATE WHEN I CONFIDE THE TRUTH TO HIM!
AND PERRY DOES...
SORRY ABOUT YOUR AMNESIA, FELLOW! ABOUT THAT POSITION SUPERMAN RECOMMENDED YOU FOR IN THE PLANET'S PRODUCTION DEPARTMENT... YOU'RE HIRED! WE'LL TRAIN YOU FOR THE JOB!
HE'LL NEVER KNOW HE'S FROM KRYPTON... SPENT 25 YEARS IN THE PHANTOM ZONE... AND HAD SUPER-POWERS BRIEFLY! BUT WHAT WILL HAPPEN WHEN IT'S TIME TO RELEASE THE NEXT PHANTOM ZONE PRISONER!?
10
THE END

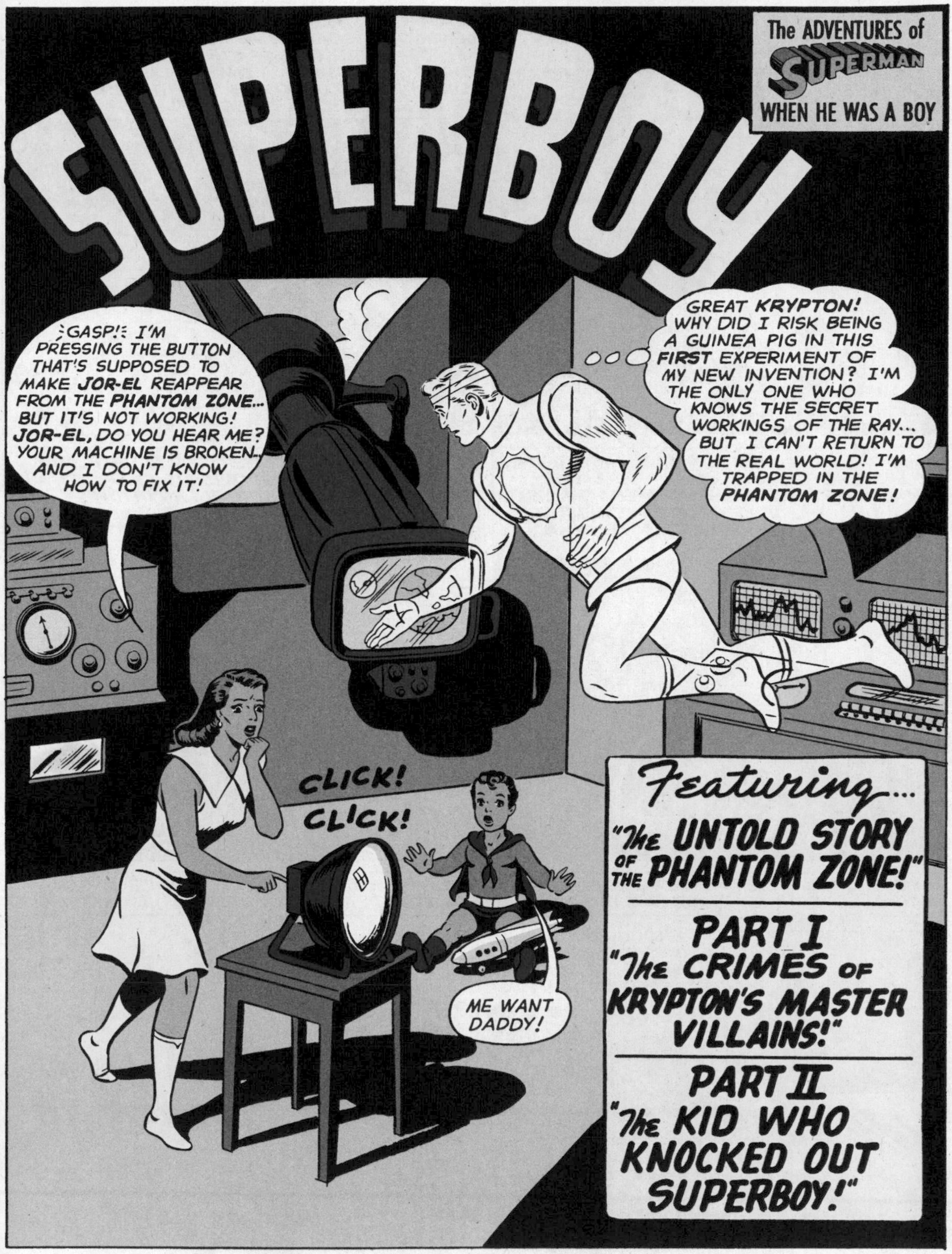
SUPERBOY
The ADVENTURES of SUPERMAN WHEN HE WAS A BOY
¡GASP!¡ I'M PRESSING THE BUTTON THAT'S SUPPOSED TO MAKE JOR-EL REAPPEAR FROM THE PHANTOM ZONE... BUT IT'S NOT WORKING! JOR-EL, DO YOU HEAR ME? YOUR MACHINE IS BROKEN... AND I DON'T KNOW HOW TO FIX IT!
GREAT KRYPTON! WHY DID I RISK BEING A GUINEA PIG IN THIS FIRST EXPERIMENT OF MY NEW INVENTION? I'M THE ONLY ONE WHO KNOWS THE SECRET WORKINGS OF THE RAY... BUT I CAN'T RETURN TO THE REAL WORLD! I'M TRAPPED IN THE PHANTOM ZONE!
CLICK! CLICK!
ME WANT DADDY!
Featuring... "The UNTOLD STORY of the PHANTOM ZONE!"
PART I "The CRIMES of KRYPTON'S MASTER VILLAINS!"
PART II "The KID WHO KNOCKED OUT SUPERBOY!"

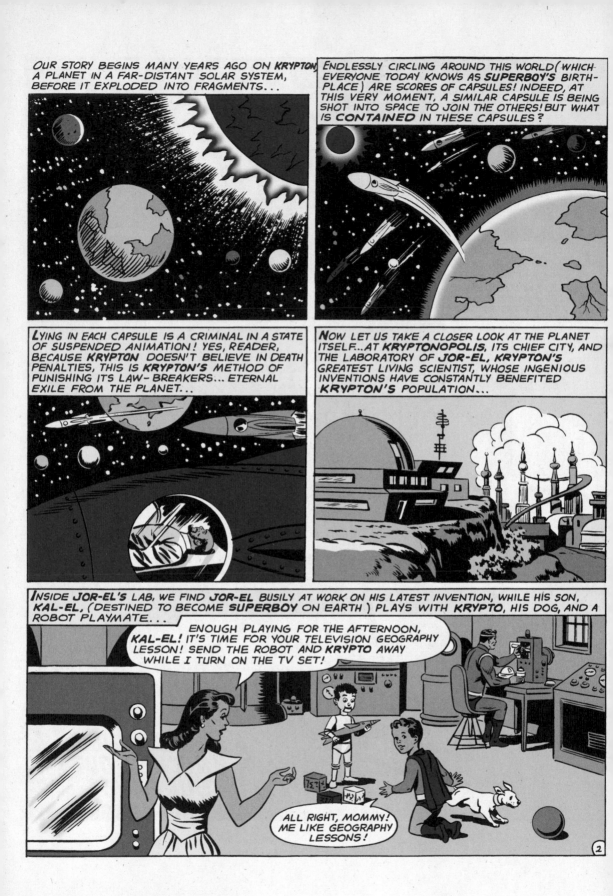

OUR STORY BEGINS MANY YEARS AGO ON *KRYPTON*, A PLANET IN A FAR-DISTANT SOLAR SYSTEM, BEFORE IT EXPLODED INTO FRAGMENTS...

ENDLESSLY CIRCLING AROUND THIS WORLD (WHICH EVERYONE TODAY KNOWS AS *SUPERBOY'S* BIRTHPLACE) ARE SCORES OF CAPSULES! INDEED, AT THIS VERY MOMENT, A SIMILAR CAPSULE IS BEING SHOT INTO SPACE TO JOIN THE OTHERS! BUT WHAT IS *CONTAINED* IN THESE CAPSULES?

LYING IN EACH CAPSULE IS A CRIMINAL IN A STATE OF SUSPENDED ANIMATION! YES, READER, BECAUSE *KRYPTON* DOESN'T BELIEVE IN DEATH PENALTIES, THIS IS *KRYPTON'S* METHOD OF PUNISHING ITS LAW-BREAKERS... ETERNAL EXILE FROM THE PLANET...

NOW LET US TAKE A CLOSER LOOK AT THE PLANET ITSELF... AT *KRYPTONOPOLIS*, ITS CHIEF CITY, AND THE LABORATORY OF *JOR-EL*, *KRYPTON'S* GREATEST LIVING SCIENTIST, WHOSE INGENIOUS INVENTIONS HAVE CONSTANTLY BENEFITED *KRYPTON'S* POPULATION...

INSIDE *JOR-EL'S* LAB, WE FIND *JOR-EL* BUSILY AT WORK ON HIS LATEST INVENTION, WHILE HIS SON, *KAL-EL*, (DESTINED TO BECOME *SUPERBOY* ON EARTH) PLAYS WITH *KRYPTO*, HIS DOG, AND A ROBOT PLAYMATE...

ENOUGH PLAYING FOR THE AFTERNOON, *KAL-EL*! IT'S TIME FOR YOUR TELEVISION GEOGRAPHY LESSON! SEND THE ROBOT AND *KRYPTO* AWAY WHILE I TURN ON THE TV SET!

ALL RIGHT, MOMMY! ME LIKE GEOGRAPHY LESSONS!

2

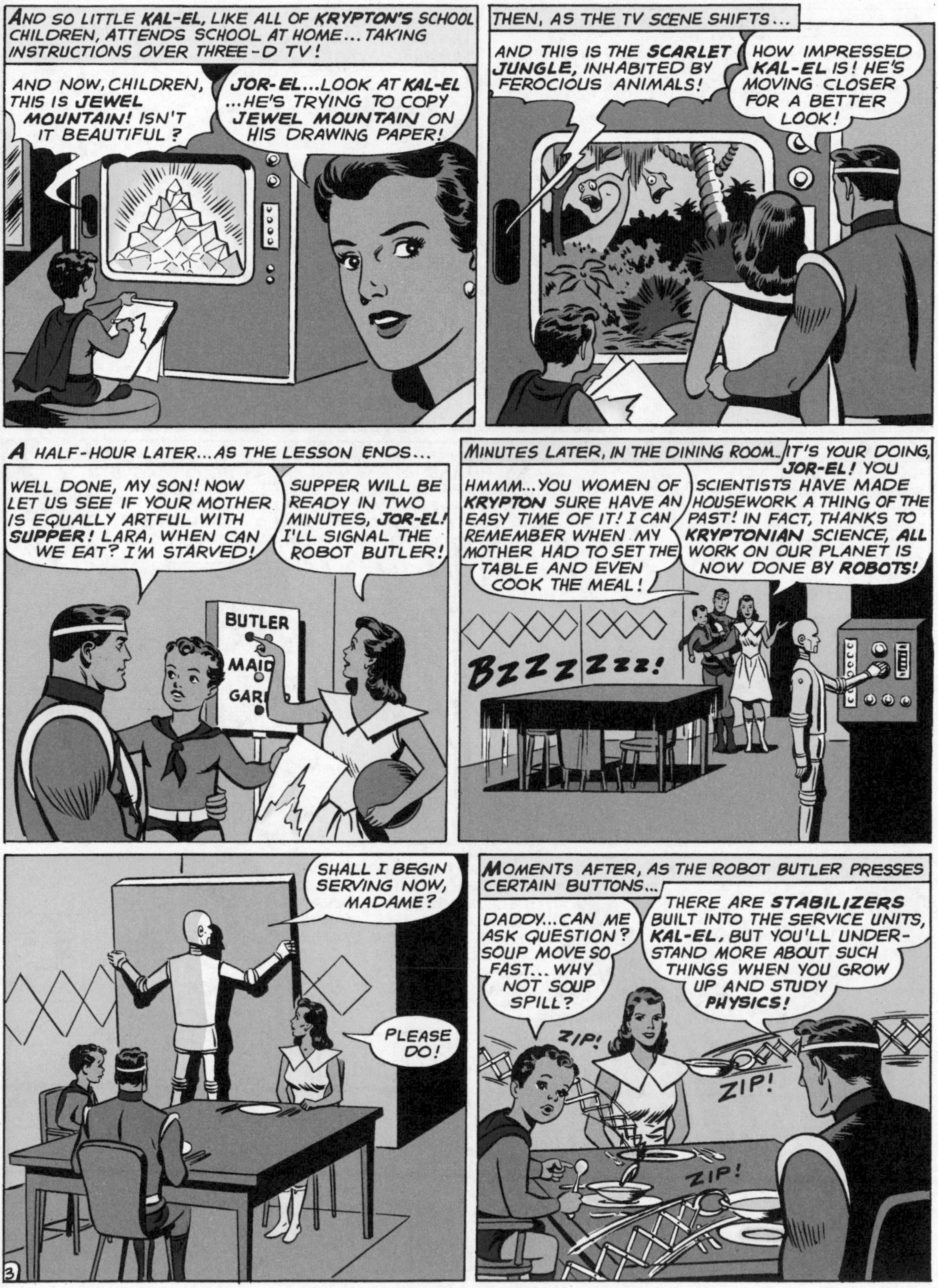
AND SO LITTLE KAL-EL, LIKE ALL OF KRYPTON'S SCHOOL CHILDREN, ATTENDS SCHOOL AT HOME... TAKING INSTRUCTIONS OVER THREE-D TV!
AND NOW, CHILDREN, THIS IS JEWEL MOUNTAIN! ISN'T IT BEAUTIFUL?
JOR-EL... LOOK AT KAL-EL ...HE'S TRYING TO COPY JEWEL MOUNTAIN ON HIS DRAWING PAPER!
THEN, AS THE TV SCENE SHIFTS...
AND THIS IS THE SCARLET JUNGLE, INHABITED BY FEROCIOUS ANIMALS!
HOW IMPRESSED KAL-EL IS! HE'S MOVING CLOSER FOR A BETTER LOOK!
A HALF-HOUR LATER... AS THE LESSON ENDS...
WELL DONE, MY SON! NOW LET US SEE IF YOUR MOTHER IS EQUALLY ARTFUL WITH SUPPER! LARA, WHEN CAN WE EAT? I'M STARVED!
SUPPER WILL BE READY IN TWO MINUTES, JOR-EL! I'LL SIGNAL THE ROBOT BUTLER!
BUTLER
MAID
GAR
MINUTES LATER, IN THE DINING ROOM...
HMMM... YOU WOMEN OF KRYPTON SURE HAVE AN EASY TIME OF IT! I CAN REMEMBER WHEN MY MOTHER HAD TO SET THE TABLE AND EVEN COOK THE MEAL!
IT'S YOUR DOING, JOR-EL! YOU SCIENTISTS HAVE MADE HOUSEWORK A THING OF THE PAST! IN FACT, THANKS TO KRYPTONIAN SCIENCE, ALL WORK ON OUR PLANET IS NOW DONE BY ROBOTS!
BZZZZZZ!
SHALL I BEGIN SERVING NOW, MADAME?
PLEASE DO!
3
MOMENTS AFTER, AS THE ROBOT BUTLER PRESSES CERTAIN BUTTONS...
DADDY... CAN ME ASK QUESTION? SOUP MOVE SO FAST... WHY NOT SOUP SPILL?
THERE ARE STABILIZERS BUILT INTO THE SERVICE UNITS, KAL-EL, BUT YOU'LL UNDERSTAND MORE ABOUT SUCH THINGS WHEN YOU GROW UP AND STUDY PHYSICS!
ZIP!
ZIP!
ZIP!

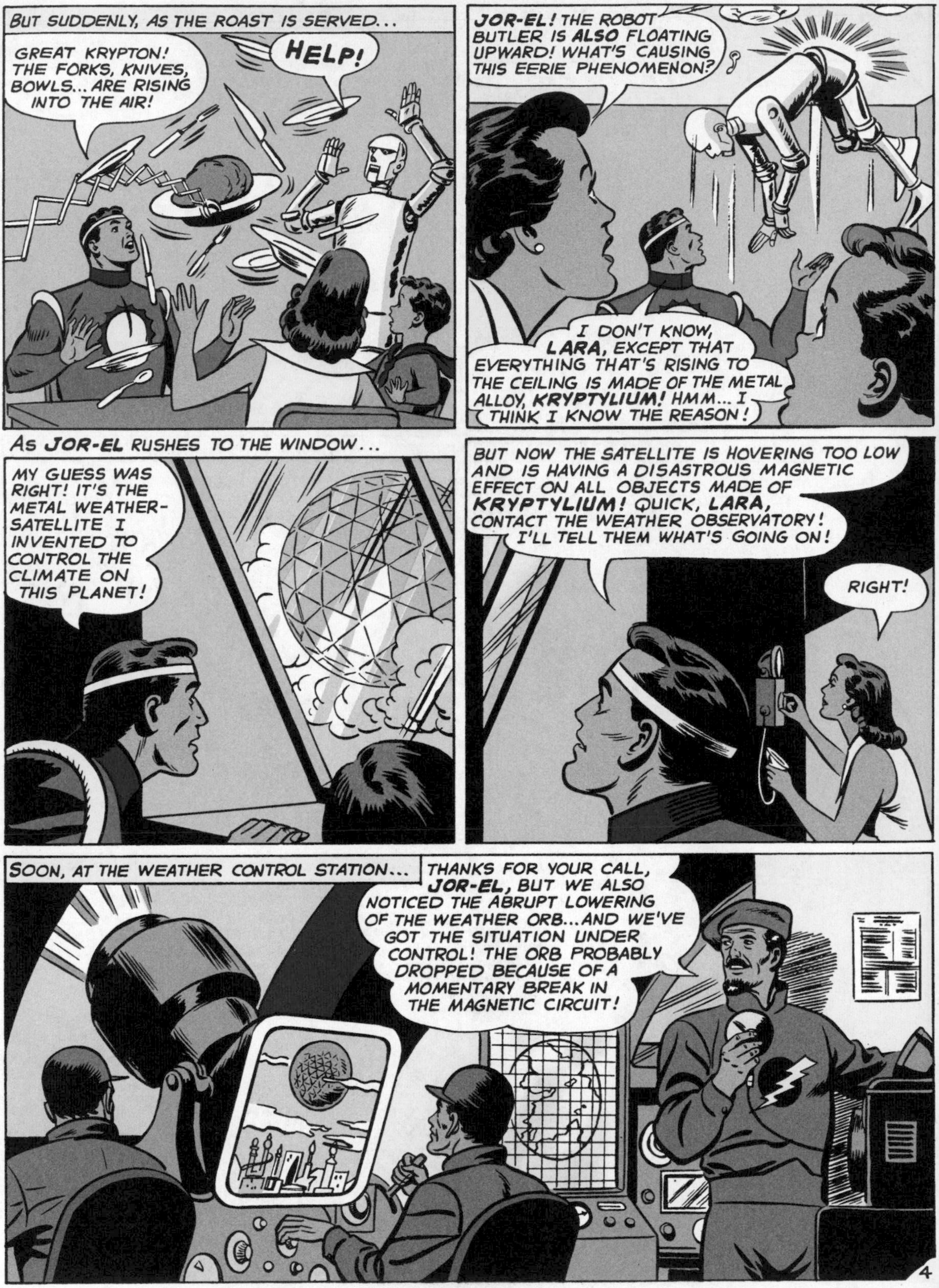

BUT SUDDENLY, AS THE ROAST IS SERVED...
GREAT KRYPTON! THE FORKS, KNIVES, BOWLS... ARE RISING INTO THE AIR!
HELP!
JOR-EL! THE ROBOT BUTLER IS ALSO FLOATING UPWARD! WHAT'S CAUSING THIS EERIE PHENOMENON?
I DON'T KNOW, LARA, EXCEPT THAT EVERYTHING THAT'S RISING TO THE CEILING IS MADE OF THE METAL ALLOY, KRYPTYLIUM! HMM... I THINK I KNOW THE REASON!
AS JOR-EL RUSHES TO THE WINDOW...
MY GUESS WAS RIGHT! IT'S THE METAL WEATHER-SATELLITE I INVENTED TO CONTROL THE CLIMATE ON THIS PLANET!
BUT NOW THE SATELLITE IS HOVERING TOO LOW AND IS HAVING A DISASTROUS MAGNETIC EFFECT ON ALL OBJECTS MADE OF KRYPTYLIUM! QUICK, LARA, CONTACT THE WEATHER OBSERVATORY! I'LL TELL THEM WHAT'S GOING ON!
RIGHT!
SOON, AT THE WEATHER CONTROL STATION...
THANKS FOR YOUR CALL, JOR-EL, BUT WE ALSO NOTICED THE ABRUPT LOWERING OF THE WEATHER ORB...AND WE'VE GOT THE SITUATION UNDER CONTROL! THE ORB PROBABLY DROPPED BECAUSE OF A MOMENTARY BREAK IN THE MAGNETIC CIRCUIT!
4

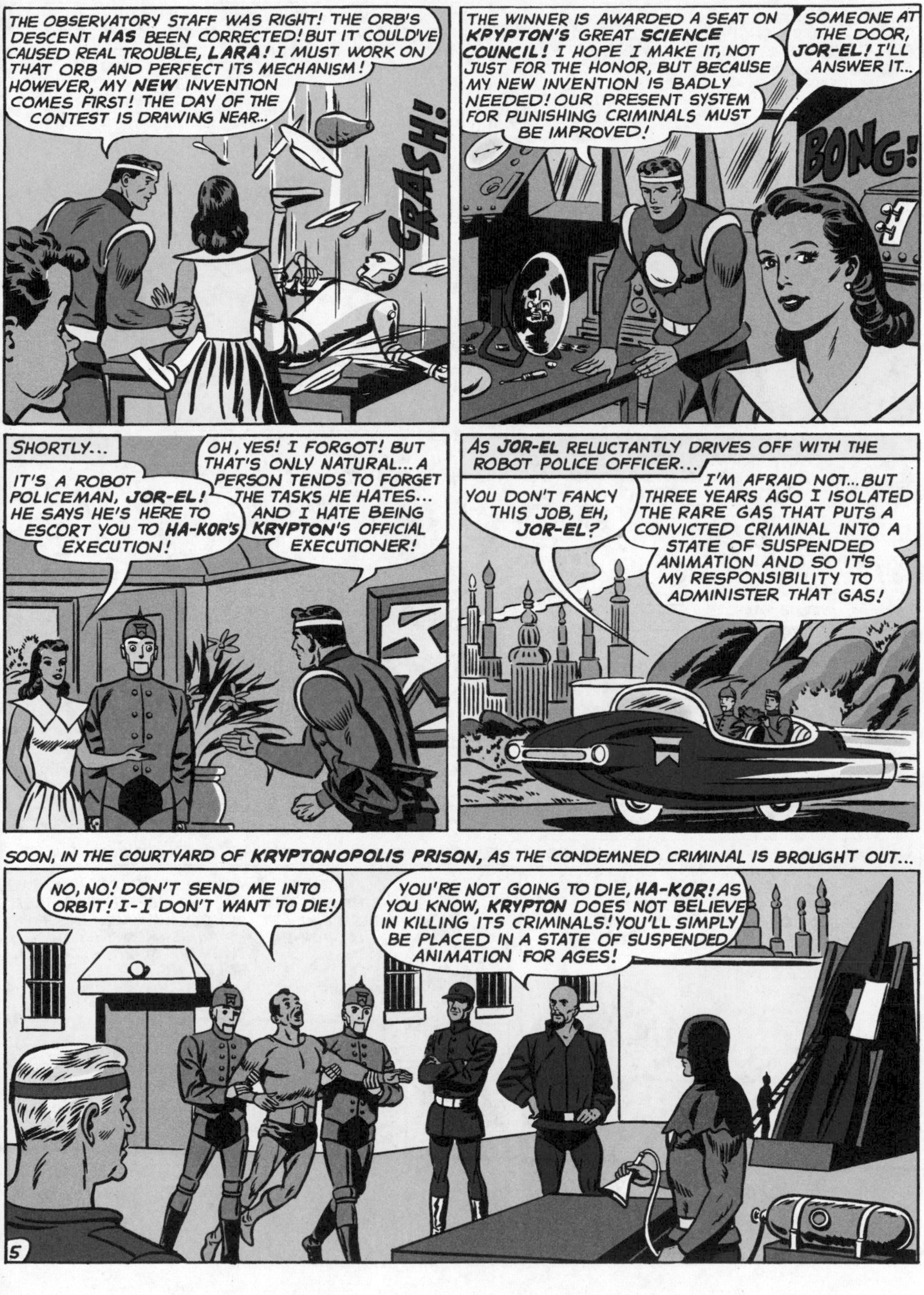
THE OBSERVATORY STAFF WAS RIGHT! THE ORB'S DESCENT HAS BEEN CORRECTED! BUT IT COULD'VE CAUSED REAL TROUBLE, LARA! I MUST WORK ON THAT ORB AND PERFECT ITS MECHANISM! HOWEVER, MY NEW INVENTION COMES FIRST! THE DAY OF THE CONTEST IS DRAWING NEAR...
CRASH!
THE WINNER IS AWARDED A SEAT ON KRYPTON'S GREAT SCIENCE COUNCIL! I HOPE I MAKE IT, NOT JUST FOR THE HONOR, BUT BECAUSE MY NEW INVENTION IS BADLY NEEDED! OUR PRESENT SYSTEM FOR PUNISHING CRIMINALS MUST BE IMPROVED!
SOMEONE AT THE DOOR, JOR-EL! I'LL ANSWER IT...
BONG!
SHORTLY...
IT'S A ROBOT POLICEMAN, JOR-EL! HE SAYS HE'S HERE TO ESCORT YOU TO HA-KOR'S EXECUTION!
OH, YES! I FORGOT! BUT THAT'S ONLY NATURAL... A PERSON TENDS TO FORGET THE TASKS HE HATES... AND I HATE BEING KRYPTON'S OFFICIAL EXECUTIONER!
AS JOR-EL RELUCTANTLY DRIVES OFF WITH THE ROBOT POLICE OFFICER...
YOU DON'T FANCY THIS JOB, EH, JOR-EL?
I'M AFRAID NOT... BUT THREE YEARS AGO I ISOLATED THE RARE GAS THAT PUTS A CONVICTED CRIMINAL INTO A STATE OF SUSPENDED ANIMATION AND SO IT'S MY RESPONSIBILITY TO ADMINISTER THAT GAS!
SOON, IN THE COURTYARD OF KRYPTONOPOLIS PRISON, AS THE CONDEMNED CRIMINAL IS BROUGHT OUT...
NO, NO! DON'T SEND ME INTO ORBIT! I-I DON'T WANT TO DIE!
YOU'RE NOT GOING TO DIE, HA-KOR! AS YOU KNOW, KRYPTON DOES NOT BELIEVE IN KILLING ITS CRIMINALS! YOU'LL SIMPLY BE PLACED IN A STATE OF SUSPENDED ANIMATION FOR AGES!
5

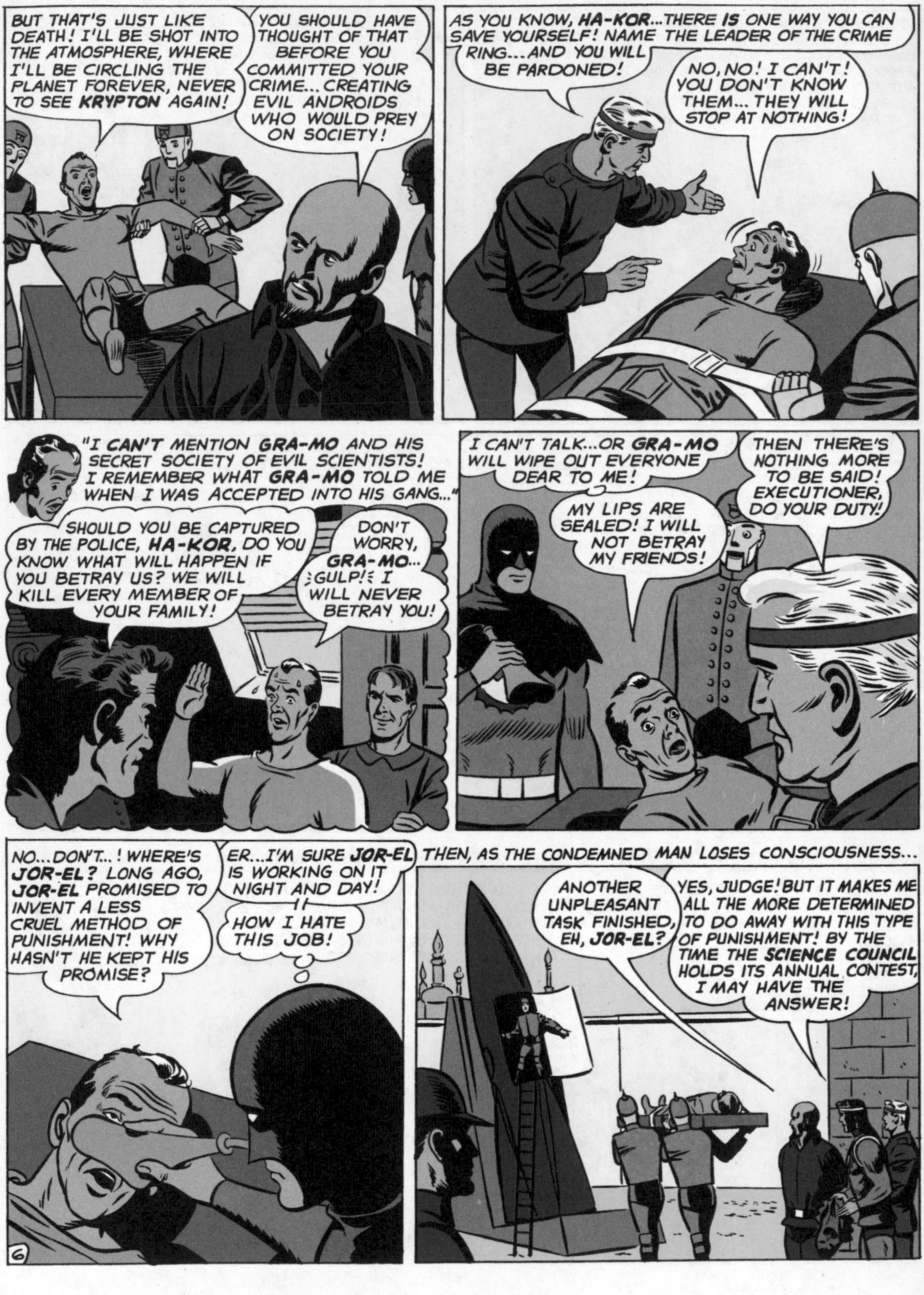

BUT THAT'S JUST LIKE DEATH! I'LL BE SHOT INTO THE ATMOSPHERE, WHERE I'LL BE CIRCLING THE PLANET FOREVER, NEVER TO SEE KRYPTON AGAIN!
YOU SHOULD HAVE THOUGHT OF THAT BEFORE YOU COMMITTED YOUR CRIME... CREATING EVIL ANDROIDS WHO WOULD PREY ON SOCIETY!
AS YOU KNOW, HA-KOR... THERE IS ONE WAY YOU CAN SAVE YOURSELF! NAME THE LEADER OF THE CRIME RING... AND YOU WILL BE PARDONED!
NO, NO! I CAN'T! YOU DON'T KNOW THEM... THEY WILL STOP AT NOTHING!
"I CAN'T MENTION GRA-MO AND HIS SECRET SOCIETY OF EVIL SCIENTISTS! I REMEMBER WHAT GRA-MO TOLD ME WHEN I WAS ACCEPTED INTO HIS GANG..."
SHOULD YOU BE CAPTURED BY THE POLICE, HA-KOR, DO YOU KNOW WHAT WILL HAPPEN IF YOU BETRAY US? WE WILL KILL EVERY MEMBER OF YOUR FAMILY!
DON'T WORRY, GRA-MO... GULP! I WILL NEVER BETRAY YOU!
I CAN'T TALK... OR GRA-MO WILL WIPE OUT EVERYONE DEAR TO ME!
MY LIPS ARE SEALED! I WILL NOT BETRAY MY FRIENDS!
THEN THERE'S NOTHING MORE TO BE SAID! EXECUTIONER, DO YOUR DUTY!
NO... DON'T...! WHERE'S JOR-EL? LONG AGO, JOR-EL PROMISED TO INVENT A LESS CRUEL METHOD OF PUNISHMENT! WHY HASN'T HE KEPT HIS PROMISE?
ER... I'M SURE JOR-EL IS WORKING ON IT NIGHT AND DAY!
HOW I HATE THIS JOB!
6
THEN, AS THE CONDEMNED MAN LOSES CONSCIOUSNESS...
ANOTHER UNPLEASANT TASK FINISHED, EH, JOR-EL?
YES, JUDGE! BUT IT MAKES ME ALL THE MORE DETERMINED TO DO AWAY WITH THIS TYPE OF PUNISHMENT! BY THE TIME THE SCIENCE COUNCIL HOLDS ITS ANNUAL CONTEST, I MAY HAVE THE ANSWER!

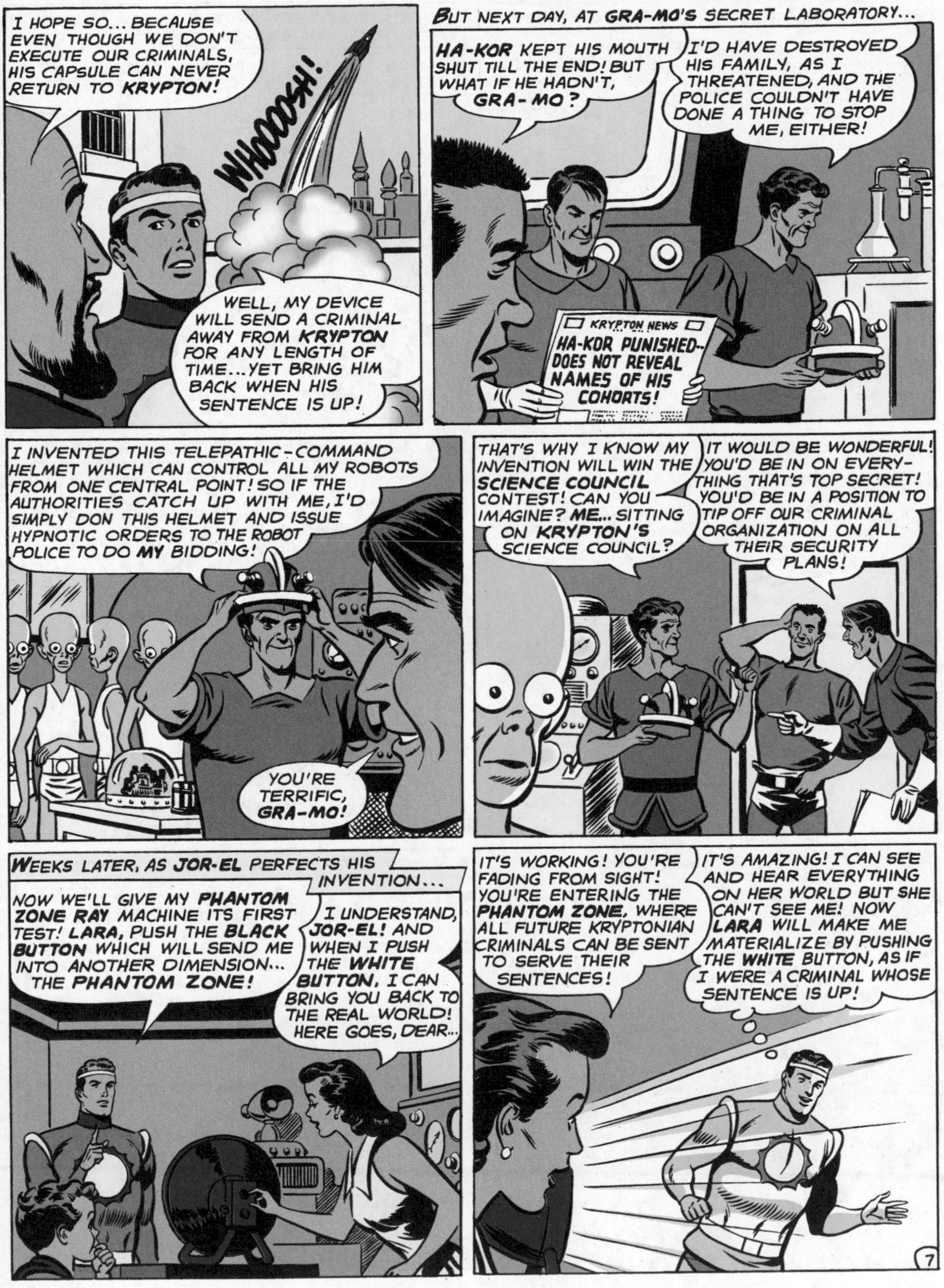
I HOPE SO... BECAUSE EVEN THOUGH WE DON'T EXECUTE OUR CRIMINALS, HIS CAPSULE CAN NEVER RETURN TO KRYPTON!
WHOOOOSH!
WELL, MY DEVICE WILL SEND A CRIMINAL AWAY FROM KRYPTON FOR ANY LENGTH OF TIME...YET BRING HIM BACK WHEN HIS SENTENCE IS UP!
BUT NEXT DAY, AT GRA-MO'S SECRET LABORATORY...
HA-KOR KEPT HIS MOUTH SHUT TILL THE END! BUT WHAT IF HE HADN'T, GRA-MO?
I'D HAVE DESTROYED HIS FAMILY, AS I THREATENED, AND THE POLICE COULDN'T HAVE DONE A THING TO STOP ME, EITHER!
KRYPTON NEWS
HA-KOR PUNISHED-- DOES NOT REVEAL NAMES OF HIS COHORTS!
I INVENTED THIS TELEPATHIC-COMMAND HELMET WHICH CAN CONTROL ALL MY ROBOTS FROM ONE CENTRAL POINT! SO IF THE AUTHORITIES CATCH UP WITH ME, I'D SIMPLY DON THIS HELMET AND ISSUE HYPNOTIC ORDERS TO THE ROBOT POLICE TO DO MY BIDDING!
YOU'RE TERRIFIC, GRA-MO!
THAT'S WHY I KNOW MY INVENTION WILL WIN THE SCIENCE COUNCIL CONTEST! CAN YOU IMAGINE? ME... SITTING ON KRYPTON'S SCIENCE COUNCIL?
IT WOULD BE WONDERFUL! YOU'D BE IN ON EVERYTHING THAT'S TOP SECRET! YOU'D BE IN A POSITION TO TIP OFF OUR CRIMINAL ORGANIZATION ON ALL THEIR SECURITY PLANS!
WEEKS LATER, AS JOR-EL PERFECTS HIS INVENTION...
NOW WE'LL GIVE MY PHANTOM ZONE RAY MACHINE ITS FIRST TEST! LARA, PUSH THE BLACK BUTTON WHICH WILL SEND ME INTO ANOTHER DIMENSION... THE PHANTOM ZONE!
I UNDERSTAND, JOR-EL! AND WHEN I PUSH THE WHITE BUTTON, I CAN BRING YOU BACK TO THE REAL WORLD! HERE GOES, DEAR...
IT'S WORKING! YOU'RE FADING FROM SIGHT! YOU'RE ENTERING THE PHANTOM ZONE, WHERE ALL FUTURE KRYPTONIAN CRIMINALS CAN BE SENT TO SERVE THEIR SENTENCES!
IT'S AMAZING! I CAN SEE AND HEAR EVERYTHING ON HER WORLD BUT SHE CAN'T SEE ME! NOW LARA WILL MAKE ME MATERIALIZE BY PUSHING THE WHITE BUTTON, AS IF I WERE A CRIMINAL WHOSE SENTENCE IS UP!
7

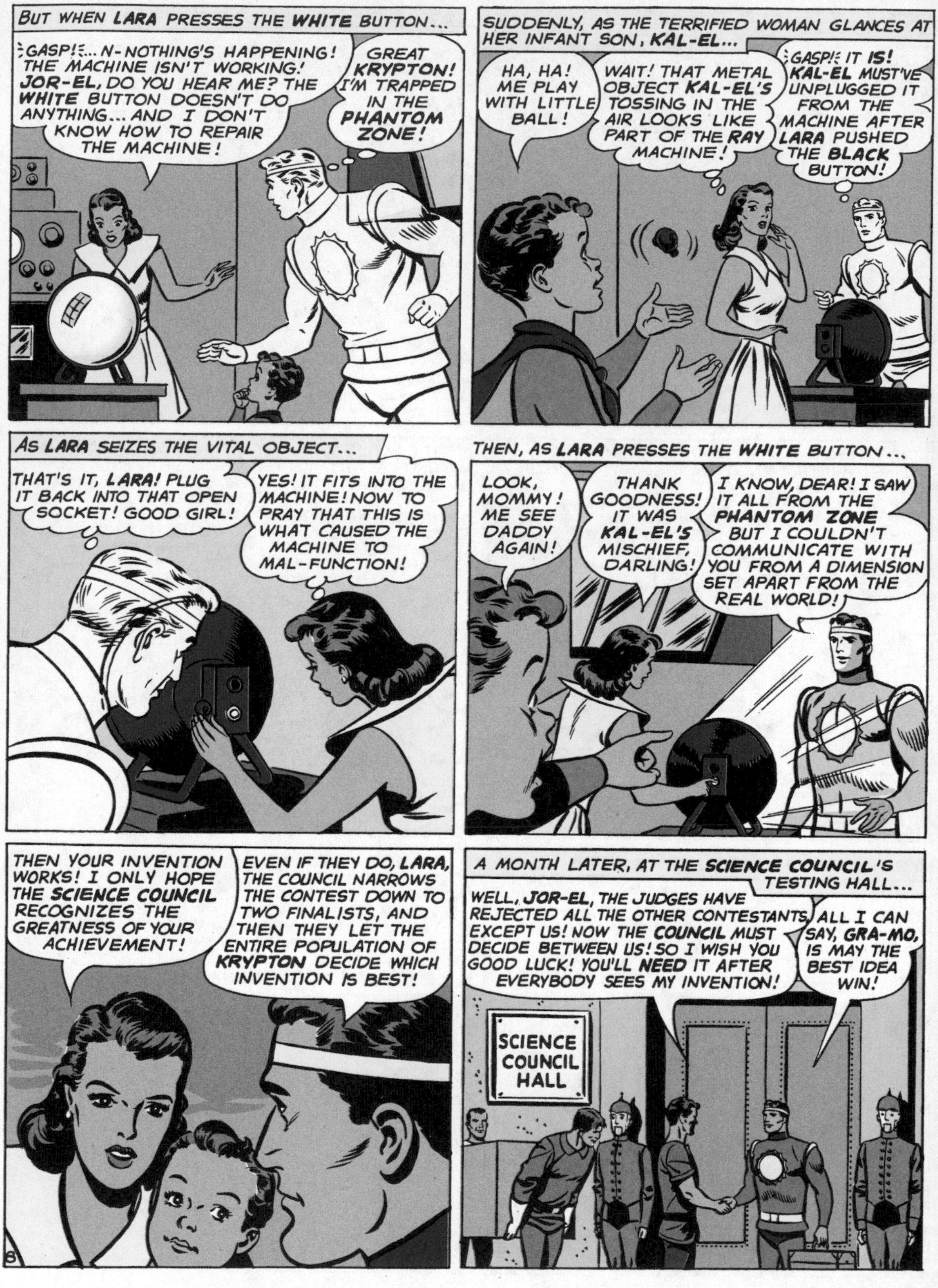
BUT WHEN LARA PRESSES THE WHITE BUTTON...
GASP! ...N-NOTHING'S HAPPENING! THE MACHINE ISN'T WORKING! JOR-EL, DO YOU HEAR ME? THE WHITE BUTTON DOESN'T DO ANYTHING... AND I DON'T KNOW HOW TO REPAIR THE MACHINE!
GREAT KRYPTON! I'M TRAPPED IN THE PHANTOM ZONE!
SUDDENLY, AS THE TERRIFIED WOMAN GLANCES AT HER INFANT SON, KAL-EL...
HA, HA! ME PLAY WITH LITTLE BALL!
WAIT! THAT METAL OBJECT KAL-EL'S TOSSING IN THE AIR LOOKS LIKE PART OF THE RAY MACHINE!
GASP! IT IS! KAL-EL MUST'VE UNPLUGGED IT FROM THE MACHINE AFTER LARA PUSHED THE BLACK BUTTON!
AS LARA SEIZES THE VITAL OBJECT...
THAT'S IT, LARA! PLUG IT BACK INTO THAT OPEN SOCKET! GOOD GIRL!
YES! IT FITS INTO THE MACHINE! NOW TO PRAY THAT THIS IS WHAT CAUSED THE MACHINE TO MAL-FUNCTION!
THEN, AS LARA PRESSES THE WHITE BUTTON...
LOOK, MOMMY! ME SEE DADDY AGAIN!
THANK GOODNESS! IT WAS KAL-EL'S MISCHIEF, DARLING!
I KNOW, DEAR! I SAW IT ALL FROM THE PHANTOM ZONE BUT I COULDN'T COMMUNICATE WITH YOU FROM A DIMENSION SET APART FROM THE REAL WORLD!
THEN YOUR INVENTION WORKS! I ONLY HOPE THE SCIENCE COUNCIL RECOGNIZES THE GREATNESS OF YOUR ACHIEVEMENT!
EVEN IF THEY DO, LARA, THE COUNCIL NARROWS THE CONTEST DOWN TO TWO FINALISTS, AND THEN THEY LET THE ENTIRE POPULATION OF KRYPTON DECIDE WHICH INVENTION IS BEST!
8
A MONTH LATER, AT THE SCIENCE COUNCIL'S TESTING HALL...
WELL, JOR-EL, THE JUDGES HAVE REJECTED ALL THE OTHER CONTESTANTS, EXCEPT US! NOW THE COUNCIL MUST DECIDE BETWEEN US! SO I WISH YOU GOOD LUCK! YOU'LL NEED IT AFTER EVERYBODY SEES MY INVENTION!
ALL I CAN SAY, GRA-MO, IS MAY THE BEST IDEA WIN!
SCIENCE COUNCIL HALL

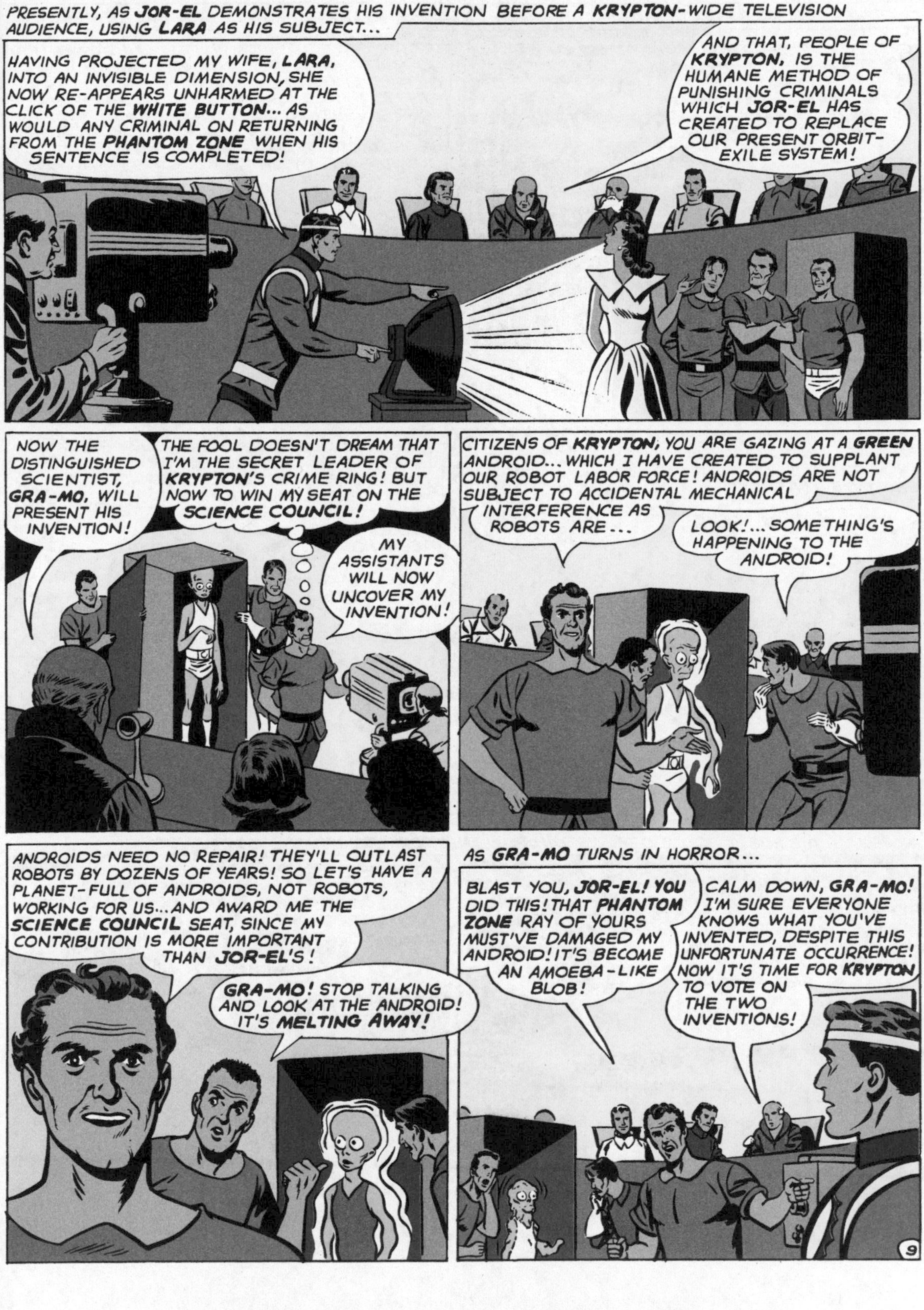
PRESENTLY, AS JOR-EL DEMONSTRATES HIS INVENTION BEFORE A KRYPTON-WIDE TELEVISION AUDIENCE, USING LARA AS HIS SUBJECT...
HAVING PROJECTED MY WIFE, LARA, INTO AN INVISIBLE DIMENSION, SHE NOW RE-APPEARS UNHARMED AT THE CLICK OF THE WHITE BUTTON... AS WOULD ANY CRIMINAL ON RETURNING FROM THE PHANTOM ZONE WHEN HIS SENTENCE IS COMPLETED!
AND THAT, PEOPLE OF KRYPTON, IS THE HUMANE METHOD OF PUNISHING CRIMINALS WHICH JOR-EL HAS CREATED TO REPLACE OUR PRESENT ORBIT-EXILE SYSTEM!
NOW THE DISTINGUISHED SCIENTIST, GRA-MO, WILL PRESENT HIS INVENTION!
THE FOOL DOESN'T DREAM THAT I'M THE SECRET LEADER OF KRYPTON'S CRIME RING! BUT NOW TO WIN MY SEAT ON THE SCIENCE COUNCIL!
MY ASSISTANTS WILL NOW UNCOVER MY INVENTION!
CITIZENS OF KRYPTON, YOU ARE GAZING AT A GREEN ANDROID... WHICH I HAVE CREATED TO SUPPLANT OUR ROBOT LABOR FORCE! ANDROIDS ARE NOT SUBJECT TO ACCIDENTAL MECHANICAL INTERFERENCE AS ROBOTS ARE...
LOOK!... SOMETHING'S HAPPENING TO THE ANDROID!
ANDROIDS NEED NO REPAIR! THEY'LL OUTLAST ROBOTS BY DOZENS OF YEARS! SO LET'S HAVE A PLANET-FULL OF ANDROIDS, NOT ROBOTS, WORKING FOR US... AND AWARD ME THE SCIENCE COUNCIL SEAT, SINCE MY CONTRIBUTION IS MORE IMPORTANT THAN JOR-EL'S!
GRA-MO! STOP TALKING AND LOOK AT THE ANDROID! IT'S MELTING AWAY!
AS GRA-MO TURNS IN HORROR...
BLAST YOU, JOR-EL! YOU DID THIS! THAT PHANTOM ZONE RAY OF YOURS MUST'VE DAMAGED MY ANDROID! IT'S BECOME AN AMOEBA-LIKE BLOB!
CALM DOWN, GRA-MO! I'M SURE EVERYONE KNOWS WHAT YOU'VE INVENTED, DESPITE THIS UNFORTUNATE OCCURRENCE! NOW IT'S TIME FOR KRYPTON TO VOTE ON THE TWO INVENTIONS!
9

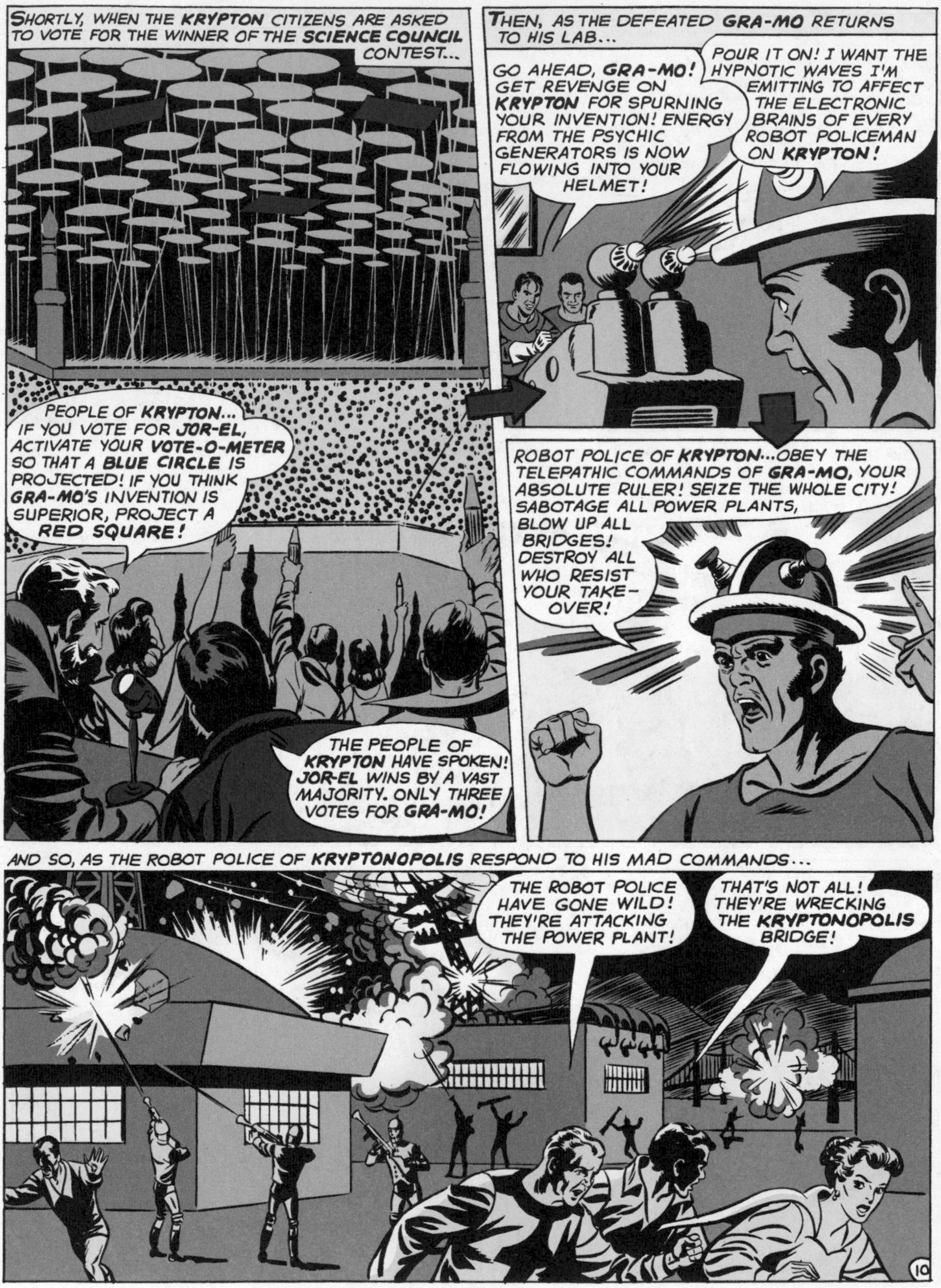
SHORTLY, WHEN THE KRYPTON CITIZENS ARE ASKED TO VOTE FOR THE WINNER OF THE SCIENCE COUNCIL CONTEST...
PEOPLE OF KRYPTON... IF YOU VOTE FOR JOR-EL, ACTIVATE YOUR VOTE-O-METER SO THAT A BLUE CIRCLE IS PROJECTED! IF YOU THINK GRA-MO'S INVENTION IS SUPERIOR, PROJECT A RED SQUARE!
THE PEOPLE OF KRYPTON HAVE SPOKEN! JOR-EL WINS BY A VAST MAJORITY. ONLY THREE VOTES FOR GRA-MO!
THEN, AS THE DEFEATED GRA-MO RETURNS TO HIS LAB...
GO AHEAD, GRA-MO! GET REVENGE ON KRYPTON FOR SPURNING YOUR INVENTION! ENERGY FROM THE PSYCHIC GENERATORS IS NOW FLOWING INTO YOUR HELMET!
POUR IT ON! I WANT THE HYPNOTIC WAVES I'M EMITTING TO AFFECT THE ELECTRONIC BRAINS OF EVERY ROBOT POLICEMAN ON KRYPTON!
ROBOT POLICE OF KRYPTON...OBEY THE TELEPATHIC COMMANDS OF GRA-MO, YOUR ABSOLUTE RULER! SEIZE THE WHOLE CITY! SABOTAGE ALL POWER PLANTS, BLOW UP ALL BRIDGES! DESTROY ALL WHO RESIST YOUR TAKE-OVER!
AND SO, AS THE ROBOT POLICE OF KRYPTONOPOLIS RESPOND TO HIS MAD COMMANDS...
THE ROBOT POLICE HAVE GONE WILD! THEY'RE ATTACKING THE POWER PLANT!
THAT'S NOT ALL! THEY'RE WRECKING THE KRYPTONOPOLIS BRIDGE!
10

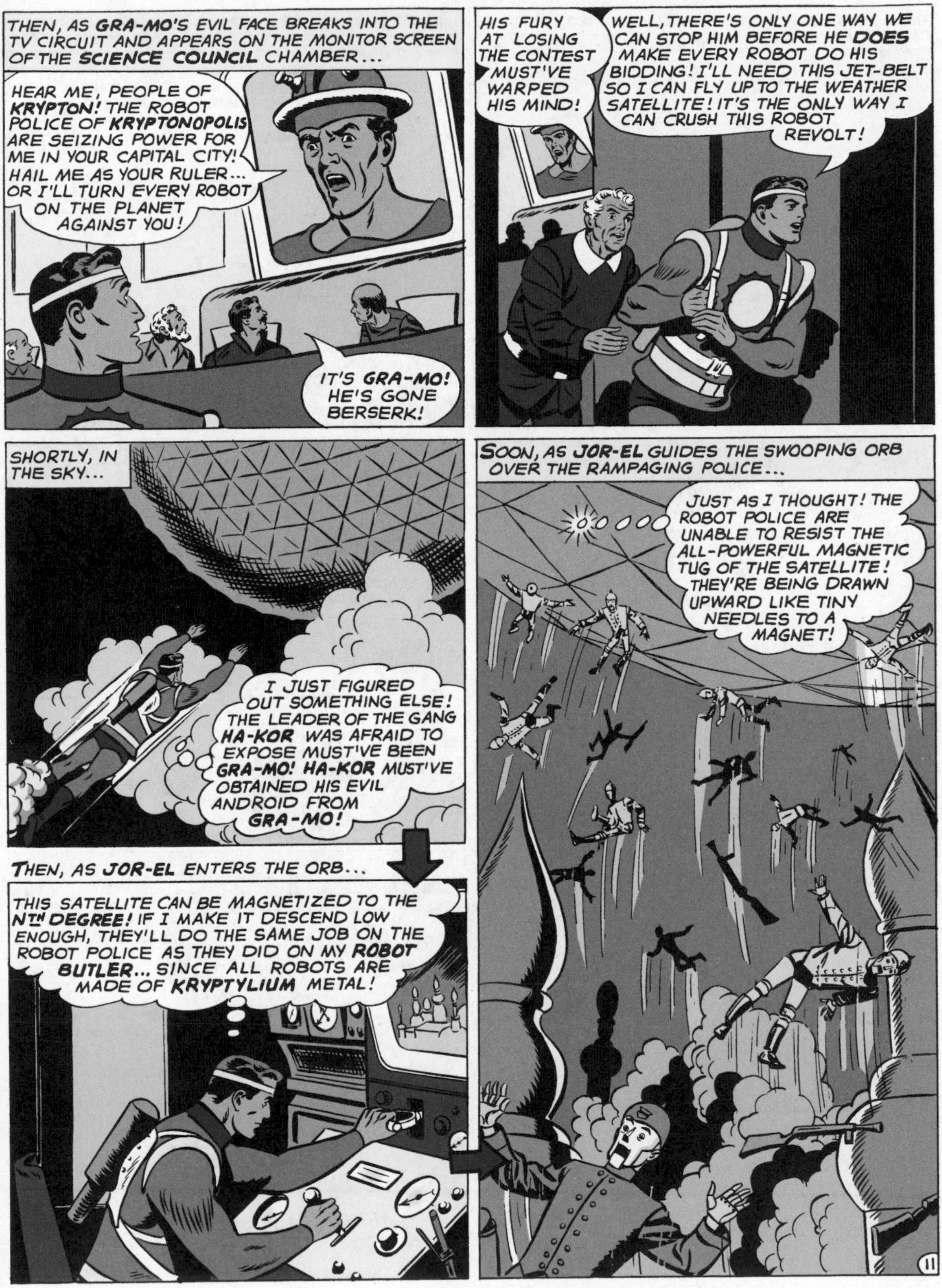

THEN, AS GRA-MO'S EVIL FACE BREAKS INTO THE TV CIRCUIT AND APPEARS ON THE MONITOR SCREEN OF THE SCIENCE COUNCIL CHAMBER...
HEAR ME, PEOPLE OF KRYPTON! THE ROBOT POLICE OF KRYPTONOPOLIS ARE SEIZING POWER FOR ME IN YOUR CAPITAL CITY! HAIL ME AS YOUR RULER... OR I'LL TURN EVERY ROBOT ON THE PLANET AGAINST YOU!
IT'S GRA-MO! HE'S GONE BERSERK!
HIS FURY AT LOSING THE CONTEST MUST'VE WARPED HIS MIND!
WELL, THERE'S ONLY ONE WAY WE CAN STOP HIM BEFORE HE DOES MAKE EVERY ROBOT DO HIS BIDDING! I'LL NEED THIS JET-BELT SO I CAN FLY UP TO THE WEATHER SATELLITE! IT'S THE ONLY WAY I CAN CRUSH THIS ROBOT REVOLT!
SHORTLY, IN THE SKY...
I JUST FIGURED OUT SOMETHING ELSE! THE LEADER OF THE GANG HA-KOR WAS AFRAID TO EXPOSE MUST'VE BEEN GRA-MO! HA-KOR MUST'VE OBTAINED HIS EVIL ANDROID FROM GRA-MO!
THEN, AS JOR-EL ENTERS THE ORB...
THIS SATELLITE CAN BE MAGNETIZED TO THE NTH DEGREE! IF I MAKE IT DESCEND LOW ENOUGH, THEY'LL DO THE SAME JOB ON THE ROBOT POLICE AS THEY DID ON MY ROBOT BUTLER... SINCE ALL ROBOTS ARE MADE OF KRYPTYLIUM METAL!
SOON, AS JOR-EL GUIDES THE SWOOPING ORB OVER THE RAMPAGING POLICE...
JUST AS I THOUGHT! THE ROBOT POLICE ARE UNABLE TO RESIST THE ALL-POWERFUL MAGNETIC TUG OF THE SATELLITE! THEY'RE BEING DRAWN UPWARD LIKE TINY NEEDLES TO A MAGNET!
11

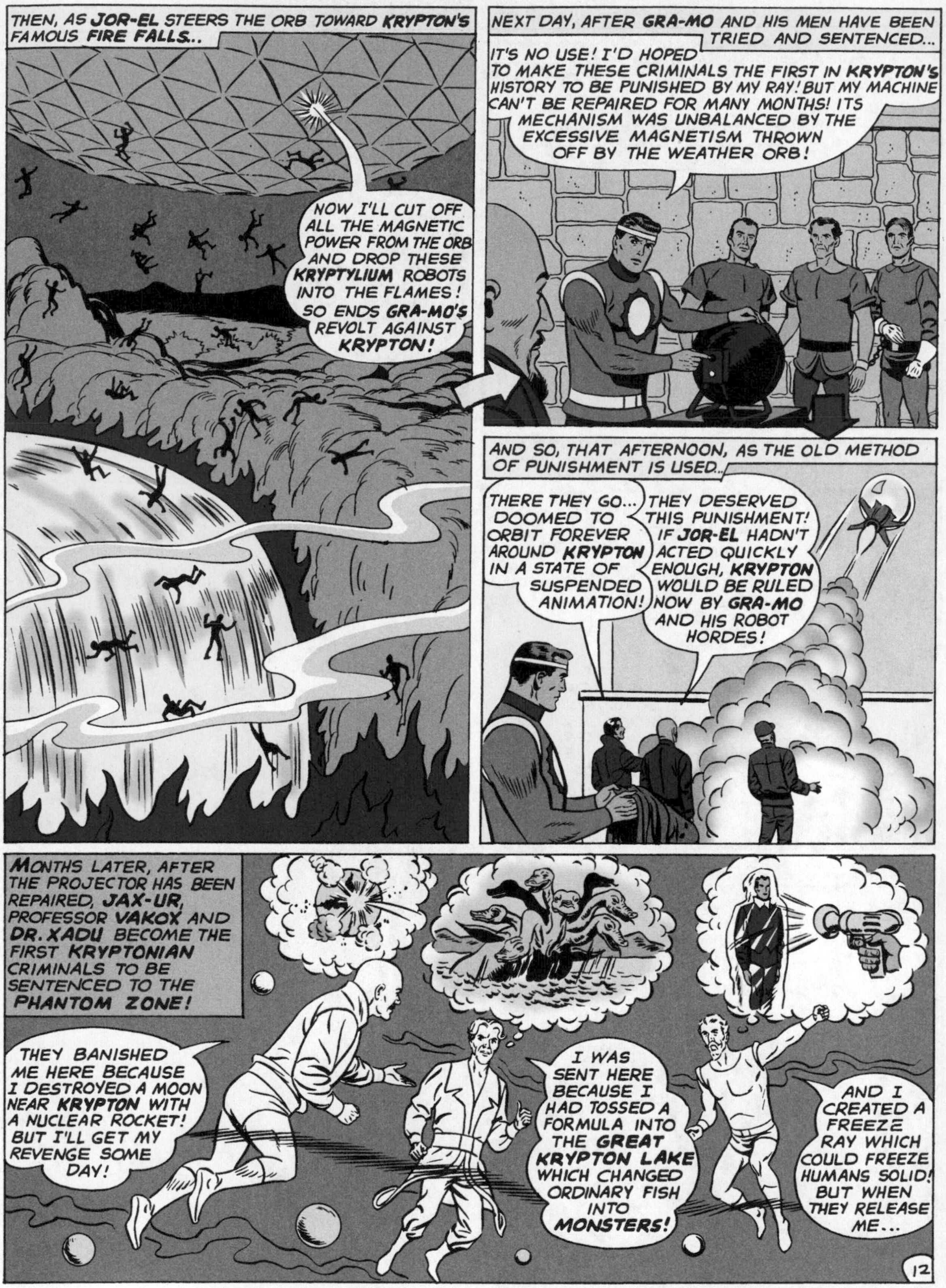
THEN, AS JOR-EL STEERS THE ORB TOWARD KRYPTON'S FAMOUS FIRE FALLS..
NOW I'LL CUT OFF ALL THE MAGNETIC POWER FROM THE ORB AND DROP THESE KRYPTYLIUM ROBOTS INTO THE FLAMES! SO ENDS GRA-MO'S REVOLT AGAINST KRYPTON!
NEXT DAY, AFTER GRA-MO AND HIS MEN HAVE BEEN TRIED AND SENTENCED...
IT'S NO USE! I'D HOPED TO MAKE THESE CRIMINALS THE FIRST IN KRYPTON'S HISTORY TO BE PUNISHED BY MY RAY! BUT MY MACHINE CAN'T BE REPAIRED FOR MANY MONTHS! ITS MECHANISM WAS UNBALANCED BY THE EXCESSIVE MAGNETISM THROWN OFF BY THE WEATHER ORB!
AND SO, THAT AFTERNOON, AS THE OLD METHOD OF PUNISHMENT IS USED...
THERE THEY GO... DOOMED TO ORBIT FOREVER AROUND KRYPTON IN A STATE OF SUSPENDED ANIMATION!
THEY DESERVED THIS PUNISHMENT! IF JOR-EL HADN'T ACTED QUICKLY ENOUGH, KRYPTON WOULD BE RULED NOW BY GRA-MO AND HIS ROBOT HORDES!
MONTHS LATER, AFTER THE PROJECTOR HAS BEEN REPAIRED, JAX-UR, PROFESSOR VAKOX AND DR. XADU BECOME THE FIRST KRYPTONIAN CRIMINALS TO BE SENTENCED TO THE PHANTOM ZONE!
THEY BANISHED ME HERE BECAUSE I DESTROYED A MOON NEAR KRYPTON WITH A NUCLEAR ROCKET! BUT I'LL GET MY REVENGE SOME DAY!
I WAS SENT HERE BECAUSE I HAD TOSSED A FORMULA INTO THE GREAT KRYPTON LAKE WHICH CHANGED ORDINARY FISH INTO MONSTERS!
AND I CREATED A FREEZE RAY WHICH COULD FREEZE HUMANS SOLID! BUT WHEN THEY RELEASE ME...
12

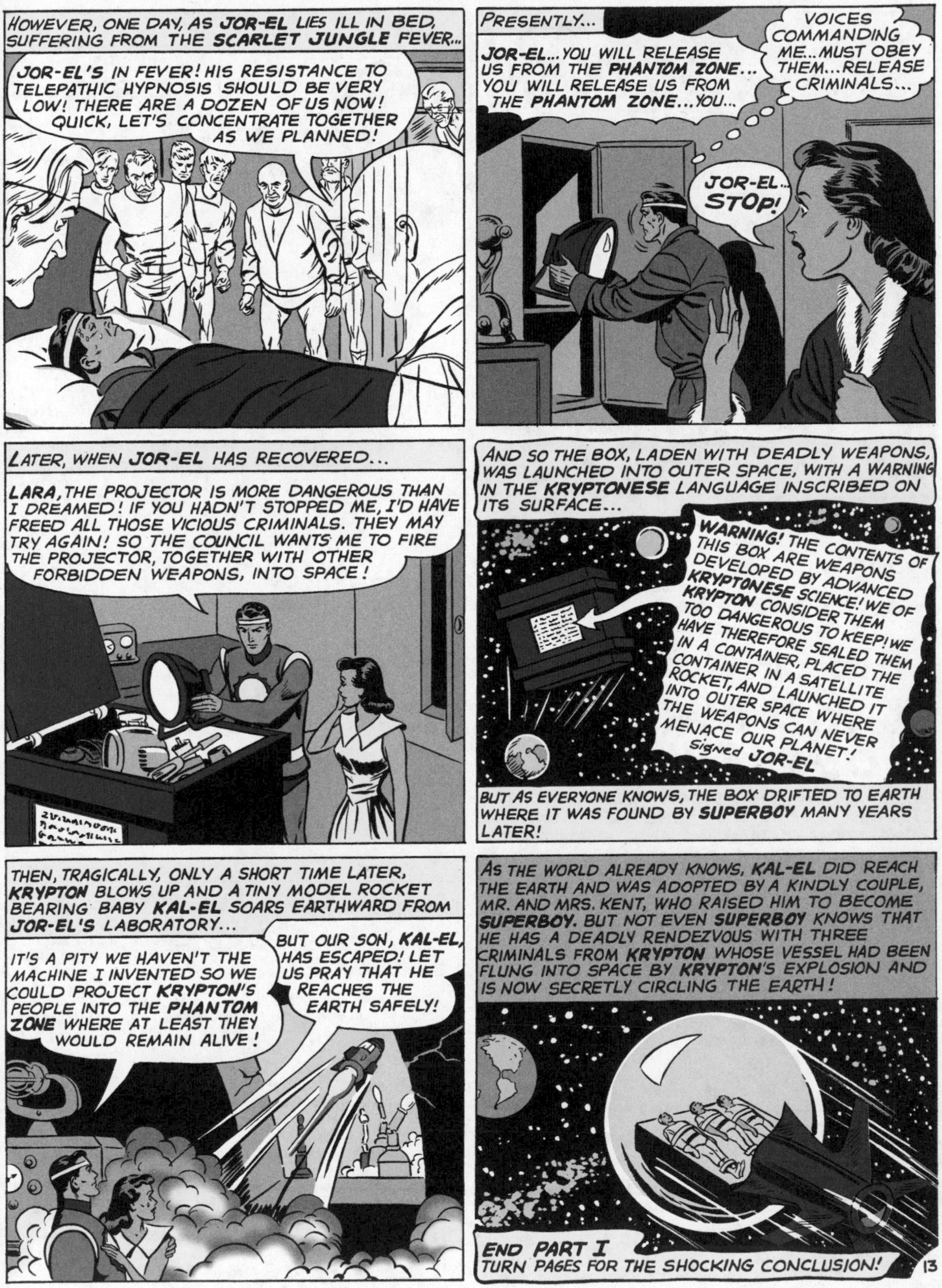
HOWEVER, ONE DAY, AS JOR-EL LIES ILL IN BED, SUFFERING FROM THE SCARLET JUNGLE FEVER...
JOR-EL'S IN FEVER! HIS RESISTANCE TO TELEPATHIC HYPNOSIS SHOULD BE VERY LOW! THERE ARE A DOZEN OF US NOW! QUICK, LET'S CONCENTRATE TOGETHER AS WE PLANNED!
PRESENTLY...
JOR-EL... YOU WILL RELEASE US FROM THE PHANTOM ZONE... YOU WILL RELEASE US FROM THE PHANTOM ZONE... YOU...
VOICES COMMANDING ME... MUST OBEY THEM... RELEASE CRIMINALS...
JOR-EL... STOP!
LATER, WHEN JOR-EL HAS RECOVERED...
LARA, THE PROJECTOR IS MORE DANGEROUS THAN I DREAMED! IF YOU HADN'T STOPPED ME, I'D HAVE FREED ALL THOSE VICIOUS CRIMINALS. THEY MAY TRY AGAIN! SO THE COUNCIL WANTS ME TO FIRE THE PROJECTOR, TOGETHER WITH OTHER FORBIDDEN WEAPONS, INTO SPACE!
AND SO THE BOX, LADEN WITH DEADLY WEAPONS, WAS LAUNCHED INTO OUTER SPACE, WITH A WARNING IN THE KRYPTONESE LANGUAGE INSCRIBED ON ITS SURFACE...
WARNING! THE CONTENTS OF THIS BOX ARE WEAPONS DEVELOPED BY ADVANCED KRYPTONESE SCIENCE! WE OF KRYPTON CONSIDER THEM TOO DANGEROUS TO KEEP! WE HAVE THEREFORE SEALED THEM IN A CONTAINER, PLACED THE CONTAINER IN A SATELLITE ROCKET, AND LAUNCHED IT INTO OUTER SPACE WHERE THE WEAPONS CAN NEVER MENACE OUR PLANET! Signed JOR-EL
BUT AS EVERYONE KNOWS, THE BOX DRIFTED TO EARTH WHERE IT WAS FOUND BY SUPERBOY MANY YEARS LATER!
THEN, TRAGICALLY, ONLY A SHORT TIME LATER, KRYPTON BLOWS UP AND A TINY MODEL ROCKET BEARING BABY KAL-EL SOARS EARTHWARD FROM JOR-EL'S LABORATORY...
IT'S A PITY WE HAVEN'T THE MACHINE I INVENTED SO WE COULD PROJECT KRYPTON'S PEOPLE INTO THE PHANTOM ZONE WHERE AT LEAST THEY WOULD REMAIN ALIVE!
BUT OUR SON, KAL-EL, HAS ESCAPED! LET US PRAY THAT HE REACHES THE EARTH SAFELY!
AS THE WORLD ALREADY KNOWS, KAL-EL DID REACH THE EARTH AND WAS ADOPTED BY A KINDLY COUPLE, MR. AND MRS. KENT, WHO RAISED HIM TO BECOME SUPERBOY. BUT NOT EVEN SUPERBOY KNOWS THAT HE HAS A DEADLY RENDEZVOUS WITH THREE CRIMINALS FROM KRYPTON WHOSE VESSEL HAD BEEN FLUNG INTO SPACE BY KRYPTON'S EXPLOSION AND IS NOW SECRETLY CIRCLING THE EARTH!
END PART I
TURN PAGES FOR THE SHOCKING CONCLUSION!
13

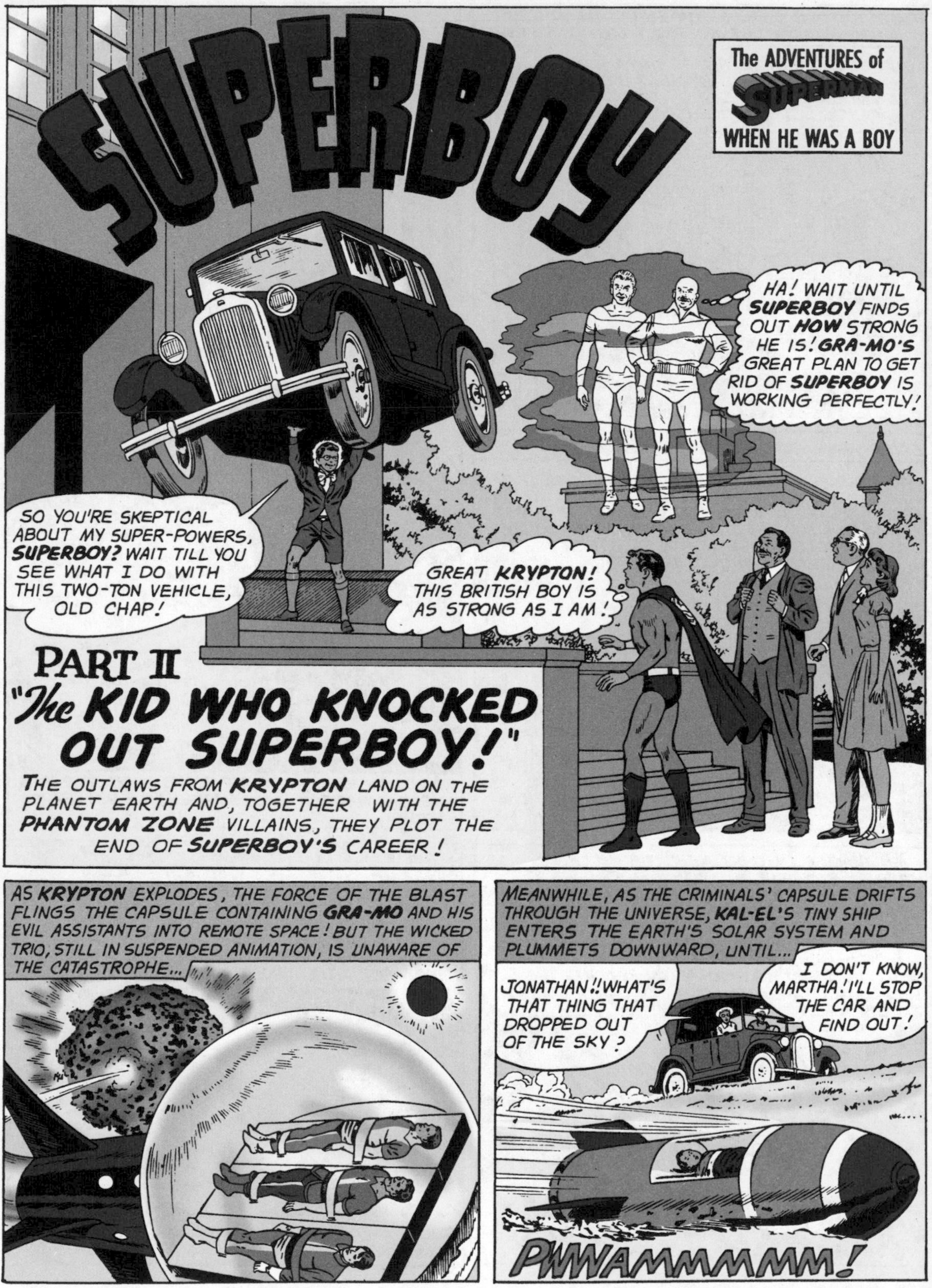
SUPERBOY
The ADVENTURES of SUPERMAN WHEN HE WAS A BOY
HA! WAIT UNTIL SUPERBOY FINDS OUT HOW STRONG HE IS! GRA-MO'S GREAT PLAN TO GET RID OF SUPERBOY IS WORKING PERFECTLY!
SO YOU'RE SKEPTICAL ABOUT MY SUPER-POWERS, SUPERBOY? WAIT TILL YOU SEE WHAT I DO WITH THIS TWO-TON VEHICLE, OLD CHAP!
GREAT KRYPTON! THIS BRITISH BOY IS AS STRONG AS I AM!
PART II
"The KID WHO KNOCKED OUT SUPERBOY!"
THE OUTLAWS FROM KRYPTON LAND ON THE PLANET EARTH AND, TOGETHER WITH THE PHANTOM ZONE VILLAINS, THEY PLOT THE END OF SUPERBOY'S CAREER!
AS KRYPTON EXPLODES, THE FORCE OF THE BLAST FLINGS THE CAPSULE CONTAINING GRA-MO AND HIS EVIL ASSISTANTS INTO REMOTE SPACE! BUT THE WICKED TRIO, STILL IN SUSPENDED ANIMATION, IS UNAWARE OF THE CATASTROPHE...
MEANWHILE, AS THE CRIMINALS' CAPSULE DRIFTS THROUGH THE UNIVERSE, KAL-EL'S TINY SHIP ENTERS THE EARTH'S SOLAR SYSTEM AND PLUMMETS DOWNWARD, UNTIL...
JONATHAN!! WHAT'S THAT THING THAT DROPPED OUT OF THE SKY?
I DON'T KNOW, MARTHA! I'LL STOP THE CAR AND FIND OUT!
PWWAMMMMMM!

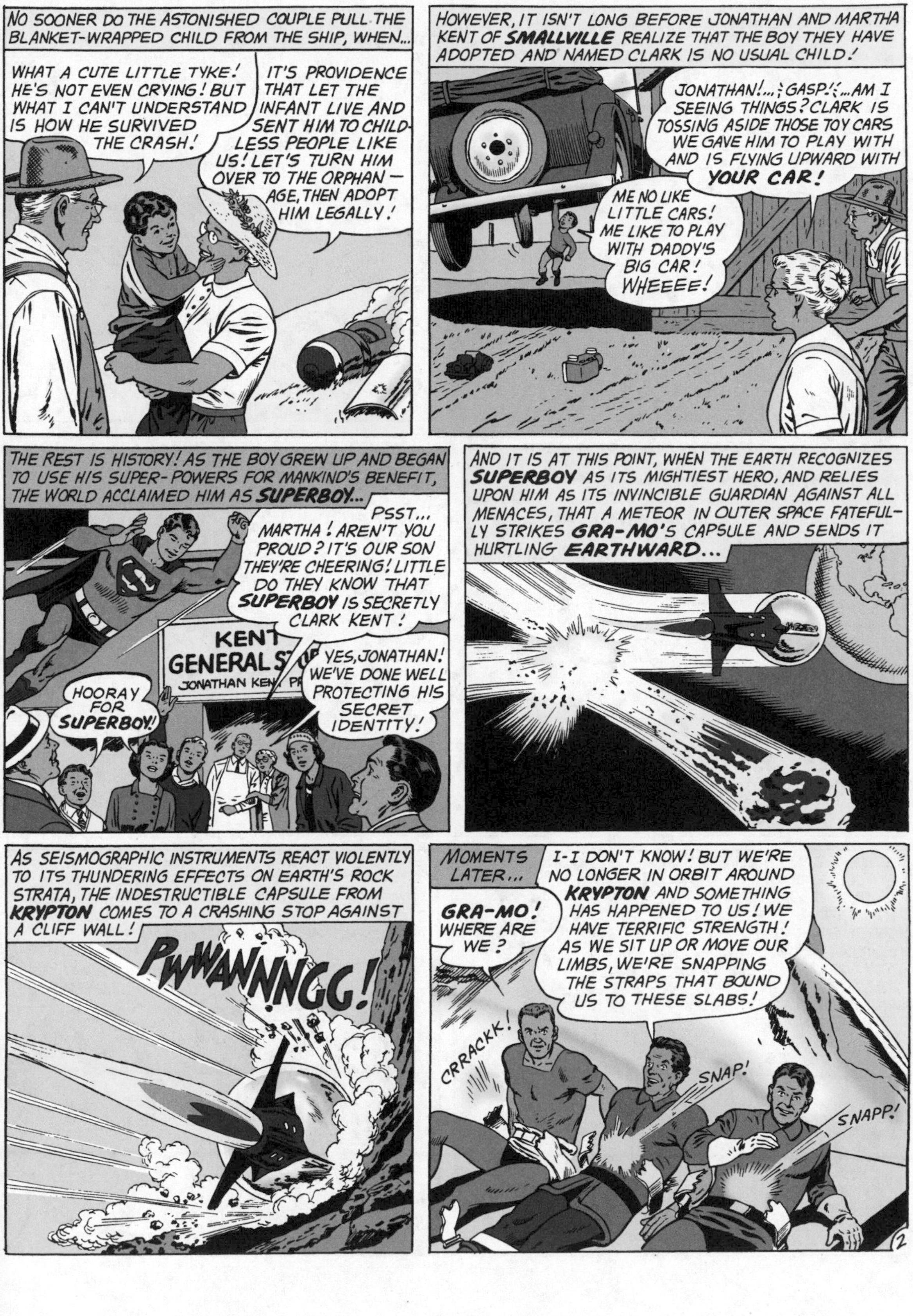
NO SOONER DO THE ASTONISHED COUPLE PULL THE BLANKET-WRAPPED CHILD FROM THE SHIP, WHEN...
WHAT A CUTE LITTLE TYKE! HE'S NOT EVEN CRYING! BUT WHAT I CAN'T UNDERSTAND IS HOW HE SURVIVED THE CRASH!
IT'S PROVIDENCE THAT LET THE INFANT LIVE AND SENT HIM TO CHILDLESS PEOPLE LIKE US! LET'S TURN HIM OVER TO THE ORPHANAGE, THEN ADOPT HIM LEGALLY!
HOWEVER, IT ISN'T LONG BEFORE JONATHAN AND MARTHA KENT OF SMALLVILLE REALIZE THAT THE BOY THEY HAVE ADOPTED AND NAMED CLARK IS NO USUAL CHILD!
JONATHAN!...GASP!...AM I SEEING THINGS? CLARK IS TOSSING ASIDE THOSE TOY CARS WE GAVE HIM TO PLAY WITH AND IS FLYING UPWARD WITH YOUR CAR!
ME NO LIKE LITTLE CARS! ME LIKE TO PLAY WITH DADDY'S BIG CAR! WHEEEE!
THE REST IS HISTORY! AS THE BOY GREW UP AND BEGAN TO USE HIS SUPER-POWERS FOR MANKIND'S BENEFIT, THE WORLD ACCLAIMED HIM AS SUPERBOY...
PSST... MARTHA! AREN'T YOU PROUD? IT'S OUR SON THEY'RE CHEERING! LITTLE DO THEY KNOW THAT SUPERBOY IS SECRETLY CLARK KENT!
KENT
GENERAL ST
JONATHAN KEN
HOORAY FOR SUPERBOY!
YES, JONATHAN! WE'VE DONE WELL PROTECTING HIS SECRET IDENTITY!
AND IT IS AT THIS POINT, WHEN THE EARTH RECOGNIZES SUPERBOY AS ITS MIGHTIEST HERO, AND RELIES UPON HIM AS ITS INVINCIBLE GUARDIAN AGAINST ALL MENACES, THAT A METEOR IN OUTER SPACE FATEFULLY STRIKES GRA-MO'S CAPSULE AND SENDS IT HURTLING EARTHWARD...
AS SEISMOGRAPHIC INSTRUMENTS REACT VIOLENTLY TO ITS THUNDERING EFFECTS ON EARTH'S ROCK STRATA, THE INDESTRUCTIBLE CAPSULE FROM KRYPTON COMES TO A CRASHING STOP AGAINST A CLIFF WALL!
PWWANNNGG!
MOMENTS LATER...
GRA-MO! WHERE ARE WE?
I-I DON'T KNOW! BUT WE'RE NO LONGER IN ORBIT AROUND KRYPTON AND SOMETHING HAS HAPPENED TO US! WE HAVE TERRIFIC STRENGTH! AS WE SIT UP OR MOVE OUR LIMBS, WE'RE SNAPPING THE STRAPS THAT BOUND US TO THESE SLABS!
CRRACKK!
SNAP!
SNAPP!
2

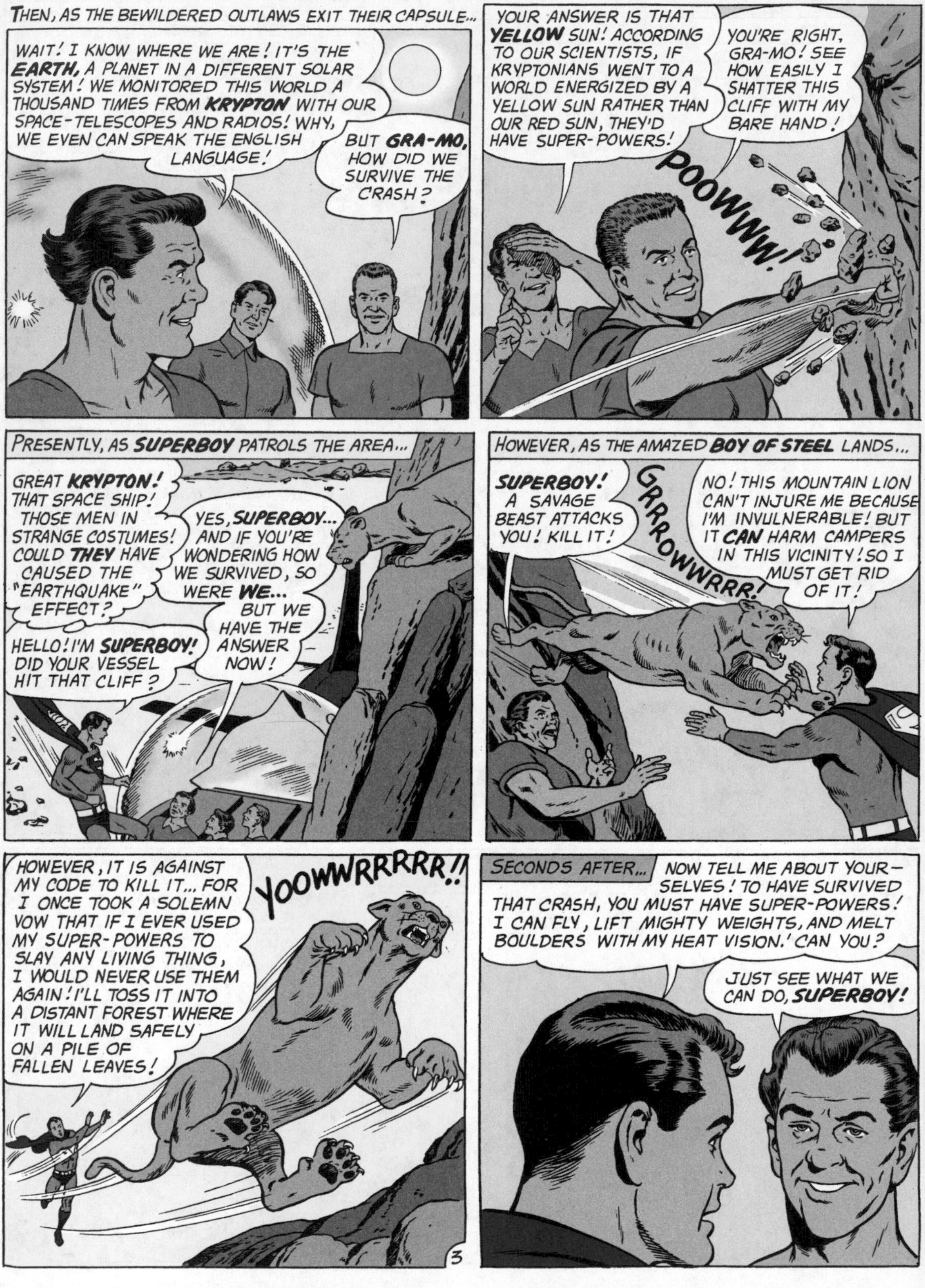
THEN, AS THE BEWILDERED OUTLAWS EXIT THEIR CAPSULE...
WAIT! I KNOW WHERE WE ARE! IT'S THE EARTH, A PLANET IN A DIFFERENT SOLAR SYSTEM! WE MONITORED THIS WORLD A THOUSAND TIMES FROM KRYPTON WITH OUR SPACE-TELESCOPES AND RADIOS! WHY, WE EVEN CAN SPEAK THE ENGLISH LANGUAGE!
BUT GRA-MO, HOW DID WE SURVIVE THE CRASH?
YOUR ANSWER IS THAT YELLOW SUN! ACCORDING TO OUR SCIENTISTS, IF KRYPTONIANS WENT TO A WORLD ENERGIZED BY A YELLOW SUN RATHER THAN OUR RED SUN, THEY'D HAVE SUPER-POWERS!
YOU'RE RIGHT, GRA-MO! SEE HOW EASILY I SHATTER THIS CLIFF WITH MY BARE HAND!
POOWWW!
PRESENTLY, AS SUPERBOY PATROLS THE AREA...
GREAT KRYPTON! THAT SPACE SHIP! THOSE MEN IN STRANGE COSTUMES! COULD THEY HAVE CAUSED THE "EARTHQUAKE" EFFECT?
HELLO! I'M SUPERBOY! DID YOUR VESSEL HIT THAT CLIFF?
YES, SUPERBOY... AND IF YOU'RE WONDERING HOW WE SURVIVED, SO WERE WE...
BUT WE HAVE THE ANSWER NOW!
HOWEVER, AS THE AMAZED BOY OF STEEL LANDS...
SUPERBOY! A SAVAGE BEAST ATTACKS YOU! KILL IT!
GRRROWWRRR!
NO! THIS MOUNTAIN LION CAN'T INJURE ME BECAUSE I'M INVULNERABLE! BUT IT CAN HARM CAMPERS IN THIS VICINITY! SO I MUST GET RID OF IT!
HOWEVER, IT IS AGAINST MY CODE TO KILL IT... FOR I ONCE TOOK A SOLEMN VOW THAT IF I EVER USED MY SUPER-POWERS TO SLAY ANY LIVING THING, I WOULD NEVER USE THEM AGAIN! I'LL TOSS IT INTO A DISTANT FOREST WHERE IT WILL LAND SAFELY ON A PILE OF FALLEN LEAVES!
YOOWWRRRRR!!
3
SECONDS AFTER...
NOW TELL ME ABOUT YOURSELVES! TO HAVE SURVIVED THAT CRASH, YOU MUST HAVE SUPER-POWERS! I CAN FLY, LIFT MIGHTY WEIGHTS, AND MELT BOULDERS WITH MY HEAT VISION! CAN YOU?
JUST SEE WHAT WE CAN DO, SUPERBOY!

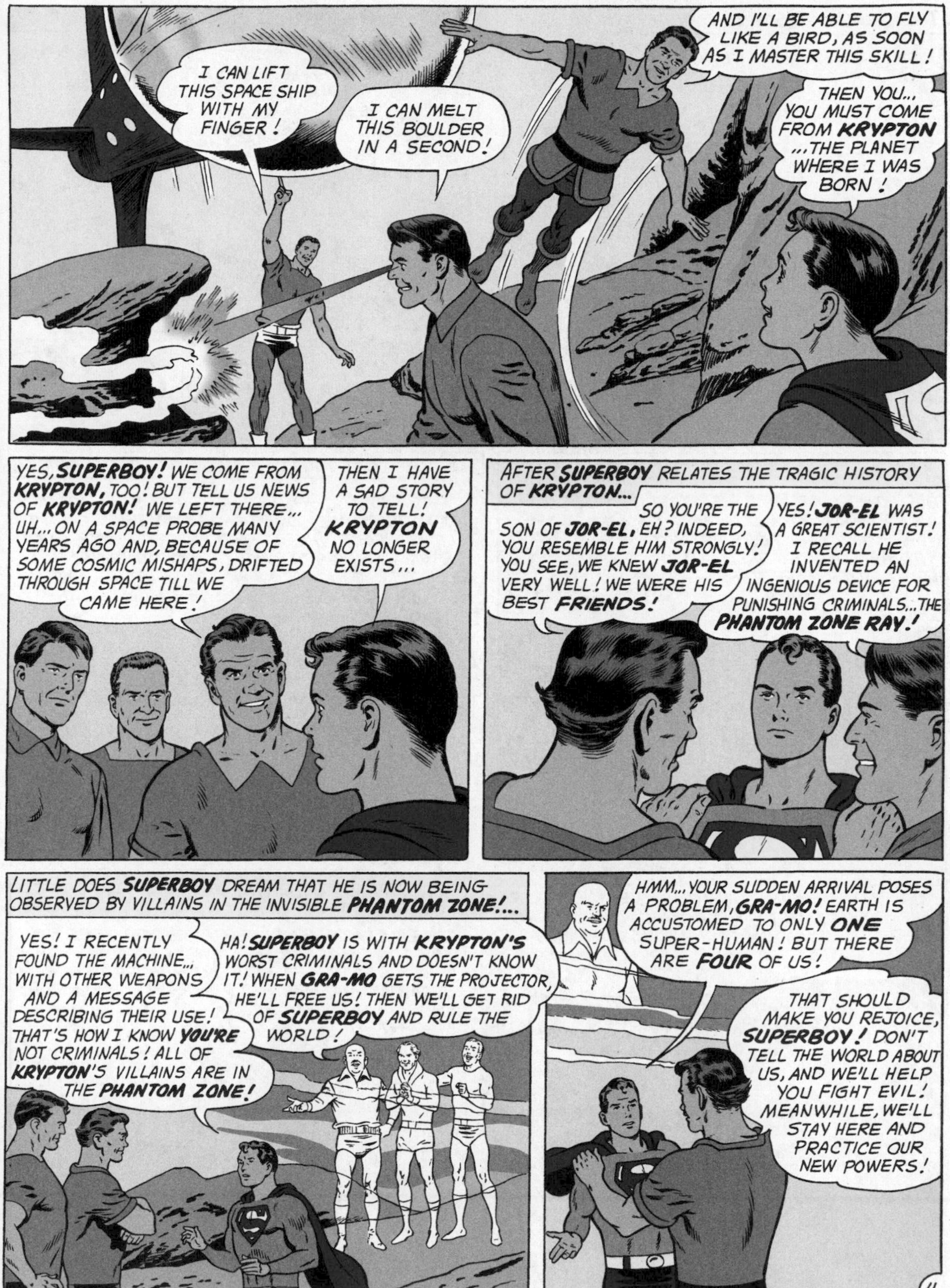
I CAN LIFT THIS SPACE SHIP WITH MY FINGER!
I CAN MELT THIS BOULDER IN A SECOND!
AND I'LL BE ABLE TO FLY LIKE A BIRD, AS SOON AS I MASTER THIS SKILL!
THEN YOU... YOU MUST COME FROM KRYPTON ...THE PLANET WHERE I WAS BORN!
YES, SUPERBOY! WE COME FROM KRYPTON, TOO! BUT TELL US NEWS OF KRYPTON! WE LEFT THERE... UH... ON A SPACE PROBE MANY YEARS AGO AND, BECAUSE OF SOME COSMIC MISHAPS, DRIFTED THROUGH SPACE TILL WE CAME HERE!
THEN I HAVE A SAD STORY TO TELL! KRYPTON NO LONGER EXISTS...
AFTER SUPERBOY RELATES THE TRAGIC HISTORY OF KRYPTON...
SO YOU'RE THE SON OF JOR-EL, EH? INDEED, YOU RESEMBLE HIM STRONGLY! YOU SEE, WE KNEW JOR-EL VERY WELL! WE WERE HIS BEST FRIENDS!
YES! JOR-EL WAS A GREAT SCIENTIST! I RECALL HE INVENTED AN INGENIOUS DEVICE FOR PUNISHING CRIMINALS... THE PHANTOM ZONE RAY!
LITTLE DOES SUPERBOY DREAM THAT HE IS NOW BEING OBSERVED BY VILLAINS IN THE INVISIBLE PHANTOM ZONE!...
YES! I RECENTLY FOUND THE MACHINE... WITH OTHER WEAPONS AND A MESSAGE DESCRIBING THEIR USE! THAT'S HOW I KNOW YOU'RE NOT CRIMINALS! ALL OF KRYPTON'S VILLAINS ARE IN THE PHANTOM ZONE!
HA! SUPERBOY IS WITH KRYPTON'S WORST CRIMINALS AND DOESN'T KNOW IT! WHEN GRA-MO GETS THE PROJECTOR, HE'LL FREE US! THEN WE'LL GET RID OF SUPERBOY AND RULE THE WORLD!
HMM... YOUR SUDDEN ARRIVAL POSES A PROBLEM, GRA-MO! EARTH IS ACCUSTOMED TO ONLY ONE SUPER-HUMAN! BUT THERE ARE FOUR OF US!
THAT SHOULD MAKE YOU REJOICE, SUPERBOY! DON'T TELL THE WORLD ABOUT US, AND WE'LL HELP YOU FIGHT EVIL! MEANWHILE, WE'LL STAY HERE AND PRACTICE OUR NEW POWERS!
4

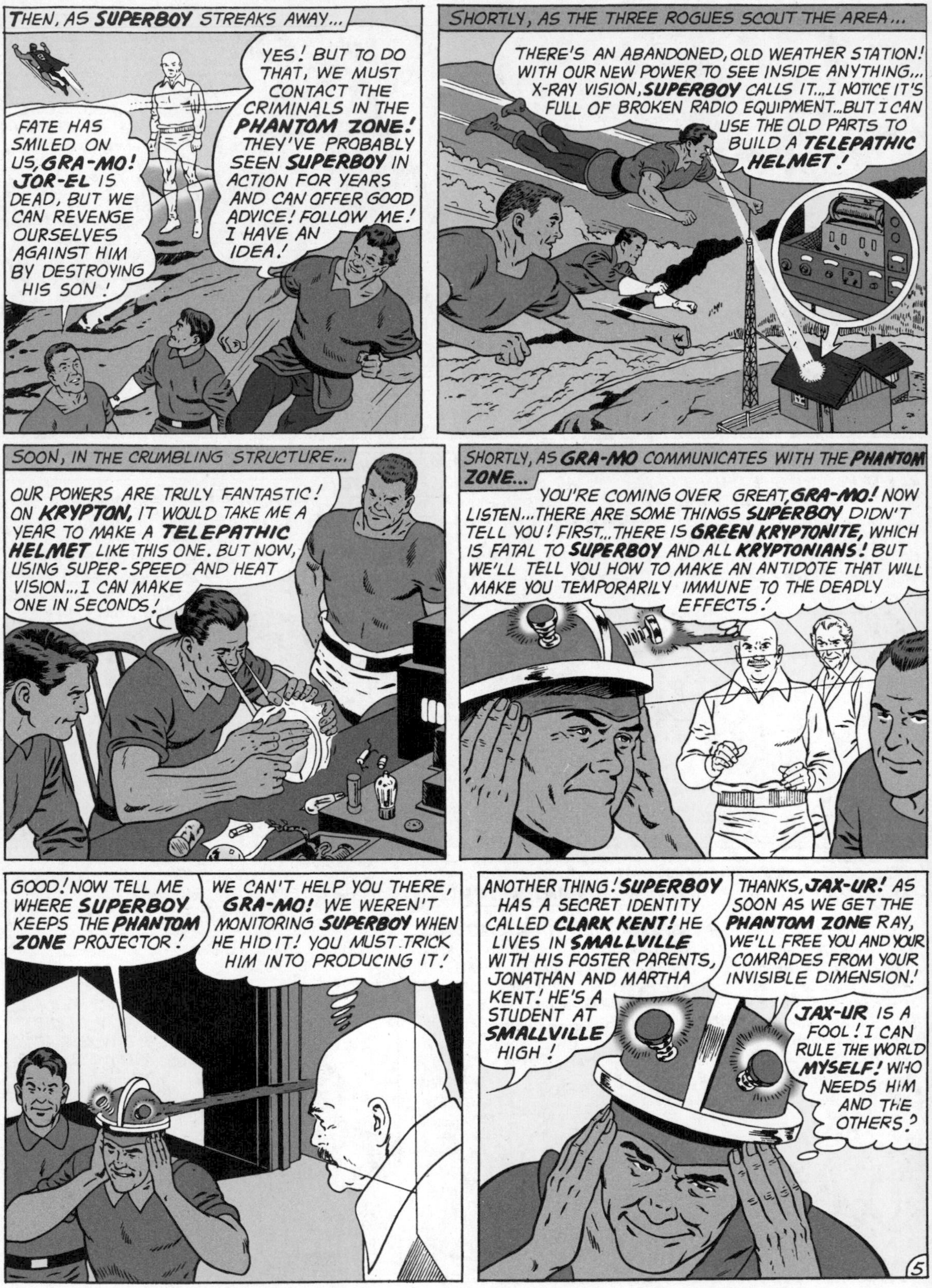
THEN, AS SUPERBOY STREAKS AWAY...
FATE HAS SMILED ON US, GRA-MO! JOR-EL IS DEAD, BUT WE CAN REVENGE OURSELVES AGAINST HIM BY DESTROYING HIS SON!
YES! BUT TO DO THAT, WE MUST CONTACT THE CRIMINALS IN THE PHANTOM ZONE! THEY'VE PROBABLY SEEN SUPERBOY IN ACTION FOR YEARS AND CAN OFFER GOOD ADVICE! FOLLOW ME! I HAVE AN IDEA!
SHORTLY, AS THE THREE ROGUES SCOUT THE AREA...
THERE'S AN ABANDONED, OLD WEATHER STATION! WITH OUR NEW POWER TO SEE INSIDE ANYTHING... X-RAY VISION, SUPERBOY CALLS IT...I NOTICE IT'S FULL OF BROKEN RADIO EQUIPMENT...BUT I CAN USE THE OLD PARTS TO BUILD A TELEPATHIC HELMET!
SOON, IN THE CRUMBLING STRUCTURE...
OUR POWERS ARE TRULY FANTASTIC! ON KRYPTON, IT WOULD TAKE ME A YEAR TO MAKE A TELEPATHIC HELMET LIKE THIS ONE. BUT NOW, USING SUPER-SPEED AND HEAT VISION...I CAN MAKE ONE IN SECONDS!
SHORTLY, AS GRA-MO COMMUNICATES WITH THE PHANTOM ZONE...
YOU'RE COMING OVER GREAT, GRA-MO! NOW LISTEN...THERE ARE SOME THINGS SUPERBOY DIDN'T TELL YOU! FIRST...THERE IS GREEN KRYPTONITE, WHICH IS FATAL TO SUPERBOY AND ALL KRYPTONIANS! BUT WE'LL TELL YOU HOW TO MAKE AN ANTIDOTE THAT WILL MAKE YOU TEMPORARILY IMMUNE TO THE DEADLY EFFECTS!
GOOD! NOW TELL ME WHERE SUPERBOY KEEPS THE PHANTOM ZONE PROJECTOR!
WE CAN'T HELP YOU THERE, GRA-MO! WE WEREN'T MONITORING SUPERBOY WHEN HE HID IT! YOU MUST TRICK HIM INTO PRODUCING IT!
ANOTHER THING! SUPERBOY HAS A SECRET IDENTITY CALLED CLARK KENT! HE LIVES IN SMALLVILLE WITH HIS FOSTER PARENTS, JONATHAN AND MARTHA KENT! HE'S A STUDENT AT SMALLVILLE HIGH!
THANKS, JAX-UR! AS SOON AS WE GET THE PHANTOM ZONE RAY, WE'LL FREE YOU AND YOUR COMRADES FROM YOUR INVISIBLE DIMENSION!
JAX-UR IS A FOOL! I CAN RULE THE WORLD MYSELF! WHO NEEDS HIM AND THE OTHERS?
5

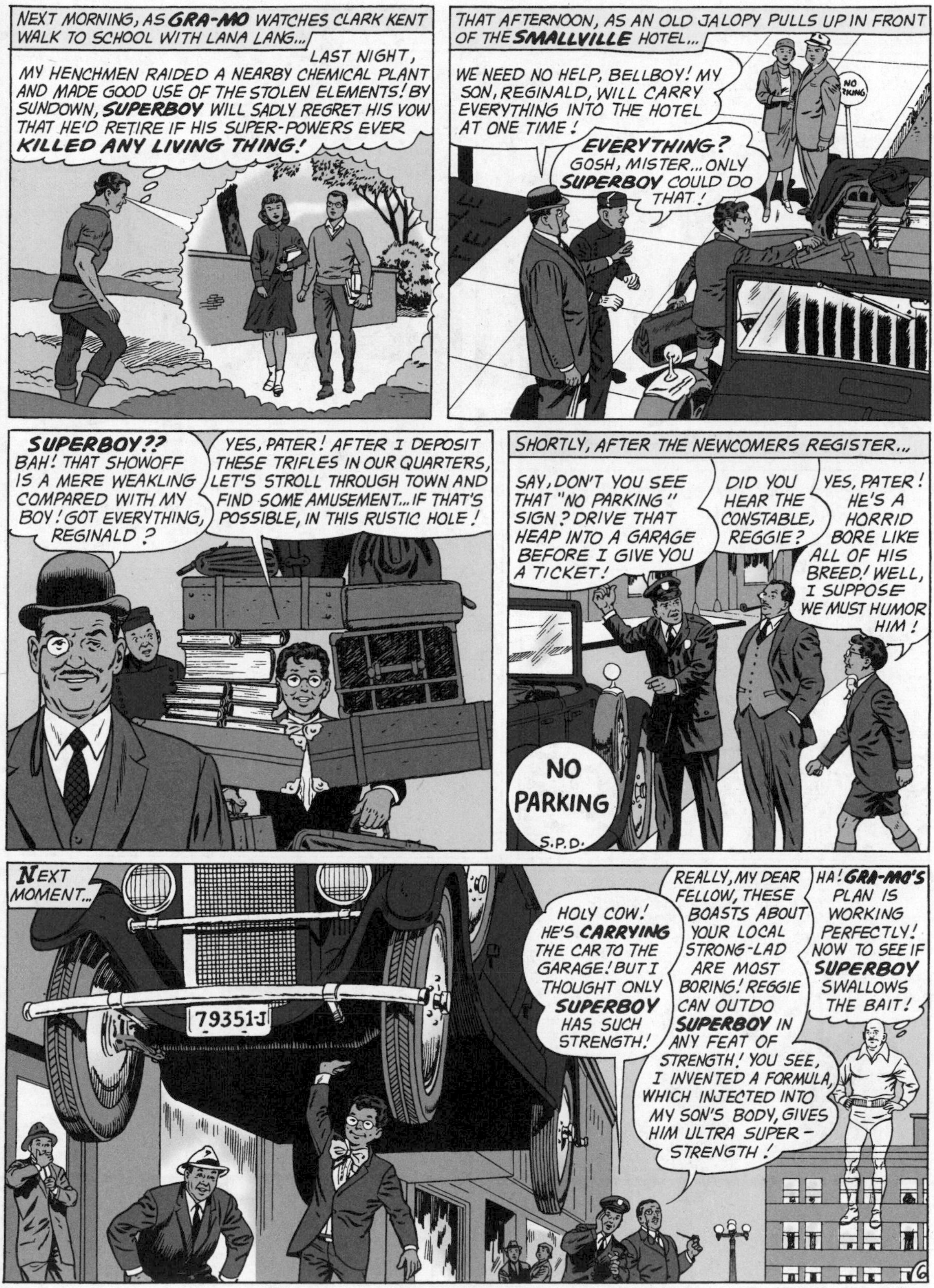
NEXT MORNING, AS GRA-MO WATCHES CLARK KENT WALK TO SCHOOL WITH LANA LANG...
LAST NIGHT, MY HENCHMEN RAIDED A NEARBY CHEMICAL PLANT AND MADE GOOD USE OF THE STOLEN ELEMENTS! BY SUNDOWN, SUPERBOY WILL SADLY REGRET HIS VOW THAT HE'D RETIRE IF HIS SUPER-POWERS EVER KILLED ANY LIVING THING!
THAT AFTERNOON, AS AN OLD JALOPY PULLS UP IN FRONT OF THE SMALLVILLE HOTEL...
WE NEED NO HELP, BELLBOY! MY SON, REGINALD, WILL CARRY EVERYTHING INTO THE HOTEL AT ONE TIME!
EVERYTHING? GOSH, MISTER... ONLY SUPERBOY COULD DO THAT!
SUPERBOY?? BAH! THAT SHOWOFF IS A MERE WEAKLING COMPARED WITH MY BOY! GOT EVERYTHING, REGINALD?
YES, PATER! AFTER I DEPOSIT THESE TRIFLES IN OUR QUARTERS, LET'S STROLL THROUGH TOWN AND FIND SOME AMUSEMENT... IF THAT'S POSSIBLE, IN THIS RUSTIC HOLE!
SHORTLY, AFTER THE NEWCOMERS REGISTER...
SAY, DON'T YOU SEE THAT "NO PARKING" SIGN? DRIVE THAT HEAP INTO A GARAGE BEFORE I GIVE YOU A TICKET!
DID YOU HEAR THE CONSTABLE, REGGIE?
YES, PATER! HE'S A HORRID BORE LIKE ALL OF HIS BREED! WELL, I SUPPOSE WE MUST HUMOR HIM!
NO PARKING
S.P.D.
NEXT MOMENT...
HOLY COW! HE'S CARRYING THE CAR TO THE GARAGE! BUT I THOUGHT ONLY SUPERBOY HAS SUCH STRENGTH!
REALLY, MY DEAR FELLOW, THESE BOASTS ABOUT YOUR LOCAL STRONG-LAD ARE MOST BORING! REGGIE CAN OUTDO SUPERBOY IN ANY FEAT OF STRENGTH! YOU SEE, I INVENTED A FORMULA, WHICH INJECTED INTO MY SON'S BODY, GIVES HIM ULTRA SUPER-STRENGTH!
HA! GRA-MO'S PLAN IS WORKING PERFECTLY! NOW TO SEE IF SUPERBOY SWALLOWS THE BAIT!
79351-J
6

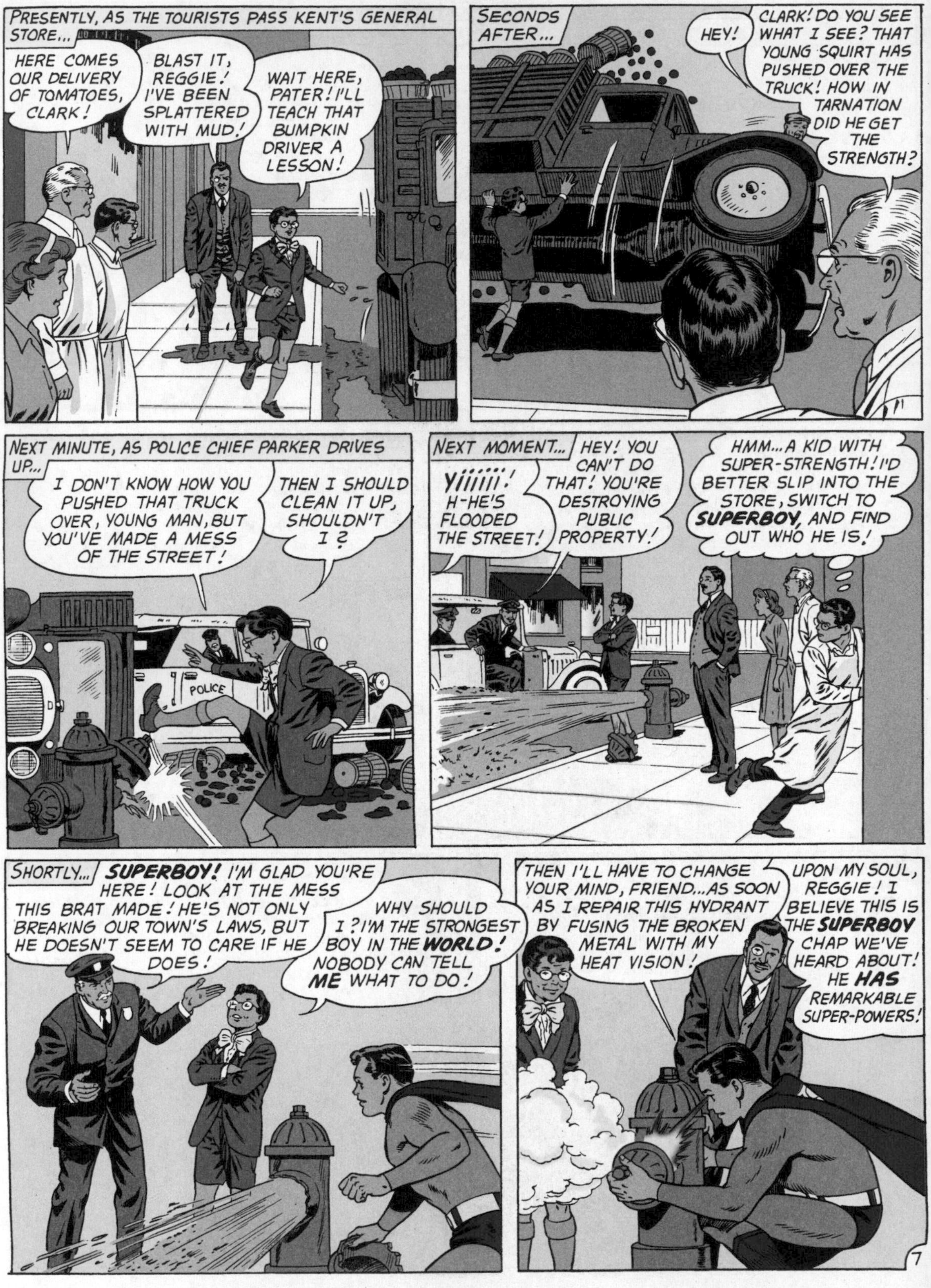
PRESENTLY, AS THE TOURISTS PASS KENT'S GENERAL STORE...
HERE COMES OUR DELIVERY OF TOMATOES, CLARK!
BLAST IT, REGGIE! I'VE BEEN SPLATTERED WITH MUD!
WAIT HERE, PATER! I'LL TEACH THAT BUMPKIN DRIVER A LESSON!
SECONDS AFTER...
HEY!
CLARK! DO YOU SEE WHAT I SEE? THAT YOUNG SQUIRT HAS PUSHED OVER THE TRUCK! HOW IN TARNATION DID HE GET THE STRENGTH?
NEXT MINUTE, AS POLICE CHIEF PARKER DRIVES UP...
I DON'T KNOW HOW YOU PUSHED THAT TRUCK OVER, YOUNG MAN, BUT YOU'VE MADE A MESS OF THE STREET!
THEN I SHOULD CLEAN IT UP, SHOULDN'T I?
POLICE
NEXT MOMENT...
YIIIIII! H-HE'S FLOODED THE STREET!
HEY! YOU CAN'T DO THAT! YOU'RE DESTROYING PUBLIC PROPERTY!
HMM...A KID WITH SUPER-STRENGTH! I'D BETTER SLIP INTO THE STORE, SWITCH TO SUPERBOY, AND FIND OUT WHO HE IS!
SHORTLY...
SUPERBOY! I'M GLAD YOU'RE HERE! LOOK AT THE MESS THIS BRAT MADE! HE'S NOT ONLY BREAKING OUR TOWN'S LAWS, BUT HE DOESN'T SEEM TO CARE IF HE DOES!
WHY SHOULD I? I'M THE STRONGEST BOY IN THE WORLD! NOBODY CAN TELL ME WHAT TO DO!
THEN I'LL HAVE TO CHANGE YOUR MIND, FRIEND...AS SOON AS I REPAIR THIS HYDRANT BY FUSING THE BROKEN METAL WITH MY HEAT VISION!
UPON MY SOUL, REGGIE! I BELIEVE THIS IS THE SUPERBOY CHAP WE'VE HEARD ABOUT! HE HAS REMARKABLE SUPER-POWERS!
7

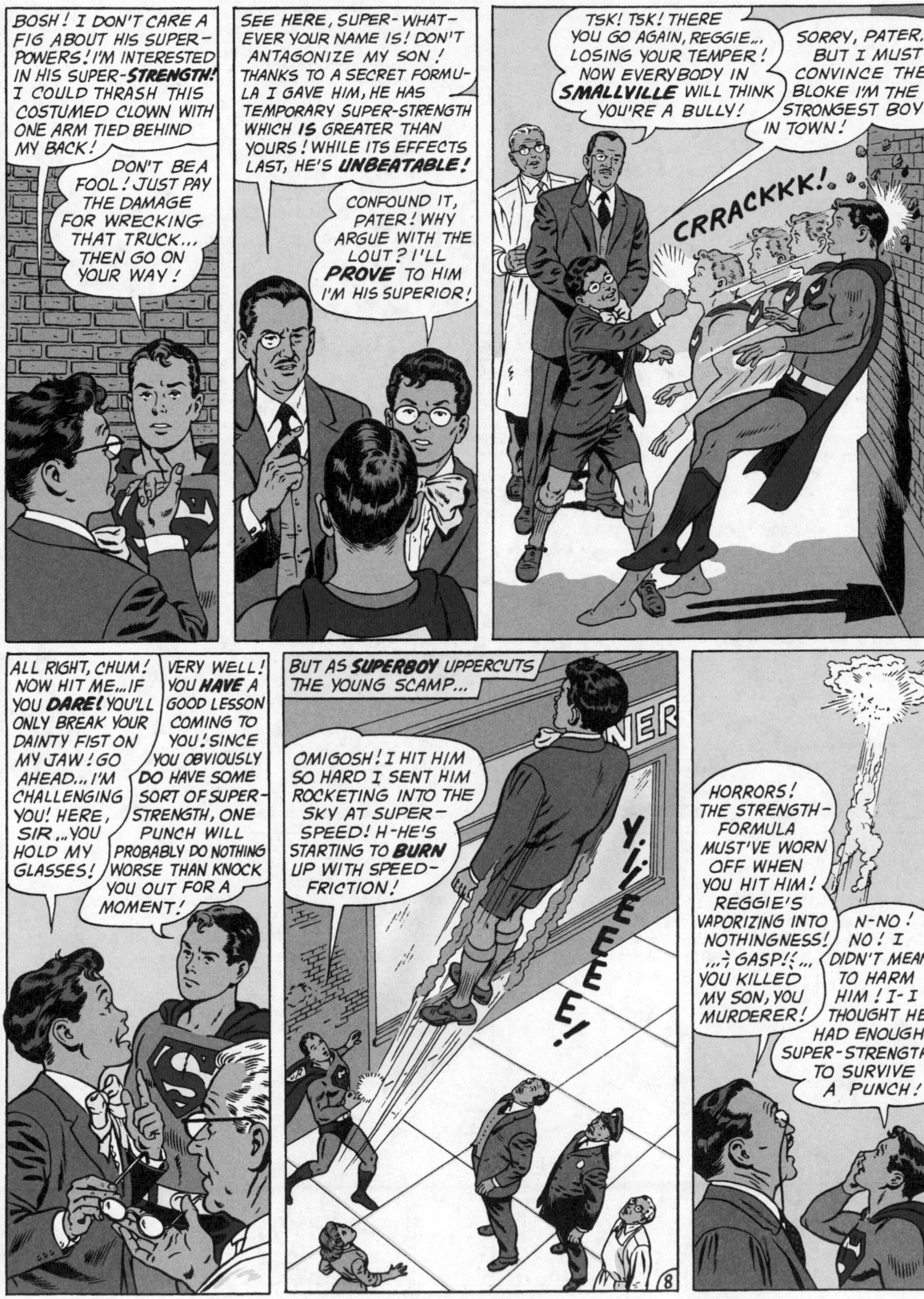

BOSH! I DON'T CARE A FIG ABOUT HIS SUPER-POWERS! I'M INTERESTED IN HIS SUPER-STRENGTH! I COULD THRASH THIS COSTUMED CLOWN WITH ONE ARM TIED BEHIND MY BACK!
DON'T BE A FOOL! JUST PAY THE DAMAGE FOR WRECKING THAT TRUCK... THEN GO ON YOUR WAY!
SEE HERE, SUPER-WHAT-EVER YOUR NAME IS! DON'T ANTAGONIZE MY SON! THANKS TO A SECRET FORMULA I GAVE HIM, HE HAS TEMPORARY SUPER-STRENGTH WHICH IS GREATER THAN YOURS! WHILE ITS EFFECTS LAST, HE'S UNBEATABLE!
CONFOUND IT, PATER! WHY ARGUE WITH THE LOUT? I'LL PROVE TO HIM I'M HIS SUPERIOR!
TSK! TSK! THERE YOU GO AGAIN, REGGIE... LOSING YOUR TEMPER! NOW EVERYBODY IN SMALLVILLE WILL THINK YOU'RE A BULLY!
SORRY, PATER... BUT I MUST CONVINCE THE BLOKE I'M THE STRONGEST BOY IN TOWN!
CRRACKKK!
ALL RIGHT, CHUM! NOW HIT ME...IF YOU DARE! YOU'LL ONLY BREAK YOUR DAINTY FIST ON MY JAW! GO AHEAD... I'M CHALLENGING YOU! HERE, SIR... YOU HOLD MY GLASSES!
VERY WELL! YOU HAVE A GOOD LESSON COMING TO YOU! SINCE YOU OBVIOUSLY DO HAVE SOME SORT OF SUPER-STRENGTH, ONE PUNCH WILL PROBABLY DO NOTHING WORSE THAN KNOCK YOU OUT FOR A MOMENT!
BUT AS SUPERBOY UPPERCUTS THE YOUNG SCAMP...
OMIGOSH! I HIT HIM SO HARD I SENT HIM ROCKETING INTO THE SKY AT SUPER-SPEED! H-HE'S STARTING TO BURN UP WITH SPEED-FRICTION!
YIIEEEEE!
8
HORRORS! THE STRENGTH-FORMULA MUST'VE WORN OFF WHEN YOU HIT HIM! REGGIE'S VAPORIZING INTO NOTHINGNESS! ...GASP!... YOU KILLED MY SON, YOU MURDERER!
N-NO! NO! I DIDN'T MEAN TO HARM HIM! I-I THOUGHT HE HAD ENOUGH SUPER-STRENGTH TO SURVIVE A PUNCH!

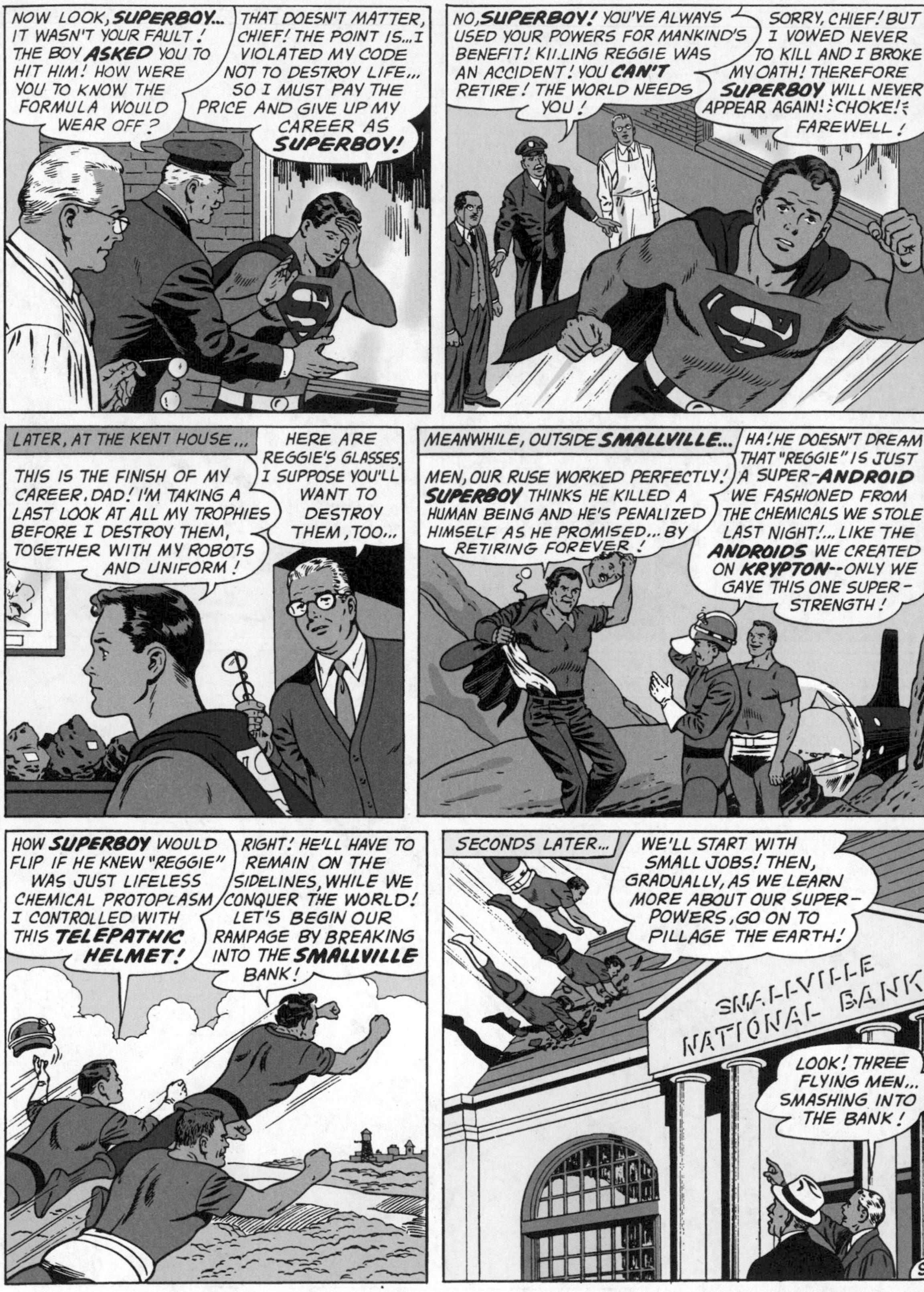
NOW LOOK, SUPERBOY... IT WASN'T YOUR FAULT! THE BOY ASKED YOU TO HIT HIM! HOW WERE YOU TO KNOW THE FORMULA WOULD WEAR OFF?
THAT DOESN'T MATTER, CHIEF! THE POINT IS...I VIOLATED MY CODE NOT TO DESTROY LIFE... SO I MUST PAY THE PRICE AND GIVE UP MY CAREER AS SUPERBOY!
NO, SUPERBOY! YOU'VE ALWAYS USED YOUR POWERS FOR MANKIND'S BENEFIT! KILLING REGGIE WAS AN ACCIDENT! YOU CAN'T RETIRE! THE WORLD NEEDS YOU!
SORRY, CHIEF! BUT I VOWED NEVER TO KILL AND I BROKE MY OATH! THEREFORE SUPERBOY WILL NEVER APPEAR AGAIN! CHOKE! FAREWELL!
LATER, AT THE KENT HOUSE...
THIS IS THE FINISH OF MY CAREER, DAD! I'M TAKING A LAST LOOK AT ALL MY TROPHIES BEFORE I DESTROY THEM, TOGETHER WITH MY ROBOTS AND UNIFORM!
HERE ARE REGGIE'S GLASSES. I SUPPOSE YOU'LL WANT TO DESTROY THEM, TOO...
MEANWHILE, OUTSIDE SMALLVILLE...
MEN, OUR RUSE WORKED PERFECTLY! SUPERBOY THINKS HE KILLED A HUMAN BEING AND HE'S PENALIZED HIMSELF AS HE PROMISED... BY RETIRING FOREVER!
HA! HE DOESN'T DREAM THAT "REGGIE" IS JUST A SUPER-ANDROID WE FASHIONED FROM THE CHEMICALS WE STOLE LAST NIGHT!... LIKE THE ANDROIDS WE CREATED ON KRYPTON--ONLY WE GAVE THIS ONE SUPER-STRENGTH!
HOW SUPERBOY WOULD FLIP IF HE KNEW "REGGIE" WAS JUST LIFELESS CHEMICAL PROTOPLASM I CONTROLLED WITH THIS TELEPATHIC HELMET!
RIGHT! HE'LL HAVE TO REMAIN ON THE SIDELINES, WHILE WE CONQUER THE WORLD! LET'S BEGIN OUR RAMPAGE BY BREAKING INTO THE SMALLVILLE BANK!
SECONDS LATER...
WE'LL START WITH SMALL JOBS! THEN, GRADUALLY, AS WE LEARN MORE ABOUT OUR SUPER-POWERS, GO ON TO PILLAGE THE EARTH!
SMALLVILLE NATIONAL BANK
LOOK! THREE FLYING MEN... SMASHING INTO THE BANK!
9

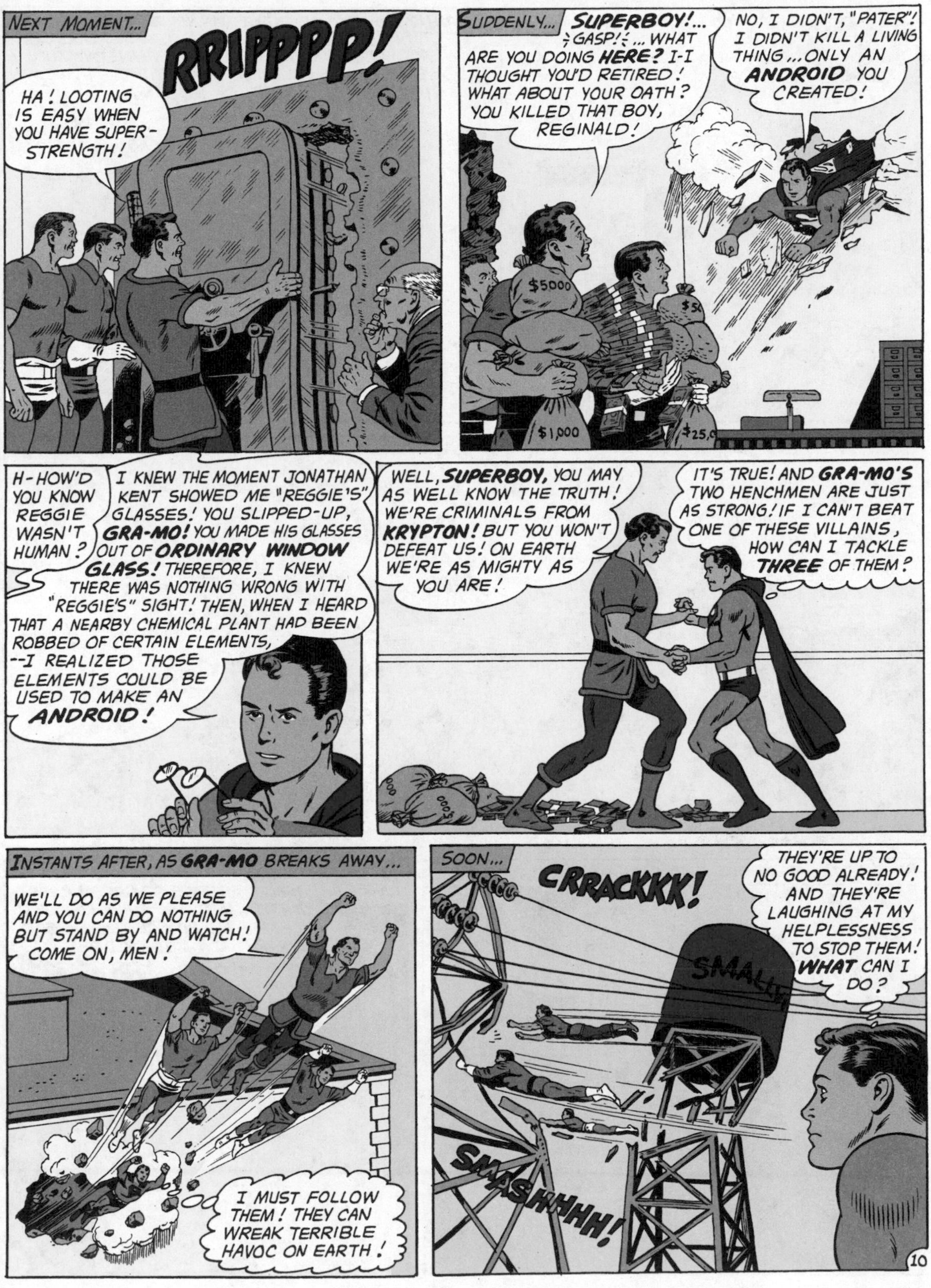
NEXT MOMENT...
RRIPPPP!
HA! LOOTING IS EASY WHEN YOU HAVE SUPER-STRENGTH!
SUDDENLY...
SUPERBOY!... GASP! ... WHAT ARE YOU DOING HERE? I-I THOUGHT YOU'D RETIRED! WHAT ABOUT YOUR OATH? YOU KILLED THAT BOY, REGINALD!
NO, I DIDN'T, "PATER"! I DIDN'T KILL A LIVING THING ... ONLY AN ANDROID YOU CREATED!
$5000
$1,000
H-HOW'D YOU KNOW REGGIE WASN'T HUMAN?
I KNEW THE MOMENT JONATHAN KENT SHOWED ME "REGGIE'S" GLASSES! YOU SLIPPED-UP, GRA-MO! YOU MADE HIS GLASSES OUT OF ORDINARY WINDOW GLASS! THEREFORE, I KNEW THERE WAS NOTHING WRONG WITH "REGGIE'S" SIGHT! THEN, WHEN I HEARD THAT A NEARBY CHEMICAL PLANT HAD BEEN ROBBED OF CERTAIN ELEMENTS, --I REALIZED THOSE ELEMENTS COULD BE USED TO MAKE AN ANDROID!
WELL, SUPERBOY, YOU MAY AS WELL KNOW THE TRUTH! WE'RE CRIMINALS FROM KRYPTON! BUT YOU WON'T DEFEAT US! ON EARTH WE'RE AS MIGHTY AS YOU ARE!
IT'S TRUE! AND GRA-MO'S TWO HENCHMEN ARE JUST AS STRONG! IF I CAN'T BEAT ONE OF THESE VILLAINS, HOW CAN I TACKLE THREE OF THEM?
INSTANTS AFTER, AS GRA-MO BREAKS AWAY...
WE'LL DO AS WE PLEASE AND YOU CAN DO NOTHING BUT STAND BY AND WATCH! COME ON, MEN!
I MUST FOLLOW THEM! THEY CAN WREAK TERRIBLE HAVOC ON EARTH!
SOON...
CRRACKKK!
THEY'RE UP TO NO GOOD ALREADY! AND THEY'RE LAUGHING AT MY HELPLESSNESS TO STOP THEM! WHAT CAN I DO?
SMASHHHHH!
10

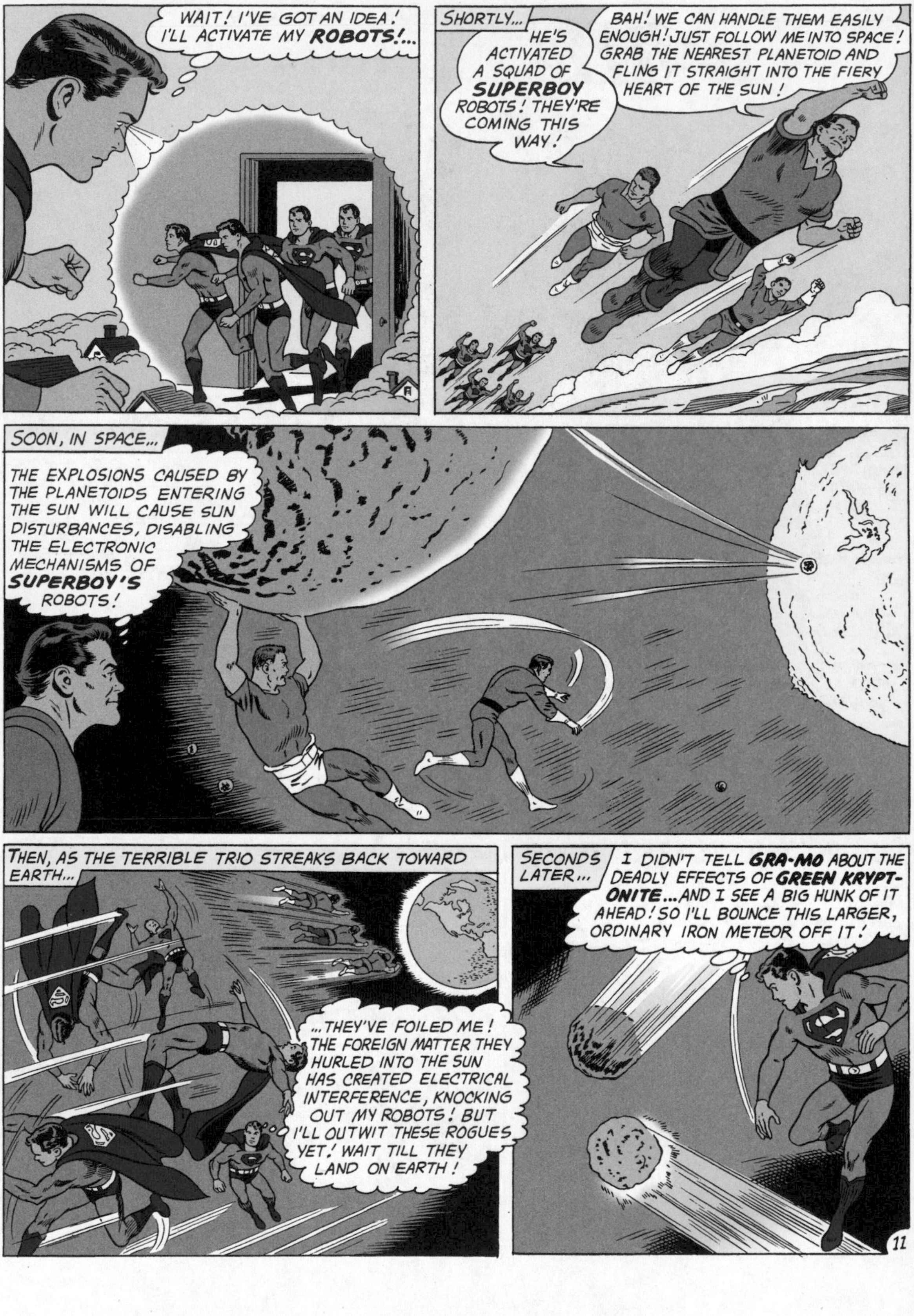

WAIT! I'VE GOT AN IDEA! I'LL ACTIVATE MY ROBOTS!...
SHORTLY...
HE'S ACTIVATED A SQUAD OF SUPERBOY ROBOTS! THEY'RE COMING THIS WAY!
BAH! WE CAN HANDLE THEM EASILY ENOUGH! JUST FOLLOW ME INTO SPACE! GRAB THE NEAREST PLANETOID AND FLING IT STRAIGHT INTO THE FIERY HEART OF THE SUN!
SOON, IN SPACE...
THE EXPLOSIONS CAUSED BY THE PLANETOIDS ENTERING THE SUN WILL CAUSE SUN DISTURBANCES, DISABLING THE ELECTRONIC MECHANISMS OF SUPERBOY'S ROBOTS!
THEN, AS THE TERRIBLE TRIO STREAKS BACK TOWARD EARTH...
...THEY'VE FOILED ME! THE FOREIGN MATTER THEY HURLED INTO THE SUN HAS CREATED ELECTRICAL INTERFERENCE, KNOCKING OUT MY ROBOTS! BUT I'LL OUTWIT THESE ROGUES YET! WAIT TILL THEY LAND ON EARTH!
SECONDS LATER...
I DIDN'T TELL GRA-MO ABOUT THE DEADLY EFFECTS OF GREEN KRYPTONITE...AND I SEE A BIG HUNK OF IT AHEAD! SO I'LL BOUNCE THIS LARGER, ORDINARY IRON METEOR OFF IT!
11

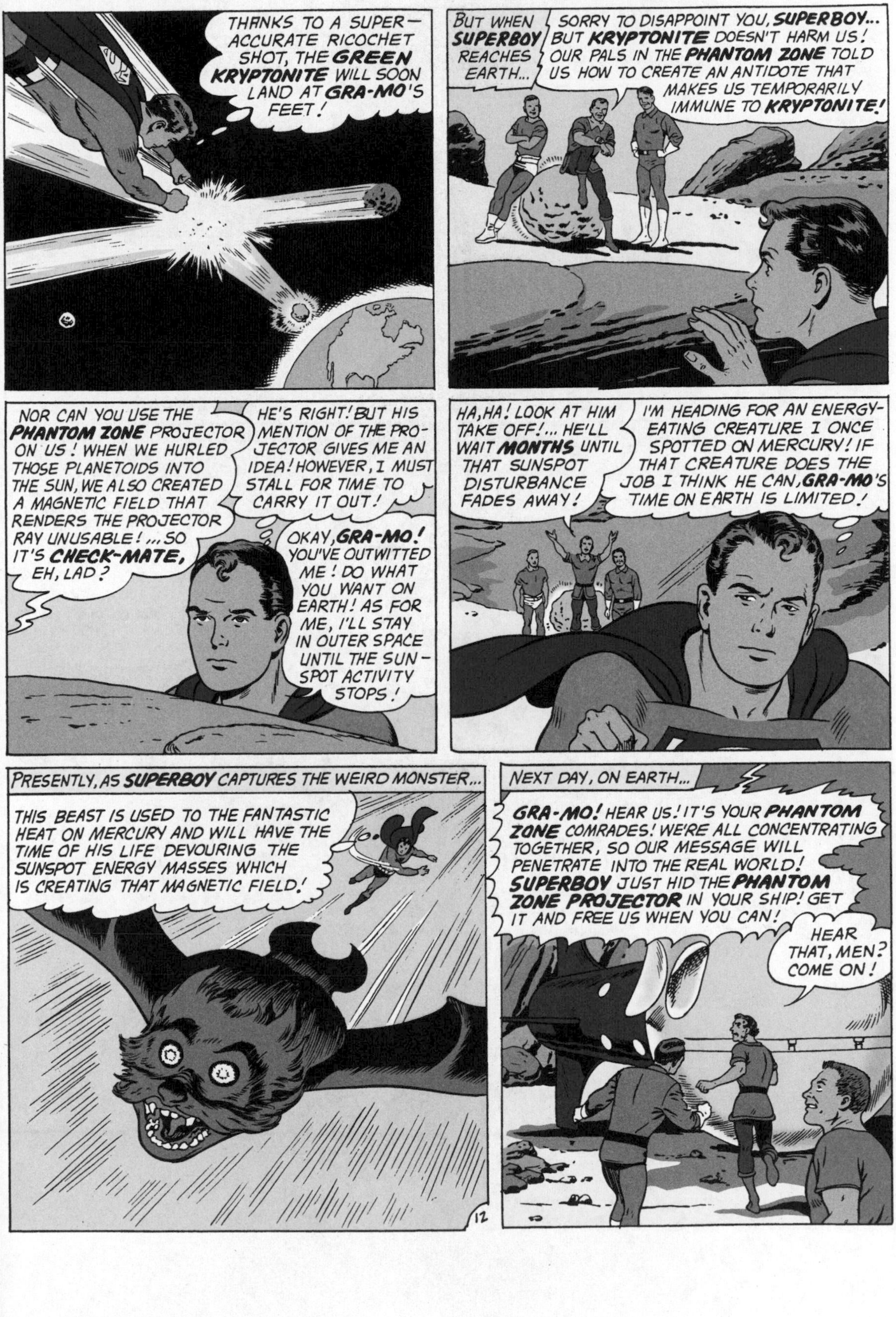
THANKS TO A SUPER-ACCURATE RICOCHET SHOT, THE GREEN KRYPTONITE WILL SOON LAND AT GRA-MO'S FEET!
BUT WHEN SUPERBOY REACHES EARTH...
SORRY TO DISAPPOINT YOU, SUPERBOY... BUT KRYPTONITE DOESN'T HARM US! OUR PALS IN THE PHANTOM ZONE TOLD US HOW TO CREATE AN ANTIDOTE THAT MAKES US TEMPORARILY IMMUNE TO KRYPTONITE!
NOR CAN YOU USE THE PHANTOM ZONE PROJECTOR ON US! WHEN WE HURLED THOSE PLANETOIDS INTO THE SUN, WE ALSO CREATED A MAGNETIC FIELD THAT RENDERS THE PROJECTOR RAY UNUSABLE! ... SO IT'S CHECK-MATE, EH, LAD?
HE'S RIGHT! BUT HIS MENTION OF THE PROJECTOR GIVES ME AN IDEA! HOWEVER, I MUST STALL FOR TIME TO CARRY IT OUT!
OKAY, GRA-MO! YOU'VE OUTWITTED ME! DO WHAT YOU WANT ON EARTH! AS FOR ME, I'LL STAY IN OUTER SPACE UNTIL THE SUNSPOT ACTIVITY STOPS!
HA, HA! LOOK AT HIM TAKE OFF! ... HE'LL WAIT MONTHS UNTIL THAT SUNSPOT DISTURBANCE FADES AWAY!
I'M HEADING FOR AN ENERGY-EATING CREATURE I ONCE SPOTTED ON MERCURY! IF THAT CREATURE DOES THE JOB I THINK HE CAN, GRA-MO'S TIME ON EARTH IS LIMITED!
PRESENTLY, AS SUPERBOY CAPTURES THE WEIRD MONSTER...
THIS BEAST IS USED TO THE FANTASTIC HEAT ON MERCURY AND WILL HAVE THE TIME OF HIS LIFE DEVOURING THE SUNSPOT ENERGY MASSES WHICH IS CREATING THAT MAGNETIC FIELD!
12
NEXT DAY, ON EARTH...
GRA-MO! HEAR US! IT'S YOUR PHANTOM ZONE COMRADES! WE'RE ALL CONCENTRATING TOGETHER, SO OUR MESSAGE WILL PENETRATE INTO THE REAL WORLD! SUPERBOY JUST HID THE PHANTOM ZONE PROJECTOR IN YOUR SHIP! GET IT AND FREE US WHEN YOU CAN!
HEAR THAT, MEN? COME ON!

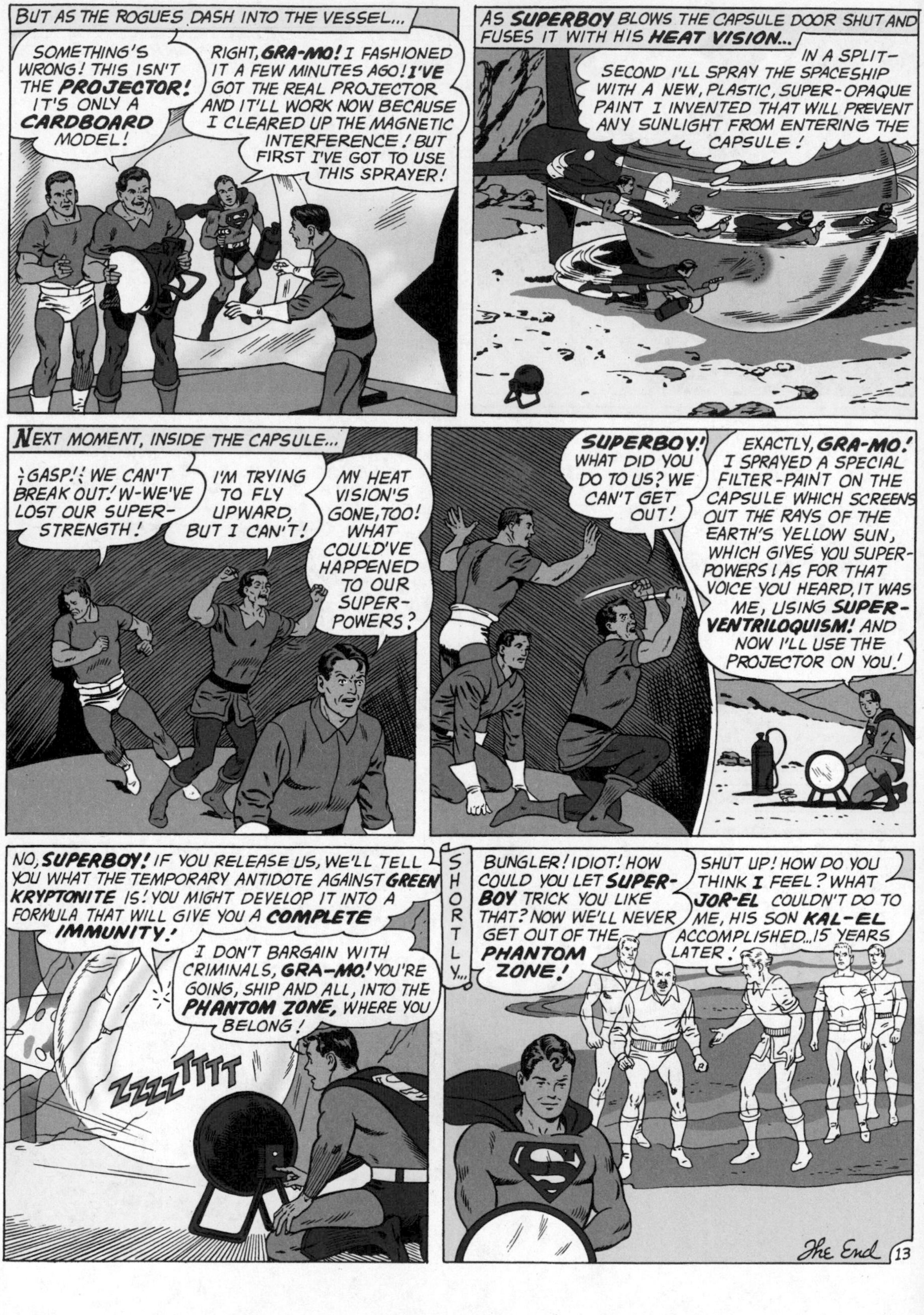
BUT AS THE ROGUES DASH INTO THE VESSEL...
SOMETHING'S WRONG! THIS ISN'T THE PROJECTOR! IT'S ONLY A CARDBOARD MODEL!
RIGHT, GRA-MO! I FASHIONED IT A FEW MINUTES AGO! I'VE GOT THE REAL PROJECTOR AND IT'LL WORK NOW BECAUSE I CLEARED UP THE MAGNETIC INTERFERENCE! BUT FIRST I'VE GOT TO USE THIS SPRAYER!
AS SUPERBOY BLOWS THE CAPSULE DOOR SHUT AND FUSES IT WITH HIS HEAT VISION...
IN A SPLIT-SECOND I'LL SPRAY THE SPACESHIP WITH A NEW, PLASTIC, SUPER-OPAQUE PAINT I INVENTED THAT WILL PREVENT ANY SUNLIGHT FROM ENTERING THE CAPSULE!
NEXT MOMENT, INSIDE THE CAPSULE...
GASP! WE CAN'T BREAK OUT! W-WE'VE LOST OUR SUPER-STRENGTH!
I'M TRYING TO FLY UPWARD, BUT I CAN'T!
MY HEAT VISION'S GONE, TOO! WHAT COULD'VE HAPPENED TO OUR SUPER-POWERS?
SUPERBOY! WHAT DID YOU DO TO US? WE CAN'T GET OUT!
EXACTLY, GRA-MO! I SPRAYED A SPECIAL FILTER-PAINT ON THE CAPSULE WHICH SCREENS OUT THE RAYS OF THE EARTH'S YELLOW SUN, WHICH GIVES YOU SUPER-POWERS! AS FOR THAT VOICE YOU HEARD, IT WAS ME, USING SUPER-VENTRILOQUISM! AND NOW I'LL USE THE PROJECTOR ON YOU!
NO, SUPERBOY! IF YOU RELEASE US, WE'LL TELL YOU WHAT THE TEMPORARY ANTIDOTE AGAINST GREEN KRYPTONITE IS! YOU MIGHT DEVELOP IT INTO A FORMULA THAT WILL GIVE YOU A COMPLETE IMMUNITY!
I DON'T BARGAIN WITH CRIMINALS, GRA-MO! YOU'RE GOING, SHIP AND ALL, INTO THE PHANTOM ZONE, WHERE YOU BELONG!
ZZZZTTTT
SHORTLY...
BUNGLER! IDIOT! HOW COULD YOU LET SUPERBOY TRICK YOU LIKE THAT? NOW WE'LL NEVER GET OUT OF THE PHANTOM ZONE!
SHUT UP! HOW DO YOU THINK I FEEL? WHAT JOR-EL COULDN'T DO TO ME, HIS SON KAL-EL ACCOMPLISHED...15 YEARS LATER!
The End
13

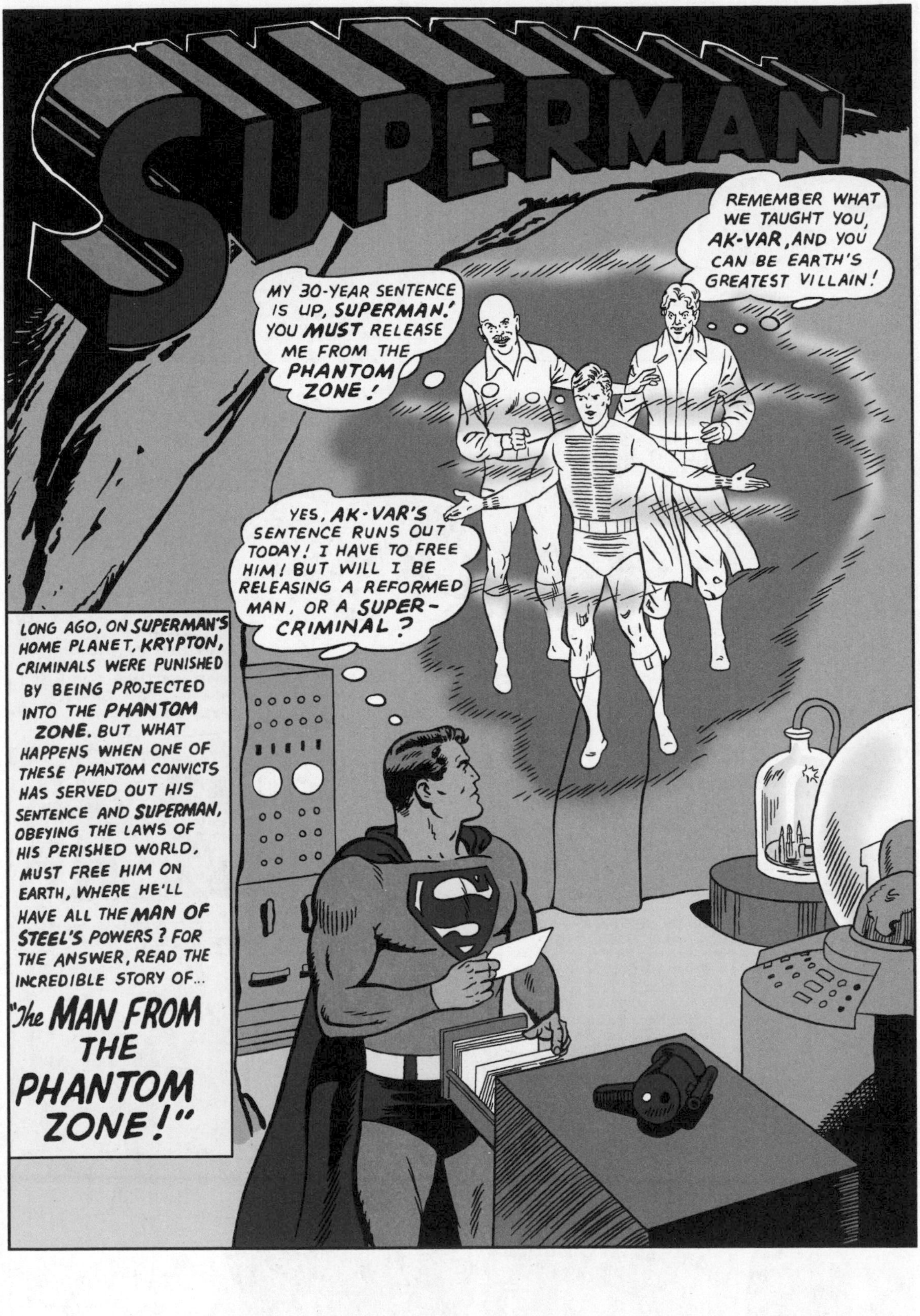
SUPERMAN
MY 30-YEAR SENTENCE IS UP, SUPERMAN! YOU MUST RELEASE ME FROM THE PHANTOM ZONE!
REMEMBER WHAT WE TAUGHT YOU, AK-VAR, AND YOU CAN BE EARTH'S GREATEST VILLAIN!
YES, AK-VAR'S SENTENCE RUNS OUT TODAY! I HAVE TO FREE HIM! BUT WILL I BE RELEASING A REFORMED MAN, OR A SUPER-CRIMINAL?
LONG AGO, ON SUPERMAN'S HOME PLANET, KRYPTON, CRIMINALS WERE PUNISHED BY BEING PROJECTED INTO THE PHANTOM ZONE. BUT WHAT HAPPENS WHEN ONE OF THESE PHANTOM CONVICTS HAS SERVED OUT HIS SENTENCE AND SUPERMAN, OBEYING THE LAWS OF HIS PERISHED WORLD, MUST FREE HIM ON EARTH, WHERE HE'LL HAVE ALL THE MAN OF STEEL'S POWERS? FOR THE ANSWER, READ THE INCREDIBLE STORY OF...
"The MAN FROM THE PHANTOM ZONE!"

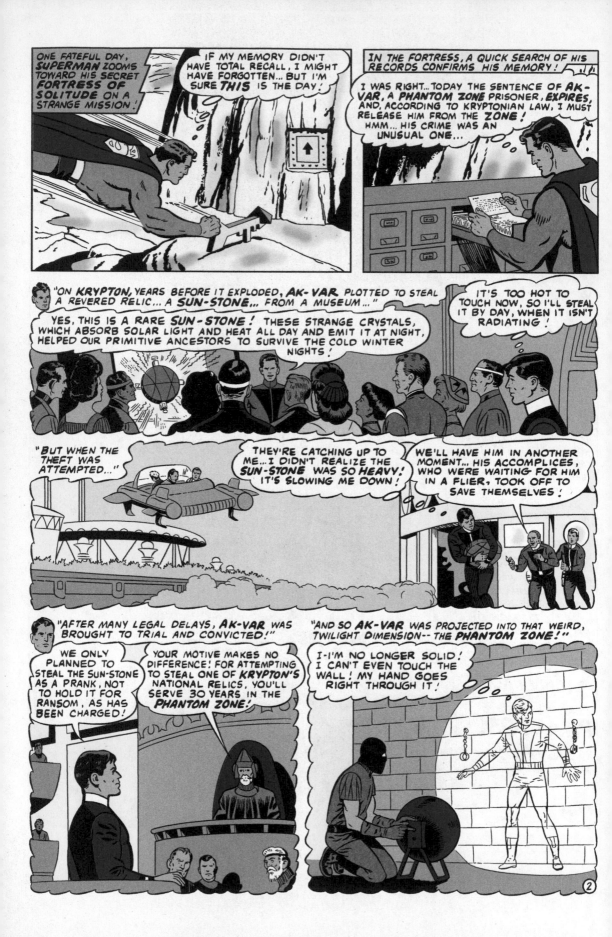

ONE FATEFUL DAY, SUPERMAN ZOOMS TOWARD HIS SECRET FORTRESS OF SOLITUDE ON A STRANGE MISSION!

IF MY MEMORY DIDN'T HAVE TOTAL RECALL, I MIGHT HAVE FORGOTTEN... BUT I'M SURE THIS IS THE DAY!

IN THE FORTRESS, A QUICK SEARCH OF HIS RECORDS CONFIRMS HIS MEMORY!

I WAS RIGHT... TODAY THE SENTENCE OF AK-VAR, A PHANTOM ZONE PRISONER, EXPIRES, AND, ACCORDING TO KRYPTONIAN LAW, I MUST RELEASE HIM FROM THE ZONE! HMM... HIS CRIME WAS AN UNUSUAL ONE...

"ON KRYPTON, YEARS BEFORE IT EXPLODED, AK-VAR PLOTTED TO STEAL A REVERED RELIC... A SUN-STONE... FROM A MUSEUM..."

YES, THIS IS A RARE SUN-STONE! THESE STRANGE CRYSTALS, WHICH ABSORB SOLAR LIGHT AND HEAT ALL DAY AND EMIT IT AT NIGHT, HELPED OUR PRIMITIVE ANCESTORS TO SURVIVE THE COLD WINTER NIGHTS!

IT'S TOO HOT TO TOUCH NOW, SO I'LL STEAL IT BY DAY, WHEN IT ISN'T RADIATING!

"BUT WHEN THE THEFT WAS ATTEMPTED..."

THEY'RE CATCHING UP TO ME... I DIDN'T REALIZE THE SUN-STONE WAS SO HEAVY! IT'S SLOWING ME DOWN!

WE'LL HAVE HIM IN ANOTHER MOMENT... HIS ACCOMPLICES, WHO WERE WAITING FOR HIM IN A FLIER, TOOK OFF TO SAVE THEMSELVES!

"AFTER MANY LEGAL DELAYS, AK-VAR WAS BROUGHT TO TRIAL AND CONVICTED!"

WE ONLY PLANNED TO STEAL THE SUN-STONE AS A PRANK, NOT TO HOLD IT FOR RANSOM, AS HAS BEEN CHARGED!

YOUR MOTIVE MAKES NO DIFFERENCE! FOR ATTEMPTING TO STEAL ONE OF KRYPTON'S NATIONAL RELICS, YOU'LL SERVE 30 YEARS IN THE PHANTOM ZONE!

"AND SO AK-VAR WAS PROJECTED INTO THAT WEIRD, TWILIGHT DIMENSION-- THE PHANTOM ZONE!"

I-I'M NO LONGER SOLID! I CAN'T EVEN TOUCH THE WALL! MY HAND GOES RIGHT THROUGH IT!

②

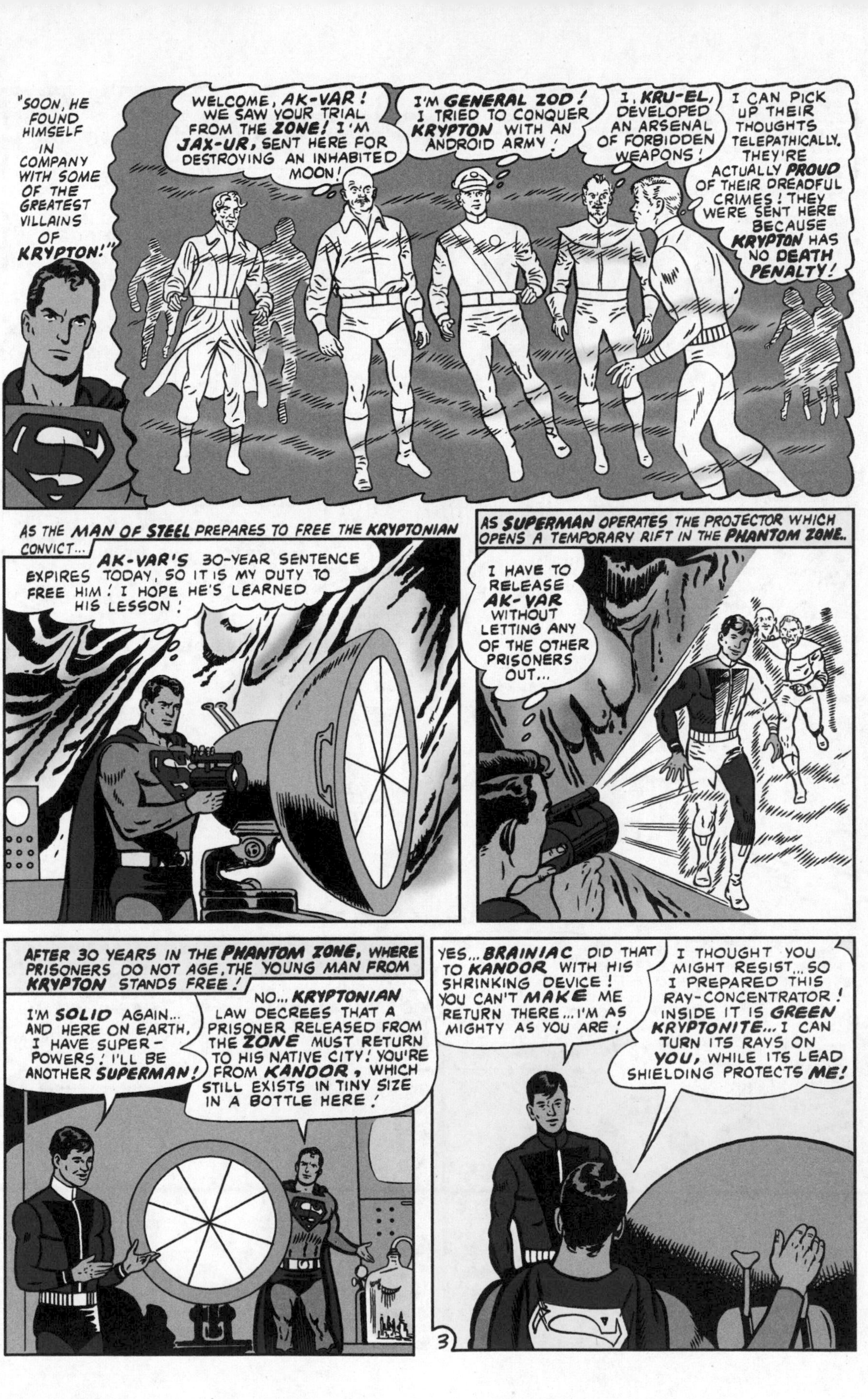
"SOON, HE FOUND HIMSELF IN COMPANY WITH SOME OF THE GREATEST VILLAINS OF KRYPTON!"
WELCOME, AK-VAR! WE SAW YOUR TRIAL FROM THE ZONE! I'M JAX-UR, SENT HERE FOR DESTROYING AN INHABITED MOON!
I'M GENERAL ZOD! I TRIED TO CONQUER KRYPTON WITH AN ANDROID ARMY!
I, KRU-EL, DEVELOPED AN ARSENAL OF FORBIDDEN WEAPONS!
I CAN PICK UP THEIR THOUGHTS TELEPATHICALLY. THEY'RE ACTUALLY PROUD OF THEIR DREADFUL CRIMES! THEY WERE SENT HERE BECAUSE KRYPTON HAS NO DEATH PENALTY!
AS THE MAN OF STEEL PREPARES TO FREE THE KRYPTONIAN CONVICT...
AK-VAR'S 30-YEAR SENTENCE EXPIRES TODAY, SO IT IS MY DUTY TO FREE HIM! I HOPE HE'S LEARNED HIS LESSON!
AS SUPERMAN OPERATES THE PROJECTOR WHICH OPENS A TEMPORARY RIFT IN THE PHANTOM ZONE..
I HAVE TO RELEASE AK-VAR WITHOUT LETTING ANY OF THE OTHER PRISONERS OUT...
AFTER 30 YEARS IN THE PHANTOM ZONE, WHERE PRISONERS DO NOT AGE, THE YOUNG MAN FROM KRYPTON STANDS FREE!
I'M SOLID AGAIN... AND HERE ON EARTH, I HAVE SUPER-POWERS! I'LL BE ANOTHER SUPERMAN!
NO... KRYPTONIAN LAW DECREES THAT A PRISONER RELEASED FROM THE ZONE MUST RETURN TO HIS NATIVE CITY! YOU'RE FROM KANDOR, WHICH STILL EXISTS IN TINY SIZE IN A BOTTLE HERE!
YES... BRAINIAC DID THAT TO KANDOR WITH HIS SHRINKING DEVICE! YOU CAN'T MAKE ME RETURN THERE... I'M AS MIGHTY AS YOU ARE!
I THOUGHT YOU MIGHT RESIST... SO I PREPARED THIS RAY-CONCENTRATOR! INSIDE IT IS GREEN KRYPTONITE... I CAN TURN ITS RAYS ON YOU, WHILE ITS LEAD SHIELDING PROTECTS ME!
3

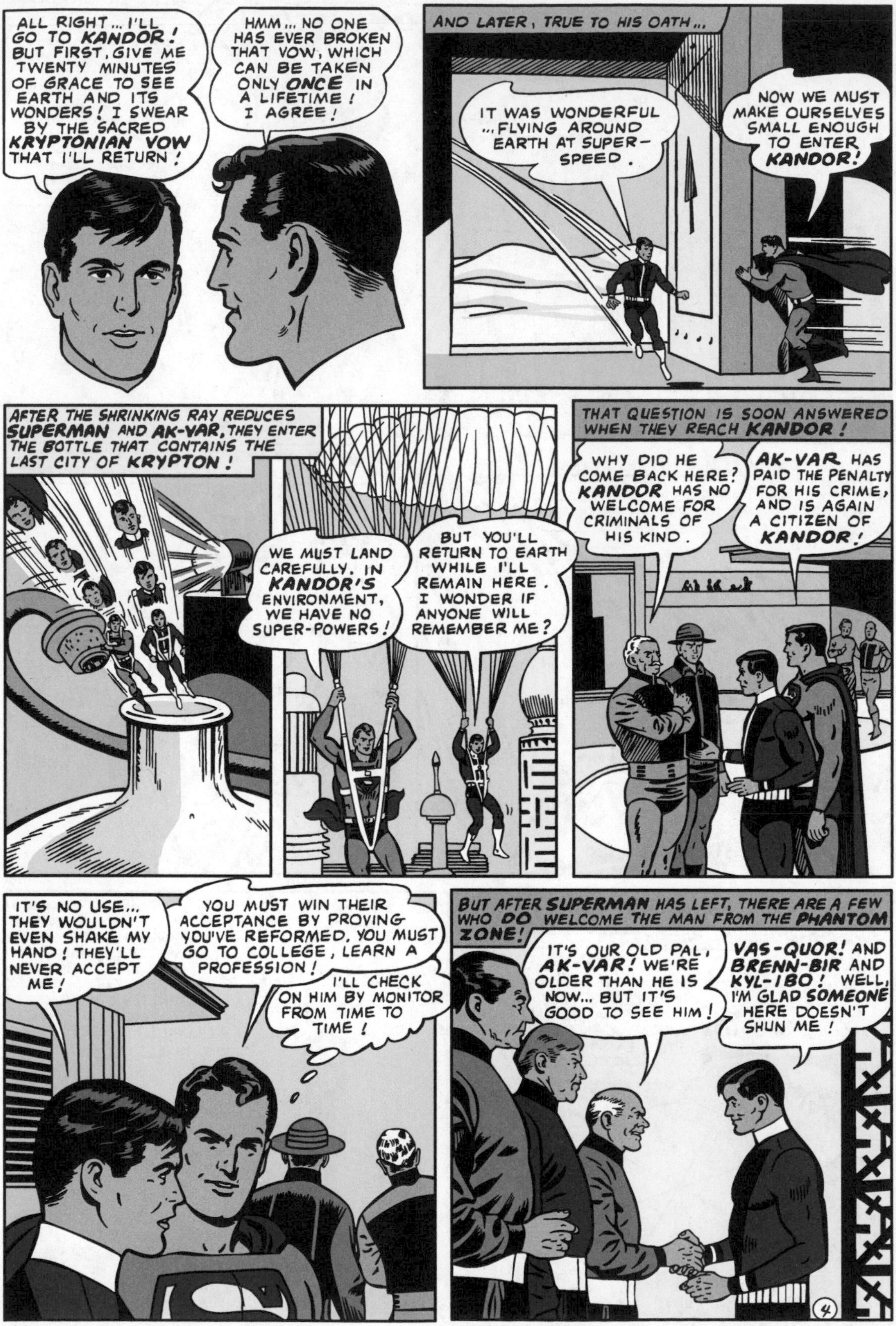
ALL RIGHT... I'LL GO TO KANDOR! BUT FIRST, GIVE ME TWENTY MINUTES OF GRACE TO SEE EARTH AND ITS WONDERS! I SWEAR BY THE SACRED KRYPTONIAN VOW THAT I'LL RETURN!
HMM... NO ONE HAS EVER BROKEN THAT VOW, WHICH CAN BE TAKEN ONLY ONCE IN A LIFETIME! I AGREE!
AND LATER, TRUE TO HIS OATH...
IT WAS WONDERFUL ...FLYING AROUND EARTH AT SUPER-SPEED.
NOW WE MUST MAKE OURSELVES SMALL ENOUGH TO ENTER KANDOR!
AFTER THE SHRINKING RAY REDUCES SUPERMAN AND AK-VAR, THEY ENTER THE BOTTLE THAT CONTAINS THE LAST CITY OF KRYPTON!
WE MUST LAND CAREFULLY. IN KANDOR'S ENVIRONMENT, WE HAVE NO SUPER-POWERS!
BUT YOU'LL RETURN TO EARTH WHILE I'LL REMAIN HERE. I WONDER IF ANYONE WILL REMEMBER ME?
THAT QUESTION IS SOON ANSWERED WHEN THEY REACH KANDOR!
WHY DID HE COME BACK HERE? KANDOR HAS NO WELCOME FOR CRIMINALS OF HIS KIND.
AK-VAR HAS PAID THE PENALTY FOR HIS CRIME, AND IS AGAIN A CITIZEN OF KANDOR!
IT'S NO USE... THEY WOULDN'T EVEN SHAKE MY HAND! THEY'LL NEVER ACCEPT ME!
YOU MUST WIN THEIR ACCEPTANCE BY PROVING YOU'VE REFORMED. YOU MUST GO TO COLLEGE, LEARN A PROFESSION!
I'LL CHECK ON HIM BY MONITOR FROM TIME TO TIME!
BUT AFTER SUPERMAN HAS LEFT, THERE ARE A FEW WHO DO WELCOME THE MAN FROM THE PHANTOM ZONE!
IT'S OUR OLD PAL, AK-VAR! WE'RE OLDER THAN HE IS NOW... BUT IT'S GOOD TO SEE HIM!
VAS-QUOR! AND BRENN-BIR AND KYL-IBO! WELL, I'M GLAD SOMEONE HERE DOESN'T SHUN ME!
4

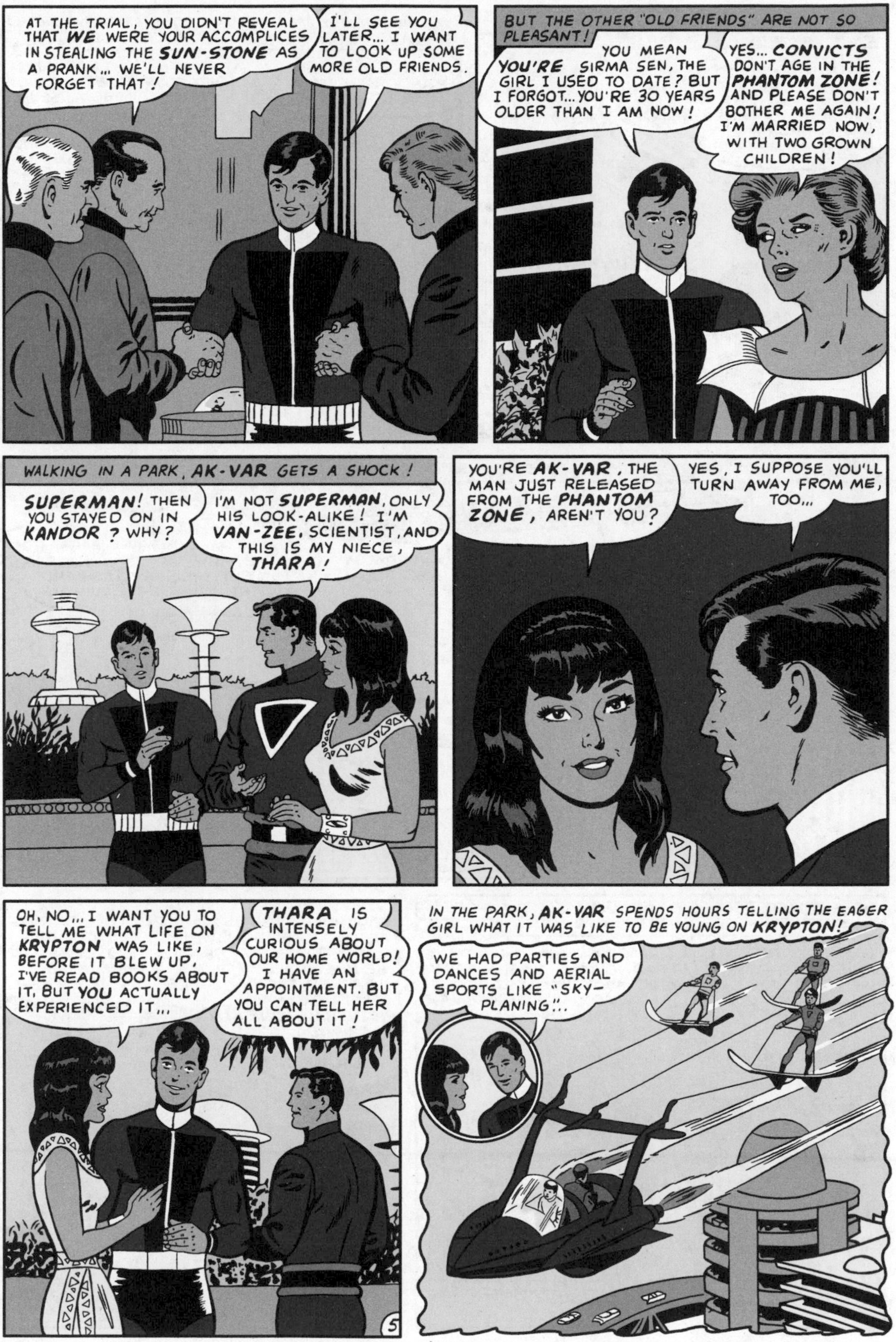
AT THE TRIAL, YOU DIDN'T REVEAL THAT WE WERE YOUR ACCOMPLICES IN STEALING THE SUN-STONE AS A PRANK... WE'LL NEVER FORGET THAT!
I'LL SEE YOU LATER... I WANT TO LOOK UP SOME MORE OLD FRIENDS.
BUT THE OTHER "OLD FRIENDS" ARE NOT SO PLEASANT!
YOU MEAN YOU'RE SIRMA SEN, THE GIRL I USED TO DATE? BUT I FORGOT... YOU'RE 30 YEARS OLDER THAN I AM NOW!
YES... CONVICTS DON'T AGE IN THE PHANTOM ZONE! AND PLEASE DON'T BOTHER ME AGAIN! I'M MARRIED NOW, WITH TWO GROWN CHILDREN!
WALKING IN A PARK, AK-VAR GETS A SHOCK!
SUPERMAN! THEN YOU STAYED ON IN KANDOR? WHY?
I'M NOT SUPERMAN, ONLY HIS LOOK-ALIKE! I'M VAN-ZEE, SCIENTIST, AND THIS IS MY NIECE, THARA!
YOU'RE AK-VAR, THE MAN JUST RELEASED FROM THE PHANTOM ZONE, AREN'T YOU?
YES, I SUPPOSE YOU'LL TURN AWAY FROM ME, TOO...
OH, NO... I WANT YOU TO TELL ME WHAT LIFE ON KRYPTON WAS LIKE, BEFORE IT BLEW UP. I'VE READ BOOKS ABOUT IT, BUT YOU ACTUALLY EXPERIENCED IT...
THARA IS INTENSELY CURIOUS ABOUT OUR HOME WORLD! I HAVE AN APPOINTMENT. BUT YOU CAN TELL HER ALL ABOUT IT!
5
IN THE PARK, AK-VAR SPENDS HOURS TELLING THE EAGER GIRL WHAT IT WAS LIKE TO BE YOUNG ON KRYPTON!
WE HAD PARTIES AND DANCES AND AERIAL SPORTS LIKE "SKY-PLANING"...

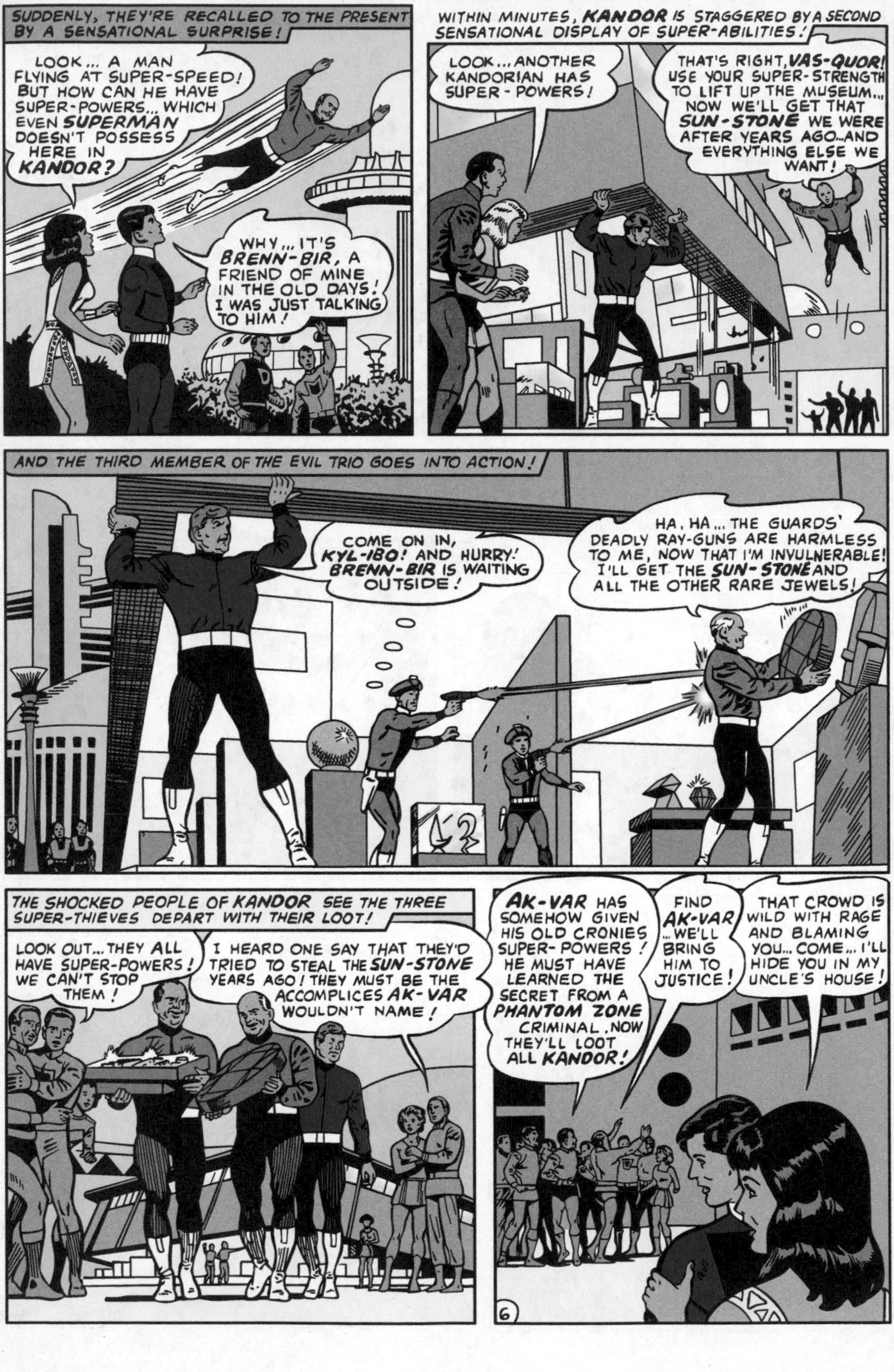
SUDDENLY, THEY'RE RECALLED TO THE PRESENT BY A SENSATIONAL SURPRISE!
LOOK... A MAN FLYING AT SUPER-SPEED! BUT HOW CAN HE HAVE SUPER-POWERS... WHICH EVEN SUPERMAN DOESN'T POSSESS HERE IN KANDOR?
WHY... IT'S BRENN-BIR, A FRIEND OF MINE IN THE OLD DAYS! I WAS JUST TALKING TO HIM!
WITHIN MINUTES, KANDOR IS STAGGERED BY A SECOND SENSATIONAL DISPLAY OF SUPER-ABILITIES!
LOOK... ANOTHER KANDORIAN HAS SUPER-POWERS!
THAT'S RIGHT, VAS-QUOR! USE YOUR SUPER-STRENGTH TO LIFT UP THE MUSEUM... NOW WE'LL GET THAT SUN-STONE WE WERE AFTER YEARS AGO...AND EVERYTHING ELSE WE WANT!
AND THE THIRD MEMBER OF THE EVIL TRIO GOES INTO ACTION!
COME ON IN, KYL-IBO! AND HURRY! BRENN-BIR IS WAITING OUTSIDE!
HA, HA... THE GUARDS' DEADLY RAY-GUNS ARE HARMLESS TO ME, NOW THAT I'M INVULNERABLE! I'LL GET THE SUN-STONE AND ALL THE OTHER RARE JEWELS!
THE SHOCKED PEOPLE OF KANDOR SEE THE THREE SUPER-THIEVES DEPART WITH THEIR LOOT!
LOOK OUT... THEY ALL HAVE SUPER-POWERS! WE CAN'T STOP THEM!
I HEARD ONE SAY THAT THEY'D TRIED TO STEAL THE SUN-STONE YEARS AGO! THEY MUST BE THE ACCOMPLICES AK-VAR WOULDN'T NAME!
AK-VAR HAS SOMEHOW GIVEN HIS OLD CRONIES SUPER-POWERS! HE MUST HAVE LEARNED THE SECRET FROM A PHANTOM ZONE CRIMINAL. NOW THEY'LL LOOT ALL KANDOR!
FIND AK-VAR ...WE'LL BRING HIM TO JUSTICE!
THAT CROWD IS WILD WITH RAGE AND BLAMING YOU... COME... I'LL HIDE YOU IN MY UNCLE'S HOUSE!
6

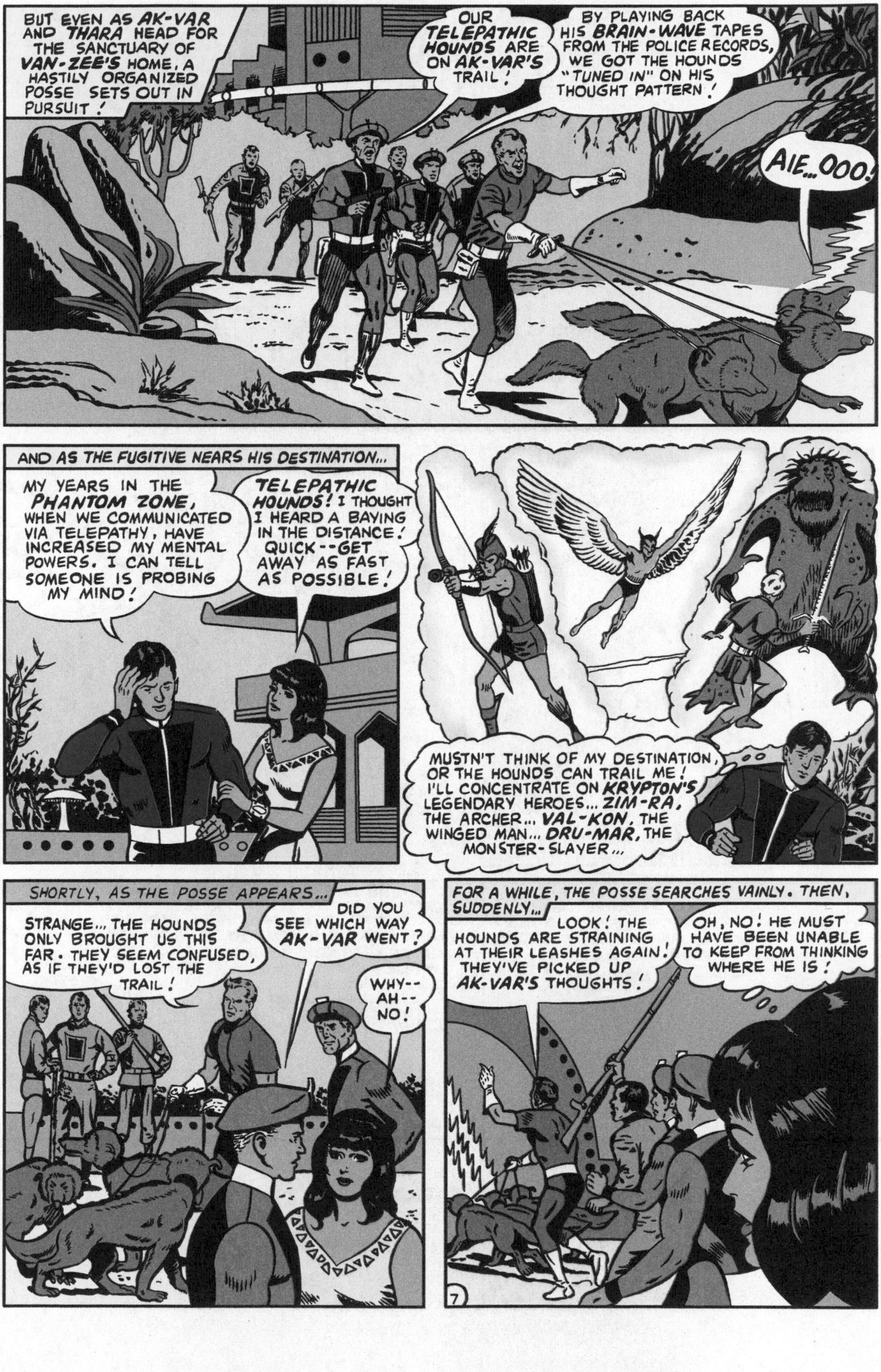
BUT EVEN AS AK-VAR AND THARA HEAD FOR THE SANCTUARY OF VAN-ZEE'S HOME, A HASTILY ORGANIZED POSSE SETS OUT IN PURSUIT!
OUR TELEPATHIC HOUNDS ARE ON AK-VAR'S TRAIL!
BY PLAYING BACK HIS BRAIN-WAVE TAPES FROM THE POLICE RECORDS, WE GOT THE HOUNDS "TUNED IN" ON HIS THOUGHT PATTERN!
AIE...OOO!
AND AS THE FUGITIVE NEARS HIS DESTINATION...
MY YEARS IN THE PHANTOM ZONE, WHEN WE COMMUNICATED VIA TELEPATHY, HAVE INCREASED MY MENTAL POWERS. I CAN TELL SOMEONE IS PROBING MY MIND!
TELEPATHIC HOUNDS! I THOUGHT I HEARD A BAYING IN THE DISTANCE! QUICK--GET AWAY AS FAST AS POSSIBLE!
MUSTN'T THINK OF MY DESTINATION, OR THE HOUNDS CAN TRAIL ME! I'LL CONCENTRATE ON KRYPTON'S LEGENDARY HEROES... ZIM-RA, THE ARCHER... VAL-KON, THE WINGED MAN... DRU-MAR, THE MONSTER-SLAYER...
SHORTLY, AS THE POSSE APPEARS...
STRANGE... THE HOUNDS ONLY BROUGHT US THIS FAR. THEY SEEM CONFUSED, AS IF THEY'D LOST THE TRAIL!
DID YOU SEE WHICH WAY AK-VAR WENT?
WHY-- AH-- NO!
FOR A WHILE, THE POSSE SEARCHES VAINLY. THEN, SUDDENLY...
LOOK! THE HOUNDS ARE STRAINING AT THEIR LEASHES AGAIN! THEY'VE PICKED UP AK-VAR'S THOUGHTS!
OH, NO! HE MUST HAVE BEEN UNABLE TO KEEP FROM THINKING WHERE HE IS!
7

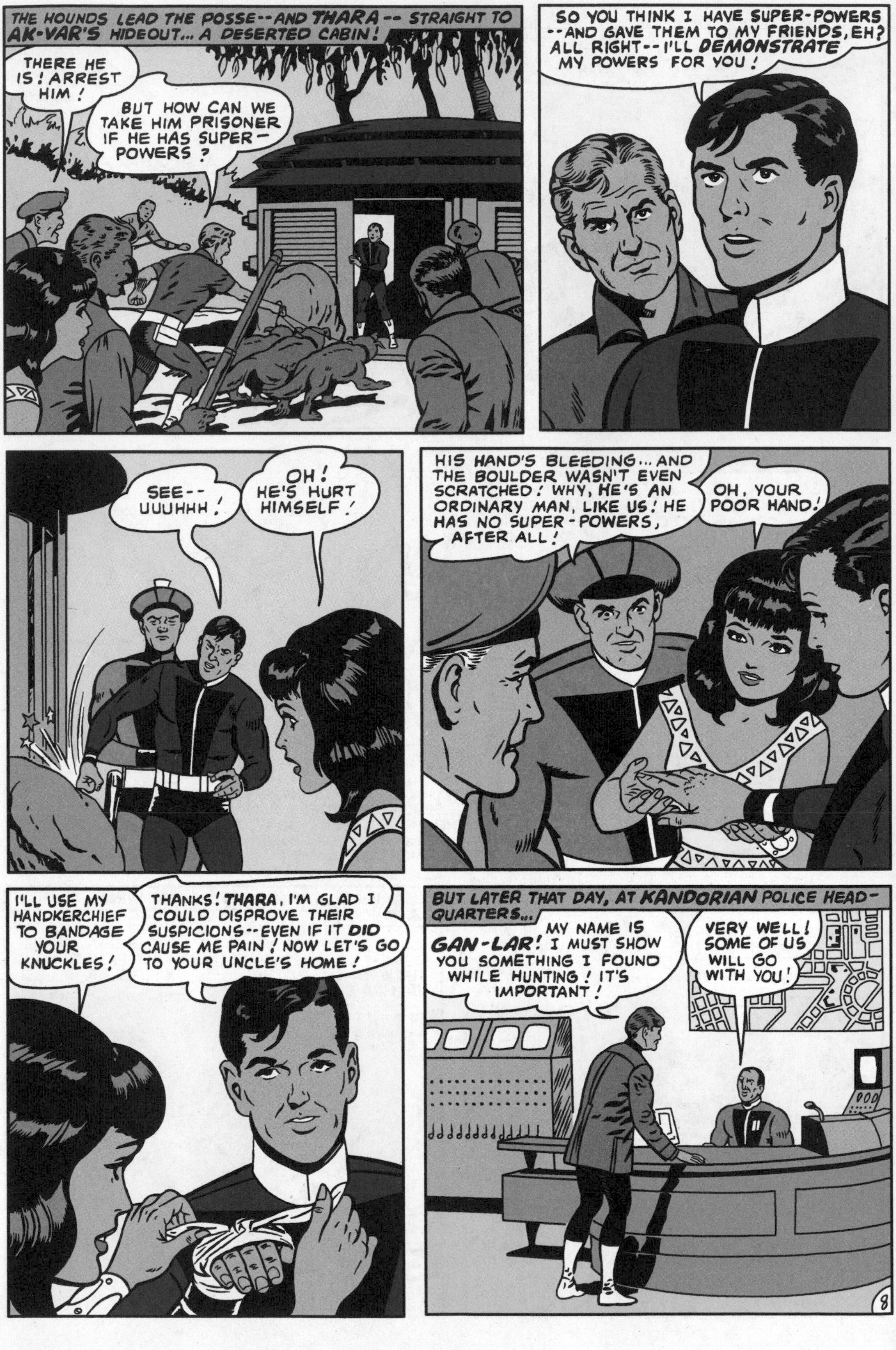
THE HOUNDS LEAD THE POSSE--AND THARA-- STRAIGHT TO AK-VAR'S HIDEOUT... A DESERTED CABIN!
THERE HE IS! ARREST HIM!
BUT HOW CAN WE TAKE HIM PRISONER IF HE HAS SUPER-POWERS?
SO YOU THINK I HAVE SUPER-POWERS --AND GAVE THEM TO MY FRIENDS, EH? ALL RIGHT--I'LL DEMONSTRATE MY POWERS FOR YOU!
SEE-- UUUHHH!
OH! HE'S HURT HIMSELF!
HIS HAND'S BLEEDING... AND THE BOULDER WASN'T EVEN SCRATCHED! WHY, HE'S AN ORDINARY MAN, LIKE US! HE HAS NO SUPER-POWERS, AFTER ALL!
OH, YOUR POOR HAND!
I'LL USE MY HANDKERCHIEF TO BANDAGE YOUR KNUCKLES!
THANKS! THARA, I'M GLAD I COULD DISPROVE THEIR SUSPICIONS--EVEN IF IT DID CAUSE ME PAIN! NOW LET'S GO TO YOUR UNCLE'S HOME!
BUT LATER THAT DAY, AT KANDORIAN POLICE HEAD-QUARTERS...
MY NAME IS GAN-LAR! I MUST SHOW YOU SOMETHING I FOUND WHILE HUNTING! IT'S IMPORTANT!
VERY WELL! SOME OF US WILL GO WITH YOU!
8

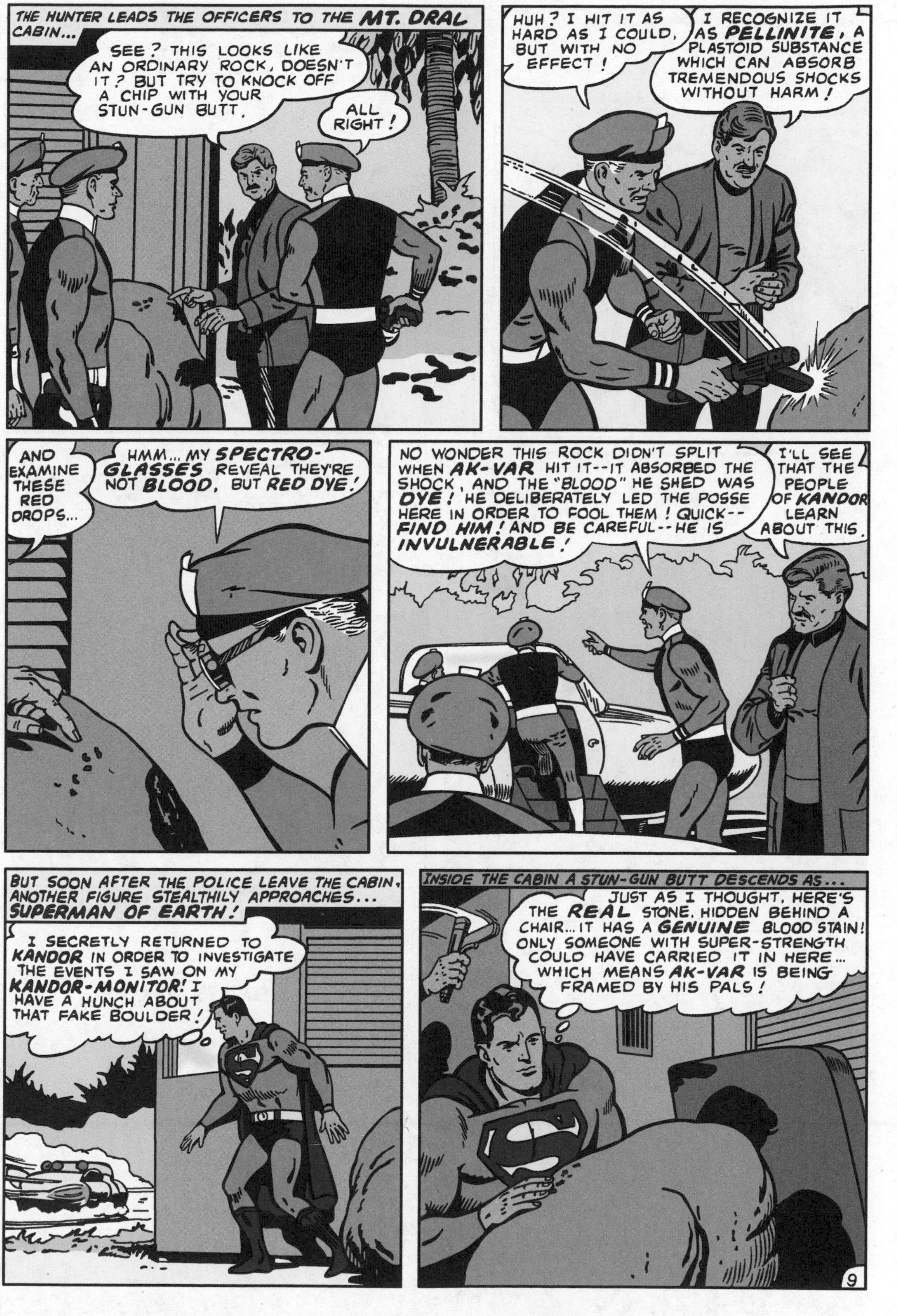
THE HUNTER LEADS THE OFFICERS TO THE MT. DRAL CABIN...
SEE? THIS LOOKS LIKE AN ORDINARY ROCK, DOESN'T IT? BUT TRY TO KNOCK OFF A CHIP WITH YOUR STUN-GUN BUTT.
ALL RIGHT!
HUH? I HIT IT AS HARD AS I COULD, BUT WITH NO EFFECT!
I RECOGNIZE IT AS PELLINITE, A PLASTOID SUBSTANCE WHICH CAN ABSORB TREMENDOUS SHOCKS WITHOUT HARM!
AND EXAMINE THESE RED DROPS...
HMM... MY SPECTRO-GLASSES REVEAL THEY'RE NOT BLOOD, BUT RED DYE!
NO WONDER THIS ROCK DIDN'T SPLIT WHEN AK-VAR HIT IT--IT ABSORBED THE SHOCK, AND THE "BLOOD" HE SHED WAS DYE! HE DELIBERATELY LED THE POSSE HERE IN ORDER TO FOOL THEM! QUICK--FIND HIM! AND BE CAREFUL--HE IS INVULNERABLE!
I'LL SEE THAT THE PEOPLE OF KANDOR LEARN ABOUT THIS.
BUT SOON AFTER THE POLICE LEAVE THE CABIN, ANOTHER FIGURE STEALTHILY APPROACHES... SUPERMAN OF EARTH!
I SECRETLY RETURNED TO KANDOR IN ORDER TO INVESTIGATE THE EVENTS I SAW ON MY KANDOR-MONITOR! I HAVE A HUNCH ABOUT THAT FAKE BOULDER!
INSIDE THE CABIN A STUN-GUN BUTT DESCENDS AS...
JUST AS I THOUGHT. HERE'S THE REAL STONE, HIDDEN BEHIND A CHAIR... IT HAS A GENUINE BLOOD STAIN! ONLY SOMEONE WITH SUPER-STRENGTH COULD HAVE CARRIED IT IN HERE... WHICH MEANS AK-VAR IS BEING FRAMED BY HIS PALS!
9

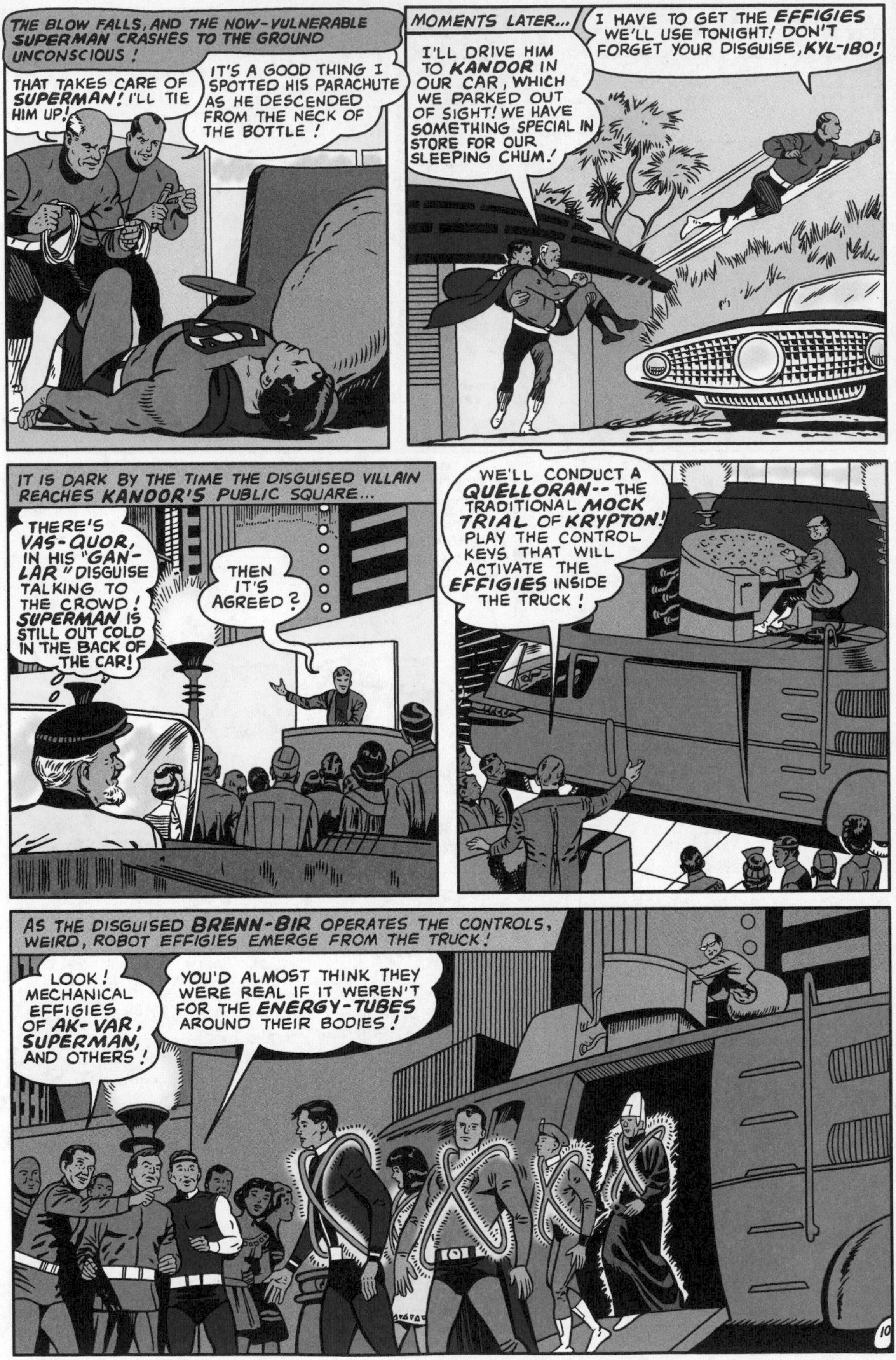
THE BLOW FALLS, AND THE NOW-VULNERABLE SUPERMAN CRASHES TO THE GROUND UNCONSCIOUS!
THAT TAKES CARE OF SUPERMAN! I'LL TIE HIM UP!
IT'S A GOOD THING I SPOTTED HIS PARACHUTE AS HE DESCENDED FROM THE NECK OF THE BOTTLE!
MOMENTS LATER...
I'LL DRIVE HIM TO KANDOR IN OUR CAR, WHICH WE PARKED OUT OF SIGHT! WE HAVE SOMETHING SPECIAL IN STORE FOR OUR SLEEPING CHUM!
I HAVE TO GET THE EFFIGIES WE'LL USE TONIGHT! DON'T FORGET YOUR DISGUISE, KYL-IBO!
IT IS DARK BY THE TIME THE DISGUISED VILLAIN REACHES KANDOR'S PUBLIC SQUARE...
THERE'S VAS-QUOR, IN HIS "GAN-LAR" DISGUISE TALKING TO THE CROWD! SUPERMAN IS STILL OUT COLD IN THE BACK OF THE CAR!
THEN IT'S AGREED?
WE'LL CONDUCT A QUELLORAN-- THE TRADITIONAL MOCK TRIAL OF KRYPTON! PLAY THE CONTROL KEYS THAT WILL ACTIVATE THE EFFIGIES INSIDE THE TRUCK!
AS THE DISGUISED BRENN-BIR OPERATES THE CONTROLS, WEIRD, ROBOT EFFIGIES EMERGE FROM THE TRUCK!
LOOK! MECHANICAL EFFIGIES OF AK-VAR, SUPERMAN, AND OTHERS!
YOU'D ALMOST THINK THEY WERE REAL IF IT WEREN'T FOR THE ENERGY-TUBES AROUND THEIR BODIES!
10

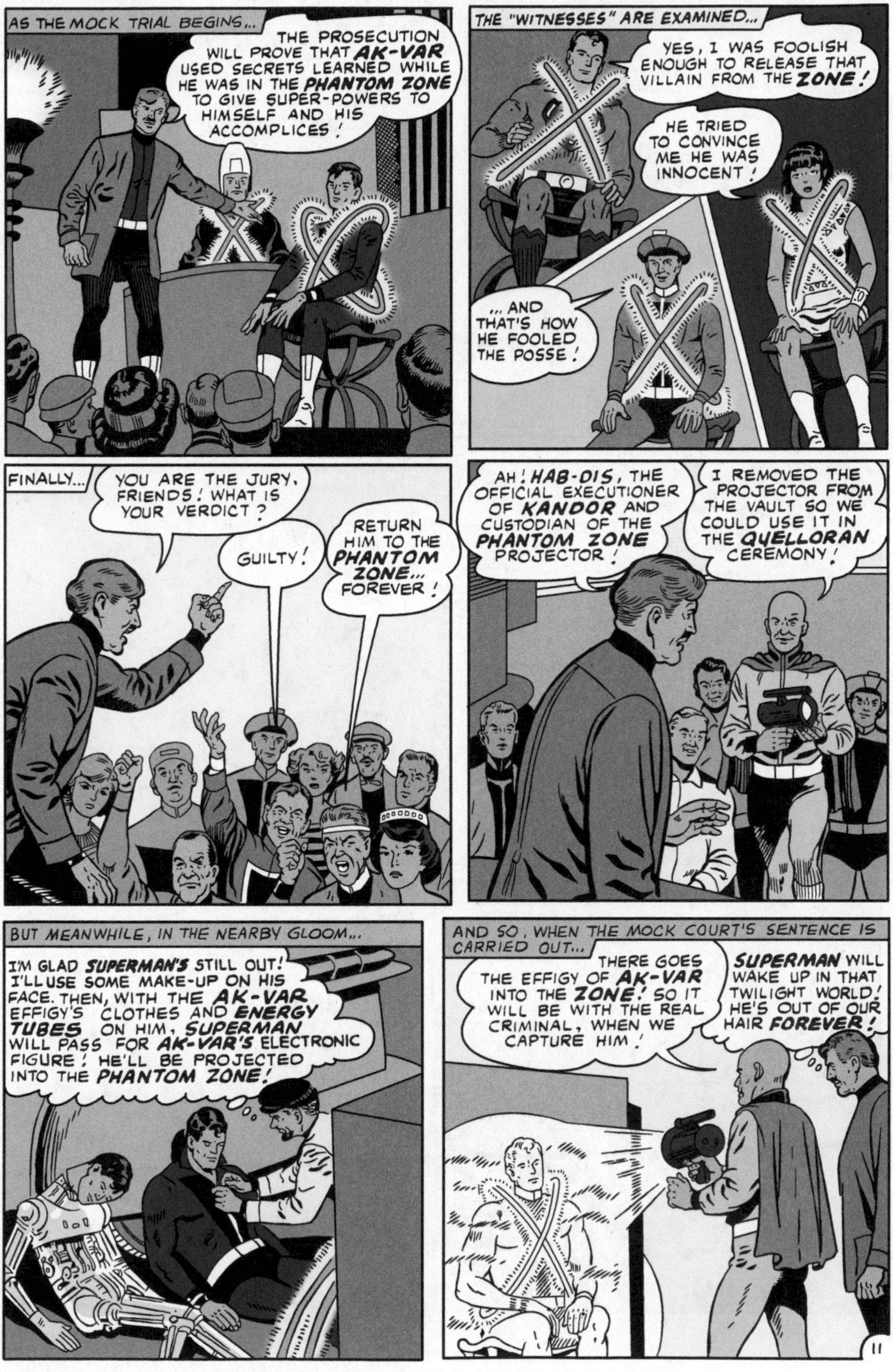
AS THE MOCK TRIAL BEGINS...
THE PROSECUTION WILL PROVE THAT AK-VAR USED SECRETS LEARNED WHILE HE WAS IN THE PHANTOM ZONE TO GIVE SUPER-POWERS TO HIMSELF AND HIS ACCOMPLICES!
THE "WITNESSES" ARE EXAMINED...
YES, I WAS FOOLISH ENOUGH TO RELEASE THAT VILLAIN FROM THE ZONE!
HE TRIED TO CONVINCE ME HE WAS INNOCENT!
...AND THAT'S HOW HE FOOLED THE POSSE!
FINALLY...
YOU ARE THE JURY, FRIENDS! WHAT IS YOUR VERDICT?
GUILTY!
RETURN HIM TO THE PHANTOM ZONE... FOREVER!
AH! HAB-DIS, THE OFFICIAL EXECUTIONER OF KANDOR AND CUSTODIAN OF THE PHANTOM ZONE PROJECTOR!
I REMOVED THE PROJECTOR FROM THE VAULT SO WE COULD USE IT IN THE QUELLORAN CEREMONY!
BUT MEANWHILE, IN THE NEARBY GLOOM...
I'M GLAD SUPERMAN'S STILL OUT! I'LL USE SOME MAKE-UP ON HIS FACE. THEN, WITH THE AK-VAR EFFIGY'S CLOTHES AND ENERGY TUBES ON HIM, SUPERMAN WILL PASS FOR AK-VAR'S ELECTRONIC FIGURE! HE'LL BE PROJECTED INTO THE PHANTOM ZONE!
AND SO, WHEN THE MOCK COURT'S SENTENCE IS CARRIED OUT...
THERE GOES THE EFFIGY OF AK-VAR INTO THE ZONE! SO IT WILL BE WITH THE REAL CRIMINAL, WHEN WE CAPTURE HIM!
SUPERMAN WILL WAKE UP IN THAT TWILIGHT WORLD! HE'S OUT OF OUR HAIR FOREVER!
11

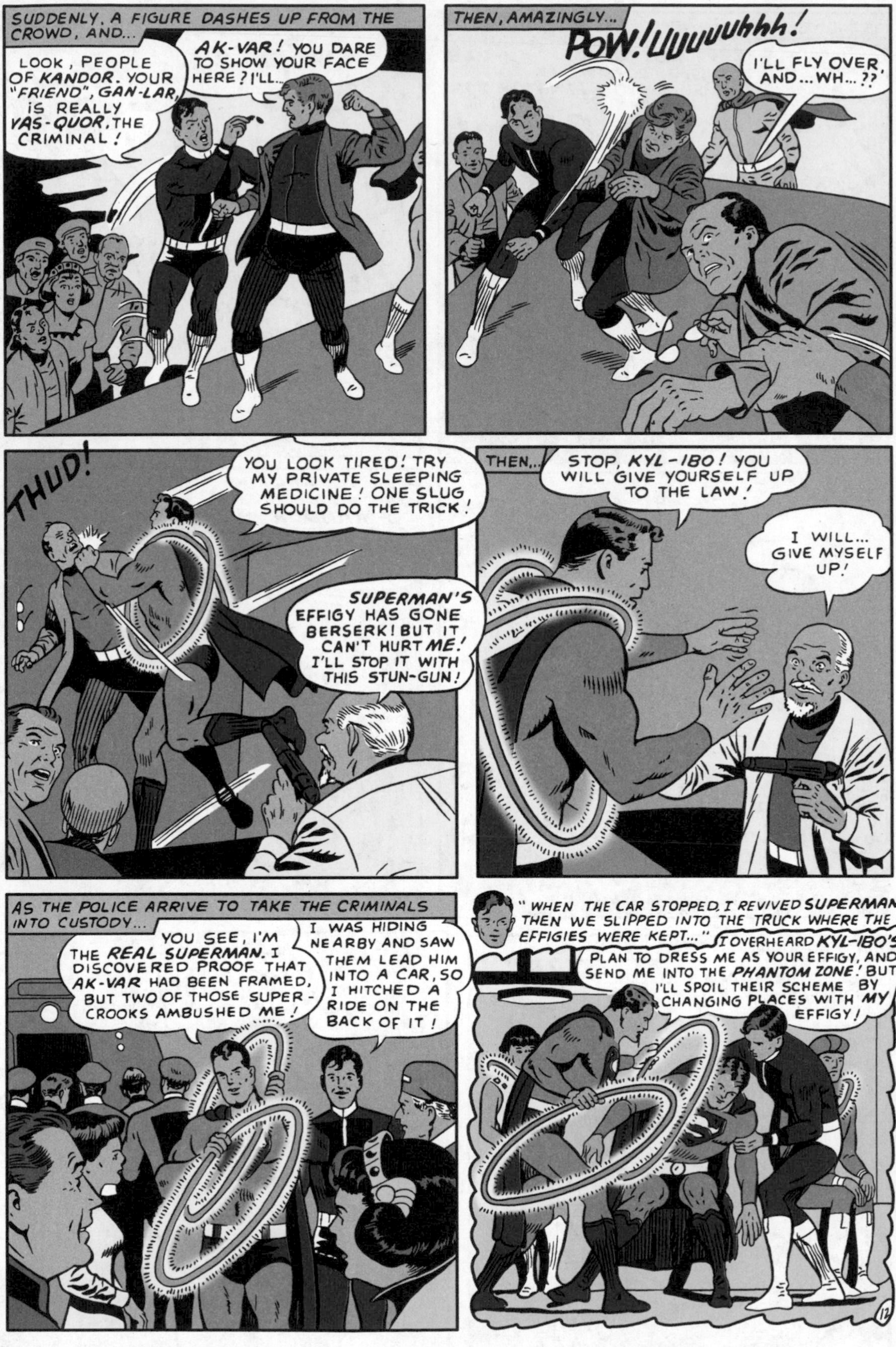
SUDDENLY, A FIGURE DASHES UP FROM THE CROWD, AND...
LOOK, PEOPLE OF KANDOR. YOUR "FRIEND", GAN-LAR, IS REALLY VAS-QUOR, THE CRIMINAL!
AK-VAR! YOU DARE TO SHOW YOUR FACE HERE? I'LL...
THEN, AMAZINGLY...
POW! UUUUUhhh!
I'LL FLY OVER, AND... WH...??
THUD!
YOU LOOK TIRED! TRY MY PRIVATE SLEEPING MEDICINE! ONE SLUG SHOULD DO THE TRICK!
SUPERMAN'S EFFIGY HAS GONE BERSERK! BUT IT CAN'T HURT ME! I'LL STOP IT WITH THIS STUN-GUN!
THEN...
STOP, KYL-IBO! YOU WILL GIVE YOURSELF UP TO THE LAW!
I WILL... GIVE MYSELF UP!
AS THE POLICE ARRIVE TO TAKE THE CRIMINALS INTO CUSTODY...
YOU SEE, I'M THE REAL SUPERMAN. I DISCOVERED PROOF THAT AK-VAR HAD BEEN FRAMED, BUT TWO OF THOSE SUPER-CROOKS AMBUSHED ME!
I WAS HIDING NEARBY AND SAW THEM LEAD HIM INTO A CAR, SO I HITCHED A RIDE ON THE BACK OF IT!
"WHEN THE CAR STOPPED, I REVIVED SUPERMAN THEN WE SLIPPED INTO THE TRUCK WHERE THE EFFIGIES WERE KEPT..."
I OVERHEARD KYL-IBO'S PLAN TO DRESS ME AS YOUR EFFIGY, AND SEND ME INTO THE PHANTOM ZONE! BUT I'LL SPOIL THEIR SCHEME BY CHANGING PLACES WITH MY EFFIGY!
12

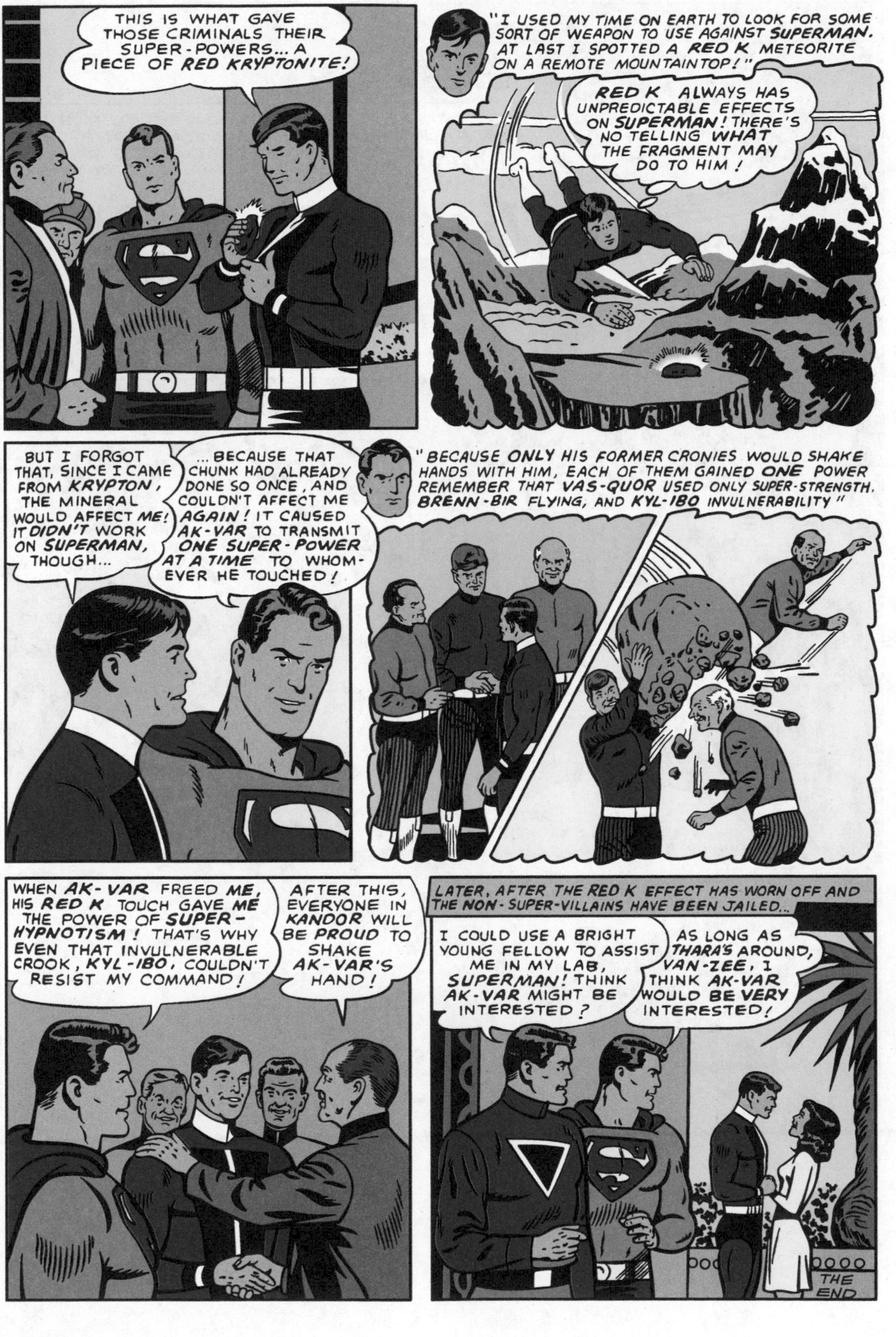
THIS IS WHAT GAVE THOSE CRIMINALS THEIR SUPER-POWERS... A PIECE OF RED KRYPTONITE!
"I USED MY TIME ON EARTH TO LOOK FOR SOME SORT OF WEAPON TO USE AGAINST SUPERMAN. AT LAST I SPOTTED A RED K METEORITE ON A REMOTE MOUNTAINTOP!"
RED K ALWAYS HAS UNPREDICTABLE EFFECTS ON SUPERMAN! THERE'S NO TELLING WHAT THE FRAGMENT MAY DO TO HIM!
BUT I FORGOT THAT, SINCE I CAME FROM KRYPTON, THE MINERAL WOULD AFFECT ME! IT DIDN'T WORK ON SUPERMAN, THOUGH...
...BECAUSE THAT CHUNK HAD ALREADY DONE SO ONCE, AND COULDN'T AFFECT ME AGAIN! IT CAUSED AK-VAR TO TRANSMIT ONE SUPER-POWER AT A TIME TO WHOMEVER HE TOUCHED!
"BECAUSE ONLY HIS FORMER CRONIES WOULD SHAKE HANDS WITH HIM, EACH OF THEM GAINED ONE POWER REMEMBER THAT VAS-QUOR USED ONLY SUPER-STRENGTH, BRENN-BIR FLYING, AND KYL-IBO INVULNERABILITY"
WHEN AK-VAR FREED ME, HIS RED K TOUCH GAVE ME THE POWER OF SUPER-HYPNOTISM! THAT'S WHY EVEN THAT INVULNERABLE CROOK, KYL-IBO, COULDN'T RESIST MY COMMAND!
AFTER THIS, EVERYONE IN KANDOR WILL BE PROUD TO SHAKE AK-VAR'S HAND!
LATER, AFTER THE RED K EFFECT HAS WORN OFF AND THE NON-SUPER-VILLAINS HAVE BEEN JAILED...
I COULD USE A BRIGHT YOUNG FELLOW TO ASSIST ME IN MY LAB, SUPERMAN! THINK AK-VAR MIGHT BE INTERESTED?
AS LONG AS THARA'S AROUND, VAN-ZEE, I THINK AK-VAR WOULD BE VERY INTERESTED!
THE END

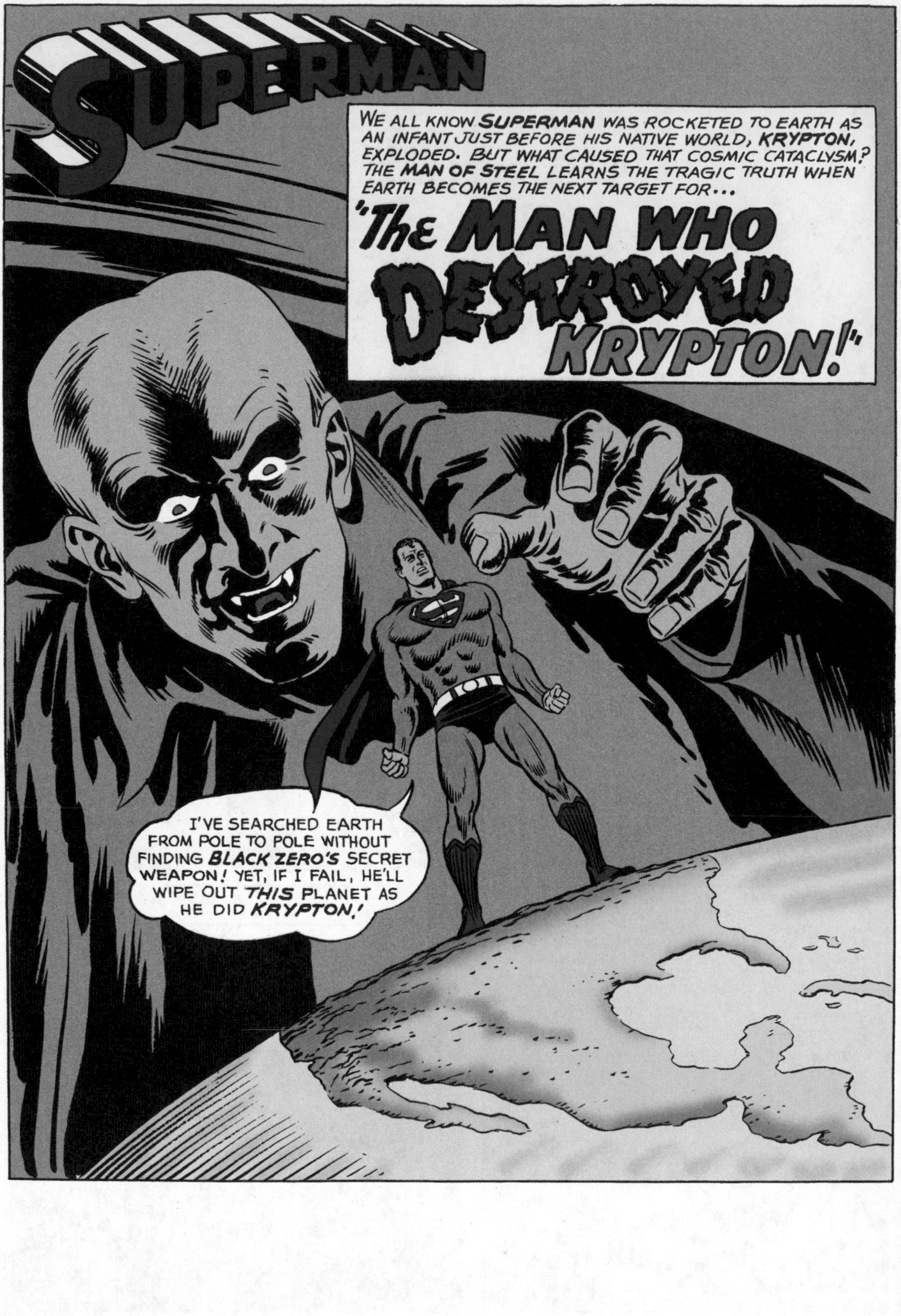
SUPERMAN
WE ALL KNOW SUPERMAN WAS ROCKETED TO EARTH AS AN INFANT JUST BEFORE HIS NATIVE WORLD, KRYPTON, EXPLODED. BUT WHAT CAUSED THAT COSMIC CATACLYSM? THE MAN OF STEEL LEARNS THE TRAGIC TRUTH WHEN EARTH BECOMES THE NEXT TARGET FOR...
"The MAN WHO DESTROYED KRYPTON!"
I'VE SEARCHED EARTH FROM POLE TO POLE WITHOUT FINDING BLACK ZERO'S SECRET WEAPON! YET, IF I FAIL, HE'LL WIPE OUT THIS PLANET AS HE DID KRYPTON!

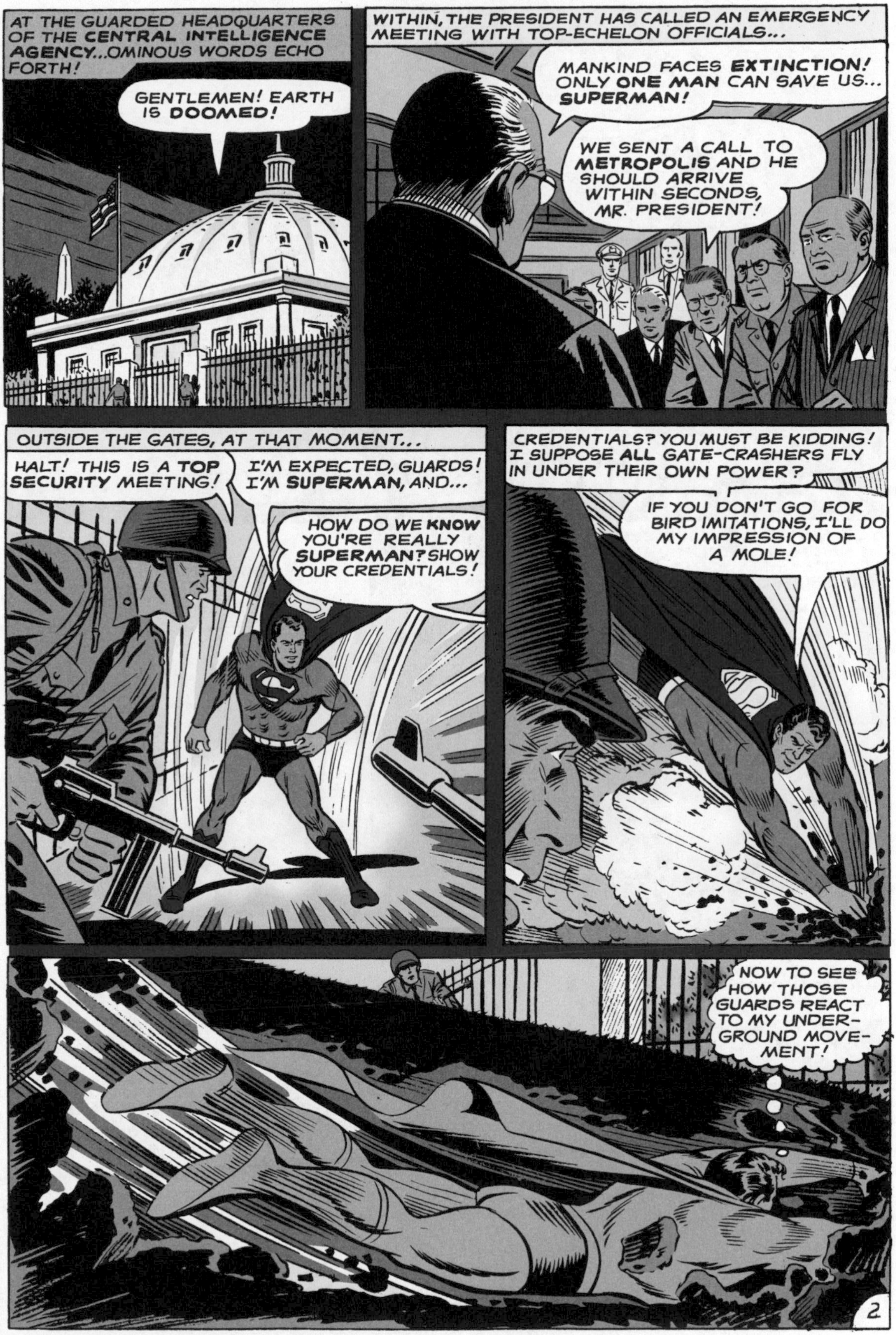
AT THE GUARDED HEADQUARTERS OF THE CENTRAL INTELLIGENCE AGENCY...OMINOUS WORDS ECHO FORTH!
GENTLEMEN! EARTH IS DOOMED!
WITHIN, THE PRESIDENT HAS CALLED AN EMERGENCY MEETING WITH TOP-ECHELON OFFICIALS...
MANKIND FACES EXTINCTION! ONLY ONE MAN CAN SAVE US... SUPERMAN!
WE SENT A CALL TO METROPOLIS AND HE SHOULD ARRIVE WITHIN SECONDS, MR. PRESIDENT!
OUTSIDE THE GATES, AT THAT MOMENT...
HALT! THIS IS A TOP SECURITY MEETING!
I'M EXPECTED, GUARDS! I'M SUPERMAN, AND...
HOW DO WE KNOW YOU'RE REALLY SUPERMAN? SHOW YOUR CREDENTIALS!
CREDENTIALS? YOU MUST BE KIDDING! I SUPPOSE ALL GATE-CRASHERS FLY IN UNDER THEIR OWN POWER?
IF YOU DON'T GO FOR BIRD IMITATIONS, I'LL DO MY IMPRESSION OF A MOLE!
NOW TO SEE HOW THOSE GUARDS REACT TO MY UNDER-GROUND MOVE-MENT!
2

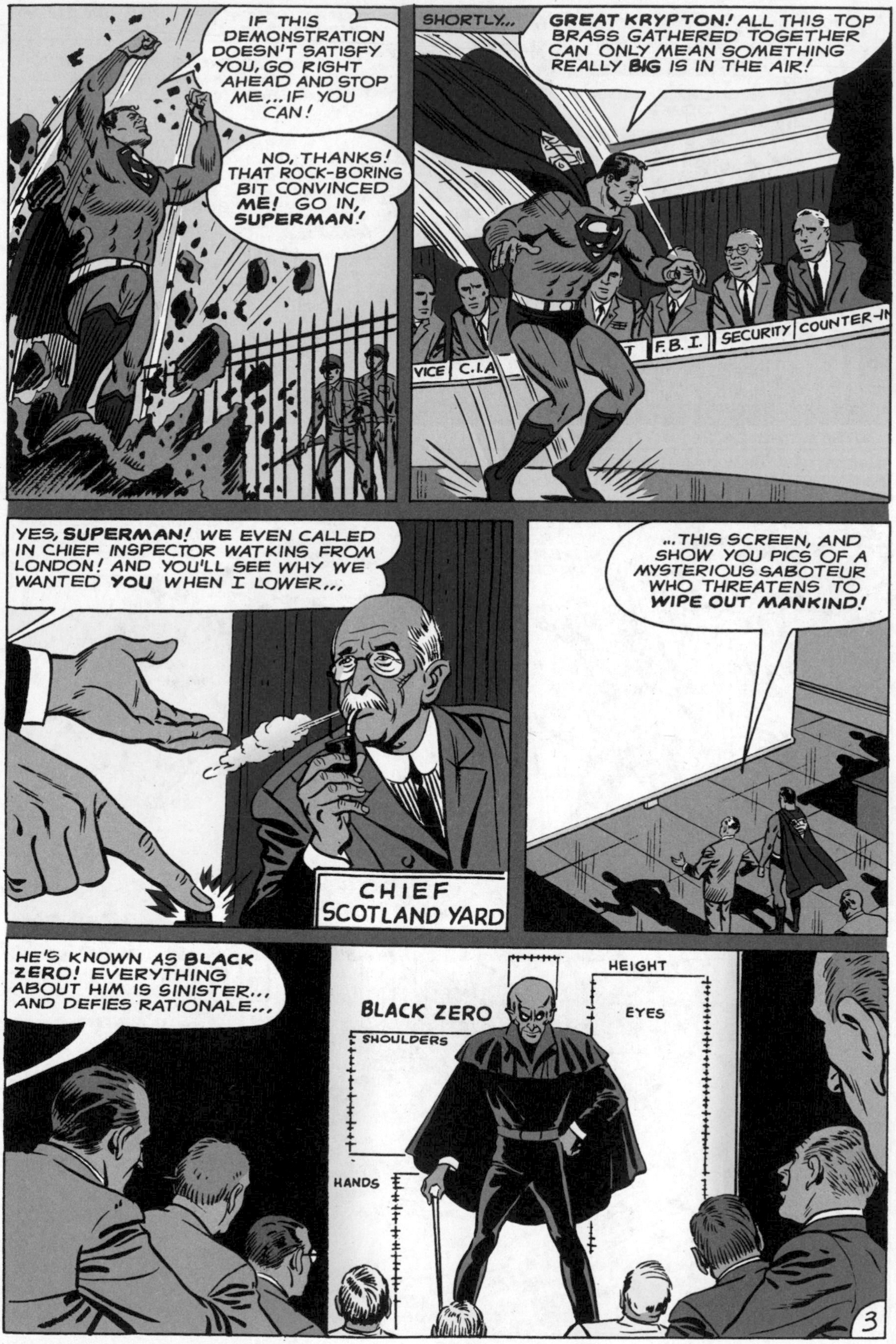
IF THIS DEMONSTRATION DOESN'T SATISFY YOU, GO RIGHT AHEAD AND STOP ME... IF YOU CAN!
NO, THANKS! THAT ROCK-BORING BIT CONVINCED ME! GO IN, SUPERMAN!
SHORTLY...
GREAT KRYPTON! ALL THIS TOP BRASS GATHERED TOGETHER CAN ONLY MEAN SOMETHING REALLY BIG IS IN THE AIR!
VICE
C.I.A
F.B.I.
SECURITY
COUNTER-IN
YES, SUPERMAN! WE EVEN CALLED IN CHIEF INSPECTOR WATKINS FROM LONDON! AND YOU'LL SEE WHY WE WANTED YOU WHEN I LOWER...
CHIEF
SCOTLAND YARD
...THIS SCREEN, AND SHOW YOU PICS OF A MYSTERIOUS SABOTEUR WHO THREATENS TO WIPE OUT MANKIND!
HE'S KNOWN AS BLACK ZERO! EVERYTHING ABOUT HIM IS SINISTER... AND DEFIES RATIONALE...
BLACK ZERO
HEIGHT
EYES
SHOULDERS
HANDS
3

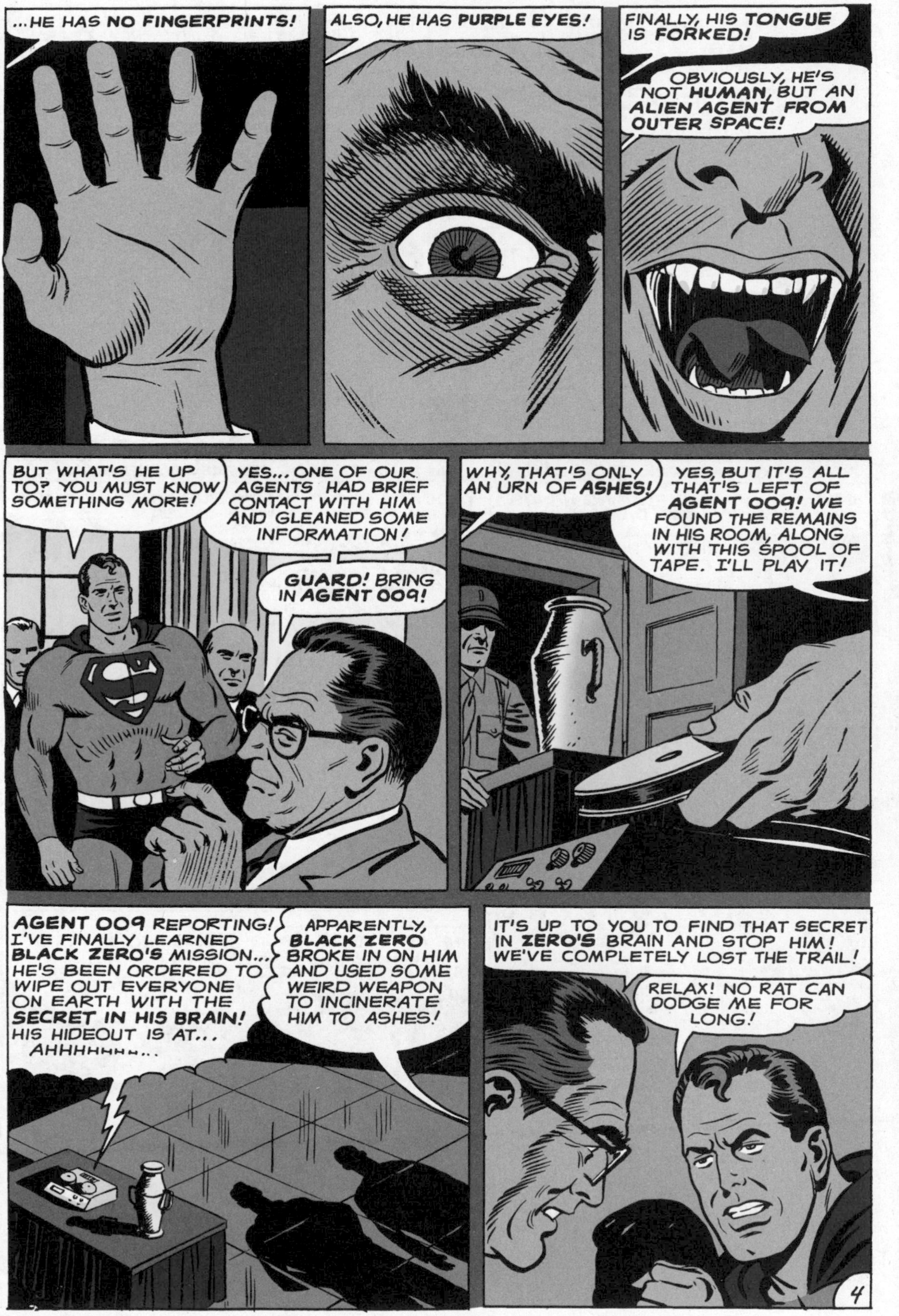
...HE HAS NO FINGERPRINTS!
ALSO, HE HAS PURPLE EYES!
FINALLY, HIS TONGUE IS FORKED!
OBVIOUSLY, HE'S NOT HUMAN, BUT AN ALIEN AGENT FROM OUTER SPACE!
BUT WHAT'S HE UP TO? YOU MUST KNOW SOMETHING MORE!
YES... ONE OF OUR AGENTS HAD BRIEF CONTACT WITH HIM AND GLEANED SOME INFORMATION!
GUARD! BRING IN AGENT 009!
WHY, THAT'S ONLY AN URN OF ASHES!
YES, BUT IT'S ALL THAT'S LEFT OF AGENT 009! WE FOUND THE REMAINS IN HIS ROOM, ALONG WITH THIS SPOOL OF TAPE. I'LL PLAY IT!
AGENT 009 REPORTING! I'VE FINALLY LEARNED BLACK ZERO'S MISSION... HE'S BEEN ORDERED TO WIPE OUT EVERYONE ON EARTH WITH THE SECRET IN HIS BRAIN! HIS HIDEOUT IS AT... AHHHHHHH...
APPARENTLY, BLACK ZERO BROKE IN ON HIM AND USED SOME WEIRD WEAPON TO INCINERATE HIM TO ASHES!
IT'S UP TO YOU TO FIND THAT SECRET IN ZERO'S BRAIN AND STOP HIM! WE'VE COMPLETELY LOST THE TRAIL!
RELAX! NO RAT CAN DODGE ME FOR LONG!
4

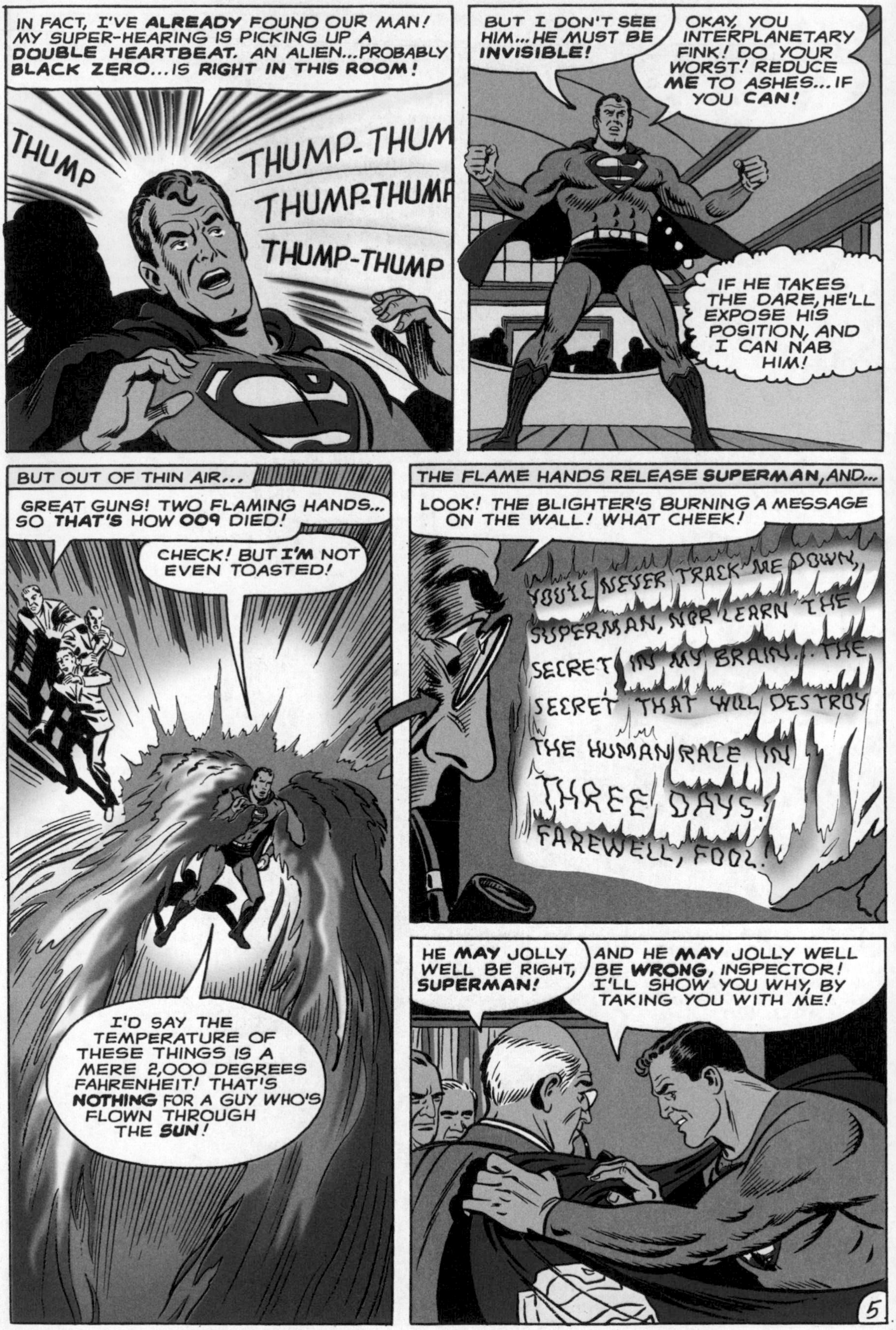
IN FACT, I'VE ALREADY FOUND OUR MAN! MY SUPER-HEARING IS PICKING UP A DOUBLE HEARTBEAT. AN ALIEN...PROBABLY BLACK ZERO...IS RIGHT IN THIS ROOM!
THUMP
THUMP-THUM
THUMP-THUMP
THUMP-THUMP
BUT I DON'T SEE HIM...HE MUST BE INVISIBLE!
OKAY, YOU INTERPLANETARY FINK! DO YOUR WORST! REDUCE ME TO ASHES...IF YOU CAN!
IF HE TAKES THE DARE, HE'LL EXPOSE HIS POSITION, AND I CAN NAB HIM!
BUT OUT OF THIN AIR...
GREAT GUNS! TWO FLAMING HANDS... SO THAT'S HOW 009 DIED!
CHECK! BUT I'M NOT EVEN TOASTED!
I'D SAY THE TEMPERATURE OF THESE THINGS IS A MERE 2,000 DEGREES FAHRENHEIT! THAT'S NOTHING FOR A GUY WHO'S FLOWN THROUGH THE SUN!
THE FLAME HANDS RELEASE SUPERMAN, AND...
LOOK! THE BLIGHTER'S BURNING A MESSAGE ON THE WALL! WHAT CHEEK!
YOU'LL NEVER TRACK ME DOWN, SUPERMAN, NOR LEARN THE SECRET IN MY BRAIN. THE SECRET THAT WILL DESTROY THE HUMAN RACE IN THREE DAYS! FAREWELL, FOOL!
HE MAY JOLLY WELL BE RIGHT, SUPERMAN!
AND HE MAY JOLLY WELL BE WRONG, INSPECTOR! I'LL SHOW YOU WHY, BY TAKING YOU WITH ME!
5

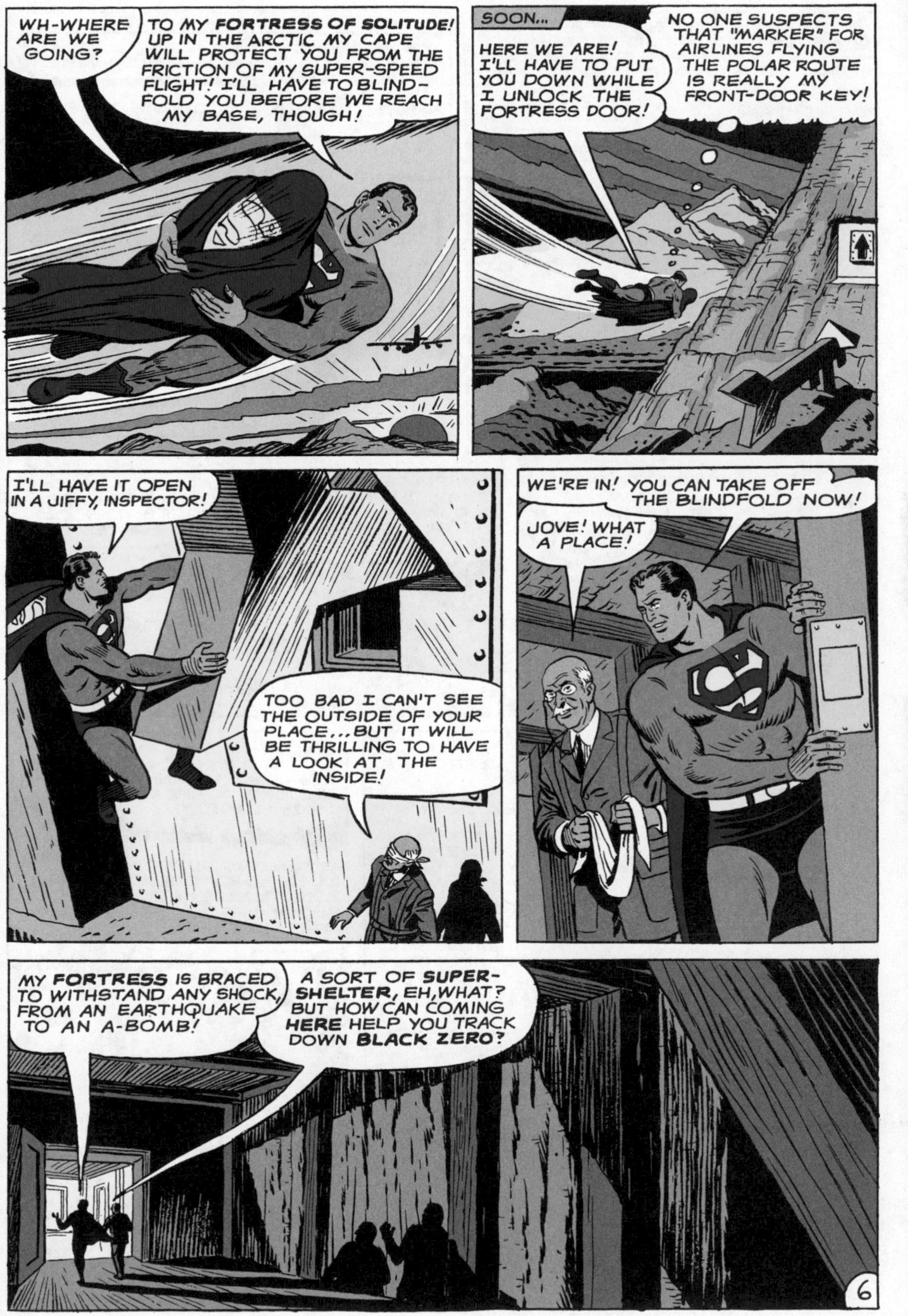
WH-WHERE ARE WE GOING?
TO MY FORTRESS OF SOLITUDE! UP IN THE ARCTIC MY CAPE WILL PROTECT YOU FROM THE FRICTION OF MY SUPER-SPEED FLIGHT! I'LL HAVE TO BLIND-FOLD YOU BEFORE WE REACH MY BASE, THOUGH!
SOON...
HERE WE ARE! I'LL HAVE TO PUT YOU DOWN WHILE I UNLOCK THE FORTRESS DOOR!
NO ONE SUSPECTS THAT "MARKER" FOR AIRLINES FLYING THE POLAR ROUTE IS REALLY MY FRONT-DOOR KEY!
I'LL HAVE IT OPEN IN A JIFFY, INSPECTOR!
TOO BAD I CAN'T SEE THE OUTSIDE OF YOUR PLACE... BUT IT WILL BE THRILLING TO HAVE A LOOK AT THE INSIDE!
WE'RE IN! YOU CAN TAKE OFF THE BLINDFOLD NOW!
JOVE! WHAT A PLACE!
MY FORTRESS IS BRACED TO WITHSTAND ANY SHOCK, FROM AN EARTHQUAKE TO AN A-BOMB!
A SORT OF SUPER-SHELTER, EH, WHAT? BUT HOW CAN COMING HERE HELP YOU TRACK DOWN BLACK ZERO?
6

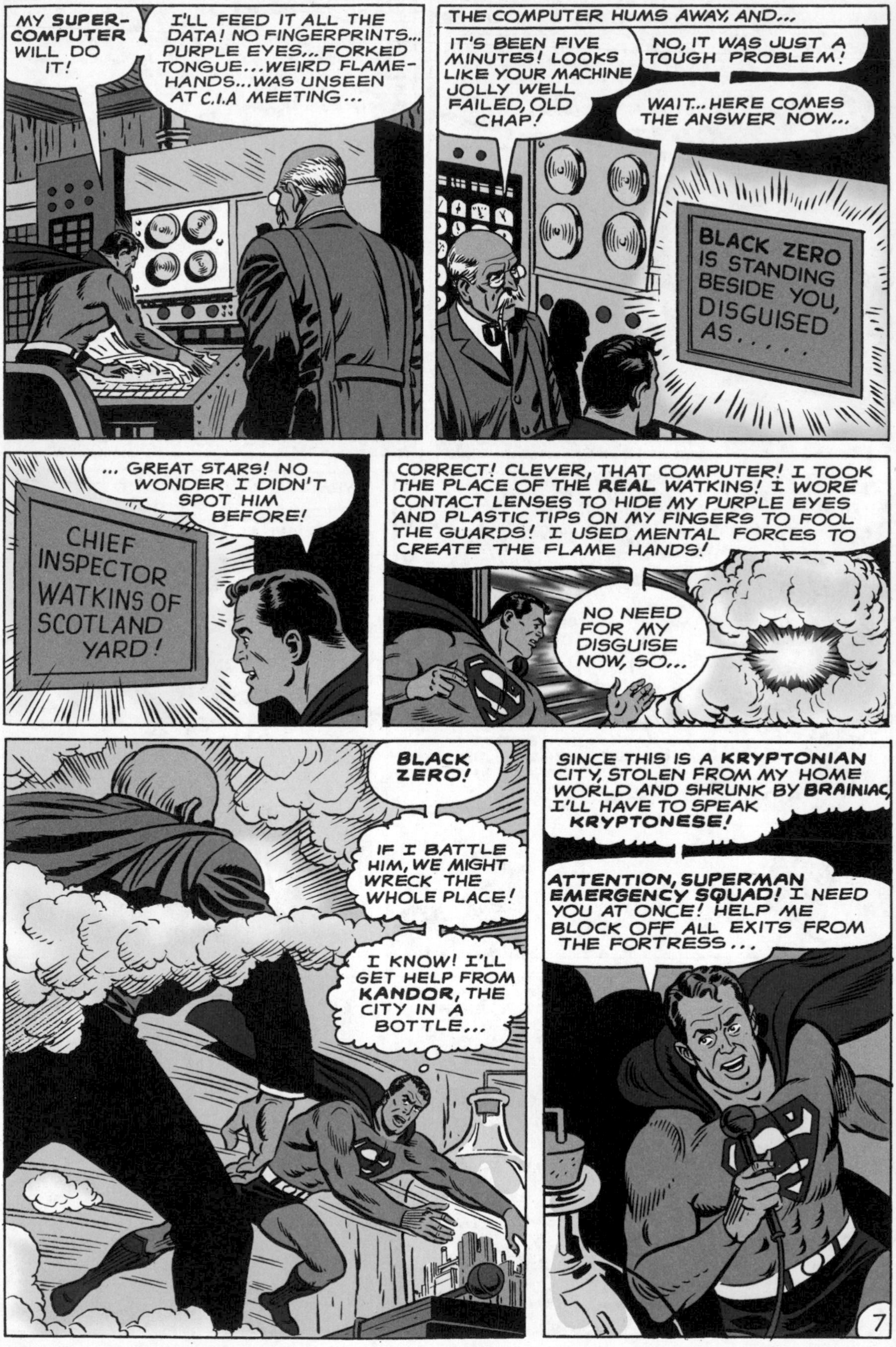
MY SUPER-COMPUTER WILL DO IT!
I'LL FEED IT ALL THE DATA! NO FINGERPRINTS... PURPLE EYES... FORKED TONGUE... WEIRD FLAME-HANDS... WAS UNSEEN AT C.I.A MEETING...
THE COMPUTER HUMS AWAY, AND...
IT'S BEEN FIVE MINUTES! LOOKS LIKE YOUR MACHINE JOLLY WELL FAILED, OLD CHAP!
NO, IT WAS JUST A TOUGH PROBLEM!
WAIT... HERE COMES THE ANSWER NOW...
BLACK ZERO IS STANDING BESIDE YOU, DISGUISED AS.....
... GREAT STARS! NO WONDER I DIDN'T SPOT HIM BEFORE!
CHIEF INSPECTOR WATKINS OF SCOTLAND YARD!
CORRECT! CLEVER, THAT COMPUTER! I TOOK THE PLACE OF THE REAL WATKINS! I WORE CONTACT LENSES TO HIDE MY PURPLE EYES AND PLASTIC TIPS ON MY FINGERS TO FOOL THE GUARDS! I USED MENTAL FORCES TO CREATE THE FLAME HANDS!
NO NEED FOR MY DISGUISE NOW, SO...
BLACK ZERO!
IF I BATTLE HIM, WE MIGHT WRECK THE WHOLE PLACE!
I KNOW! I'LL GET HELP FROM KANDOR, THE CITY IN A BOTTLE...
SINCE THIS IS A KRYPTONIAN CITY, STOLEN FROM MY HOME WORLD AND SHRUNK BY BRAINIAC, I'LL HAVE TO SPEAK KRYPTONESE!
ATTENTION, SUPERMAN EMERGENCY SQUAD! I NEED YOU AT ONCE! HELP ME BLOCK OFF ALL EXITS FROM THE FORTRESS...
7

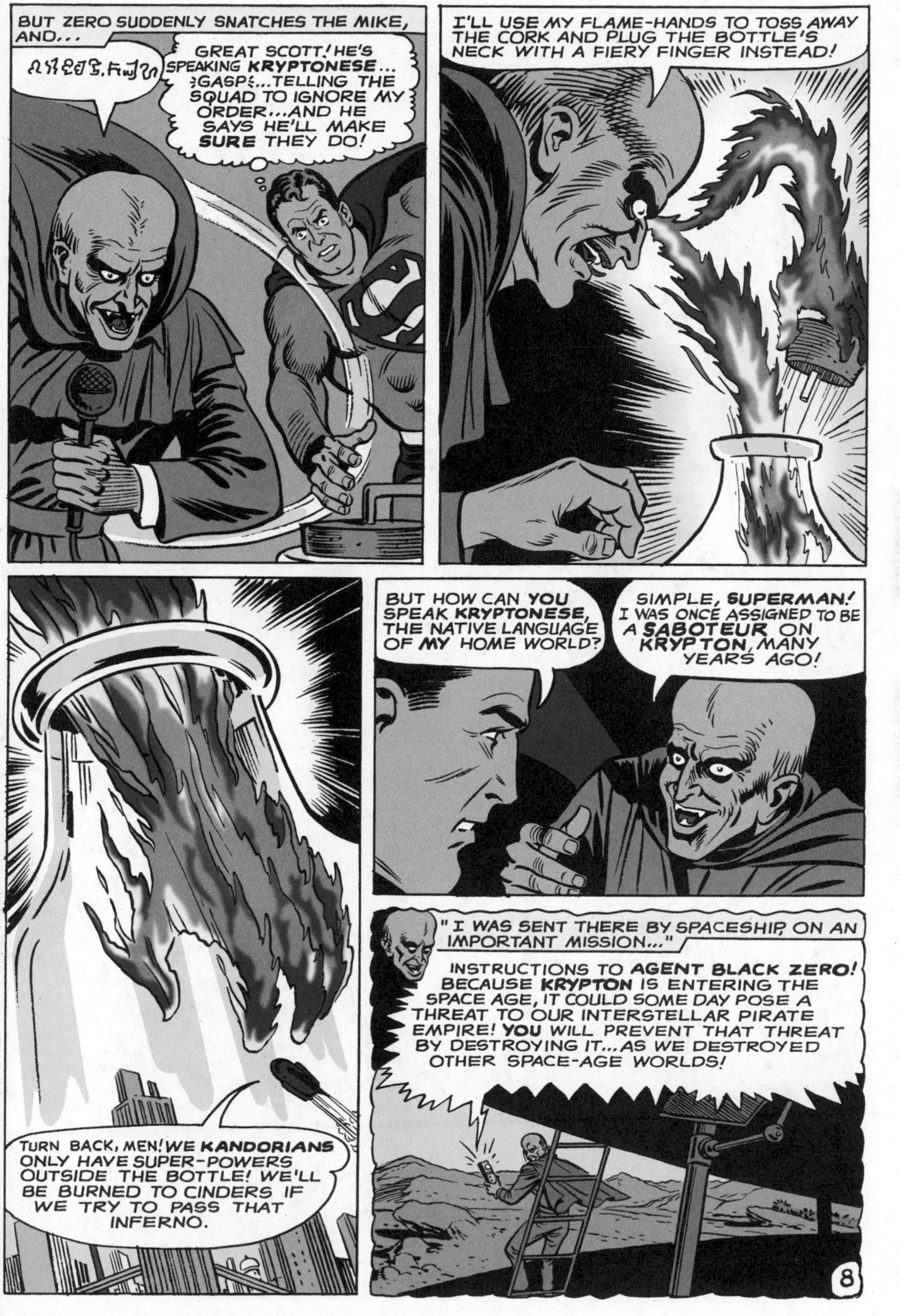
BUT ZERO SUDDENLY SNATCHES THE MIKE, AND...
GREAT SCOTT! HE'S SPEAKING KRYPTONESE... GASP!...TELLING THE SQUAD TO IGNORE MY ORDER...AND HE SAYS HE'LL MAKE SURE THEY DO!
I'LL USE MY FLAME-HANDS TO TOSS AWAY THE CORK AND PLUG THE BOTTLE'S NECK WITH A FIERY FINGER INSTEAD!
TURN BACK, MEN! WE KANDORIANS ONLY HAVE SUPER-POWERS OUTSIDE THE BOTTLE! WE'LL BE BURNED TO CINDERS IF WE TRY TO PASS THAT INFERNO.
BUT HOW CAN YOU SPEAK KRYPTONESE, THE NATIVE LANGUAGE OF MY HOME WORLD?
SIMPLE, SUPERMAN! I WAS ONCE ASSIGNED TO BE A SABOTEUR ON KRYPTON, MANY YEARS AGO!
"I WAS SENT THERE BY SPACESHIP, ON AN IMPORTANT MISSION..."
INSTRUCTIONS TO AGENT BLACK ZERO! BECAUSE KRYPTON IS ENTERING THE SPACE AGE, IT COULD SOME DAY POSE A THREAT TO OUR INTERSTELLAR PIRATE EMPIRE! YOU WILL PREVENT THAT THREAT BY DESTROYING IT...AS WE DESTROYED OTHER SPACE-AGE WORLDS!
8

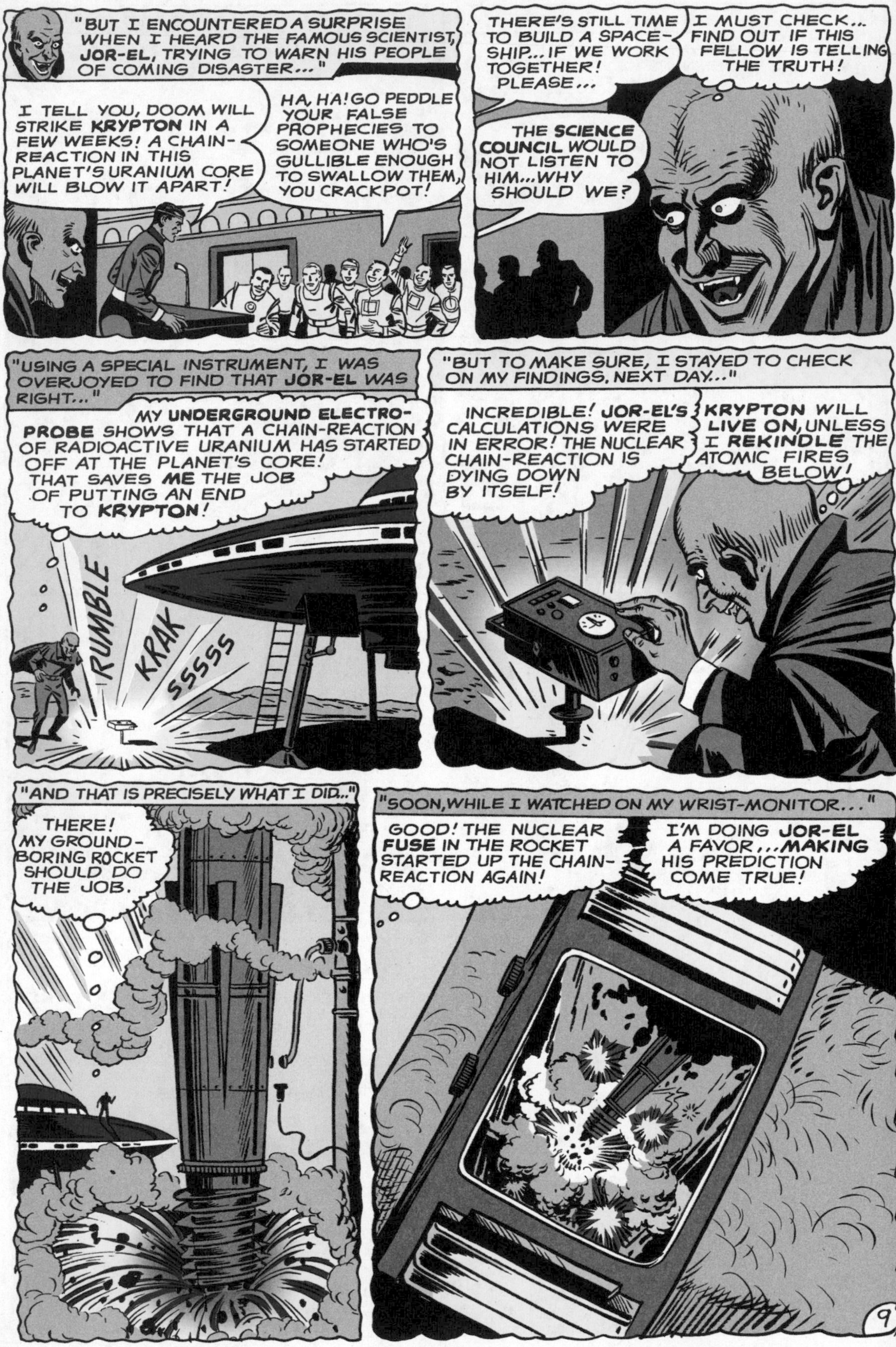
"BUT I ENCOUNTERED A SURPRISE WHEN I HEARD THE FAMOUS SCIENTIST, JOR-EL, TRYING TO WARN HIS PEOPLE OF COMING DISASTER..."
I TELL YOU, DOOM WILL STRIKE KRYPTON IN A FEW WEEKS! A CHAIN-REACTION IN THIS PLANET'S URANIUM CORE WILL BLOW IT APART!
HA, HA! GO PEDDLE YOUR FALSE PROPHECIES TO SOMEONE WHO'S GULLIBLE ENOUGH TO SWALLOW THEM, YOU CRACKPOT!
THERE'S STILL TIME TO BUILD A SPACE-SHIP... IF WE WORK TOGETHER! PLEASE...
I MUST CHECK... FIND OUT IF THIS FELLOW IS TELLING THE TRUTH!
THE SCIENCE COUNCIL WOULD NOT LISTEN TO HIM... WHY SHOULD WE?
"USING A SPECIAL INSTRUMENT, I WAS OVERJOYED TO FIND THAT JOR-EL WAS RIGHT..."
MY UNDERGROUND ELECTRO-PROBE SHOWS THAT A CHAIN-REACTION OF RADIOACTIVE URANIUM HAS STARTED OFF AT THE PLANET'S CORE! THAT SAVES ME THE JOB OF PUTTING AN END TO KRYPTON!
RUMBLE
KRAK
SSSSS
"BUT TO MAKE SURE, I STAYED TO CHECK ON MY FINDINGS, NEXT DAY..."
INCREDIBLE! JOR-EL'S CALCULATIONS WERE IN ERROR! THE NUCLEAR CHAIN-REACTION IS DYING DOWN BY ITSELF!
KRYPTON WILL LIVE ON, UNLESS I REKINDLE THE ATOMIC FIRES BELOW!
"AND THAT IS PRECISELY WHAT I DID..."
THERE! MY GROUND-BORING ROCKET SHOULD DO THE JOB.
"SOON, WHILE I WATCHED ON MY WRIST-MONITOR..."
GOOD! THE NUCLEAR FUSE IN THE ROCKET STARTED UP THE CHAIN-REACTION AGAIN!
I'M DOING JOR-EL A FAVOR,.. MAKING HIS PREDICTION COME TRUE!
9

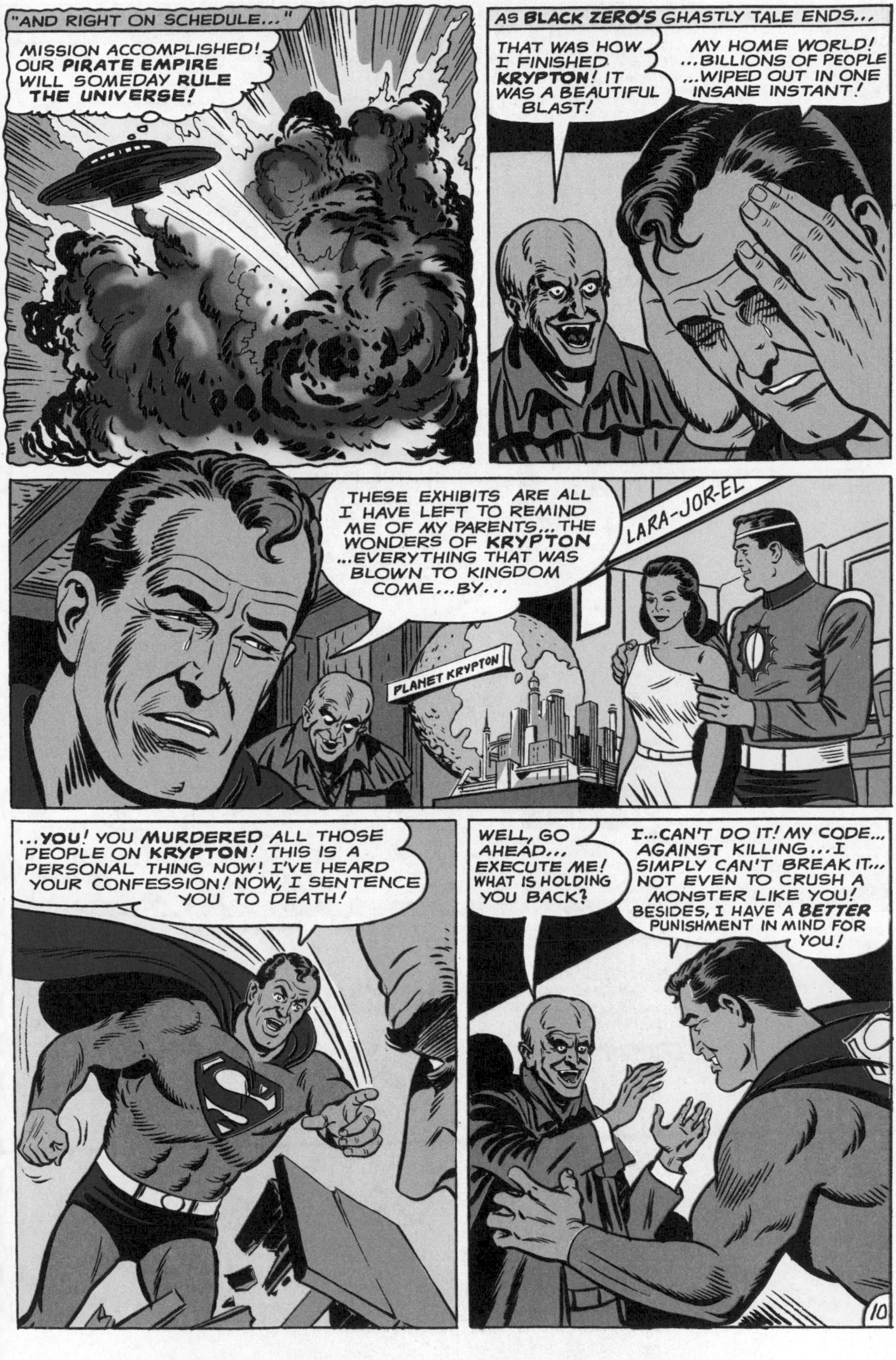
"AND RIGHT ON SCHEDULE..."
MISSION ACCOMPLISHED! OUR PIRATE EMPIRE WILL SOMEDAY RULE THE UNIVERSE!
AS BLACK ZERO'S GHASTLY TALE ENDS...
THAT WAS HOW I FINISHED KRYPTON! IT WAS A BEAUTIFUL BLAST!
MY HOME WORLD! ...BILLIONS OF PEOPLE ...WIPED OUT IN ONE INSANE INSTANT!
THESE EXHIBITS ARE ALL I HAVE LEFT TO REMIND ME OF MY PARENTS... THE WONDERS OF KRYPTON ...EVERYTHING THAT WAS BLOWN TO KINGDOM COME...BY...
LARA-JOR-EL
PLANET KRYPTON
...YOU! YOU MURDERED ALL THOSE PEOPLE ON KRYPTON! THIS IS A PERSONAL THING NOW! I'VE HEARD YOUR CONFESSION! NOW, I SENTENCE YOU TO DEATH!
WELL, GO AHEAD... EXECUTE ME! WHAT IS HOLDING YOU BACK?
I...CAN'T DO IT! MY CODE... AGAINST KILLING... I SIMPLY CAN'T BREAK IT... NOT EVEN TO CRUSH A MONSTER LIKE YOU! BESIDES, I HAVE A BETTER PUNISHMENT IN MIND FOR YOU!
10

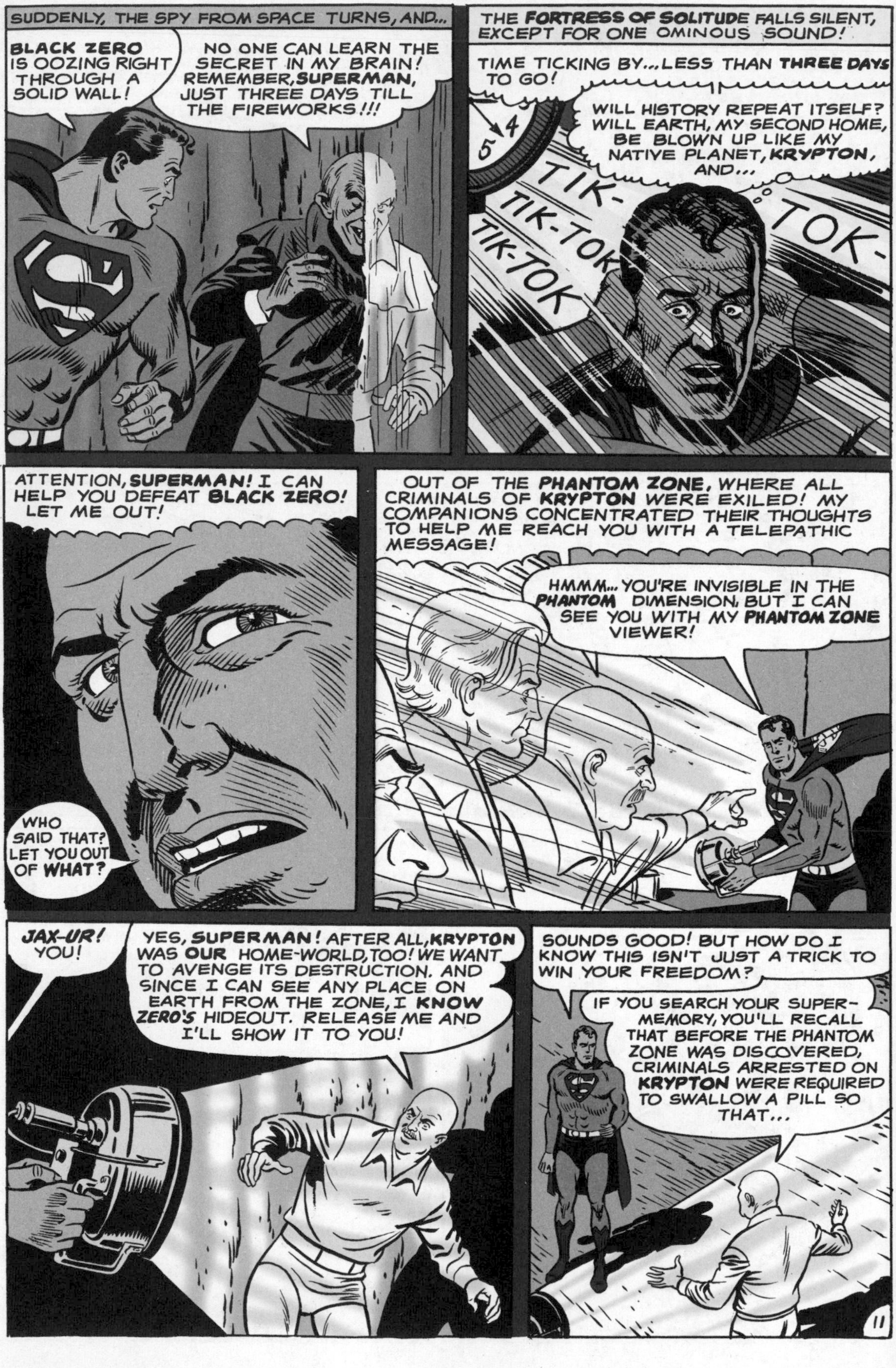

SUDDENLY, THE SPY FROM SPACE TURNS, AND...
BLACK ZERO IS OOZING RIGHT THROUGH A SOLID WALL!
NO ONE CAN LEARN THE SECRET IN MY BRAIN! REMEMBER, SUPERMAN, JUST THREE DAYS TILL THE FIREWORKS!!!
THE FORTRESS OF SOLITUDE FALLS SILENT, EXCEPT FOR ONE OMINOUS SOUND!
TIME TICKING BY... LESS THAN THREE DAYS TO GO!
WILL HISTORY REPEAT ITSELF? WILL EARTH, MY SECOND HOME, BE BLOWN UP LIKE MY NATIVE PLANET, KRYPTON, AND...
TIK-TOK-
TIK-TOK
TIK-TOK
ATTENTION, SUPERMAN! I CAN HELP YOU DEFEAT BLACK ZERO! LET ME OUT!
WHO SAID THAT? LET YOU OUT OF WHAT?
OUT OF THE PHANTOM ZONE, WHERE ALL CRIMINALS OF KRYPTON WERE EXILED! MY COMPANIONS CONCENTRATED THEIR THOUGHTS TO HELP ME REACH YOU WITH A TELEPATHIC MESSAGE!
HMMM... YOU'RE INVISIBLE IN THE PHANTOM DIMENSION, BUT I CAN SEE YOU WITH MY PHANTOM ZONE VIEWER!
JAX-UR! YOU!
YES, SUPERMAN! AFTER ALL, KRYPTON WAS OUR HOME-WORLD, TOO! WE WANT TO AVENGE ITS DESTRUCTION. AND SINCE I CAN SEE ANY PLACE ON EARTH FROM THE ZONE, I KNOW ZERO'S HIDEOUT. RELEASE ME AND I'LL SHOW IT TO YOU!
SOUNDS GOOD! BUT HOW DO I KNOW THIS ISN'T JUST A TRICK TO WIN YOUR FREEDOM?
IF YOU SEARCH YOUR SUPER-MEMORY, YOU'LL RECALL THAT BEFORE THE PHANTOM ZONE WAS DISCOVERED, CRIMINALS ARRESTED ON KRYPTON WERE REQUIRED TO SWALLOW A PILL SO THAT...
11

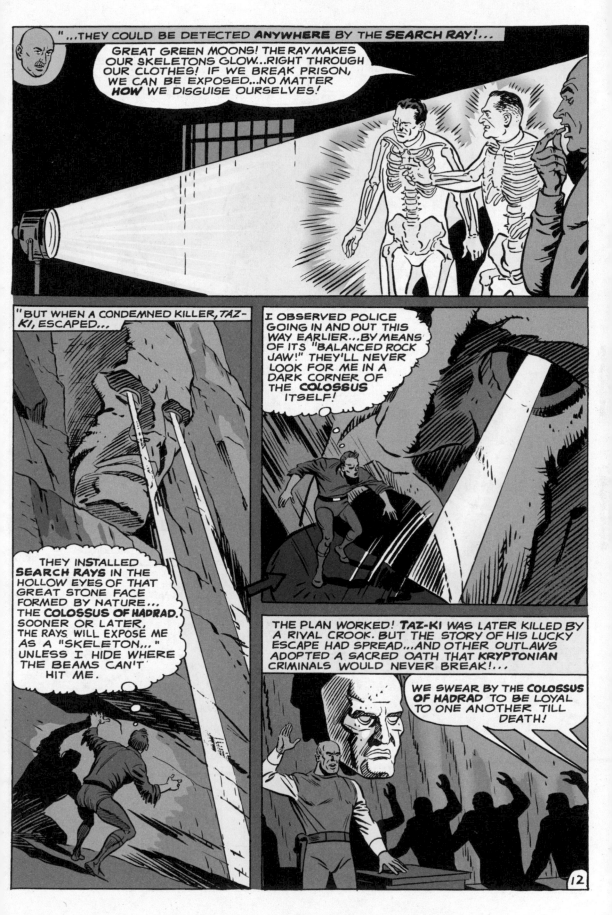

"...THEY COULD BE DETECTED *ANYWHERE* BY THE *SEARCH RAY*!...

GREAT GREEN MOONS! THE RAY MAKES OUR SKELETONS GLOW...RIGHT THROUGH OUR CLOTHES! IF WE BREAK PRISON, WE CAN BE EXPOSED...NO MATTER *HOW* WE DISGUISE OURSELVES!

"BUT WHEN A CONDEMNED KILLER, *TAZ-KI*, ESCAPED..."

I OBSERVED POLICE GOING IN AND OUT THIS WAY EARLIER...BY MEANS OF ITS "BALANCED ROCK JAW!" THEY'LL NEVER LOOK FOR ME IN A DARK CORNER OF THE *COLOSSUS* ITSELF!

THEY INSTALLED *SEARCH RAYS* IN THE HOLLOW EYES OF THAT GREAT STONE FACE FORMED BY NATURE... THE *COLOSSUS OF HADRAD*. SOONER OR LATER, THE RAYS WILL EXPOSE ME AS A "SKELETON..." UNLESS I HIDE WHERE THE BEAMS CAN'T HIT ME.

THE PLAN WORKED! *TAZ-KI* WAS LATER KILLED BY A RIVAL CROOK. BUT THE STORY OF HIS LUCKY ESCAPE HAD SPREAD...AND OTHER OUTLAWS ADOPTED A SACRED OATH THAT *KRYPTONIAN* CRIMINALS WOULD NEVER BREAK!...

WE SWEAR BY THE *COLOSSUS OF HADRAD* TO BE LOYAL TO ONE ANOTHER TILL DEATH!

12

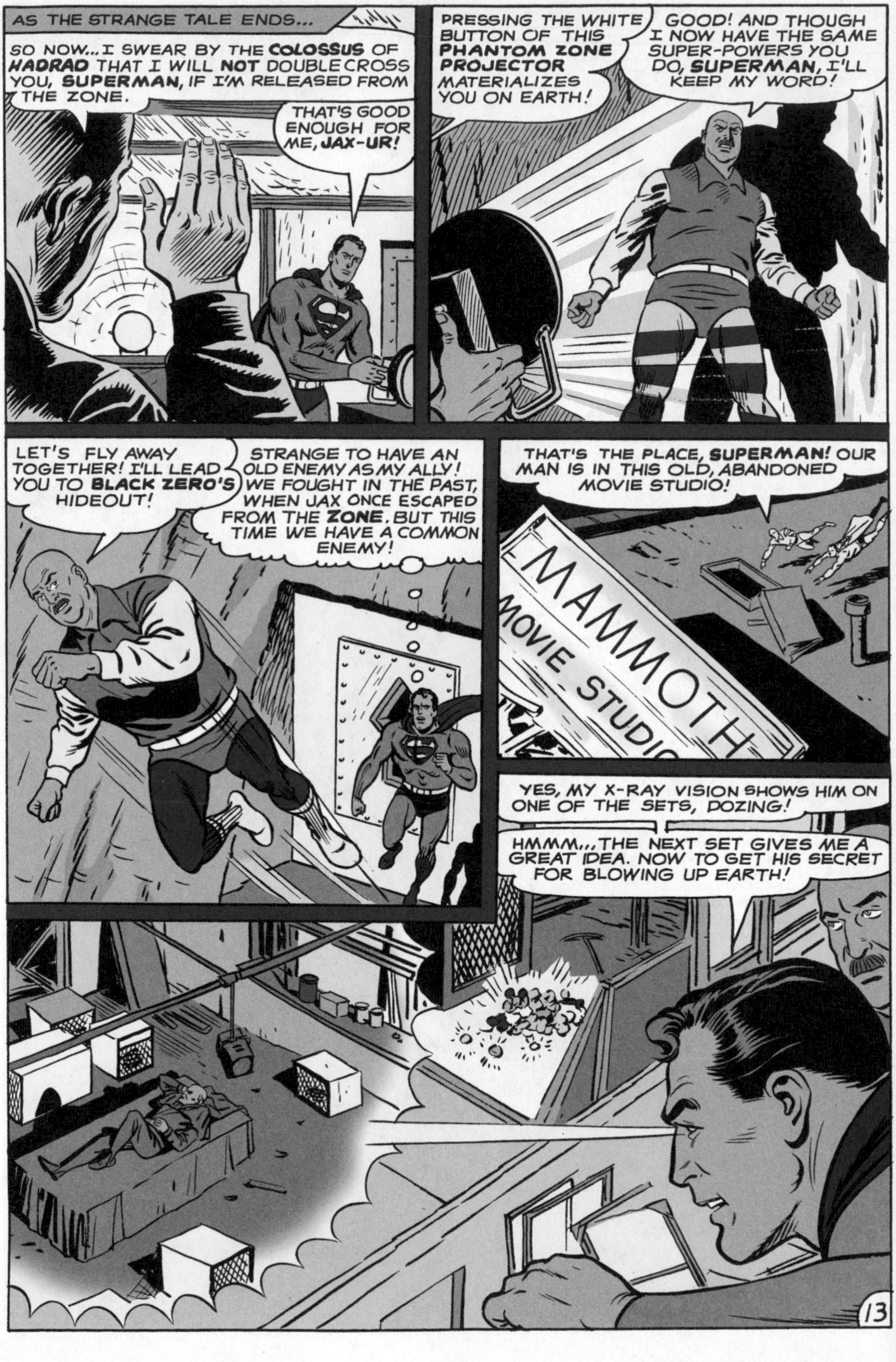
AS THE STRANGE TALE ENDS...
SO NOW...I SWEAR BY THE COLOSSUS OF HADRAD THAT I WILL NOT DOUBLE CROSS YOU, SUPERMAN, IF I'M RELEASED FROM THE ZONE.
THAT'S GOOD ENOUGH FOR ME, JAX-UR!
PRESSING THE WHITE BUTTON OF THIS PHANTOM ZONE PROJECTOR MATERIALIZES YOU ON EARTH!
GOOD! AND THOUGH I NOW HAVE THE SAME SUPER-POWERS YOU DO, SUPERMAN, I'LL KEEP MY WORD!
LET'S FLY AWAY TOGETHER! I'LL LEAD YOU TO BLACK ZERO'S HIDEOUT!
STRANGE TO HAVE AN OLD ENEMY AS MY ALLY! WE FOUGHT IN THE PAST, WHEN JAX ONCE ESCAPED FROM THE ZONE. BUT THIS TIME WE HAVE A COMMON ENEMY!
THAT'S THE PLACE, SUPERMAN! OUR MAN IS IN THIS OLD, ABANDONED MOVIE STUDIO!
MAMMOTH MOVIE STUDIO
YES, MY X-RAY VISION SHOWS HIM ON ONE OF THE SETS, DOZING!
HMMM...THE NEXT SET GIVES ME A GREAT IDEA. NOW TO GET HIS SECRET FOR BLOWING UP EARTH!
13

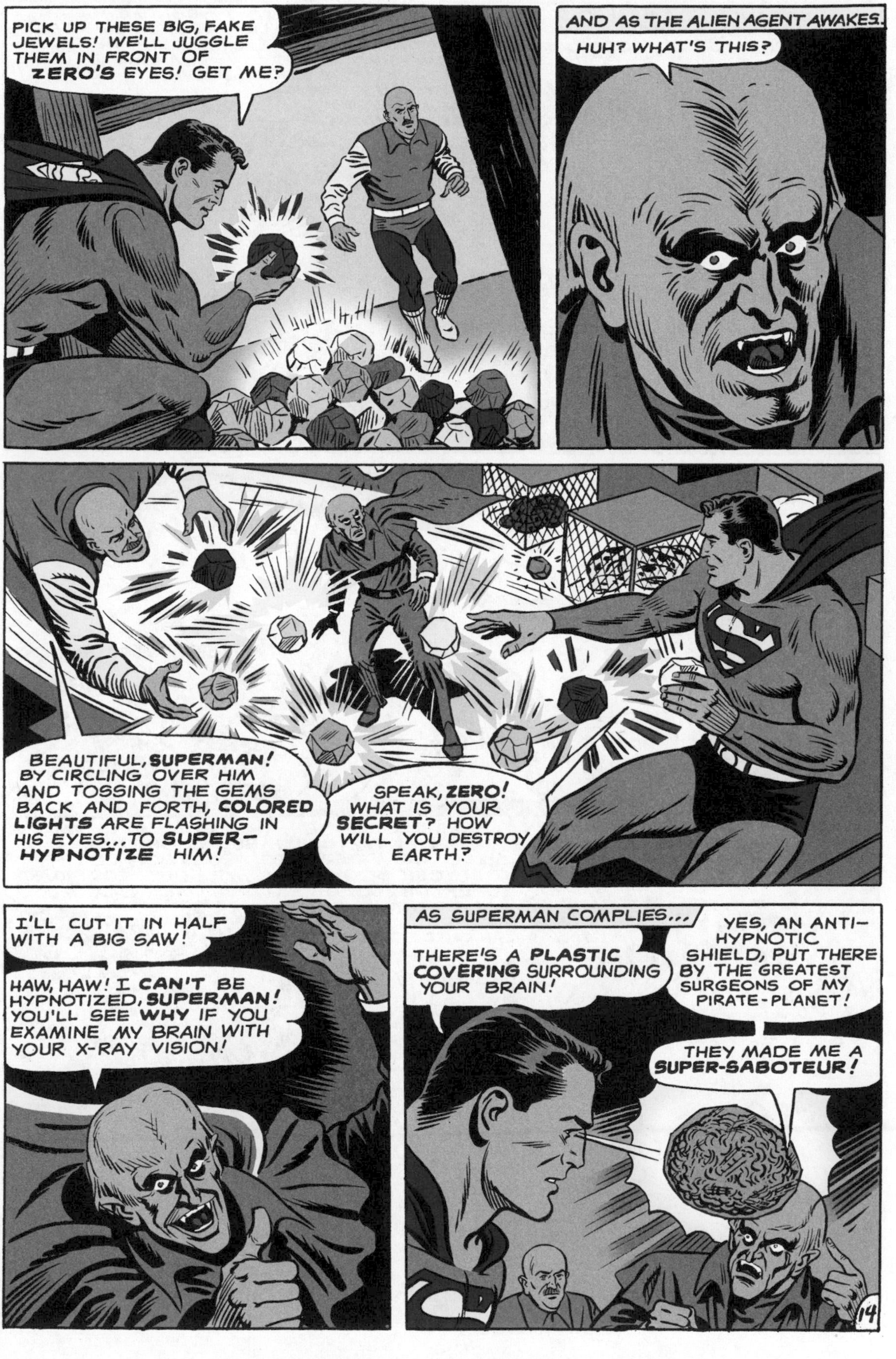
PICK UP THESE BIG, FAKE JEWELS! WE'LL JUGGLE THEM IN FRONT OF ZERO'S EYES! GET ME?
AND AS THE ALIEN AGENT AWAKES.
HUH? WHAT'S THIS?
BEAUTIFUL, SUPERMAN! BY CIRCLING OVER HIM AND TOSSING THE GEMS BACK AND FORTH, COLORED LIGHTS ARE FLASHING IN HIS EYES...TO SUPER-HYPNOTIZE HIM!
SPEAK, ZERO! WHAT IS YOUR SECRET? HOW WILL YOU DESTROY EARTH?
I'LL CUT IT IN HALF WITH A BIG SAW!
HAW, HAW! I CAN'T BE HYPNOTIZED, SUPERMAN! YOU'LL SEE WHY IF YOU EXAMINE MY BRAIN WITH YOUR X-RAY VISION!
AS SUPERMAN COMPLIES...
THERE'S A PLASTIC COVERING SURROUNDING YOUR BRAIN!
YES, AN ANTI-HYPNOTIC SHIELD, PUT THERE BY THE GREATEST SURGEONS OF MY PIRATE-PLANET!
THEY MADE ME A SUPER-SABOTEUR!
14

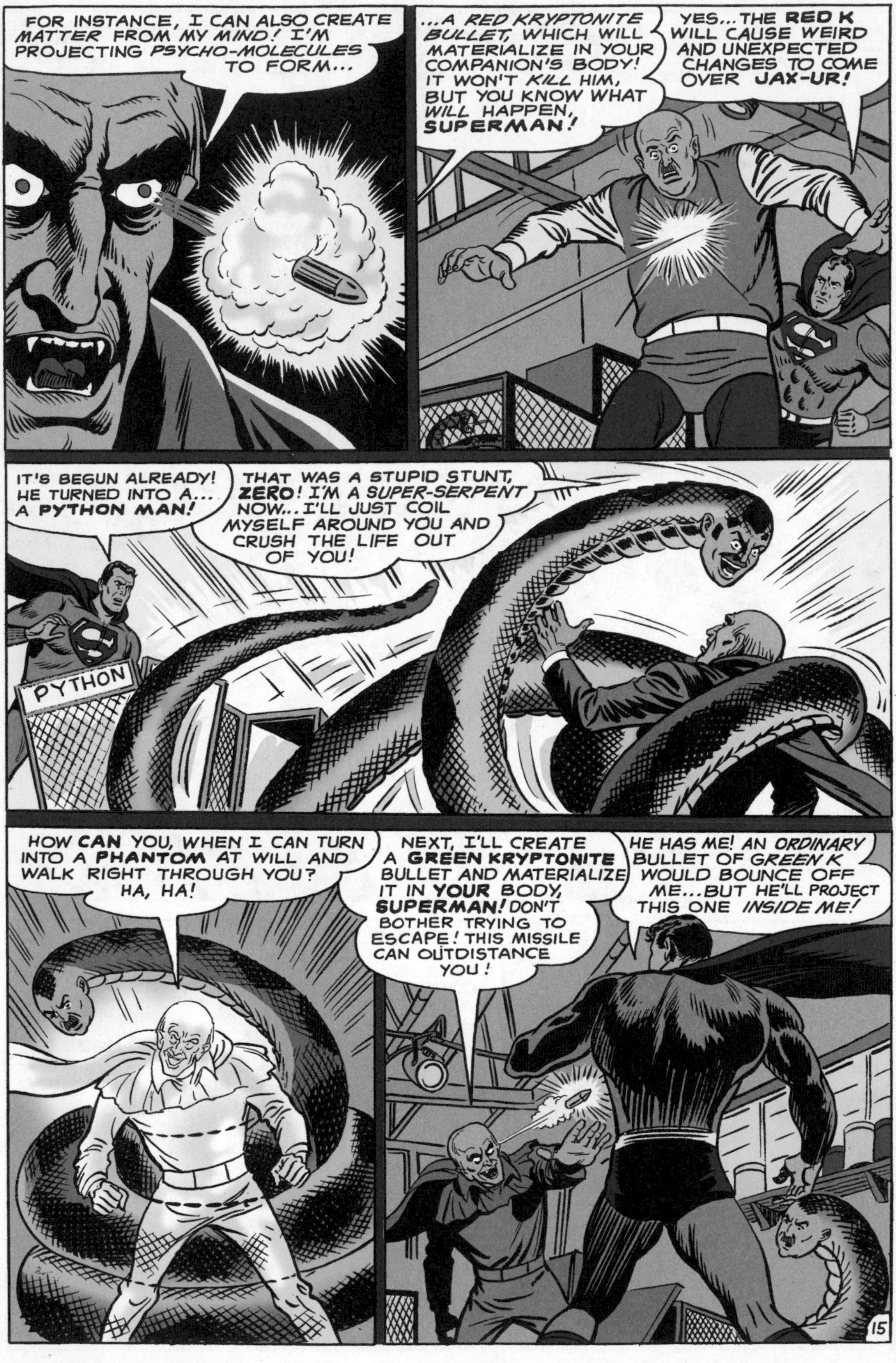
FOR INSTANCE, I CAN ALSO CREATE MATTER FROM MY MIND! I'M PROJECTING PSYCHO-MOLECULES TO FORM...
...A RED KRYPTONITE BULLET, WHICH WILL MATERIALIZE IN YOUR COMPANION'S BODY! IT WON'T KILL HIM, BUT YOU KNOW WHAT WILL HAPPEN, SUPERMAN!
YES... THE RED K WILL CAUSE WEIRD AND UNEXPECTED CHANGES TO COME OVER JAX-UR!
IT'S BEGUN ALREADY! HE TURNED INTO A... A PYTHON MAN!
THAT WAS A STUPID STUNT, ZERO! I'M A SUPER-SERPENT NOW... I'LL JUST COIL MYSELF AROUND YOU AND CRUSH THE LIFE OUT OF YOU!
PYTHON
HOW CAN YOU, WHEN I CAN TURN INTO A PHANTOM AT WILL AND WALK RIGHT THROUGH YOU? HA, HA!
NEXT, I'LL CREATE A GREEN KRYPTONITE BULLET AND MATERIALIZE IT IN YOUR BODY, SUPERMAN! DON'T BOTHER TRYING TO ESCAPE! THIS MISSILE CAN OUTDISTANCE YOU!
HE HAS ME! AN ORDINARY BULLET OF GREEN K WOULD BOUNCE OFF ME... BUT HE'LL PROJECT THIS ONE INSIDE ME!
15

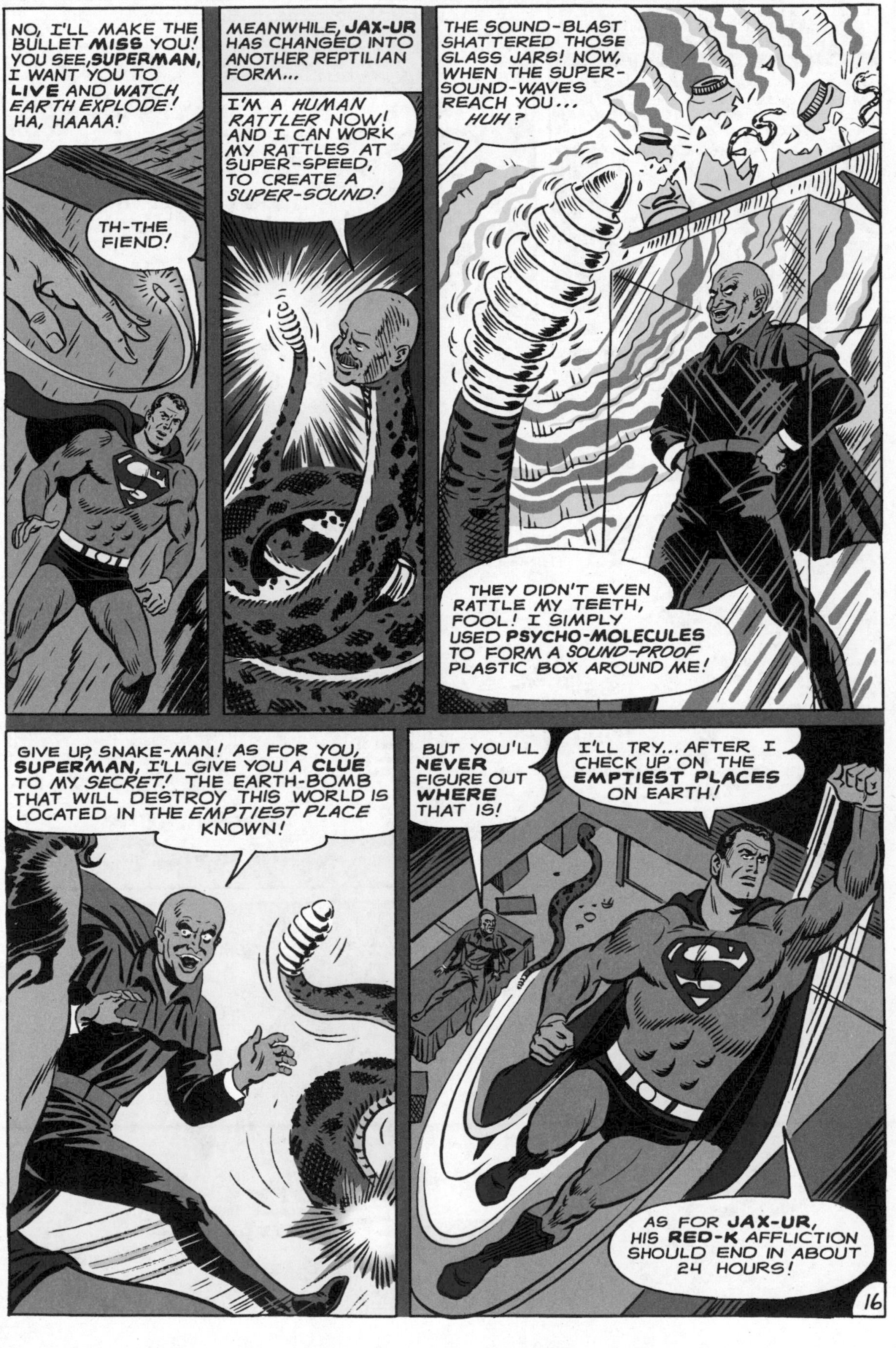
NO, I'LL MAKE THE BULLET MISS YOU! YOU SEE, SUPERMAN, I WANT YOU TO LIVE AND WATCH EARTH EXPLODE! HA, HAAAA!
TH-THE FIEND!
MEANWHILE, JAX-UR HAS CHANGED INTO ANOTHER REPTILIAN FORM...
I'M A HUMAN RATTLER NOW! AND I CAN WORK MY RATTLES AT SUPER-SPEED, TO CREATE A SUPER-SOUND!
THE SOUND-BLAST SHATTERED THOSE GLASS JARS! NOW, WHEN THE SUPER-SOUND-WAVES REACH YOU... HUH?
THEY DIDN'T EVEN RATTLE MY TEETH, FOOL! I SIMPLY USED PSYCHO-MOLECULES TO FORM A SOUND-PROOF PLASTIC BOX AROUND ME!
GIVE UP, SNAKE-MAN! AS FOR YOU, SUPERMAN, I'LL GIVE YOU A CLUE TO MY SECRET! THE EARTH-BOMB THAT WILL DESTROY THIS WORLD IS LOCATED IN THE EMPTIEST PLACE KNOWN!
BUT YOU'LL NEVER FIGURE OUT WHERE THAT IS!
I'LL TRY... AFTER I CHECK UP ON THE EMPTIEST PLACES ON EARTH!
AS FOR JAX-UR, HIS RED-K AFFLICTION SHOULD END IN ABOUT 24 HOURS!
16

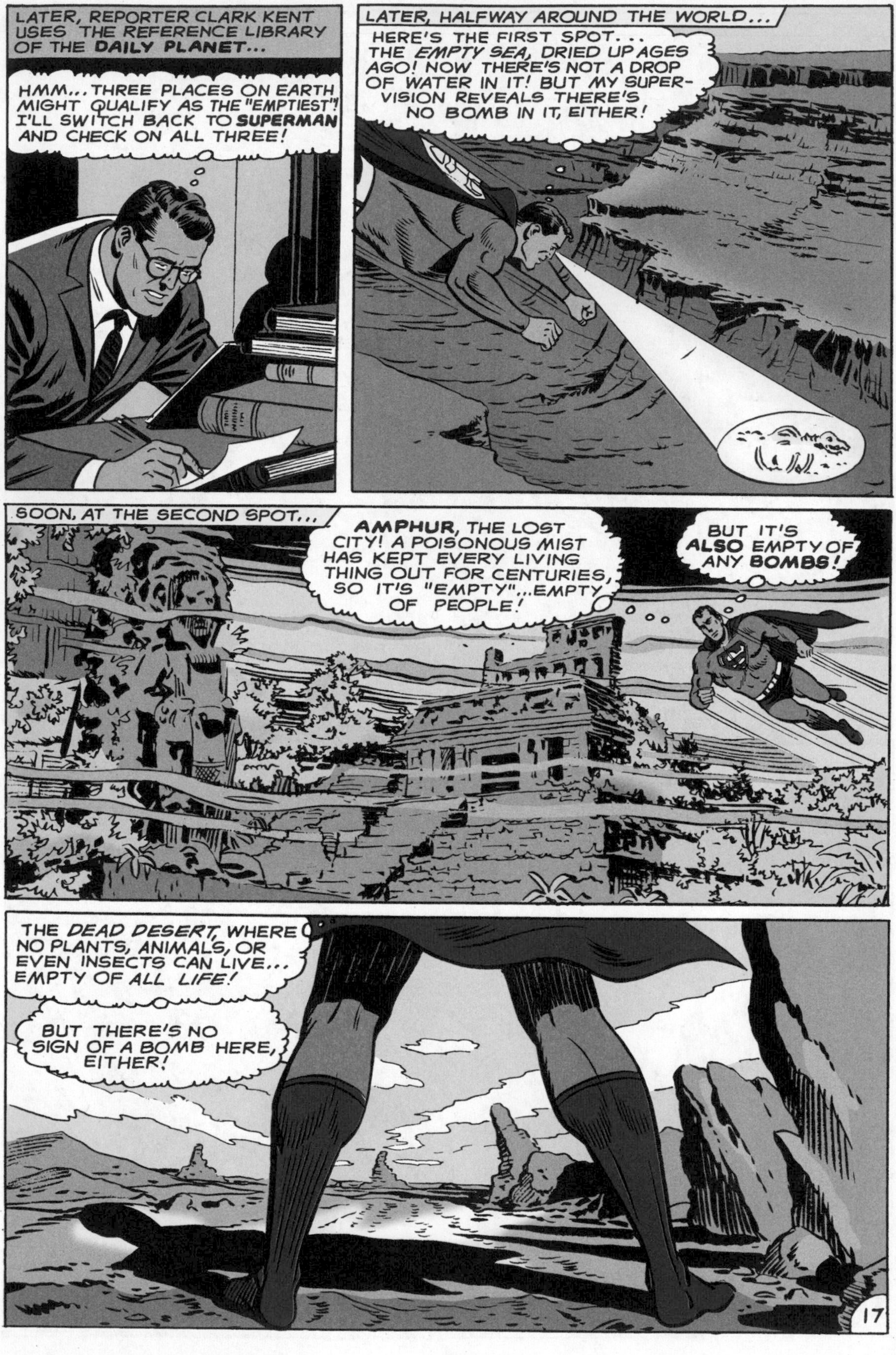
LATER, REPORTER CLARK KENT USES THE REFERENCE LIBRARY OF THE DAILY PLANET...
HMM... THREE PLACES ON EARTH MIGHT QUALIFY AS THE "EMPTIEST"! I'LL SWITCH BACK TO SUPERMAN AND CHECK ON ALL THREE!
LATER, HALFWAY AROUND THE WORLD...
HERE'S THE FIRST SPOT... THE EMPTY SEA, DRIED UP AGES AGO! NOW THERE'S NOT A DROP OF WATER IN IT! BUT MY SUPER-VISION REVEALS THERE'S NO BOMB IN IT, EITHER!
SOON, AT THE SECOND SPOT...
AMPHUR, THE LOST CITY! A POISONOUS MIST HAS KEPT EVERY LIVING THING OUT FOR CENTURIES, SO IT'S "EMPTY"... EMPTY OF PEOPLE!
BUT IT'S ALSO EMPTY OF ANY BOMBS!
THE DEAD DESERT, WHERE NO PLANTS, ANIMALS, OR EVEN INSECTS CAN LIVE... EMPTY OF ALL LIFE!
BUT THERE'S NO SIGN OF A BOMB HERE, EITHER!
17

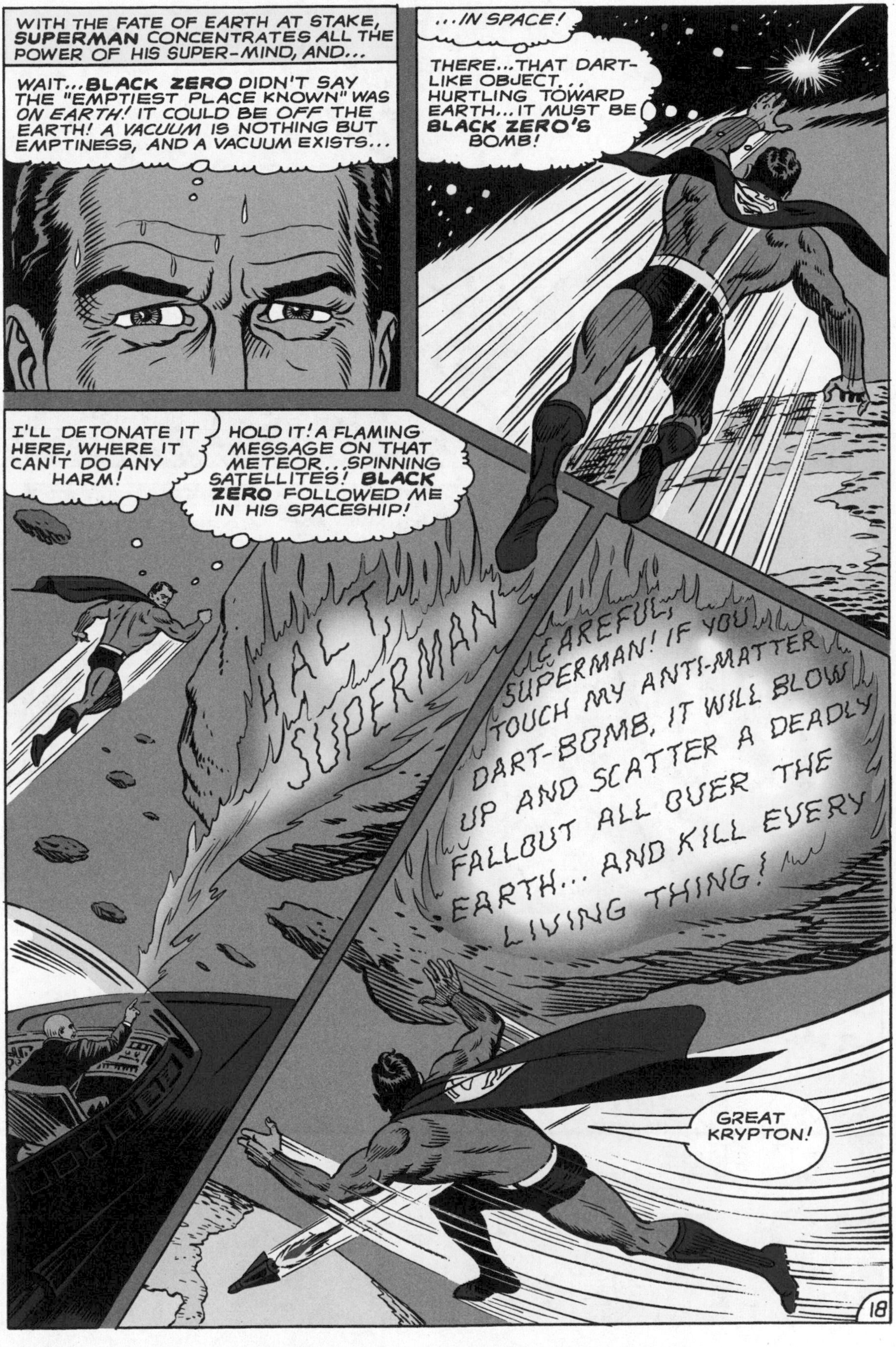
WITH THE FATE OF EARTH AT STAKE, SUPERMAN CONCENTRATES ALL THE POWER OF HIS SUPER-MIND, AND...
WAIT...BLACK ZERO DIDN'T SAY THE "EMPTIEST PLACE KNOWN" WAS ON EARTH! IT COULD BE OFF THE EARTH! A VACUUM IS NOTHING BUT EMPTINESS, AND A VACUUM EXISTS...
...IN SPACE!
THERE...THAT DART-LIKE OBJECT... HURTLING TOWARD EARTH...IT MUST BE BLACK ZERO'S BOMB!
I'LL DETONATE IT HERE, WHERE IT CAN'T DO ANY HARM!
HOLD IT! A FLAMING MESSAGE ON THAT METEOR...SPINNING SATELLITES! BLACK ZERO FOLLOWED ME IN HIS SPACESHIP!
HALT, SUPERMAN
CAREFUL, SUPERMAN! IF YOU TOUCH MY ANTI-MATTER DART-BOMB, IT WILL BLOW UP AND SCATTER A DEADLY FALLOUT ALL OVER THE EARTH... AND KILL EVERY LIVING THING!
GREAT KRYPTON!
18

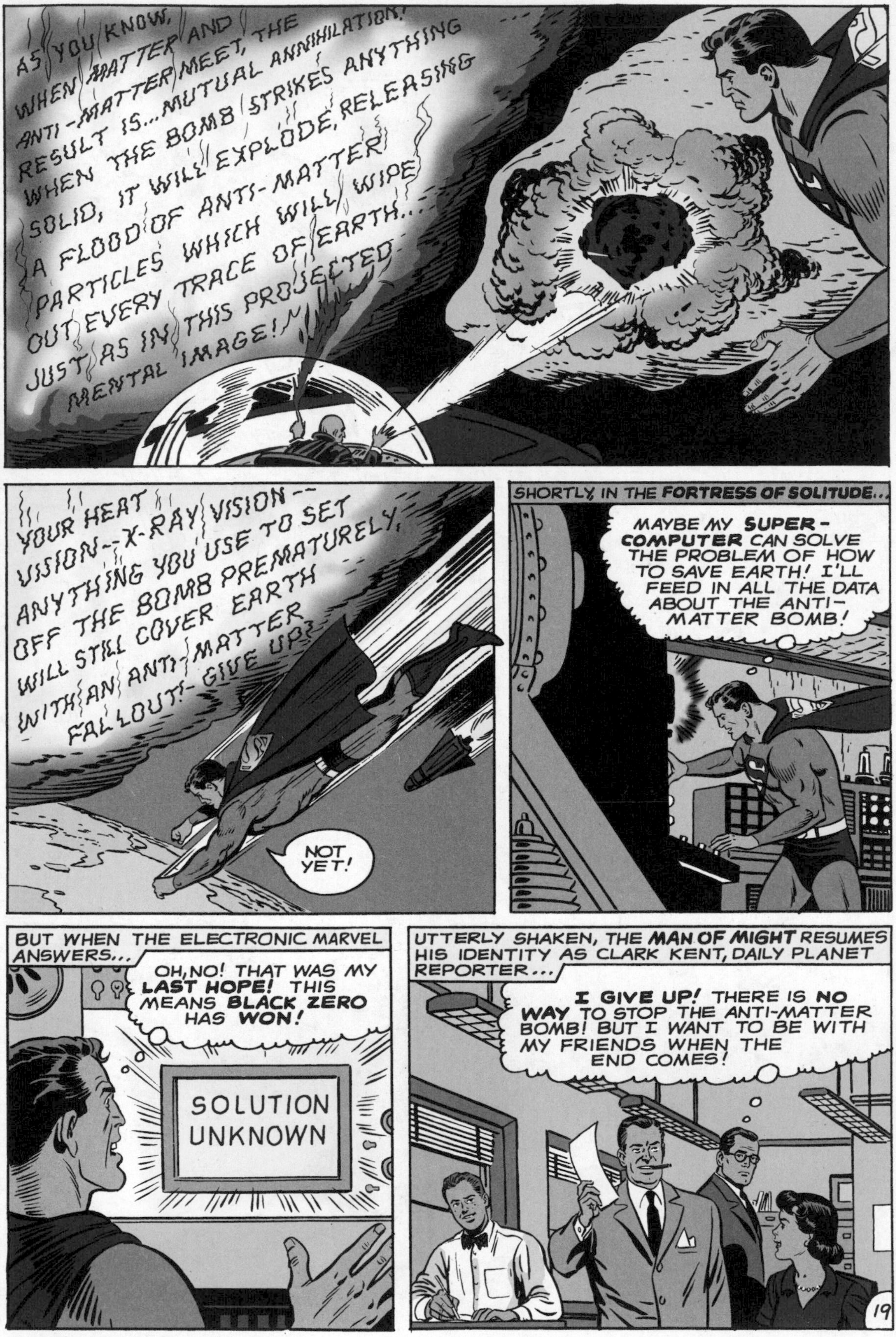

AS YOU KNOW, WHEN MATTER AND ANTI-MATTER MEET, THE RESULT IS...MUTUAL ANNIHILATION! WHEN THE BOMB STRIKES ANYTHING SOLID, IT WILL EXPLODE, RELEASING A FLOOD OF ANTI-MATTER PARTICLES WHICH WILL WIPE OUT EVERY TRACE OF EARTH... JUST AS IN THIS PROJECTED MENTAL IMAGE!
YOUR HEAT VISION--X-RAY VISION--ANYTHING YOU USE TO SET OFF THE BOMB PREMATURELY, WILL STILL COVER EARTH WITH AN ANTI-MATTER FALLOUT! GIVE UP!
NOT YET!
SHORTLY, IN THE FORTRESS OF SOLITUDE...
MAYBE MY SUPER-COMPUTER CAN SOLVE THE PROBLEM OF HOW TO SAVE EARTH! I'LL FEED IN ALL THE DATA ABOUT THE ANTI-MATTER BOMB!
BUT WHEN THE ELECTRONIC MARVEL ANSWERS...
OH, NO! THAT WAS MY LAST HOPE! THIS MEANS BLACK ZERO HAS WON!
SOLUTION UNKNOWN
UTTERLY SHAKEN, THE MAN OF MIGHT RESUMES HIS IDENTITY AS CLARK KENT, DAILY PLANET REPORTER...
I GIVE UP! THERE IS NO WAY TO STOP THE ANTI-MATTER BOMB! BUT I WANT TO BE WITH MY FRIENDS WHEN THE END COMES!
19

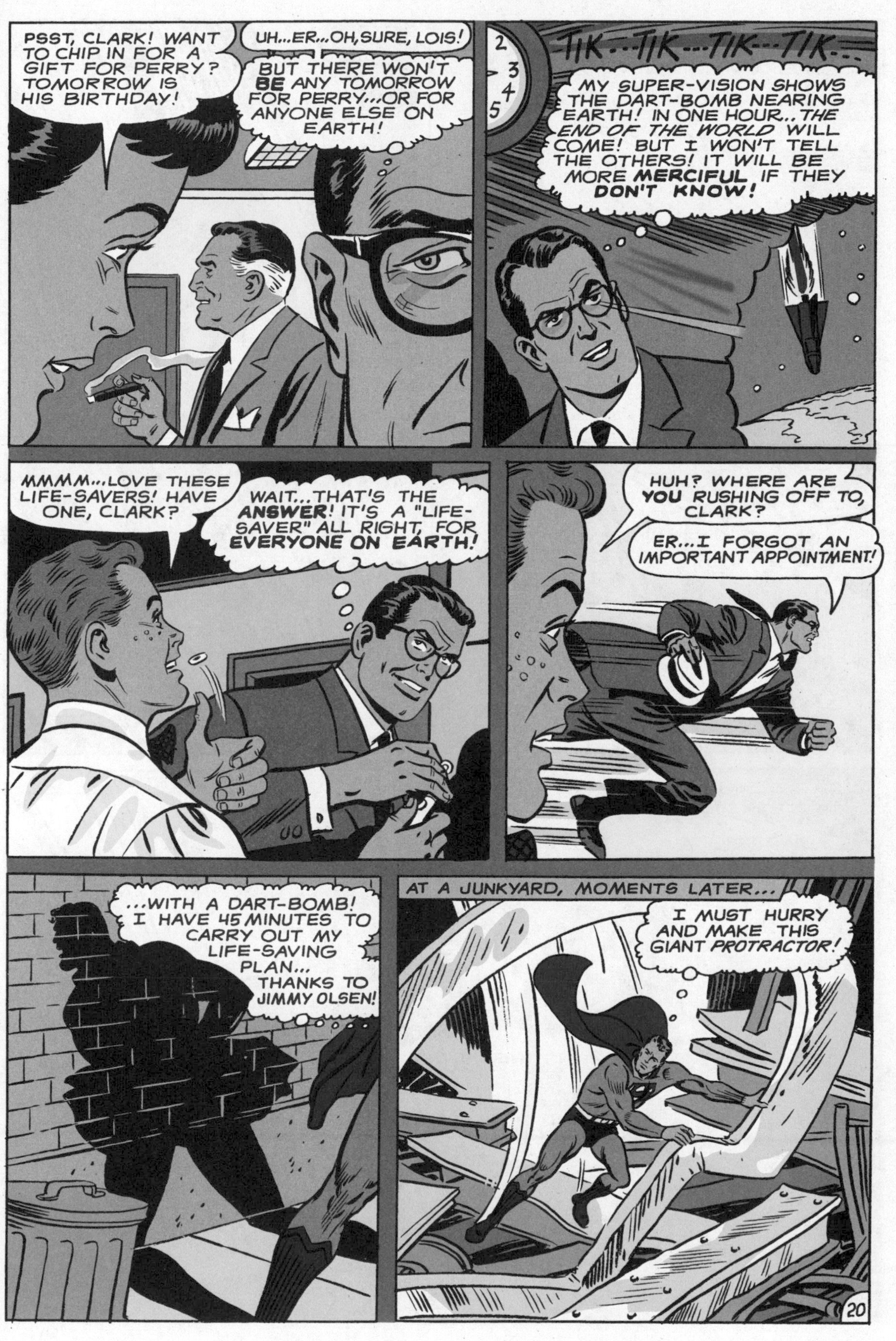
PSST, CLARK! WANT TO CHIP IN FOR A GIFT FOR PERRY? TOMORROW IS HIS BIRTHDAY!
UH...ER...OH, SURE, LOIS!
BUT THERE WON'T **BE** ANY TOMORROW FOR PERRY...OR FOR ANYONE ELSE ON EARTH!
TIK...TIK...TIK...TIK...
MY SUPER-VISION SHOWS THE DART-BOMB NEARING EARTH! IN ONE HOUR... *THE END OF THE WORLD* WILL COME! BUT I WON'T TELL THE OTHERS! IT WILL BE MORE **MERCIFUL** IF THEY **DON'T KNOW!**
MMMM...LOVE THESE LIFE-SAVERS! HAVE ONE, CLARK?
WAIT...THAT'S THE **ANSWER**! IT'S A "LIFE-SAVER" ALL RIGHT, FOR **EVERYONE ON EARTH**!
HUH? WHERE ARE **YOU** RUSHING OFF TO, CLARK?
ER...I FORGOT AN IMPORTANT APPOINTMENT!
...WITH A DART-BOMB! I HAVE 45 MINUTES TO CARRY OUT MY LIFE-SAVING PLAN... THANKS TO JIMMY OLSEN!
AT A JUNKYARD, MOMENTS LATER...
I MUST HURRY AND MAKE THIS GIANT *PROTRACTOR*!
20

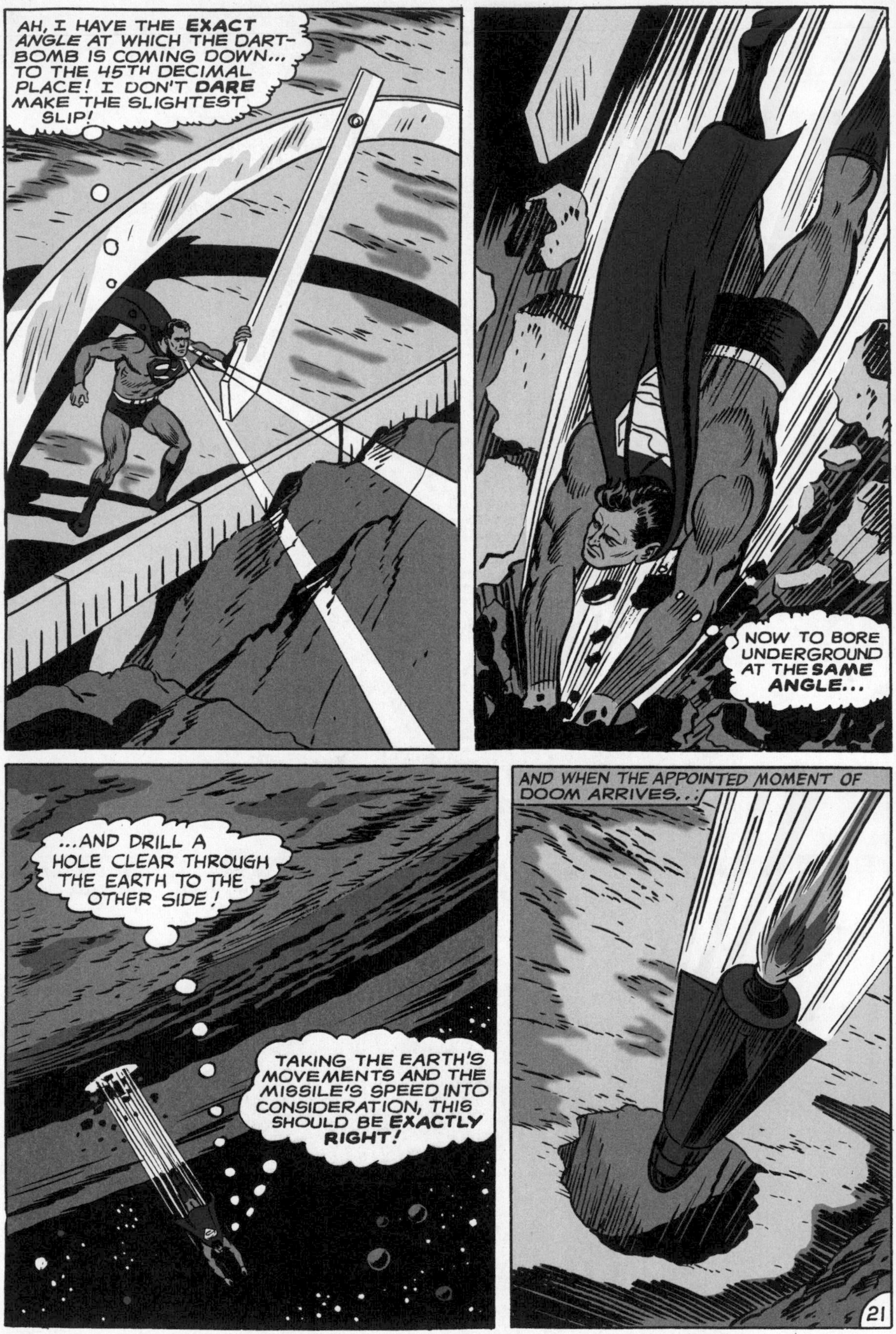
AH, I HAVE THE EXACT ANGLE AT WHICH THE DART-BOMB IS COMING DOWN... TO THE 45TH DECIMAL PLACE! I DON'T DARE MAKE THE SLIGHTEST SLIP!
NOW TO BORE UNDERGROUND AT THE SAME ANGLE...
...AND DRILL A HOLE CLEAR THROUGH THE EARTH TO THE OTHER SIDE!
TAKING THE EARTH'S MOVEMENTS AND THE MISSILE'S SPEED INTO CONSIDERATION, THIS SHOULD BE EXACTLY RIGHT!
AND WHEN THE APPOINTED MOMENT OF DOOM ARRIVES...
21

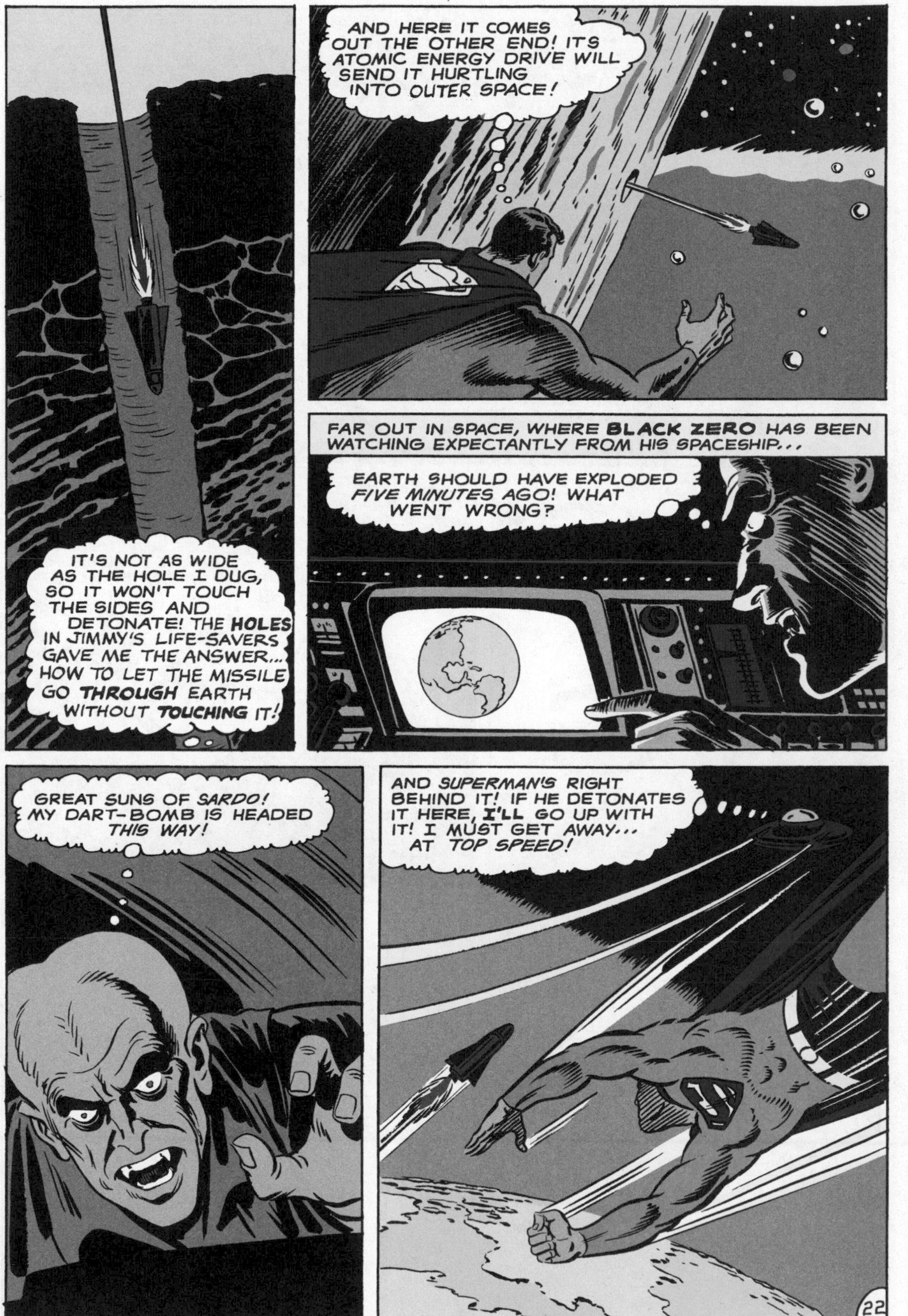
AND HERE IT COMES OUT THE OTHER END! ITS ATOMIC ENERGY DRIVE WILL SEND IT HURTLING INTO OUTER SPACE!
IT'S NOT AS WIDE AS THE HOLE I DUG, SO IT WON'T TOUCH THE SIDES AND DETONATE! THE HOLES IN JIMMY'S LIFE-SAVERS GAVE ME THE ANSWER... HOW TO LET THE MISSILE GO THROUGH EARTH WITHOUT TOUCHING IT!
FAR OUT IN SPACE, WHERE BLACK ZERO HAS BEEN WATCHING EXPECTANTLY FROM HIS SPACESHIP...
EARTH SHOULD HAVE EXPLODED FIVE MINUTES AGO! WHAT WENT WRONG?
GREAT SUNS OF SARDO! MY DART-BOMB IS HEADED THIS WAY!
AND SUPERMAN'S RIGHT BEHIND IT! IF HE DETONATES IT HERE, I'LL GO UP WITH IT! I MUST GET AWAY... AT TOP SPEED!
22

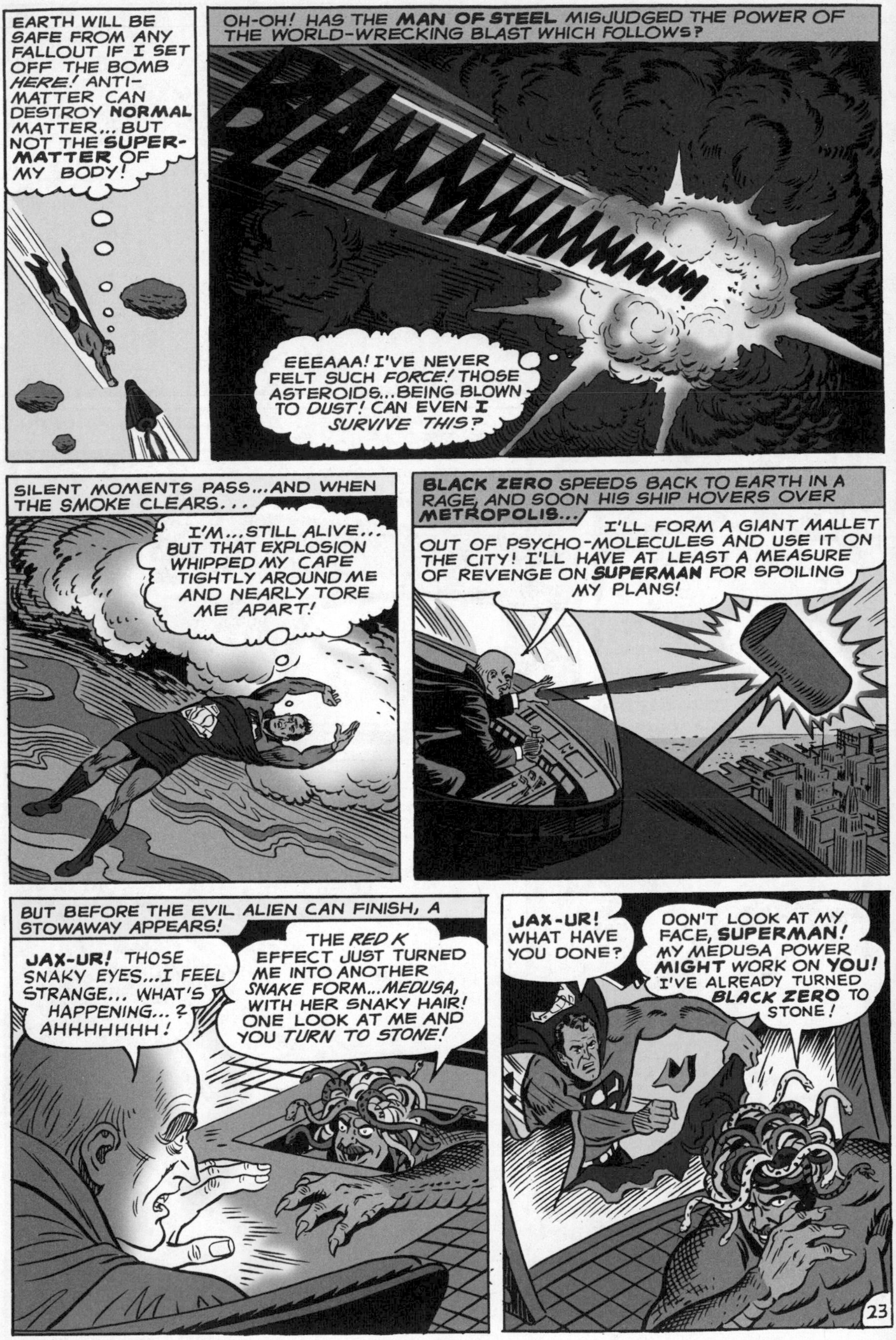
EARTH WILL BE SAFE FROM ANY FALLOUT IF I SET OFF THE BOMB HERE! ANTI-MATTER CAN DESTROY NORMAL MATTER... BUT NOT THE SUPER-MATTER OF MY BODY!
OH-OH! HAS THE MAN OF STEEL MISJUDGED THE POWER OF THE WORLD-WRECKING BLAST WHICH FOLLOWS?
BLAMMMMMMMMMM
EEEAAA! I'VE NEVER FELT SUCH FORCE! THOSE ASTEROIDS...BEING BLOWN TO DUST! CAN EVEN I SURVIVE THIS?
SILENT MOMENTS PASS...AND WHEN THE SMOKE CLEARS...
I'M...STILL ALIVE... BUT THAT EXPLOSION WHIPPED MY CAPE TIGHTLY AROUND ME AND NEARLY TORE ME APART!
BLACK ZERO SPEEDS BACK TO EARTH IN A RAGE, AND SOON HIS SHIP HOVERS OVER METROPOLIS...
I'LL FORM A GIANT MALLET OUT OF PSYCHO-MOLECULES AND USE IT ON THE CITY! I'LL HAVE AT LEAST A MEASURE OF REVENGE ON SUPERMAN FOR SPOILING MY PLANS!
BUT BEFORE THE EVIL ALIEN CAN FINISH, A STOWAWAY APPEARS!
JAX-UR! THOSE SNAKY EYES...I FEEL STRANGE... WHAT'S HAPPENING...? AHHHHHHH!
THE RED K EFFECT JUST TURNED ME INTO ANOTHER SNAKE FORM...MEDUSA, WITH HER SNAKY HAIR! ONE LOOK AT ME AND YOU TURN TO STONE!
JAX-UR! WHAT HAVE YOU DONE?
DON'T LOOK AT MY FACE, SUPERMAN! MY MEDUSA POWER MIGHT WORK ON YOU! I'VE ALREADY TURNED BLACK ZERO TO STONE!
23

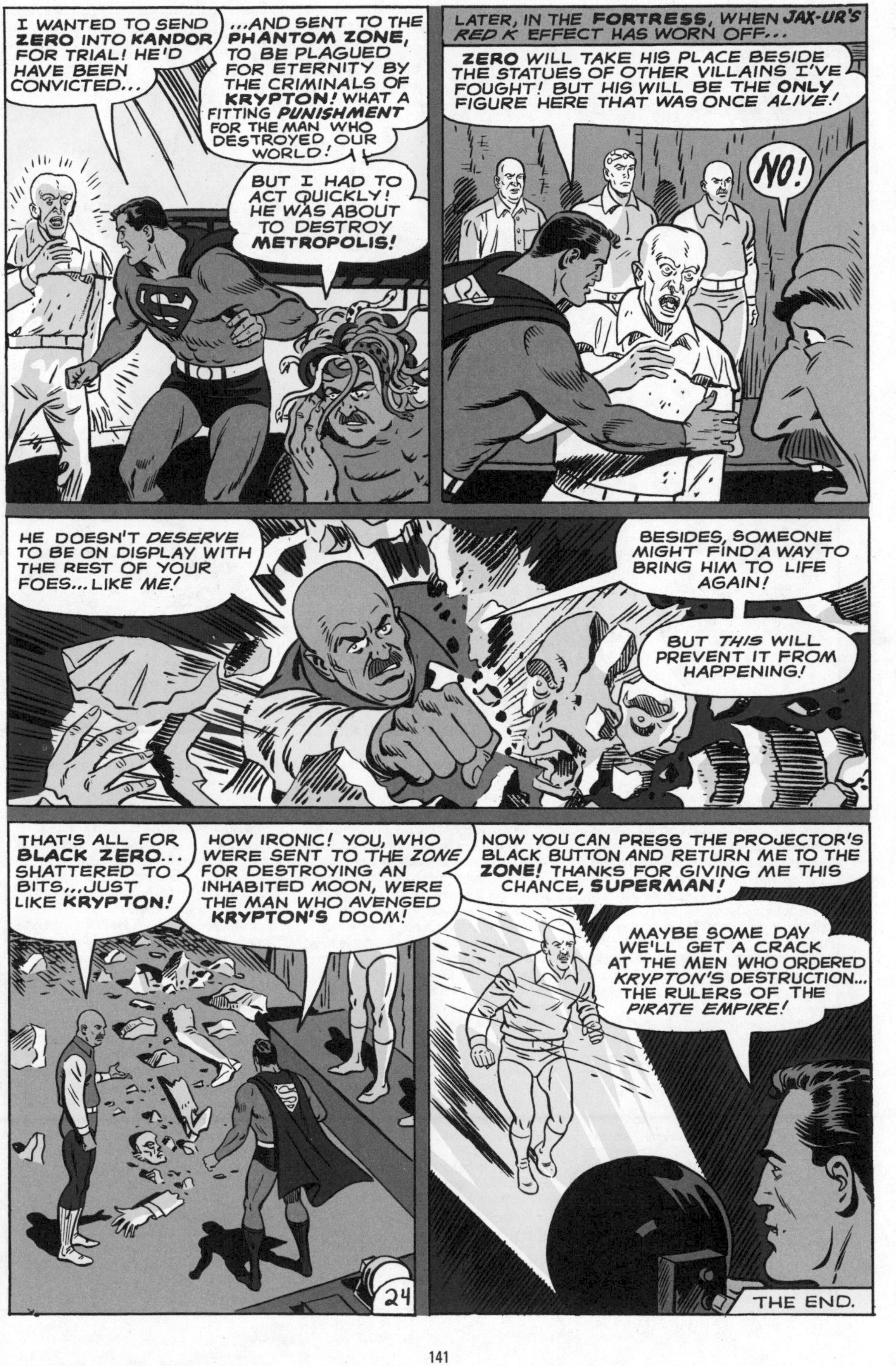
I WANTED TO SEND ZERO INTO KANDOR FOR TRIAL! HE'D HAVE BEEN CONVICTED...
...AND SENT TO THE PHANTOM ZONE, TO BE PLAGUED FOR ETERNITY BY THE CRIMINALS OF KRYPTON! WHAT A FITTING PUNISHMENT FOR THE MAN WHO DESTROYED OUR WORLD!
BUT I HAD TO ACT QUICKLY! HE WAS ABOUT TO DESTROY METROPOLIS!
LATER, IN THE FORTRESS, WHEN JAX-UR'S RED K EFFECT HAS WORN OFF...
ZERO WILL TAKE HIS PLACE BESIDE THE STATUES OF OTHER VILLAINS I'VE FOUGHT! BUT HIS WILL BE THE ONLY FIGURE HERE THAT WAS ONCE ALIVE!
NO!
HE DOESN'T DESERVE TO BE ON DISPLAY WITH THE REST OF YOUR FOES... LIKE ME!
BESIDES, SOMEONE MIGHT FIND A WAY TO BRING HIM TO LIFE AGAIN!
BUT THIS WILL PREVENT IT FROM HAPPENING!
THAT'S ALL FOR BLACK ZERO... SHATTERED TO BITS... JUST LIKE KRYPTON!
HOW IRONIC! YOU, WHO WERE SENT TO THE ZONE FOR DESTROYING AN INHABITED MOON, WERE THE MAN WHO AVENGED KRYPTON'S DOOM!
NOW YOU CAN PRESS THE PROJECTOR'S BLACK BUTTON AND RETURN ME TO THE ZONE! THANKS FOR GIVING ME THIS CHANCE, SUPERMAN!
MAYBE SOME DAY WE'LL GET A CRACK AT THE MEN WHO ORDERED KRYPTON'S DESTRUCTION... THE RULERS OF THE PIRATE EMPIRE!
24
THE END.

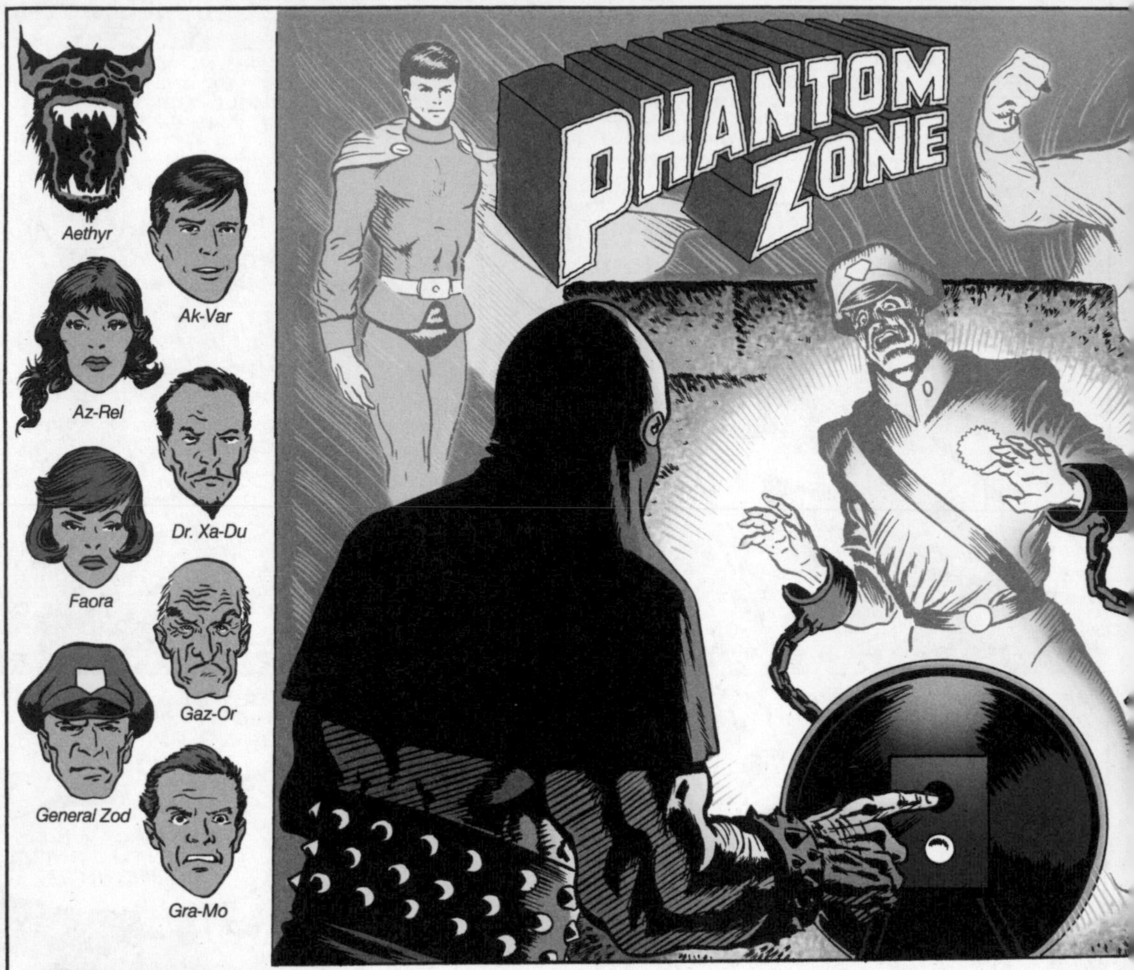
PHANTOM ZONE
Aethyr
Ak-Var
Az-Rel
Dr. Xa-Du
Faora
Gaz-Or
General Zod
Gra-Mo

HISTORY

The Phantom Zone is an eerie twilight dimension in which people can exist as incorporeal phantoms, able to see into the universe from which they have been exiled, but incapable of touching or having any influence on anything in it. They do not eat, drink, or sleep, and cannot talk, communicating by telepathy. It appears they can touch each other to a small degree, but not enough to harm one another. All in all, it is a terrible existence, in which one is denied all normal pleasures, and which can go on indefinitely, for in the Zone no one ever ages.

The Phantom Zone is only the outermost limit of the universe of a godlike being called Aethyr. Anyone penetrating deeper into its realm finds that all things there are shaped—and exist or not—by Aethyr's whim.

Only Superman (see *Superman II*) has traveled through the entire dimensional universe to escape from it and emerge in the universe of his birth.

Yet the truth about Aethyr's realm was not suspected by Jor-El (see *Jor-El*) when he discovered it while trying to find a way to save the people of Krypton (see *Krypton*) from the coming cataclysm he knew would shatter that planet. He could not condemn the whole race to the hideous existence in this dimension, but it occurred to him that it would be a perfect place to exile the worst criminals, since Krypton had no capital punishment.

Jor-El presented this plan to the ruling Science Council as his bid for membership in that body. His opponent in the election was *Gra-Mo,* secretly head of a criminal organization. He proposed replacing Krypton's robot police with androids—but the android he displayed proved defective, and the election went to Jor-El. Gra-Mo then used his telepathic control helmet to take command of the robot police—only to be defeated by Jor-El, who used a weather satellite to magnetically seize the robots and dump them in the Fire-Falls. Gra-Mo was apprehended and he and his gang became the last criminals to be sent into orbit in suspended animation as punishment.

Placed against a wall, shackled by specially treated chains that would not be affected by the Phantom Zone Projector, a criminal began his sentence in the hellish twilight world. Pressing the black button sent one into the Zone; pressing the white button could free a criminal. A Zone-o-Phone was invented to permit communication with criminals up for parole.

Later, in Argo City, after the destruction of Krypton (see *Supergirl*), Jor-El's brother Zor-El created another projector. And in the city of Kandor (see *Kandor*), Nim-El, Jor-El's twin, independently discovered the Zone.

The major Phantom Zone inhabitants are:

Jax-Ur, first criminal to be exiled there. A former co-worker with Jor-El at Krypton's Space Center, Jax-Ur created a nuclear missile with which he planned to destroy a huge meteor as a test. Instead, it went astray and struck Wegthor, one of Krypton's moons, which had been colonized. For this, Jax was sent to the Zone for life—but with hope of parole. He first appeared in ADVENTURE COMICS #289.

Dr. Xa-Du, convicted of conducting forbidden experiments in suspended animation, resulting in the deaths of the subjects who volunteered for the test. His wife, Erndine Ze-Da, was later convicted and sent into the Zone. They eventually escaped, but were tricked by Superboy, who exiled them on a red-sun planet. Years later, they returned, with a new power which worked when they gripped each other's hands. Superman imprisoned them on separate worlds in different galaxies. Dr. Xa-Du first appeared in ADVENTURE COMICS #283.

Faora Hu-Ul, a man-hating master of Horu-Kanu, the deadliest of the Kryptonian martial arts, who also had the power to produce psychic bolts that could cause great pain—or death. She lured men to a special concentration camp where she tortured them to death. When she escaped from the Zone, she posed as the ghost of Katie Porter, dead wife of Jackson Porter. Super-

Jax-Ur

Jer-Em

Kru-El

Mon-El

Nadira

Nam-Ek

Quex-Ul

Va-Kox

man, realizing Porter's mind was permanently affected by her mental influence, sent him into the Zone with her. Faora first appeared in ACTION COMICS #471.

General Dru-Zod, in charge of Krypton's space program until it was canceled after the destruction of Wegthor. He then set out to seize power by creating his own army of artificial men, all doubles of himself. Not the best of scientists, Zod produced only imperfect doubles—Bizarro versions of himself (see *Bizarro*). They were destroyed and Zod sent to the Zone. General Zod first appeared in ADVENTURE COMICS #283.

Professor Va-Kox, who conducted an experiment on the Great Krypton Lake that polluted it and changed all life in it into dangerous monsters. Va-Kox first appeared in SUPERBOY #104.

Az-Rel and *Nadira,* who were banished from their homeland, Bokos, Isle of Thieves, because of their dangerous psychic powers. They were sent to the Zone for using these powers for crime. Both first appeared in THE PHANTOM ZONE #1. They were killed during a mass escape from the Zone.

Kru-El, Jor-El's cousin, who created forbidden weapons. Jor-El himself captured him and sent him into the Zone. Kru-El first appeared in ACTION COMICS #297.

Ak-Var, convicted of stealing a revered relic, the sun-stone, and the one criminal known to have reformed after his release

from the Zone (see *Nightwing and Flamebird*).

Gaz-Or, the worst of the lot. Old and dying, this criminal decided to take Krypton with him by using a quake machine to shake it apart. Jor-El stopped him and Gaz-Or was sentenced to life in the Zone—without hope of parole. He first appeared in ADVENTURE COMICS #323.

Quex-Ul, convicted of killing rare Rondors, animals with horns that could cure many ailments, then using their horns to set up a Hall of Healing, thus enriching himself. He confessed and was sent to the Zone, but was released by Superman when his time was up. He then tried to get revenge on Superman, son of Jor-El, who had headed the Justice Council that convicted him. He set up a Gold Kryptonite trap deep in the sea. Superman, however, learned that Quex-Ul had been under the hypnotic control of one Rog-Ar, the real Rondor killer. Quex-Ul, finding this out, exposed himself to the Gold K to save Superman. Losing both his powers and his memory, he went to work in the *Daily Planet*'s production department (see *Daily Planet*). Later, exiled with Superman into the Zone by escaping villains, Quex-Ul recovered his powers and memory and used them to sacrifice his life for Superman. Quex-Ul first appeared in SUPERMAN #157.

Much later, when Zor-El found a way to take Argo City under a yellow sun where its

people became super-powered, *Jer-Em,* a religious fanatic, undid this and ultimately doomed the city. For this he was exiled into the Zone. Later, during a mass escape, he exposed himself to Kryptonite and died. He first appeared in ACTION COMICS #309.

The forbidden weapons cache eventually fell to Earth and was found by Superboy. This story, introducing the Zone, appeared in ADVENTURE COMICS #283. Subsequently, the Boy of Steel sent others into the Zone, the first being *Mon-El*—to save his life (see *Mon-El*). When Gra-Mo and his gang reached Earth, Superboy sent them into the Zone. Gra-Mo first appeared in SUPERBOY #104.

Nam-Ek was another who killed a Rondor—but he used its horn to make a serum to render himself immortal. It also made him a human Rondor—hideous and foul-smelling. He outlived Krypton and finally came to Earth, where he fought Superman. The Man of Steel used Nam-Ek's horn to stop a plague, then he, too, was exiled into the Zone. Nam-Ek first appeared in SUPERMAN #282.